A. Erdely

A Comedy of Wisdoms:
Common Sense and Beyond

A. Erdely

A Comedy of Wisdoms: Common Sense and Beyond

ATE

Cover Picture: Thinker: Photograph by Mr. Riccardo Lazet, Meldepad 10, 3193 Rotterdam, Netherlands

Harlequin: Courtesy of Mr. Tiziano Trivella, Lingua, Cultura e Tradizioni Bergamasche, Bergamo, Italy

Bibliographic information published by the Deutsche Nationalbibliothek
The Deutsche Nationalbibliothek lists this publication in the Deutsche Nationalbibliografie; detailed bibliographic data are available in the Internet at http://dnb.d-nb.de.

A catalogue record for this book is available from the British Library

ISBN 978-3-89781-170-6

AT Edition Berlin 2010

Distribution/Contact:
Fresnostr. 2 48159 Münster 0 251 / 20 07 96 10
e-Mail: ate@at-edition.de http://www.at-edition.de

To Gabi,

a fountain of practical wisdoms

Foreword

You are about to read the account of a seminar the subject of which was wisdoms.

The seminar was never held. No one seems to have thought of organizing one on the subject. There are countless seminars on business, finance, marketing, technology (I attended and even led several dozen); there are symposia on ethics, religion, philosophy - but none on wisdoms.

So I decided to fill the gap and create an imaginary symposium.

Yet, I do not believe there is such a thing called Wisdom. There are only *wisdoms,* wise or unwise behaviour. As defined here, wisdoms are nothing esoteric or otherworldly, that some old men possess or a select few are born with. Wisdoms are actions, attitudes, based on common sense, on insight, on the ability to think judiciously utilizing knowledge, experience and understanding. Wisdoms can be communicated, learned and applied by anyone, at any age.

We live in a complex, dynamic age, that values success, but also gropes, openly or covertly, for more harmony, more security, more purpose. Wisdoms help to attain those things. Moralists warn us against ruthless egotisms, pessimists against a gradual slide into decadence, even into barbarism. Wisdoms can definitely deflect such dangers.

Wisdoms come in different forms. We have the down-to-earth, practical ones. Then we have the sophisticated ones, that make us understand broad perspectives, deep relationships. We have traditional wisdoms and recent, modern ones, co-existing side by side. Wisdoms either crystallize out of long experience and study, or they emerge suddenly from a flash of insight.

But: are all wisdoms unconditionally valid? I put to myself that question as I set out to order some notes I began to jot down when young, and then continued to do so while living and working on four continents. My notes were meant to capture wise thoughts, my own and those of others. While ordering the notes, however, I realized that some of the wisdoms I recorded no longer seemed to have the universal importance I assigned to them earlier. Other wisdoms still seemed perfectly valid; but then so were their opposites, depending on the context in which I considered them. I became increasingly fascinated. This book emerged out of that fascination. It now extends well beyond the original notes out which it was born: it became a systematic search for and a lively debate on wisdoms, in which I cordially invite you to participate.

I decided to locate my fictitious seminar in Italy (where I live in the summer). But the location is irrelevant, and you will not find the venue, Piavello, on the map. I also decided that there will be two main characters attending the seminar, whom I named "Actus" and "Spectus". "Actus" is a doer, a man of *action,* a pragmatist. "Spectus" is an observer, a *spectator,* an intellectual who *speculates* about what he reads and sees. The two characters often differ in their perceptions and judgments, supplying dramatic tension to the seminar. There are also many other participants actively contributing to the drama - but let me not anticipate. You will meet them all as you read on.

The idea of using a fictitious dialog or seminar to treat a broad subject is not new. It is an excellent way to present differing views on the same issue, since you can put one opinion in the mouth of one character and the contrary opinion in the mouth of another. It is a literary tool famously used by Plato, Galileo, Erasmus - so I am in good company. However, I differ from my illustrious "predecessors" by introducing modern gadgets and techniques they could not have dreamt of, or would have considered below their dignity to employ. Thus, my seminar turns out to be somewhat unusual. It is a treatise and a bit of theatre, all in one.

You can read this book in two ways. As a play, following the plot as it develops. You will find that the sessions grow gradually more challenging, the characters more subtle, their opinions more sophisticated - though I took care that they remain lucid at all times. Or as a reference book: to do that, look up a key word in the register and see what the book has to say about the situation. I will be happy if you did either one or the other. I will have attained my purpose if you did both.

You will find many quotations in the original language in which they were uttered. I could have translated them in footnotes, but decided against it. Footnotes disrupt the fluency of the text. All quotations are commented and explained in the text anyway. And non-English readers will appreciate finding wisdoms, here and there, expressed in their mother-tongue. So will the polyglots. So will those who love Latin.

One last remark. Wisdom is a serious matter, yet I tried to be both earnest and amusing about it. This book is a bundle of serious thoughts wrapped in a light package. So, as I leave the stage to my characters, I hope that they will give you food for thought as well as provide you with entertainment. For we would all be wiser if we thought more deeply about certain things; but we should not forget, from time to time, to also have some honest fun.

And now: let the curtain rise!

A.E.

The evening before

Prologue

Large, comfortably and tastefully furnished terrace of a first class hotel in Middle Italy. At the back is the main building, with "Grand Hotel Piavello" written on the façade. Beautiful view of forest-covered hills with castle ruins, medieval towns, stately villas. Further away a large, brilliant lake, difficult to tell which. The spot and the scenery makes contemplative persons want to meditate. Active spirits feel relaxed, but also inspired to start new activities.

It is late afternoon.

There are only two guests sitting on the terrace. One is dressed casually in slacks, short-sleeved shirt, textile shoes; he has a glass of "Amaro Averna" before him. The other wears a light grey business suit, nice tie, polished shoes; he drinks a cappuccino. This reveals him to be a foreigner, for no Italian would drink one after noon.

The two guests obviously have a feeling they have met before. Strangely, there is even a certain resemblance between them. They seem to realise this and find it odd. The man drinking Amaro keeps contemplating the scenery, without undertaking anything. But the cappuccino-man, who has stared fixedly at the other for some time, decides to do something about the situation.

Cappuccino-man. Excuse me. May I present myself? My name is Actus. I have the feeling we have met before.

Amaro-man. *Turns toward Actus with a smile.* I am sure we did. But I can't say when and where. My name is Spectus.

Actus. *Takes a printed sheet out of his pocket and glances at it.* Spectus ? Then you are here for the symposium. Your name is on the list of participants.

Spectus. Yes. I came for the symposium.

Act. So did I. Beautiful spot, this, isn't it? I am glad Eclectus has chosen this venue. It is so relaxing. *(Takes a sip of cappuccino.)* Even though I wouldn't want to stay here for too long. Just long enough to recharge the batteries. Staying too long would become boring.

Spe. Boring? I am sorry, but I can't agree with you. I could sit here for days, thinking, reading, or just contemplating this beautiful view. They say the colours of the sunset are different every evening.

Act. Are they? Well, I wouldn't have the patience to look at sunsets every evening. Once you have seen a few sunsets, you have seen them all.

Pause.

Act. I wonder when the other participants will be arriving. Have you seen any of the others yet?

Spe. No.

Act. *Looks at his list again.* This is the oddest list of participants I have ever seen. Full of historic-sounding names, and names that sound like pseudonyms. I think a secretary mixed up the list with some other register.

Spe. Yes, I have been wondering about that, too.

Act. Incidentally: the invitation is rather unspecific. The purpose of this seminar is not quite clear. At least not to me. Do you happen to know any details?

Spe. I am afraid not.

Act. *Frowns.* I am a bit worried about that. I dislike vagueness. *(Sips his coffee.)* Anyway: this promises to be quite an event. It says here, in the invitation: "Seminar language will be English. However, participants will be allowed to contribute in French, German, Italian, and Spanish. Use of Latin is optional, and may be substituted by English. Contributions originally formulated in oriental and other languages will be directly translated into English." Sounds a bit like the UN, don't you think?

Spe. With the exception that Latin, to my knowledge, is not used at the UN.

They both smile. Another pause.

Act. *Gets up.* Well, it was nice meeting you. I think I will take a short walk and then look at the evening news on television. I want to get to bed early to be fit for tomorrow. I guess the others will be arriving during the evening. *(Grins.)* And if not, well, then the two of us will have to start this symposium!

Spe. *Looks at Actus, as if suddenly hit by an idea.* A rather interesting conjecture.

Act. *Somewhat taken aback.* What do you mean, an interesting conjecture? It was a joke. A silly one, too, I admit.

Spe. I know you meant it to be. But what if it is *not* a joke? What if Eclectus intended just the two of us to come here and discuss with each other?

Act. *Stares at Spectus in amazement.* Now that is ridiculous. Don't forget: there is a long list of participants.

Spe. I know. But we both found that list somewhat odd. It might be humbug.

Act. *Explodes.* Humbug? Excuse me, but that is nonsense! A seminar is not a dialogue between two people. It is a formal event, with lots of participants, having different backgrounds, specific views, and ready to discuss them with others. Besides: Eclectus wrote he would be chairing this symposium; there is no need to chair a chat between two people.

Spe. Maybe Eclectus thinks that two individuals, with different views and dispositions, as you and I seem to be, each expounding and defending his own point of view, can provide sufficient stuff for a seminar.

Act. I cannot imagine Eclectus doing a thing like that. I would consider it a dirty trick.

Spe. *Continues to ponder, despite Actus' objections.* Don't you find it strange that we have been left in the dark about the purpose of this seminar, as you rightly pointed out?

Act. I do. But I am sure Eclectus will specify the purpose tomorrow morning. He surely had a reason for not having done so in the invitation. He is a pragmatic and practical fellow. He knows what he is doing.

Spe. *Gazes at Actus.* Your perception of Eclectus is somewhat different from mine. I have often experienced him in a brooding, contemplative mood.

Act. *Grows impatient.* No-one organizes a seminar to brood and contemplate. Seminars are about examining the ways certain things are being done and finding ways to do them better. Brooding and contemplating are just a luxury. Action is a necessity.

Spe. You are quoting Henri Bergson.

Act. Am I? I didn't realize I was quoting anyone. *(He suddenly freezes, seeming to remember something. He takes out his list of participants and looks at it.)* Funny. There is a Bergson attending this seminar. Henri. *(Remains motionless for a second, then puts the list back in his pocket.)* Anyway, it cannot be *the* philosopher Henri Bergson. He has been dead for decades.

Pause.

Act. *Dismisses the oddity.* Whatever. I have got to go. I don't want to miss the evening news.

Spe. Let me not keep you. See you in the morning.

Act. Yes, see you *and* the others in the morning, *(Waves at Spectus with slight irony.)* I wish you a peaceful and serene contemplation of the sunset.

Spe. *Waves back.* I hope there is plenty of exciting action in the news.

Actus leaves for his room. Spectus takes a sip of Amaro and turns to look at the sunset, which is just beginning to paint beautiful, lively colours on the horizon.

The first day

Kickoff with surprise

Modern, elegant, huge seminar-room at the Grand Hotel Piavello. The room has a horseshoe shape made of curved glass windows. Closing off the horseshoe is a white wall with large screens for the projection of slides. The room is evidently on the roof of the hotel, for through the windows there is a stupendous roundabout view at the landscape outside.

Projected unto the wall are photographs of three well-known paintings: the Flagellation of Christ by Piero della Francesca, the Mona Lisa, and Giorgione's Tempest. There is also a fourth slide, representing a scene from Commedia dell'Arte.

At the foot of the wall is a long, green-draped table, evidently reserved for the moderators. But there is just one folded cardboard in the middle of the desk, with "Eclectus, Chairman" written on it. The seat behind the name plate is empty.

Just in front of the moderators' table, in the first row, are two desks with swivel chairs, allowing to face either the front or the back of the room. On one of the desks there is a folded cardboard with the name "Actus", on the other a similar cardboard with the name "Spectus". Behind these are rows of other desks, each with a name-plate, extending to the back of the seminar-room.

Actus and Spectus have not yet arrived, but all other participants obviously have. The room is full. Every desk is occupied. But there is something odd. With a room that full, one would expect a lively chat among the participants, as is usual before the beginning of a seminar. But there is not a sound. Each participant seems merely to sit there, saying nothing. Looking at them more closely, there is another oddity: the participants are clothed in many different attires, from different epochs, as if they meant to participate not at a modern seminar, but at some fancy-dress ball or carnival event.

It is a quarter to eight. The symposium is supposed to start at eight.

At this moment, Actus and Spectus enter the seminar-room together, coming obviously from breakfast. Actus is somewhat less formal than last night, since the invitation for the seminar specifies leisure dress; he wears grey trousers and a grey pullover. Spectus is dressed quite informally, very much like last night.

Both are about to say a loud and courteous "good-morning", when in a flash they realise the odd atmosphere in the room. There is a moment of frozen silence. Actus is the first to react.

Actus. What the devil?!

Spectus. *Continues to stare at the room. However, after a moment, he starts grinning.*

Act. *Walks up to one of the participants and looks at him closely. Then he slowly extends a finger and pokes the man first in the chest, then in the face. He turns back to Spectus with a mixture of puzzlement and anger on his face.* Wax! These are wax dummies! What the hell does Eclectus think he is doing?

Spe. *Continues to grin.* I think you said yesterday that he knows exactly what he is doing.

Act. Just what do you mean?

Spe. *Stops grinning, but still looks amused.* You remember our conversation last night?

Act. What about it?

Spe. I suggested that Eclectus may want a discussion just between the two of us. This is exactly what is going to happen. These other participants here are nothing but decoration. Scenery.

Act. *Very angry.* Decoration? Scenery? Now hold it! Do you mean I came here just to have a pleasant talk with you? I gave up important meetings to participate at this symposium. I would not have come at all if it hadn't been Eclectus who invited. I have no time to lose. I didn't come here to play a role in a farce and sit around with a bunch of Madame Tussaud´s dummies.

Spe. *Smiles.* I can understand your objections. But I am sure Eclectus thought this over. The guy has fantasy.

Act. *Continues to be angry.* Eclectus does *not* have fantasy. How can he? He was obliged all his life to be objective and keep to facts. How can such a fellow develop fantasy?

Spe. Maybe he was born with it and kept it under cover, waiting for an opportunity to let it out.

Act. Well, this monkey business is not the appropriate way to let out his fantasy, in case he has got one. And where *is* Eclectus, anyway? And what, may I ask, is the aim of this so-called symposium? Eclectus cannot expect us to find it out on our own.

Spe. I think that is precisely what he wants us to do.

Act. But we have no clue whatever.

Spe. *Thoughtful.* Maybe the clue is ourselves. You are, obviously, a man of action. I like to contemplate - not only sunsets. Maybe Eclectus wants us, somehow, to combine action and contemplation. Your views with mine. Maybe you unwittingly hit on the clue last night, on the terrace, when you paraphrased Bergson - remember?

There is a noise at the back. One of the wax figures suddenly begins to glow. Before him, on the desk, is a folded cardboard with a name: Henri Bergson. The figure suddenly loses its waxy appearance and now looks quite human. It leans slightly forward looking at Actus and Spectus, and to the consternation of both begins to talk.

Henri Bergson. La spéculation est un luxe. L'action est une nécessité. *(Having said that, the figure suddenly becomes rigid. It is, once more, nothing but a wax dummy.)*

Actus and Spectus stare at the figure with disbelief, breathing heavily. The first to react is Actus. He walks up to the dummy and pokes a finger in its face.

Act. Wax. Just wax. This is unbelievable. Absurd.

Spe. *Somewhat pale.* I don't know how this trick works. But now I am sure of one thing: we are about to embark on some clever happening, orchestrated by Eclectus. I told you not to underestimate the guy. *(Puffs, shaking off his consternation.)* I am afraid we just have to get used to the fact that these waxy fellows here can talk. I was wrong: they are not just scenery.

They are actors in Eclectus' game.

Act. *Has by now surmounted his shock and becomes angry again.* Well, damn the fellow. He is not to play games. He is supposed to conduct an international seminar.

Spe. *Thoughtful.* Maybe "game" is indeed not the right word. This may turn out to be much more than a game: an unusual, sophisticated symposium.

Act. The only sophistication I see around here are these eerie dummies.

Spe. They are eerie, yes. But there must be some plausible explanation of how they are made to come to life and talk. Electronics, microchips, artificial intelligence, whatever. These dummies are obviously programmed to repeat what the persons they represent said or wrote in their lifetime. So they are here for some purpose. Though, so far, we miss the purpose.

Pause. Then, suddenly, there is the deep, pleasant sound of a large gong being struck somewhere behind the scene. It obviously signals the beginning of the symposium.

Act. *Sighs.* Well, here we go. This utterly odd seminar begins. Consisting of two men of flesh and blood, who do not know why they are here, and a bunch of talking wax figures. Hurrah!

Actus and Spectus walk to the desks in the front row bearing their names and sit down. The chair of Eclectus remains empty.

Session 1: The two main characters present themselves

After the gong: silence. Nothing happens.

Actus. *Taps nervously with his pencil on his empty note-pad.*

Spectus. *Keeps looking intently at the projections on the wall.*

Act. *Suddenly explodes.* Now this is ridiculous! No official welcome. No chairman. No specified purpose. Nothing.

Spe. *Is torn from his contemplation of the slides.* Then do something about it.

Act. Me? But it is up to Eclectus to do something about it! It is his invitation. His seminar. He ought to come and start chairing it.

Spe. He will not come. If we just sat here and waited, we would be like Beckett's Estragon and Vladimir, waiting for Godot.

Act. Even Beckett is more amusing than this silly symposium. *(As he says this, he quickly swivels around to face the dummies, to see if any of them reacts to the mention of Beckett's name. But there is no reaction.)* Mr Beckett obviously does not participate. Well, you can't invite everybody.

Spe. I guess there is a good reason why Beckett is not here. He was a nihilist, and nihilism seems out of place here. I am sure this symposium has some constructive purpose. So let us adopt a positive attitude.

Act. I don't see how you can adopt a positive attitude about something you don't know the purpose of. Activity is meaningless without a purpose.

Spe. *Looks intently at the paintings and the Commedia dell'Arte scene, projected on the wall.* I wonder if the slides up there are meant to give us a clue about the purpose.

Act. I doubt that. Those slides are just decoration. All three paintings up there are by Italian painters. Commedia dell'Arte was born here. Since we are in Italy, it is natural that we get surrounded by Italian art. Those slides are just a sort of greeting by the organisers.

Spe. I wonder. They may be up there to convey some message. Hidden from us, for now.

Act. A hidden message? Ah, that reminds me of a cartoon I once saw. Leonardo da Vinci has half-finished painting Mona Lisa's face and is about to paint her smiling mouth. The real Mona Lisa sits there as a model, grinning. Leonardo says: "If it is so funny, Lisa, what about sharing the joke with me?"

Spe. *Laughs, then suddenly snaps his fingers.* That's it! I think I have got it.

Act. Got what?

Spe. The clue.

Act. You mean this symposium is about finding out what joke Mona Lisa told Leonardo da Vinci?

Spe. *Laughs.* Not quite. *(Becomes serious.)* Look at those paintings. Do you see any common link?

Act. No.

Spe. But there is one. These pictures, you see, belong to the most controversial art works in history. Generations of experts have been trying to interpret them. Not one of them fully succeeded. And do you know why? Because the artists distilled into these paintings a tremendous amount of personal experiences. Experiences so diverse that we can impossibly reconstruct them all.

Act. But what's the clue?

Spe. The clue is that this symposium is about what those paintings are about: personal experiences that need to be expressed, interpreted, analysed.

Act. And where, pray, are we supposed to find such experiences?

Spe. To begin with: within ourselves.

Act. Aha. And I guess you are supposed to articulate experiences derived from your high-flying intellectual speculations, whereas I am supposed to utter experiences I gathered during a down-to-earth life in business. Correct?

Spe. That is, more or less, the basic idea. And since our backgrounds and experiences differ, so will the conclusions we derive from them. The result may be a fascinating dialog.

Act. You almost sound as if we are meant to be different characters in some kind of play.

Spe. *Enthusiastic.* But of course! My dear Actus, you just hit on the message of the Commedia dell'Arte slide up there. We *are* supposed to be characters in a play. Only: it is much more than a play. We are asked to act out some kind of intellectual adventure. And we shall necessarily have to improvise, like the actors in Commedia dell'Arte had to. That is what that slide up there is trying to tell us.

Act. Does it? Well, I am not keen to play Arlecchino. Even less, Pantalone: that would be the ultimate affront. I prefer to remain my own sober self.

Spe. *Smiles.* Sometimes it is more amusing to act out a role rather than to be one's own sober self.

Act. You may be a born actor. I am not.

Spe. Then act your own self. The important thing is that you don't get boring. A good actor is one who keeps the audience from coughing.

Act. We have no audience. And these dummies don't cough.

Spe. But who knows what audiences our play may reach, once we have finished it?

Act. *Thoughtful.* Hmm. - But, Spectus, as far as I know, the actors of Commedia dell'Arte had a rough script of the story they were about to present. They didn't entirely improvise. But we haven't got a script. Not even a rough one. So there the comparison ends.

Spe. *Scratches his chin.* We may find a script.

Act. Well, then, start looking for it.

Pause. Both of them are thinking.

Act. Let us face it, Spectus, we are two characters in a play without a plot. I don't even see what we should do next.

Spe. Well, use your experience. What is usually the first step in a seminar?

Act. A welcome speech by the Chairman.

Spe. Forget it. What's the next step after that?

Act. The participants briefly present themselves.

Spe. So why don't we do that?

Act. All right, let's. That will at least bring some appearance of normality into this oddity. - You begin, Spectus.

Spe. *Stands up.* My name is Spectus. I guess some would call me an intellectual. Well, maybe I am, in a way. But I am not one of those intellectuals who retire from the world. On the contrary: I participate in it, feel comfortable in it. - I actively seek the company of friends and acquaintances, since I like being with people. I like conversations, discussions, to pass on to others what I learned and learn from them in turn. - I read a lot, but am not a bookworm. For me, books are there to answer questions people around me cannot answer. But I do not let my reading isolate me. - I have no preferred subjects of study. During some months I may concentrate on one subject, then switch to another. I find that I can get familiar with, and enjoy, any interesting subject, provided I make an effort to enter into it. - I like travelling, exhibitions, concerts. I love the theatre. I enjoy good television. I also like good wines and good food. I am a fellow of leisure, but by no means indolent. - I tend to be conservative, perhaps at times even a bit sceptical. Happily, I can permit myself the luxury to look at things from all sides, listen to different views, consider different perspectives, before reaching an opinion of my own. - I think this sums me up. Thank you. *(Sits down.)*

Act. May I ask a question, Spectus?

Spe. Please do.

Act. You obviously enjoy gathering knowledge. What for?

Spe. *Thinks for a moment.* Good question. Do you know who gave one of the best answers? Bernhard de Clairvaux.

There is a noise in the room. Actus and Spectus swivel around to face it. At the back of the room a figure begins to glow and comes to life.

Bernhard de Clairvaux. *Clad in Cistercian habit. His voice, when he begins to speak, commands attention. Surprisingly, he uses excellent modern English, obviously translating his own Latin sentences.* There are many who seek knowledge for the sake of knowledge itself: that is curiosity. There are others who seek knowledge so that they get to be known for their knowledge: that is vanity. Others seek knowledge so that they can sell it: that is dishonest. There are some who seek knowledge in order to build up others: that is charity. And again there are some who seek knowledge to build up themselves: that is judiciousness. *(Bernhard sits down and takes on a waxy appearance again.)*

Spe. *Impressed.* I am truly amazed at these automata. They not only come to life when they hear their names, but they recognize the subject being discussed and search their register for the quotes that fit it. Remarkable, to say the least.

Act. *Is by this time more interested in what Bernhard said than in how he functions.* Yes, yes, quite impressive. But tell me: which intellectual category described by Bernhard do *you* belong to?

Spe. Not to any one specifically. I partly seek knowledge because I am curious. When young I enjoyed being praised for my knowledge, but with advancing age I lost that vanity. I enjoy communicating what I know to others, so I guess Bernhard would call me, within my modest limits, charitable. I also try to use knowledge to build up myself; call that judiciousness or whatever you will.

Act. And what about selling your knowledge?

Spe. *Laughs.* I think that is judged differently today than it has been in the times of Bernhard. I would have no scruples to sell my knowledge, if an occasion presents itself.

Act. I do sell my knowledge. Or, rather, my know-how. But I do not feel dishonest about it. - One last question: what is your favourite reading when you want to relax?

Spe. P.G. Wodehouse.

Act. *Enthusiastic.* Now that's amazing. So is mine. *(They smile at each other in approval of their literary preference.)*

Spe. Your turn, Actus.

Act. *Stands up.* My name is Actus. I am a natural scientist, turned businessman, then turned investment banker. I like facts, and to act on the basis of facts. I also like precision. - I like to experiment with new and better ways of doing things. My favourite activity is managing complex tasks in order to attain goals I consider worthwhile. I work for results, but I always need to know why I am doing what. I try to deliver a bit more than what is expected of me: I find this to be the best way to create goodwill. - I take for granted that everything makes sense, and if something doesn't, I am on the wrong track. - I believe that one should not escape from challenges and difficulties, but face them. I believe in ethics in the business world, and also that humour is not out of place in business. I try to be courteous and diplomatic, but never to the detriment of honesty. - I try to be articulate. I believe that not saying things clearly is like not saying them at all. If someone doesn't understand me, it is my fault, not that of the other. - I wrote two books, but they are too technical to be relevant to this seminar. - That's it in a nutshell. Thank you. *(Sits down.)*

Spe. *Smiles.* I am supposed to be the intellectual, and you are the one who writes books. I must commend you on that. - Now, may I, in turn, ask you a question?

Act. Go ahead.

Spe. Why do *you* do all this?

Act. *Laughs.* Bergson already answered that question. Action is a necessity. I do it to earn money.

Spe. *Only* for that reason?

Act. *After a short pause.* No. Not only for that reason. I *like* work. I have fun working. I like the pleasure of getting things done and the feeling of having done them well. I like, frankly, the acknowledgments that come with a thing well done. I even get a stimulus out of things that go wrong, because they challenge me to do better next time.

Spe. I see.

Pause. Neither of them speaks for a while.

Act. Well, that was seminar step number two.

Spe. Yes. The characters in the play without a plot have gained contour. At least something has been achieved.

Act. So what's next?

The deep, pleasant sound of the gong is heard again.

Spe. That's what's next. Coffee break!

Act. Great. I love Italian coffee. Especially cappuccino.

Spe. I noticed that yesterday.

They laugh, get up, and go through the door to the lobby. Through the door drifts the aroma of finest Italian coffee.

Session 2: The plot is drafted

During coffee break the projections on the wall have been changed. In the middle, there is the sketch of a gothic cathedral. On the left, written in huge letters, are the words: "Sententiae", "Sic et Non" and "Valet". On the right is the picture of a razor blade.

The gong is sounded. Actus and Spectus are not there. They appear, hastily, a few seconds late. Obviously they were unable to tear themselves away in time from the excellent Italian coffee in the lobby. As they enter, they mutter "sorry, sorry", then realize that they are talking to a collection of lifeless dummies and feel silly. They quickly go to their desks and sit down. Then they stare at the new slides on the wall.

Silence. Spectus remains calm, but Actus gets fidgety.

Spectus. Hmm. Another message. This one may be a bit more difficult to decipher than the one this morning.

Actus. Do you really think so? I think it's easy. Eclectus wants us first to solve a Roman puzzle, then erect a cathedral, and when we have finished, cut our throats with a razor blade. An exciting plot.

Spe. *Laughs.* I think Eclectus is more humane. Above all, more subtle. - Let me see. First, I think you are wrong about that puzzle being Roman. Since it is associated with a gothic cathedral, it is not Roman, but medieval Latin.

Act. Oh, fine. And how, pray, is your medieval Latin?

Spe. Rusty, but possibly adequate. - The razor does not seem to fit into the Middle Ages. Yet it might have something to do with it.

Act. I am thrilled to know what.

Spe. We shall see. - But let us start with the Latin words first. *(Both of them stare at the words intently.)*

Act. I think I can translate "sententia". It means verdict.

Spe. Yes, but it can also mean opinion. Or decision.

Act. So which meaning do we settle on?

Spe. None of these. *(Rubs his hands.)* I told you Eclectus is a subtle fellow. There is yet another meaning to "sententia", and that one has to do with the Middle Ages. In medieval times "sententia" meant a statement by an ancient, recognized authority. There were several well-known writers who collected such statements in so-called "sententiae"-books.

Act. Ergo?

Spe. Ergo, Eclectus wants us to do what the "sententiae"-writers did: collect statements. Derived from our own experiences, and from those of others, such as the people these wax dummies represent. That is why these dummies are here.

Act. Hmm. That makes some sense. - What about "Sic et Non"?

Spe. *Ponders, then brightens up.* I think I have got it. Subtle. Very subtle.

Act. You intrigue me, Holmes.

Spe. Then listen, my dear Watson. One of the greatest authors among those who wrote “sententiae”-books ordered the statements he collected in a particular way. The author was Pierre Abelard. His book was called “Sic et Non”. He had a lot of trouble because of it.

Pierre Abelard. *Briefly flares up at the back of the seminar room, but then quickly returns to wax. It is his courteous way to ask Spectus to go on with his exposé.*

Spe. Abelard’s book contained statements by reputed authorities, set side by side with other statements on the same subject from equally reputed authorities. But the statements were arranged so that they contradicted each another. Hence the title: “Sic et Non”, meaning “Yes and No”. Abelard’s book is a warning against uncritically accepting statements by ancient authorities. It is at the root of Western open-mindedness.

Act. Interesting. But what has all this got to do with us?

Spe. Clearly, Eclectus does not want us to simply collect statements, based on the experiences of various people. He wants us to compare them, set one statement against the other, spell out the differences, show the contradictions. He wants us to analyse. He wants us to debate.

Act. Your deductive powers are remarkable, Holmes. - What about “Valet”?

Spe. “Valet”, my dear Watson, means valid. Eclectus wants us to judge whether the statements we come up with are really valid. Valid, that is, in our modern world, in the light of new discoveries, new experiences.

Act. Hmm. At last things are getting somewhat clearer. - Now: what about that cathedral?

Spe. I don’t know yet. But I am sure Eclectus put it up there for a good reason. It may have something to do with our plot. With the script we are looking for.

Pause.

Act. Let me ask you a question, Spectus. Why on earth should we collect, order and contrast statements derived from our experiences and those of these dummies here? What is the point of it? I am back at my fundamental question about purpose.

Spe. We may be asked to do it for our own benefit. Or for the benefit of Eclectus. Or for the benefit of Eclectus’ friends. Or, possibly, to publish the result and to make a profit. Or all of these things combined. Think of Bernhard de Clairvaux’s many definitions of the uses of knowledge: the same applies here.

Act. Hmm. That’s too many purposes. We need something more focused. We must find a clear, concise, simple definition of what this seminar is all about.

Spe. *Thoughtful.* Define it as research.

Act. Researching what?

Spe. Truth.

Act. That sounds bombastic.

Spe. Perhaps it does.

Silence.

Spe. Listen, Actus. Why don't we define the purpose of this symposium as researching - wisdom?

Act. *Brightens.* Researching wisdom? *(Brightens even more.)* That sounds better. Much better. In fact: it sounds good.

Spe. *Becomes enthusiastic.* Yes. The key word is wisdom. Or rather wisdoms. Not the abstract concept, but its many concrete manifestations. Wisdoms derived from your experiences, from mine, and from those of the people these dummies here represent.

Act. Excellent, Spectus! Excellent.

Spe. *Happy.* We have got it, my dear Actus. We are here to systematically search for wisdoms and then critically review them. We are asked to conduct a debate on wisdoms. Quite a challenging enterprise, I dare say. But, arguably, a rewarding one.

Act. It will mean damn hard work.

Spe. I thought you said you liked work.

Act. I do.

Spe. *Solemnly.* Well then, since the organisers chose not to do it, we take matters in our own hands and define concisely the purpose of this seminar.

Act. Hear, hear!

Spe. Hard work exploring wisdoms!

Act. We have got it! By Jove, Spectus, we have got it!

Actus and Spectus stand up and begin to dance around, like Professor Higgins and Colonel Pickering in "My Fair Lady", singing "By Jove we have got it". After a while they sit down, a bit out of breath, but obviously highly satisfied. Their enthusiasm slowly changes into the realisation that they have to move on.

Act. Spectus, we now have a purpose. And a good one. But do you know what Confucius said when he was asked what his first action would be if elected prime minister?

Confucius. *Begins to glow, comes to life and stands up. Venerable old Chinese figure, impassive, long white beard, calm and clever eyes behind heavy oriental eyelids.* If I was elected prime minister, the first thing I would do is define the meaning of important words.

Act. Thank you, venerabile. And may I commend you on your excellent knowledge of English?

Confucius doesn't seem to have understood the compliment, sits down and becomes a digni-

fied Chinese wax figure again.

Spe. You want wisdom defined, is that it, Actus?

Act. Yes. Can we rely on your intellectual capacities to give us one?

Spe. *Smiles.* I prefer to consult the authorities in this particular case, if you don't mind. *(Stands up and walks over to a bookshelf, set against the wall. There are a few heavy encyclopaedias on the shelf. He picks one up and turns several pages.)* Ah, here we are. "Wisdom is the ability to act and think utilizing knowledge, experience, understanding, common sense and insight." This was Collins.

Act. Excellent definition. What else?

Spe. *Picks up another volume.* Webster says: "Wisdom is the faculty to discern right and truth and to judge and act accordingly". It also says: "Wisdom is synonymous with sound judgement, sagacity, common sense and extensive knowledge". It further says it is the "ability to discern inner qualities and internal relationships". Hmm. Frankly, this last ability I would associate with intelligence, rather than with wisdom.

Act. What about Oxford English Dictionary?

Spe. *Picks another volume.* "The combination of experience and knowledge with the ability to apply them judiciously."

Act. I like that, because it's short, but states the essential. - What do the Germans say?

Spe. *Handles two more volumes.* Wahrig says: „Einsichtige Klugheit, Lebenserfahrung, geistige und innere Reife". Duden writes: „Auf Lebenserfahrung, Reife, Gelehrsamkeit und Distanz gegenüber den Dingen beruhende, einsichtvolle Klugheit". Very much what the English say, with the interesting addition that we need distance to things to be wise.

Act. What do the French say?

Spe. *Picks up another book.* "Circonspection, retenue, maîtrise de soi. « That was Larousse.

Act. Aha. A somewhat different definition, stressing prudence and self-discipline.

Spe. Incidentally, the French also use the word for wisdom, "sagesse", to denote chastity in women and good behaviour in a child.

Act. *Smiles.* I think we should disregard those definitions. - What is wisdom in the tongue of our host country?

Spe. *Picks up another volume.* "La sapienza che deriva dall'esperienza. Capacitá di agire, valutare, consigliare con prudenza ed equilibrio."

Act. Ah! So the Italians link wisdom with the concept of balance. Interesting. - What about the Spanish?

Spe. *Picks up the last book.* Now that is odd: the Spanish do not seem to have a special word for wisdom. They only know about "sabiduria" and define it as "conocimiento profundo de las ciencias". But that is not wisdom: it is knowledge. *(Replaces the last volume, walks back* *to his desk and sits down.)* Fascinating, isn't it, in how many ways you can define wisdom. I can even add still another definition: Wisdom is the pursuit of the best ends by the best means. - So: there is not one definition of wisdom, but many. Are you disappointed, Actus?

Act. *Smiles.* No. Wisdom is obviously a many-faceted thing. It is beyond any simple definition. But that makes our quest for it more interesting. - Incidentally: how many languages do you speak?

Spe. Six. Seven, if you add my rusty Latin. You?

Act. Six. My Latin is practically non-existent. But I can recognize many Latin and Greek words, having been trained as a scientist: most scientific terms have Latin or Greek roots.

Spe. Can you recall the Greek word for wisdom, even though it has nothing to do with science?

Act. "Sophia". Every traveller to Istanbul knows that. Hagia Sophia, holy wisdom.

Spe. Correct. And can you also recall the Greek word for love?

Act. *After a moment's hesitation.* " Philo" or something?

Spe. Good. Now say "love of wisdom" in Greek.

Act. *Slowly.* Philo-sophia.

Spe. Exactly. And what do you make of that?

Act. For the moment, nothing. What should I make of it?

Spe. I will tell you. It has to do with the history of wisdom. Care to hear it?

Act. I do.

Spe. "Wisdom" originated, of course, in the Orient. The first man in history who wrote about it was an Egyptian called Ptahhotep, around 3000 B.C. *(Turns around to the room.)* Is Ptahhotep with us, by any chance? *(No reaction in the audience.)* Pity. Interesting fellow. He was actually a general; therefore a doer, as well as a wise man. He wrote a book in which he collected wise sayings. He defines in the book what a wise life is and tells us how to realize it. He is quite pragmatic about it. The sad thing is that his successors, other Egyptians who wrote books on wisdom, became increasingly esoteric. The original idea of Ptahhotep, that wisdoms have to do with everyday life, got lost.

Act. Go on.

Spe. There were men writing wisdom-books in Babylonia, but they tended to be pessimistic. Then came the Jews, and wrote things like the Book of Proverbs, the Book of Job, and the book Kohelet, the one we call Ecclesiastes. There is also an apocryphal book about the wisdoms of King Solomon. In all of these books religion is the foundation upon which wisdom is based; for the old Jews there was no wisdom without God.

Act. And then?

Spe. Then came the Greeks. They coined the term “love of wisdom”: “philosophy”, as you correctly deduced. But, for the Greeks, philosophy was largely speculative and high-brow; simple, practical wisdoms were not its main topics. And this brings me to an important point: we should not confuse wisdom with philosophy. Wisdom is partly less, partly more than philosophy. The Greeks failed to realize the difference, so they never coined a term for wisdom as distinct from philosophy. In ancient Greece a wise man was simply one who knew all about philosophy.

Act. And what happened after the Greeks?

Spe. Then came the Romans. They largely took over the ideas of the Greeks, but added some pragmatic thoughts of their own. Their main innovation was that they equated wisdom not with philosophy, but with virtue. I think this equation is still valid today.

Act. And then?

Spe. Then came the medieval church fathers. Wisdom became institutionalised, and took on a strictly religious aspect. The Church argued that only religion and faith can bring wisdom. So wisdom became strongly tinted by metaphysics.

Act. And when did our modern definitions of wisdom arise? The ones you found in the encyclopaedias?

Spe. Towards the end of the Middle Ages. People then started to realize that *fides* and *ratio,* faith and reason, were often incompatible. The result was a parting of the ways. This was accentuated by the Renaissance and completed by the Enlightenment. Wisdom became secularised, and henceforward associated with *ratio,* rather than with *fides.*

Act. Tell me, since you know so much: where does the word ”wisdom” actually come from?

Spe. From the old Nordic “wit”, which has the same root as “video”, I see. Wisdom consists in *seeing.* Wise men *see* - and thus they know.

Act. *Satisfied.* Spectus: these were interesting comments. I learned a lot. Thank you.

Spe. *Smiles.* Glad to oblige.

Act. Now: the purpose of this seminar is clear. But what about the road? We have an aim, but no road leading to it. We still lack a plot. And, incidentally, we still do not know why the picture of that cathedral is up there. What on earth does it have to do with this seminar?

Spe. Maybe it is a reminder that the builders of cathedrals didn’t know, at the outset, if their project can be realized at all. They just went ahead and started building.

Act. No, that is not a satisfactory explanation.

Actus and Spectus lapse into silence. Actus begins to look intently at the design of the cathedral on the wall. You can see that an idea is slowly taking shape in his mind. Then, suddenly, he has a flash.

Act. That’s it! I think I have got it, Spectus, my dear fellow. Tell me: how would you build a cathedral? I mean, a real one?

Spe. No idea. I am not a mason. Not even a free one.

Act. You don't have to be. Tell me: what are cathedrals built of?

Spe. Stones.

Act. Correct. Now: we are supposed to explore wisdoms. Let us compare each wisdom we find and discuss to a stone. One wisdom, one stone. Call it a wisdom-stone.

Spe. Aha?

Act. It is immaterial from what quarry such a wisdom-stone comes from. It may come from experience, knowledge, action, contemplation, from you, from me, from anyone. Not the origin matters, but where the wisdom-stone fits into the building.

Spe. Aha??

Act. Now: how would you start building a cathedral, if you were given the chance?

Spe. I would start with the foundation.

Act. Correct. And what kind of stones would you use for the foundation?

Spe. Solid ones. Probably a bit roughly hewn.

Act. Precisely. Now: how would you apply that to our case? Let me answer my own question. Our foundation would have to be built of wisdom-stones that are strong, robust, sound, unsophisticated.

Spe. You begin to fascinate me. Go on.

Act. Next, one would erect the pillars. I would associate the pillars with individuals. Pillars need to stand upright, on their own, like individuals must. So our pillars would have to be built of wisdoms that help individuals to stand erect, ensuring they don't get toppled. Wisdoms that help you to rely on yourself.

Spe. Great. Go on.

Act. Next come the walls. To build them, we need wisdoms that have to do with relationships among individuals. Wisdoms that help groups, communities, societies to function. Wisdoms for man the social animal.

Spe. And then?

Act. Then comes the roof. There we shall need delicate wisdom-stones, those that have to do with emotions and the soul. - So what have we got? A cathedral built of wisdom-stones, with roughly three levels. The foundation can be associated with the body and the senses. The pillars and walls, the middle part, with the mind. The roof with the soul. Body, mind and soul. There will be overlaps, of course. But, grosso modo, the structure is clear.

Spe. What about the towers?

Act. The towers stand somewhat separate from the main building. So they symbolize domains of their own. *(Takes a moment to think.)* I have got it! One tower we shall build out of wisdom-stones derived from the main tenets of the principal religions. The other tower with wisdom-stones based on the most important insights of the sciences. The two towers may be incompatible, or complementary - we shall see.

Spe. And the façade?

Act. The façade closes the walls in the front. It joins together the two towers. It rests on the foundation. It reaches up to the roof. Thus, it represents a summing up. The façade will be our summary. When we finished it, we have finished our cathedral - and our seminar.

Actus and Spectus fall silent. Gradually, a feeling of great satisfaction pervades them.

Spe. Actus, we found the purpose of this seminar and we succeeded in drafting a plot. Things fall into place.

Act. Yes. But we still have one last puzzle to solve. That razor up there on the wall. What the hell is that about? (*Suddenly sits up straight.)* Wait a minute! Razor! Middle Ages! That reminds me of a famous maxim.

Spe. I think I know which one you mean.

Act. *Looks back at the seminar room.* Is William of Occam participating at this seminar? *(Nothing happens.)* Maybe William of Ockham?

William of Ockham. *Comes to life. A venerable looking figure in Franciscan habit. Intelligent face, with almost modern features, sparklingly clever eyes.* Pluralites non est ponenda sine necessitate.

Act. Exactly. Thank you, William. I happen to know the current English translation of what you just said: Multiplicity ought not to be posited without necessity.

William of Ockham does not seem to appreciate that what he once wrote in Latin is now available in modern English. He slowly sits down and is nothing more than a wax dummy.

Act. *Exults.* My dear Spectus, we have the solution to that last slide. It refers to what is known as "Occam's razor". The razor stands for avoiding unnecessarily complicated mental constructions. It is a warning against pedantry, an invitation to explain things in the simplest possible terms. Eclectus wants a *lean* cathedral. We are asked to make meaningful selections. To focus on what is really important. To use our wisdom-stones with economy.

Spe. My dear Actus: congratulations. I am impressed by the way you grabbed the initiative and attacked this whole issue - after being so negative at the beginning.

Act. At the beginning I saw no sense in this symposium. Now I do.

Spe. So there is no turning back.

Act. Turning back? Who wants to turn back? We are off! As a matter of fact, we have already completed the first part of one of my favourite maxims.

Spe. Which is?

Act. Plan your work.

Spe. And what is the second part of that maxim?

Act. Work your plan!

There is a buzz from the wall. The slides disappear. Replacing them, the following message appears projected unto the wall:

Congratulations, gentlemen. You have successfully found the reason why you have been invited to this symposium. For the rest of the seminar please observe these rules: 1. We are conducting a research on wisdoms, not on philosophy, morals, techniques or know-how. 2. You are expected to draw on your own personal experiences. However, since this will not suffice: 3. You must also draw on the experiences of others. For that purpose, instead of books, you are provided with advanced cybernetic automata. Use them at your discretion. 4. You are expected to comment openly on each other's contributions, as well as on the contributions of those represented by the automata.

Good luck. And have fun.

Eclectus, Chairman

Act. Well, well. At least we are not alone. Big Brother is watching us.

Spe. I never had the feeling of being alone. This seminar is filled with all sorts of odd presences.

Act. You will end up saying this is not a seminar at all, but some spiritist séance!

Spe. *Laughs.* I did not intend to say that. But it may not be far from the truth.

The gong is struck.

Spe. *Looks at his watch.* That's the end of the morning session.

Act. *Takes out a piece of paper from his pocket.* Next on the programme is swimming, lunch and siesta. Not bad, the way these invisible organizers operate. - I don't know about you, but I am going for a swim. Mens sana in corpore sano.

Spe. Is that your first contribution to our search for wisdoms?

Act. *Smiles.* Not officially. But that maxim certainly fits somewhere into our cathedral. Either at the level of the body or at the level of the mind. Pick your choice.

Actus and Spectus laugh, rise and leave contentedly. The other participants remain seated. Obviously, they are not hungry nor do they care for a swim.

Session 3: The Foundation

Siesta time is over. Projected onto the wall of the seminar-room is the holograph of a gothic cathedral. Only the outlines of the church are shown: there are no stones within the structure, just empty space. The holograph is revolving slowly, enabling the viewer to see the entire structure three-dimensionally.

Actus and Spectus enter, obviously refreshed after a swim, lunch and siesta. They seem to be full of pep to continue. They go briskly to their desks and sit down. As they do so, the gong is struck.

Actus. Ah. No puzzles this time. Only a holograph with a clear message: start erecting a virtual cathedral made of wisdom-stones. Well: happy building, Spectus.

Spectus. Happy building, Actus. - Our first task: build the foundation. Any suggestions how to begin?

Beginnings

Act. By digging a ditch.

Spe. *Grimace.* Oh. Can't we skip the digging, please?

Act. *Laughs.* All right, let's assume the ditch is already dug, courtesy of Eclectus. That leaves us with extra energies to fill it. - Now: we said the wisdoms for the foundation should be robust, rather simple, straightforward. The kind accepted by a majority of people as quite evidently true.

Spe. Just because something is accepted by the majority of people as true does not necessarily mean that it is true.

Act. *Somewhat irritated.* Spectus: let us not get bogged down with scepticisms right at the start, otherwise we shall never get going. We must seize the day. Carpe diem!

There is a "ping" from the projection wall. Way down in one corner of the empty foundation a small, square stone has been fitted into the picture. The first wisdom-stone has been put in place.

Act. *Surprised.* Well, what do you know!

Spe. *Applauds.* Congratulations, my dear Actus! You just managed to lay the corner-stone of our cathedral. Frankly, I did not expect that the adage of a slightly degenerate Roman poet will start us off. *(Horace, author of "carpe diem", sitting at the back of the seminar-room, briefly flares up in protest against Spectus' opinion of him.)*

Act. Slightly degenerate or not, this is proof that it does not matter where a wisdom-stone originates. What matters is where it fits into our cathedral. "Carpe diem" obviously qualifies for the foundation. - The main thing is: we are off, Spetus. We made the famous first step with which even the longest journey begins.

There is another "ping" and another wisdom-stone is added to the foundation.

Spe. *Laughs.* Actus, you talk wisdom like Molière's Monsieur Jourdain talked prose: without realizing that you do so. - Incidentally: do you know whose wisdom you just quoted?

Act. No one's. I quoted a proverb.

Spe. You quoted Lao-tsu. *(A bearded wax figure at the back of the room flares up, but quickly turns to wax again.)* Many maxims uttered by great men end up as proverbs; the origin is forgotten, the wisdom lives on. - But let us try to find more wisdoms on "beginning", once we are at it.

Act. *Thinks for a second.* For the moment, the only one I can remember is called Allen's Law: Anything is easier to get into then out of. But I guess that is too trivial to qualify as a wisdom-stone.

Actus is mistaken: he earns a "ping". Eclectus, who obviously decides behind the scenes which statements qualify and which do not, knows that "Allen's Law" is a very ancient wisdom, first formulated by Aesop.

Spe. There is, incidentally, a famous warning related to Allen's Law: Beware of beginnings. Caveat principiam, said the Romans.

„Ping".

Act. Yes, that is a classic wisdom. Yet I have some doubts about its universal validity.

Spe. Ah, that's good,. Remember: we are supposed not simply to collect wisdoms, but to question and criticise them as they come up.

Act. Then here is my criticism of caveat principiam. That wisdom is certainly valid if it is meant as a warning against small bad beginnings that can obviously snowball into huge bad endings. But if accepted as unconditionally valid in every situation, it may act as a brake. It may justify inaction. It can be turned into a pretext for not beginning something that should be done, for instance keeping us from starting to change a situation that needs to be changed. It can be an excuse for keeping us from undertaking a dangerous, yet very worthwhile enterprise, or from beginning something simply because it is unfamiliar. I once read an advice that is the opposite of caveat principiam: start doing what you are afraid to do.

Actus earns a "ping". The advice he quoted was by Emerson, who is present but obviously decides not to react.

Spe. Good comments, Actus. Let me, then, suggest an alternative to caveat principiam. Another Roman maxim, since we are at it: Respice finem. Consider the outcome.

"Ping".

Act. Yes, I prefer that adage. It does not explicitly discourage us to begin something, but urges us to consider the consequences. It warns us against starting something though we are aware of the evil effects that may ensue. But it does not keep us from beginning something that may be difficult or risky, but is likely to bring substantial rewards. I would paraphrase respice finem like this: understand what you are about to do before setting out to do it.

Spe. The Germans have a poetic rendering of respice finem: Am Ende sieht's der Tor, der Klügre in der Mitte, doch der Weise sieht das Ziel beim ersten Schritte. The wise see at the beginning what fools see only at the end. - Any other wisdoms on beginnings?

Act. *Rubs his chin, thinking. His gesture makes him remember something.* What about this one: A beard well lathered is half shaved. If you begin something well, it is already half done.

Spe. That is because if you begin something well, you obviously like what you are about to do, and chances are that you will successfully complete it. There is a secret order called the Rosicrucians, whose members turned that wisdom on its head. They had a motto: Whatever you begin doing, like it.

Both Actus and Spectus earned a "ping" with their respective adages. There are now several wisdom-stones fitted into the foundation. Actus and Spectus look at them with satisfaction, as if they scored well in some electronic bingo game. They make an effort to think of other wisdoms on the subject of "beginning", but apparently have increasing difficulty finding them.

Act. So far, so good, Spectus. But have we exhausted the subject of "beginning"? And if so: how do we proceed from here?

Spe. *After a moment of thought.* Most of the wisdoms we quoted were proverbs. They seem especially well suited to build our foundation with.

Act. But we cannot possibly remember all the proverbs we need to fill the foundation.

Spe. That is true, alas. What we would ideally need is an expert on proverbs. The wit of one to convey to us the popular wisdom of the many. Something like a wise peasant. But I doubt that we can find such a one attending this seminar.

Spectus is mistaken. A wax figure begins to glow and rises slowly, heavily. White beard, old, tranquil, firm Eurasian face, with a slight stubbornness in his features. Simple clothes, difficult to tell from what epoch or geographic region. He seems to be something of a cross between a peasant and a prophet. He fixes a lucid gaze, with a hint of shrewdness, at Actus and Spectus, but says nothing. Before him, on the desk, a name-plate: Proverbius.

Actus and Spectus are visibly impressed.

Act. Well, Eclectus seems to think of everything. Chapeau. We have the character we need. Now: how do we make him talk?

Spe. *Looks thoughtfully at Proverbius.* I believe this automaton is programmed differently from the others. He is no historic figure who reacts to his name. He reacts to words, since he rose at the precise moment we needed him. So I presume we can activate him with words, just like we would surf the internet.

Act. Odd idea. Using state-of-the-art electronics to gather popular wisdom from a bearded automaton. How bizarre can you get?

Spe. Bizarre or not, let us try.

Act. *Raises a hand.* Hold it, Spectus. If this machine is a collection of proverbs, and you activate him with a word, he will throw heaps of proverbs at us containing that word. Like Google does if you search the internet. And he may do so in all European and Asian languages, including the dialects. We can then sit here until sunset before he stops, buried under heaps of proverbs, like the sorcerer's apprentice.

Spe. *Thinks about this briefly.* I am sure Eclectus foresaw this objection and did something about it. For one thing, this fellow will presumably have the courtesy to speak only in languages we understand. Then, he will probably select in his register the proverb that suits us most, tell it briefly, and then stop. He is no chatterer. He is an old peasant, and old peasants tend to be taciturn.

Act. But, to me, he looks also like a prophet. And prophets love to talk.

Spe. I don't agree. Prophets deliver messages. The shorter the message, the better. It is philosophers who love to talk. Prophets are concise.

Act. Let's hope you are right. - All right, then, let us ask him something about beginnings.

Spe. *Turns toward Proverbius and articulates slowly and clearly.* Beginnings?

Proverbius. *After a second, in which he obviously goes through the material stored in his register, speaks calmly, weighing every word, like old peasants often do.* The threshold is often the highest mountain.

"Ping".

Spe. *Enthusiastic.* It works, Actus! He not only added another stone, but I was right: he stopped after just one maxim. This fellow will be a gold mine - I mean a mine of wisdom-stones. And I like the proverb he selected. Indeed, we often have to make the greatest effort when we begin something. The first step is often the most difficult one. - Go on, Proverbius: tell us more.

Pro. To begin is easy; to persevere is difficult.

„Ping".

Act. Hey! Let me get this straight! He just claimed the first step is the most difficult. Now he says the contrary. Can't he make up his mind?

Spe. *Laughs.* My dear Actus, we have our first case of "sic et non". Two proverbs, set side by side, conveying the exact opposite wisdoms. But both are valid. Why? Because proverbs are based on the experiences of different people in different situations, so the lessons derived can be contradictory. My father used to say: If one lives long enough, one realises that many things are true - and that the opposites of many things are also true.

There is a "ping".

Act. *Smiles.* Your father was a wise man. He earned us a stone. - But, Spectus, does this mean that our foundation will be composed of wisdoms that contradict each other? Are we erecting a cathedral based on incompatibilities? De mêchant fondement jamais bon bâtiment, say the French.

Spe. On the contrary, my dear Actus. Our foundation would be "mêchant", lopsided, if it was built of wisdoms dealing only with one side of an issue. It is by taking into account opposite, but equally valid wisdoms, that we shall erect a solid foundation. - Incidentally, this fellow Proverbius is an extremely advanced automaton. Did you notice that in the proverbs he cited the word "beginning" does not actually occur? This is no dumb machine that merely reacts to recorded words. He understands the *meaning* behind the words. He comes up with answers that fit the meaning. Remarkable, to say the least. *(Looks up at the wall.)* Congratulations to you, Eclectus.

Act. *A bit impatient.* All right, Eclectus is a genius. But we must move on. I suggest we consider the subject of "beginning" as closed; we said enough on it. - Now: this morning we said that the foundation of our cathedral corresponds to the level of the body. I suggest, therefore, that we discuss wisdoms associated with parts of the body: senses, limbs, organs. I propose that we deal with the senses first, starting with the eyes. As you pointed out, the eyes are closely associated with wisdom, since the word wisdom comes from "wit", to see.

Spe. Excellent suggestion, Actus. I wonder what Proverbius has got to say. *(Turns to Proverbius.)* Seeing? Possibly also: not Seeing? Blindness?

To look, to see

Proverbius seems briefly to concentrate. He is obviously shifting through and ordering all the relevant material on the proposed subject. Since he is a truly advanced automaton, he is ready to deliver in less than a nanosecond. His "thinking" is a thousand times faster than that of Actus or Spectus. Yet he speaks slowly; but that is only a gimmick, to make him look true to the character he represents.

Pro. Many who look do not see.

Spe. *Thoughtful.* He starts with a profound truth. There is, indeed, a substantial difference between looking and seeing. Looking is a purely physical act; seeing involves understanding. There is no use having eyes in your head if your mind is blind. If we fail to apply our reason to what we are looking at, we end up not seeing, or seeing only what we want to see.

Act. And at times we accuse others of not seeing, but what we really mean is that they refuse to see *our* way. Conversely, we tend to say that someone has common sense if he sees things exactly as we do.

Spe. That is because we tend to see things not as *they* are, but as *we* are.

Act. So what practical conclusions emerge from this?

Spe. That, in order to see, we must reason when we look. That we must regularly test if another's view is not actually wiser than our own. That we must examine whether the truth lies not outside our present field of vision.

Act. Good counsels. Unfortunately, many will never heed them. I once participated at a seminar on how to deal with people holding extreme political positions. The first lesson was: do not try to change their view; it is useless.

Spe. Yes: such people do not use their own reason in order to see, but accept, without questioning it, the reasoning of some authority. They see with the eyes of those authorities, rather than with their own. They see what they are told to see. - There is a nice anecdote to illustrate this. I found it in Galileo's "Two Chief World Systems". *(Galileo has apparently not been invited, since no-one moves.)* A philosopher, follower of Aristotle, declares that all nerves in the human body converge to the heart. An anatomist invites him to assist at an autopsy. By dissecting a dead body, he clearly shows that the nerves do not converge to the heart, but to the brain. Turning to the philosopher, he asks him whether he now acknowledges his error. The philosopher replies: You have made me see this matter so plainly, that if Aristotle did not tell otherwise, I would be forced to admit it is true. - The irony of the matter is that Aristotle himself warned against such intellectual blindness. Amicus Plato sed magis amica veritas. Plato is dear to me, but dearer to me is truth. *(Two short flashes from the seminar room proceed obviously from Plato and Aristotle, but they decide not to interfere.)* - Proverbius: what else have you got for us on seeing?

Pro. One eyewitness is better than several who only heard-so.

Act. Aha. Popular wisdom holds that eyes are more reliable than ears. Yet modern psychology has proven that the eye is easily deceived. Think of all those visual tricks. So who is right: Proverbius or psychology?

Spe. Both. Proverbius' point is that when we use our eyes we depend only on ourselves. We are our own interpreters of what we see. When we use our ears, we depend on some intermediary and his interpretation. That explains the preference of popular wisdom for the eyes. Of course, we need to be able to interpret correctly what we are looking at. If we cannot, it may be preferable to listen to someone who knows better. - What else, Proverbius?

Pro. In the country of the blind, the one-eyed man is king.

Spe. That reminds me of another anecdote. A one-eyed man visits a kingdom of blind men. He tries to persuade them that there are things they cannot understand, because he can see them, but they can't. But he cannot explain to the blind what seeing actually is. So the blind finally declare that he is mad and put him to death.

Act. Hmm. I think what Proverbius means is not quite as drastic. His one-eyed man is meant to be a half-ignorant, living among the fully ignorant. The wisdom behind Proverbius' adage is this: What matters is not how *much* you see, but how much *more* you see than the others. - Go on, Proverbius.

Pro. *Is silent.*

Act. The old chap ran out of wisdoms on seeing.

Spe. I doubt it. He only applies Occam's razor to himself and leaves us to continue. So let both of us think of a few more wisdoms to conclude this topic. Let me start. - If we look at an object from just one angle, we see just one facet of it. Our view is partial. To see an object in its entirety, we must walk around it, look at it from all sides. The same applies to issues that confront us. The wise will not reach a conclusion before they have not seen and examined a problem from all sides.

Act. Unfortunately, the more sides we see of a problem, the more difficult it will be for us to reach a decision about how to solve it. Believe me, I speak from experience.

Spe. *Laughs.* That is, alas, also true. - Your turn.

Act. We agreed that seeing is different from looking. Yet, in science, there is a word that combines both. The word is "Theory". It is composed of two Greek roots. First: "thea", that means looking. It can also be found in the word "Theatre". Second: "horein", that means seeing. So: when scientists theorize, they both look *and* see.

Spe. But scientists often theorize about things in isolation. There is still too little contact between the various scientific disciplines. And that is a pity, because we cannot really see a thing unless we see it as part of a whole.

Act. Let me point out, Spectus, that science is increasingly adopting that attitude. It is indeed learning to start from the big picture and then look at the parts. Scientists tend today not to discard earlier discoveries, but to integrate them into a larger whole. Newton, today, is simply a special case of Einstein. - But we are getting too sophisticated. Let us end this topic with some simple wisdoms, as befits our foundation. - I believe that some wisdoms are right under our noses, yet we fail to see them, despite, or maybe because of, they are so obvious. It takes a truly wise man to see wisdom in the obvious and the familiar.

Spe. How true! - Here is another piece of wisdom for you. People talk of blind fate; but blind fate is often just the result of their own short-sightedness.

Act. Hmm. That is a bit sombre. Let us finish on a more positive note. - I believe that the wise have an essential quality: they walk through life with their eyes wide open. And since they do that, they spot useful things they can do, beautiful things in which they can rejoice, profound things from which they can learn. And the more they do this, the more of such things they will actually see. - But enough of looking and seeing. Let us move on to the ears. *(Turns to Proverbius.)* Hearing? Listening?

To hear, to listen

Pro. Many who hear do not listen.

Act. Ah, the acoustic equivalent of looking without seeing. - You know, it is surprising how some ancient beliefs get confirmed by modern science. Old popular wisdom makes a distinction between hearing and listening. But so does modern communications theory: it distinguishes between phonetics and semantics. Hearing is phonetics, listening is semantics. Phonetics is simply sound; semantics is meaning. Sound becomes meaning only if it penetrates into the nervous system, gets through to a so-called communication receiver, is understood there, and triggers action. If it doesn't do all this, then sound is simply unregistered noise. - This, incidentally, applies not only to humans, but also to machines. Some machines can be taught to listen, and the more they listen, the more efficient they become.

Spe. *Smiles.* At times, men can learn from machines. - But you said sound must be translated into action, otherwise it is just remains noise. We need to qualify that. One may very well register acoustic information without necessarily acting on it; it may simply be stored for later use. Or take a beautiful concert, that is certainly meaningful sound, but triggers no action, only passive enjoyment. But these are just side remarks. - Go on, Proverbius.

Pro. We listen only to what we are accustomed to hear.

Act. I can't agree with the old chap. It is precisely when we hear something new, unaccustomed, that we sit up and listen. There is a saying among marketing experts: if you want your customer to listen, surprise him. Customers listen to the novel, the unexpected. They tend not to listen when they know what you are going to tell them.

Spe. Most people hear the new, but then proceed to fit it into familiar, existing patterns. This is as if they did not listen. I think it is rare that the initial surprise of hearing a novelty translates into a corresponding action. Most people hear the new and then stick to the familiar.

Act. We disagree, Spectus, and I think I know why. What fails to trigger action is a monologue. Monologues are like noise: they do not invite a response. If you want someone to react to and act upon the novel message you are delivering to him, engage him in a dialogue. It is dialogues that lead to action.

Spe. Unless the dialogue consists of two monologues: two people merely hearing but not listening to each other. Someone defined loneliness as having to endure the presence of one who does not listen. And another fellow defined a bore as one who talks when you want him to listen.

Act. And still some other wise chap claimed that listening is an art.

Spe. *Smiles.* Ah, the name of that wise chap I can remember. It was Epictetus, two thousand years ago. *(No-one stirs in the audience.)* But, speaking of listening being an art: did you know that listening on stage is taught in actors' studios?

Act. Is it? That's interesting.

Spe. Experienced actors know that listening on stage is just as important as speaking your lines. Many young actors only think about their own text. But if an actor does not appear to listen to his fellow actors, then his own lines and actions lack motivation; they become empty words, unconnected movements. The audience senses this and will call the non-listener a bad actor. Just as they resent someone who does not listen to them in real life.

Act. Fascinating. - At any rate, good listeners are great motivators. I get more good ideas, and formulate better, if I am talking to a good listener. I even surmise that we can learn about ourselves when we talk to one who actively listens to what we say.

Spe. I agree. - Incidentally: who, do you think, are better listeners, men or women?

Act. I guess most would say it is men.

Spe. But it is women. Many men seem to resent having to listen. Maybe this is a genetic heritage. In the old days, kings, masters, prophets spoke, the people had to listen; today superiors speak, associates must listen. But men do not wish to be perceived as people or as inferior, and they manifest their independence by not listening. Women have no such scruples.

Act. Sorry, but this contradicts my own experience. Most of my male friends and colleagues are excellent listeners, and so are most of my female friends and acquaintances. I can see no difference whatever.

Spe. *Smiles.* Maybe you choose your friends carefully. - Be that as it may, let us hope that we are moving, gradually, towards societies where people readily listen to each other, irrespective of gender or social position. Though this may take time. - What else on listening?

Pro. Be prompt to listen but slow to answer.

Act. Of course one should be prompt to listen; but I see no point in letting people wait for your answer. People appreciate quick answers.

Spe. You misinterpret the old chap, Actus. What he warns against are rash answers. There is no point in listening if you give precipitated, unconsidered answers. I find the maxim is valid. - Go on, Proverbius.

Pro. If the old monkey barks, listen.

Act. What old monkey? Himself? You? Me?

Spe. *Laughs.* He means the aged. He advises to listen to what old people say. The logic of popular wisdom is straightforward: the older one gets, the more accumulated experience one has. Since experience brings wisdom, it is wise to listen to the aged. Do we agree?

Act. Only partly. It depends what kind of experiences an old person accumulated. Time does not necessarily make sages; often it just makes old people. - I think the wisdoms of the aged are only worth listening to if they provide answers to present problems. If their experiences and wisdoms only apply to issues of yesterday, then they may be of historic interest, but are not of real help. We can benefit from listening to the aged only if their wisdoms apply to all epochs, being immune to the passage of time. But it is not always easy to separate such perennial wisdoms from those that are simply out-of-date.

Spe. So what should the wise listener do?

Act. I think he should listen not only to the aged, but also to the middle-aged and the young. He should then combine what he was told into a composite opinion of his own. That opinion will likely be just, having come from the young; practical, having come from the middle aged; and humane, having come from the old. Those three criteria, taken together, will be the sign that his opinion is wise.

Spe. An excellent suggestion, Actus, you old monkey. Let us end this topic with your wise words. - Well: that takes care of eyes and ears. What's next? The nose? *(Turns to Proverbius with a somewhat doubtful expression.)* Smelling?

Pro. *Remains silent.*

Spe. Hmm. Popular wisdom has evidently nothing to say on smelling. Despite the fact that it is our most atavistic sense. Pity. - Let us try another sense organ, the tongue. *(To Proverbius.)* Tasting?

Pro. *Remains silent again.*

Spe. Obviously you can neither smell, nor taste, wisdom.

Act. *Smiles.* Nevertheless, Spectus, smelling and tasting enable us to distinguish good food from bad. So our nose and tongue wisely keep us from harm.

Spe. *Laughs.* I never considered my nose under that aspect. I must have more respect for the wise old thing. - But now to another role of the tongue. In fact: its main role. *(Turns to Proverbius.)* Speaking? And while we are at it: Lying?

To speak, to lie

Pro. That is not good language which not all understand.

Act. *Enthusiastic.* Excellent beginning, old chap. You obviously appreciate, like I do, the merits of simple language, understood by everyone. There is an old saying: prophets think like the wise, but talk like the vulgar. I am far from being a prophet, but I firmly believe that even complicated things can and should be said in a generally understandable way. If you can't do that, there are three possibilities. You have not understood what you are talking about. You are doing something wrong. Or you are simply being uncivil; for clarity of speech is a form of courtesy.

Spe. You are absolutely right, of course. But let me point out something. - I find that profound thinkers seldom formulate simply. They often use expressions beyond the grasp of most of us. It is those who interpret and disseminate the ideas of great thinkers who must use clear, understandable language. Even though there is a drawback: using simple language when trying to explain complicated things may lead to oversimplifications and distortions.

Act. Let us not confuse obscurity with profundity. Just because someone's language is convoluted and opaque, it does not mean that he is a profound thinker. There have been men with great minds and profound ideas who were quite able to convey their thoughts in a perfectly intelligible way. Conversely, there have been mediocre minds who were regarded as great simply because no-one understood what they really meant. I claim that all ideas, no matter how abstract, can be expressed and explained in rather simple terms. Every good dictionary does that. Conversely, great ideas can be spoiled, diluted, if expressed in tortured language.

Spe. *Thoughtful.* You have some valid points there, I must admit.

Act. Then let me add another. Forcing ourselves to express complex ideas in simple, understandable terms helps us clarify those complex ideas in our own minds. Thomas Huxley said something to that effect, if I recall correctly.

Thomas Henry Huxley. *Begins to glow, rises. A severe, very Victorian-looking gentleman.* Experience with popular lecturing has convinced me that the necessity of making things plain to uninstructed people is one of the best means of clearing up the obscure recesses of my mind. *(He makes an attempt to go on talking, apparently regarding Actus and Spectus as belonging to the uninstructed lot, but a mechanism inside him makes him return to wax.)*

Act. There you are. The style is Victorian, but the message is clear. - But go on, Proverbius. Give us another inspired wisdom on speaking.

Pro. Deliver your words by weight, not by number.

Act. You praise brevity, old friend, and I fully agree with you. Brevity, indeed, is the soul of wit, thus of wisdom. Most great wisdoms are formulated briefly; the shorter the formulation, the stronger the impact. In some great maxims one word alone carries the meaning. And brevity has another advantage: short sayings are easily remembered, long ones tend to be forgotten. Short sentences, furthermore, force you to be honest about what you say; in long, windy sentences you can hide all kinds of double meanings and half-truths.

Spe. But let me add an important comment. We can formulate short only if, previously, we thought long. A concisely formulated wisdom is mostly the result of a great amount of observation, experience and analysis that went before it. Primum vivere, deinde philosphari: live, before you start to philosophise. In other words: it takes time to formulate wisdoms briefly.

Act. Excellent comment, Spectus. - Tell me: do you agree with the advice that one should not formulate a sentence before finishing the thought it is meant to convey?

Spe. Not necessarily. I think half-baked ideas often mature during a good conversation. We should not keep ourselves from expressing ideas just because they are unfinished. However, there is an important proviso: let us choose very carefully the partner with whom we discuss our unfinished thoughts. - But go on, Proverbius.

Pro. Empty vessels make the most sound.

Act. He means that those who have nothing to say are often the ones who insist on saying it. Someone, I can't recall who, expressed this quite explicitly: Fools speak because they want to say something, the wise speak because they have something to say.

Spe. That was Plato. *(Plato briefly glows to confirm he indeed said it.)* But let me raise a caveat, Actus. If one only says things when one has got something to say, one will be considered a bore. The wise man will alternate grave talk with small talk, seriousness with jokes, the profound with the light. That way, the serious things he has got to say will be more readily listened to - and he will acquire the reputation of being a pleasant conversationalist.

Act. In fact, we are trying to follow that advice at this seminar, don't we?. We try to alternate the serious with the light. - Proverbius, you are supposed to be a polyglot. Tell us a well-known wisdom on speaking in several languages, just for fun.

Actus should not have said that. He conjured up the situation he himself feared at the beginning: Proverbius starts to deliver an avalanche of proverbs. But he reveals a fine irony: he chose as a wisdom the danger of words spoken inconsiderately, unable to get retracted.

Pro. Words have wings and cannot be recalled. - The arrow, once shot, does not return to the bow. - Ist das Wort der Lipp' entflohen, du greifts es nimmer mehr. - Tard la main à la bouche quand la parole est issue. - Parola detta e sasso tirato. - La palabra en la boca no torna. *(He goes on and on, switching to lesser European languages and then to Asian dialects.)*

Spe. *Laughs heartily.*

Act. *Horrified.* Stop! Enough! Please stop!

Proverbius ignores Actus.

Spe. *Continues laughing.* I am afraid your instruction will be executed to the bitter end.

Proverbius goes on for another three full minutes. At last, mercifully, he stops. His last proverb was in ancient Ethiopian.

Act. *Takes a deep breath.* Thank you, Proverbius. But now, please, let us get back to concise, one-wisdom-at-a-time normality.

Spe. *Is still highly amused.* Don't worry, Actus, this is a one-time escapade of the old fellow. He seems to possess an in-built sense of wise irony. - But there is an important lesson to be learned from what just happened: we have no control over words once we uttered them. We can control only what we have not yet said.

Act. That is undeniable. However, if we always fear the consequences of what we say, we end up valuing silence more than speech.

Spe. But that is precisely what popular wisdom advocates. Keep silent to avoid trouble. Isn't that so, Proverbius?

Pro. Speech is silver, silence is golden.

Act. Well, sorry, but I cannot agree with the old fellow. I simply cannot accept that silence is wiser than speech. This seminar would not happen if that was the case: we would just sit around here, keeping wisely silent. The view that silence is golden appeals only to those who mistrust others. But mistrust isolates. And isolation cannot be the aim of the wise. We do not live in isolation today, quite the contrary. We live in an age of widely open communications. And that presumes trust in those we communicate with.

Spe. You are suddenly in such a buoyant mood, my dear Actus. But please go on.

Act. A German author, I forget who, once said that noises are many, but there is just one silence. *(That was Kurt Tucholsky, who has not been invited.)* I do not agree. There are many kinds of silences. Silence can mean consent; it can mean denial; it can be a confession; it can be a lie. It can express scorn. It can be cowardice. It may even do harm, if you are silent when you should be speaking up.

Spe. Actus: let me offer a compromise between your view and that of Proverbius. Both silence and speech have their merits. The wise will speak or be silent depending on what the situation calls for. They will know what to say, when to say it, and when not to say it. There is a famous passage in the Bible: there is a time to speak and a time to be silent. Speech, and silence, are both a matter of timing.

Act. *Thoughtful.* I think I can go along with that.

Spe. The wise will, furthermore, also know when to stop speaking. They will stop when they said what they had to say, knowing that adding more will only water down what they said.

Act. True.

Spe. But let me add a footnote to all this. - Life would be unpleasant and drab if we went around forever controlling what we say or do not say. Especially when we are with friends, we should relax our controls. We should then say openly what is on our hearts, have our hearts in our mouths, so to speak. And we should also allow for some freely spoken nonsense. Wisdom needs, at times, to relax.

Act. *Smiles.* A wise footnote. Have you any more, Spectus?

Spe. *Raises his hand solemnly, like an Indian chief, and speaks in deep baritone.* I have spoken.

Act. In that case, Proverbius, it's your turn again.

Pro. He knows enough who knows nothing but knows to hold his tongue.

Spe. Decidedly, he insists on the merits of silence.

Act. Well, sorry, but once more I cannot agree with him. The wise will do exactly the contrary of what Proverbius suggests. I will never improve my knowledge if I do not ask questions about things I do not understand. If I am ignorant about something, I should not hold my tongue, but speak up and ask questions. - I have experienced dozens of times at seminars that some courageous fellow, who did not understand something, spoke up and asked for clarification. You could then hear a sigh of relief from other participants who also did not understand, but were ashamed to admit it. There are no silly questions, only silly answers. Popular wisdom does not seem to have arrived at this simple insight.

Proverbius obviously decides to defend popular wisdom against Actus' low opinion of it.

Pro. He that nothing questions, nothing learns.

Act. *Surprised.* Ah?

Pro. A lame tongue gets nothing.

Act. Aha??

Pro. Who is afraid to ask has no urge to learn.

Act. Jolly good.

Pro. Better ask the way than go astray.

Act. I am impressed. I misjudged you, old chap. Sorry. You are wiser than I thought.

Spe. *Laughs.* You forgot that Proverbius is a champion of "sic et non". A consummate master at looking at all sides of an issue. - But let me point out something that has to do with Proverbius' last adage. A recent study revealed that men indeed prefer to go astray, rather then ask the way, in a strange town. They are reluctant to reveal their ignorance by asking a passer-by. Women are much more pragmatic: if they lost the way, they ask. Practical wisdom can be as simple as that. - Anything else on the merit of asking questions, Proverbius?

Pro. One fool can ask a question that ten wise cannot answer.

Spe. *Thoughtful.* That is quite profound.

Act. It is. - It reminds me of a somewhat aged scientist who, at the end of the 19th Century, claimed that all scientific questions have essentially been answered. Then some foolish young scientists appeared on the scene and started to ask questions the older one never dreamt of. We should be grateful to those fools who ask new questions to which we have yet no answers. They make us reflect, and by so doing advance our wisdom. A wise man once said: we should always prefer the fertility of open questions to the finality of answers

Spe. Nice quote, that one. - Incidentally: those "fools" who ask questions are usually far from being fools. "That fellow is wise enough to play the fool; but to do that will crave a kind of wit." Shakespeare. - What else, Proverbius?

Pro. Call a spade a spade.

Act. Ah! I was wondering when that will turn up. It is a universal classic. Talk plain English. Das Kind beim Namen nennen. Parler francais. Decir al pan pan, al vino vino. Latine loqui. Talk straight, don't beat around the bush. I am all for it. - But we keep talking of talking. What about shouting? Any wisdom on shouting?

Spe. Don't.

Act. *Laughs.* That will presumably be the shortest wisdom uttered at this seminar. - But we have one more important aspect of speech to cover, before we leave this subject: lying. What can you tell us about lying, Proverbius?

Pro. A lie procures you lunch, but no dinner.

Spe. Ah, this is one version of a very ancient adage. The Jews say a lie can get you far, but not back. The Germans say lies have short legs. And some witty man, I recall, said the best liar is the one who makes a lie go the longest way. *(Samuel Butler, if present, does not react.)* All these wisdoms warn us that, sooner or later, a lie will be found out. Nevertheless: some clever and unscrupulous people succeed in hiding lies almost indefinitely.

Act. How?

Spe. In two ways. First: by hiding a lie behind other lies. There is a difficulty with this method, though: the liar must remember not only the original lie, but all the other lies behind which he hid it. So this method requires a good memory. - But there is also a second way of hiding lies.

Act. Which is?

Spe. Mixing them with the truth. There is a stunning advice from the Orient: To sell a lie, package it into a parcel of truths. Subtle politicians have been using that trick for centuries.

Act. But then the liar must remember when he lied and when he didn't. My advice is: tell the naked truth, rather than try to dress up lies. It is less exacting.

Spe. It may be less exacting, Actus. But that brings us to a moral problem the wise will have to face. Should a lie be avoided and condemned in all situations? There is an old wisdom: Better a lie that heals, than a truth that wounds.

Act. I cannot accept that. Telling the truth is always better than lying, even if the truth hurts.

Spe. I wonder about that. - Do you know what Ibsen said about this issue?

Henrik Johan Ibsen. *The great critic of conventional morals, begins to glow and rises. Huge head with flowing white hair, small spectacles, clad all in black, an umbrella in his hand.* Take away the saving lie from the average man, and you destroy his happiness. *(He takes his glasses off, wipes them, sits down heavily and returns to wax.)*

Act. But if we accept Ibsen's view, then lying becomes a question of purely subjective judgment. We are then free to decide whether lying in a given situation is desirable or not, without any moral standard to refer to.

Spe. That is true. We are confronted here with an age-old problem: the controversy between moralists and utilitarians. - For the moralist, lying is always bad. He condemns all lies out of principle, irrespective of the consequences. A simple stance. - For the utilitarian, a lie is to be judged by its results. He may tell a lie, for instance, if by doing so he can avoid a great calamity or further a just cause. If the consequences of a lie are beneficial, then, for the utilitarian, lying is no vice, but a sensible course of action. This stance requires judgment.

Act. So what, in your opinion, should a wise man rather be: a moralist or a utilitarian?

Spe. He will accept, to begin with, that there are two opposite camps. Tell me, Actus: don't you tend to judge actions by their results?

Act. Are you forcing me into the utilitarian camp?

Spe. I somehow can't see you in the strictly moralist camp. Or am I wrong?

Act. *Thinks briefly.* You are right, Spectus. This whole matter is more subtle than it seems at first sight. Let me try to formulate my stance. - I like simple, straightforward rules. I would, therefore, much prefer to proclaim that lies are always bad, no matter the circumstances. That would make me a moralist. - Yet: I cannot deny that, for me, results are very important. That means I do have a certain sympathy for utilitarianism. But, as far as lying is concerned, I restrict that sympathy and make it dependent on three conditions. First: the utilitarian liar should never tell a lie in order to promote his own interests, but always for the benefit of those for whose sake the lie is told. Second: the utilitarian liar will make sure that the benefits of his lie are substantial. He will never lie just to obtain petty benefits. Finally: the utilitarian liar will make sure that the benefits of his lie are long-lasting, not just short-term.

Spe. *Smiles.* Bravo, Actus. You just painted the profile of a remarkable person: the wise utilitarian liar who may be mistaken for a moralist.

Act. But I haven't finished yet, Spectus. - It is extremely difficult to judge, in any situation, whether all three rules I set up will apply. So, despite my sympathy for utilitarianism, I am convinced that, in most situations, it is preferable to tell the truth. Not because of some narrow moralist precept. But because telling the truth, though it may at times be hard, is likely to have the most lasting beneficial results and thus promote the utilitarian cause.

Spe. *Smiles.* Well and wisely argued. A stance that combines the best of two worlds. But let me add a few more thoughts to this complex topic of lying. - At times, people lie without realising that they do. That happens when they propagate convictions they believe to be true, without realising that they are false. Religious fanatics are the extreme case. But even philosophers and scientists are not immune, since they can propagate theses that are false, while being convinced that they are true. - And then there are cases where it is impossible to tell if something is true or a lie. Take Proust's telegram.

Act. *Surprised.* Proust's telegram?

Spe. Proust declined an invitation to a dinner party he did not want to go to, by sending a telegram that said: impossible de venir, mensonge suit. Cannot come, lie follows. That is: Proust announced beforehand that the pretext he was going to cook up for declining the invitation is going to be a lie. But was he telling the truth or was he lying?

Act. *Grimace.* Spectus, let us keep clear of this kind of futile intellectual exercise. May I remind you that are discussing simple wisdoms, not pitfalls of logic. - Proverbius: lead us back to basics. Tell us some straightforward, easily understandable wisdom on lying.

Pro. The lost cow gave a lot of milk.

Act. *Irritated.* Do you call that straightforward and easily understandable? What the devil are you talking about?

Spe. *Laughs.* He talks about the peasant's version of the angler's story. Magnifying something through a lie. The fish was enormous: what a pity it has already been eaten, so there is no proof. The lost cow was a champion in giving milk: unfortunately, since it was lost, this can't be proven. - The wisdom behind the fish and the cow story is that lying can be tempting if there is no one around who can disprove it. No-one believed Marco Polo's account about China, because no-one could disprove his story, so people automatically assumed he was lying. - But go ahead, Proverbius, tell us more.

Pro. Where there is whispering, there is lying.

Spe. Yes: if things are not discussed openly, facts are distorted and become lies.

Pro. A lie is halfway round the world while truth is still putting its boots on.

Spe. Unfortunately, that is also true. For some odd reason a lie appears to sink more readily into the human mind than truth does. - But I suggest we allow Proverbius to relax and look at an issue that is beyond the old fellow's horizon. I mean half-lies, or, if you wish, half-truths. Do you know what I am talking about, Actus?

Act. Only too well, alas. Half-truths are selective truths, and they can be extremely dangerous. Someone telling a half-truth does not actually lie, since what he says is true. But since he only tells part of the truth, he is in fact lying. Let me give an example. - A safari-traveller enquires about the animals in the forest outside the lodge. The lodge manager tells him there are deer and zebras, which is true. But he omits to tell him that there are lions, which is also true. The manager, in fact, tells the truth, yet he misinforms. If the traveller acts upon the manager's true information and goes out without a gun, he will be in acute danger of being eaten by the lions.

Spe. Good example.

Act. There are many others. The media tend to exaggerate bad news by focusing on negative tidings, suppressing the positive ones: the journalistic principle of bad news being good news. So the public thinks it is well informed, but in fact it isn't; it is only half-informed. - Statisticians can manipulate trends by focusing on data from selected years, rather than taking data from all relevant years. They can also take short term trends and extrapolate them, giving the impression that the long-term will follow from the short-term, which is practically never the case. - Interest groups can distort proportions, magnifying parts of the truth, giving the impression that those parts are the ones that matter. - And so on and so forth. Half-truths are dangerous because they are true. Yet they are whole lies.

Spe. Nothing to add to that. Except, perhaps, a famous line by William Blake: A truth that's told with bad intent / beats all the lies you can invent. *(Blake briefly flares up but goes unnoticed.)* - I think we almost finished with speaking and lying, Actus. Any concluding remark?

Act. Yes. There are people who, if you ask them for information, prefer to give you a lie, rather than admit that they do not know. I find such people extremely annoying. The wise will never be ashamed of admitting that they do not know. - Any final remark from you, Spectus?

Spe. Yes. One that may amaze you. In the language of the North American Indians there is a thing called "evidence grammar". If a speaker makes a statement, he has to choose among three grammatical forms. The form he chooses signals whether he eye-witnessed what he is telling, heard about it from someone else, or just presumes it is so. This forces the speaker to make statements of remarkable precision.

Act. *Laughs.* I now understand why a red Indian couldn't tell a lie, and why white men were accused of speaking with a forked tongue. - We covered a lot of ground, Spectus. How are we doing with our foundation?

The "pings", the acoustic acknowledgments of a wisdom-stone accepted, have ceased a while ago, but the foundation has been quietly filling up. Not only all of Proverbius' wisdoms were incorporated into the foundation, but also many of Actus' and Spectus' commentaries.

Act. Not bad. We are making progress. Now: since we finished with the head, we have to move downward. To the arms and hands. What can one do with one's hands?

Spe. Give. Receive. Take.

Act. *Turns to Proverbius.* You heard our next topics, Proverbius; start us off.

To give, to receive, to take

Pro. It is more blessed to give than to receive.

Spe. He starts, of course, with probably the best known maxim on the subject.

Act. *Thoughtful.* Yet, though so well known, I think the maxim needs qualification. The reason is that there is an essential difference between charity and reciprocity. - Charity is one-way giving, going from the giver to the receiver. It means giving freely, without any strings attached, without the giver seeking an advantage to himself. All the receiver is supposed to do is say "thanks". Charity is certainly "blessed" from a moral point of view. - Reciprocity, on the other hand, is two-way giving. It goes from the giver to the receiver, but then reverses and goes from the receiver to the giver. This leads to a dialog between givers and receivers. It promotes mutual understanding, sociability, it even furthers affection. Though it cannot be called blessed, reciprocity is certainly wise. Though charity is needed, on a scale of wise social values I would place reciprocity above charity.

Spe. But there is an old wisdom: giving in order to expect something in return is like not giving at all.

Act. Sorry, but I question that wisdom. Giving in order to expect something in return does not in any way diminish the merit of giving. There is an age-old adage: "do ut des". Give, and expect to receive. All commercial transactions are based on that principle. Contracts are based on it. Friendships are strengthened by it. Early religious sacrifices were based on it: God, accord me that, since I sacrifice to you this. There is a profound wisdom at work behind reciprocity. - Tell me this, Spectus: do you keep inviting people who never invite you back?

Spe. Hmm. No, I don't.

Act. You see? People can get accustomed to just receiving. Giving then becomes counterproductive, since the receiver ends up seeing no need at all to reciprocate. One-way giving can even create parasites, professional beggars. It can kill initiative. It can destroy the desire for self-help and self-reliance. Where charity is really needed, do it. But do not overdo it. The wise will not give indiscriminately; and in many cases they will expect something in return.

Spe. I accept what you are saying, Actus. Charity and reciprocity are indeed quite different kinds of giving. So different rules will apply to each. I suggest that we try to formulate what these rules are. - I suggest you start with reciprocity.

Act. The most important rule concerning reciprocity is: what is being given and what is being expected in return should be of the same order of magnitude. - When you give small and expect small, there is no problem. Neither is there a problem when you give big and expect small. Trouble begins when you give small but expect big; in fact, that is morally condemnable. The most delicate case, however, is to give big and expect big. There is an oriental wisdom: Small gifts make friends, but large ones make enemies. The giver of a large gift may expect something equally big in return. However, if the receiver is not in a position to reciprocate with something equivalent, then he gets into an obligation towards the giver that he cannot satisfy. This, to say the least, is uncomfortable. At times it can become unbearable.

Spe. So what will the wise do in order to avoid the pitfalls of reciprocity?

Act. Before he gives, the wise giver will make sure that the receiver is willing and able to reciprocate with something equivalent. He will consider to whom he gives, what he gives, why he gives, and how much he can expect in return. - The wise receiver, in turn, will refuse to be given if he sees no possibility to properly reciprocate.

Spe. I commend you on this clear exposé, Actus. Now it is my turn. Wise comments on charity. - To begin with, charity, unconditional giving, can fill the giver with joy. That emotional element is missing from your clear-headed reciprocity. In Asia, givers used to thank receivers for the pleasure they got out of being allowed to give. - Now to some rules. Charity must be generous, wholehearted, with no second thoughts and no strings attached. The charitable will give before being asked to give. They will not restrict their giving to material things, but will freely give moral support, suggestions, ideas, affection - and they will do all this with a smile. While giving, the charitable will never think of being reciprocated later; for if we keep thinking about reciprocity where it is out of place, we loose warmth and spontaneity, and our giving becomes a cold, calculating act.

Act. *Smiles.* Great eloquence, Spectus.

Spe. There is one more point I wish to make. Where giving is wholehearted, the gesture of giving may actually create greater benefits than the thing given.

Act. On that point I fully agree with you. There is a simple example for it, though it has nothing to do with charity, but rather with reciprocity. It is reciprocating the services of a waiter by giving a tip. Some people give large tips, but with a detached, arrogant air. Others give smaller tips, but with a smile; they make it clear that they appreciated the services of the waiter. The waiter who receives the large tip from the condescending customer will simply bow. The waiter getting a smaller tip, but accompanied by an appreciating smile and thanks, will smile back. The first waiter will be richer; the second may be happier.

Act. True. Giving tips is an art.

Spe. Giving any gift is an art. - Do you know what I consider to be the most difficult case of giving? Giving the right gift to a close friend. The closer a friend, the more difficult it is to select a present for him or her. You can't give just any old thing to a close friend; you must carefully consider what the friend needs or what will make him happy. Tel don, tel donneur. You can judge the character of a giver by knowing what he gives to whom.

Act. True. - Have you an more rules on charity?

Spe. No.

Act. Then let me add a comment, which belongs neither to charity nor to reciprocity, yet has to do with giving and receiving. - Let me quote from personal experience. There are times when I arrive at a point where I simply feel that I have given enough. Given time, know-how, effort, information, help, whatever. At that point I need to counterbalance: I need to receive. I grasp a book, listen to music, let a good meal be served to me, let myself be entertained. However, this receiving-phase never lasts very long. After a relatively short time I feel again an urge to give: the pendulum swings back. - Something similar happens in marriage. In a healthy marriage, one of the partners gives for a while, the other receives for a while. Then the roles are reversed. No marriage will last where one of the partners always gives, and the other always receives, no matter how "blessed" giving may be. - My conclusion is this. Giving without ever receiving is only for a few saintly people. Receiving without ever giving is morally unacceptable. The wise, therefore, will seek a dynamic balance between giving and receiving; the wise will alternate.

Spe. I think, Actus, that with those wise comments of yours we have exhausted the subject of giving and receiving. Or have we not?

Act. Maybe not quite. Giving is often initiated not by the giver, but by the receiver: through asking. Proverbius: have you got in your register any wisdom on asking to be given?

Pro. He that faintly asks, begs denial.

Act. True. If you ask to be given, do it with conviction. Otherwise you may create the impression that you don't really need what you are asking for. Anything else, Proverbius?

Pro. The wheel that squeaks most loudly gets most of the grease.

Spe. *Thoughtful.* That is certainly so. There are examples for that almost every day. Militants and minorities claiming vociferously to be given. They squeak as loudly as they can in order to impress the potential givers. So what should be the attitude of the wise? They should judge calmly and objectively how much grease the squeaking wheel really needs, or if it needs any grease at all. They will give according to the real need of the wheel, not the intensity of the noise it makes.

Act. A sensible suggestion. - Now, very briefly, to one last point, beyond giving and receiving, yet related to the hands. It is taking. What is taken is not given, but yielded. Taking is against the principle of reciprocity. The wise will resist it. Since they know that if they yield an inch, they will next have to yield the yard.

Spe. Indeed. There are many instances in History. - So: that takes care of the hands.

Act. Then let us move further down the body. *(Smirks)* How about - the genitals?

Spe. I think we should not deal with those.

Act. But why not? Wisdoms about the genitals would bring colour to this symposium. And Proverbius would certainly have no inhibitions about the subject. He is quite outspoken.

Spe. *Laughs.* Maybe. But statements about genitals are either trivial, or cynical, or medical. They are not really wisdoms. I veto the subject.

Act. Pity. - All right, then, let us move further down. To the legs and feet. The organs of locomotion. We can move slowly, briskly, hurriedly. Let us see what popular wisdom has to say about that. *(Turns to Proverbius.)* Moving?

To move

Pro. Chi va piano, va sano.

Act. I could have sworn he will begin with that. It was to be expected that popular wisdom recommends slow pace, rather than speed. Well, I disagree. In rural places, where most of Proverbius' wisdoms originate, you may not need to hurry. But in modern cities, where everyone is in a hurry, you simply can't afford to be slow.

Spe. And yet, some who lived in big cities agree with Proverbius. Among them one who lived in the biggest city of his time. Is Caesar Augustus with us?

Gaius Octavius Augustus. *Comes to life. Clad in beautiful armour, like his statue from the Villa Primaporta in Rome. He points approvingly at Proverbius as if supporting what the latter just said and then pronounces the famous two words:* Festina lente! *(He lowers his arm and sits down, obviously frustrated at having to say so little, excellent rhetorician as he is. He looks waxy again, though surely he would prefer to look like marble.)*

Spe. There you are. Festina lente. A wisdom that made the tour of the world. Make haste slowly. Eile mit Weile. You name the language and you will find the same proverb. On this point the greatest of Caesars and global popular wisdom fully agree.

Act. Well, sorry, but I disagree with both Augustus and global popular wisdom. Their view is outmoded. Today, speed is essential, slowness can be suicidal. Today we need to turn Proverbius' adage on its head: chi va *presto,* va sano.

Pro. *In a warning tone, obviously irritated by Actus turning one of his basic wisdoms on its head.* Haste is the sister of repentance.

Act. *Directly addressing Proverbius, as if he were human, rather than just an automaton.* No, my dear old fellow, it is slowness, not haste, that is the sister of repentance. You will repent if you are slow, because you will miss the boat. And speaking of sisters, let me quote my father, as you quoted yours a while ago, Spectus. He never tired telling me, when I was young, that speed, prompt execution, quick response, are the main qualities of a successful operator. To be appreciated, you must play quickly, he used to say.

Actus' father earns a wisdom-stone.

Spe. *Smiles.* We both had wise fathers. But let me point out something essential, to avoid misunderstandings. What Proverbius and Augustus are condemning is not speed, but haste. They equate haste with rashness, precipitation, unconsidered action. You can't deny that the chances for errors are much higher if you act in haste.

Act. Of course I don't deny it. But, regrettably, in today's world you do not have the luxury to check, slowly and comfortably, every eventuality to ensure that you operate without errors. You just have to take the risk that things might go wrong.

Spe. But errors can mean double work, inefficiency, waste. Haste makes waste, remember?

Act. *After briefly considering Spectus' objections.* Spectus, I think I see a way out of this controversy. As you rightly pointed out, it is not speed that we should condemn, but undue haste. We can be quick, yet avoid undue haste, provided we do an essential thing: keep control. It is retaining control what really matters. If we do something quicker than our means of control allow it: that is undue haste. If we do something quickly, but without losing control: that is dispatch. It is control that makes the difference between undue haste and dispatch. The key is control.

Spe. *After a brief pause.* I must praise you for that insight, Actus. Indeed: it is control that matters. I presume we shall encounter the necessity for control, time and again, as we proceed with this seminar. You hit on a major universal wisdom. - But let us hear what else Proverbius has to say on moving.

Pro. Mieux vaut un trot qui dure, qu'un galop qui se lasse.

Spe. He means that you are more likely to reach your goal at a steady trot than by trying to gallop there all the way.

Act. Unfortunately, though, we often have to gallop most of the time to reach our goal. If we decide to trot comfortably along, some other rider may get to the goal before we do.

Spe. *Smiles.* Actus, this time let *me* offer a way out of the controversy. We should certainly gallop when it is necessary, but not when it is not necessary. We should not spur our horse if he does not need to gallop. This is simply practical wisdom: spare your energies when you can, so that you will have them at your disposal when you really need them. Speed up when speed is called for, slow down when you can afford it. Find the right pace, the right rhythm, for everything you do.

Act. No objections. I can fully support what you said. - Anything else, Proverbius?

Pro. Soon ripe, soon rotten.

Act. Sorry, but once again I must disagree with you. Your adage certainly applies to vegetation. But in human affairs, if something ripens quickly, meaning it is brought to a conclusion speedily, it does not mean it will soon afterwards start rotting. Rather the contrary: human affairs may start rotting if they take too long to accomplish. We tend to lose interest in an affair that gets dragged; and losing interest is akin to rotting. - Anything else, old fellow?

Pro. *Is silent.*

Spe. We seem to have exhausted the old chap. Have you got any final wisdom to add on moving, Actus?

Act. I do. If you have the choice between taking your car or walk: walk!

Spe. *Laughs.* A surprising piece of wisdom coming from someone who prefers galloping to trotting. But I fully agree. I simply love walking. There is hardly any problem I can't find a solution to when taking a walk. Especially through a beautiful forest.

Act. Same here. - Well, we have finished with the external parts of the body. To continue, we shall have to go inside it.

The gong is struck.

Spe. Ah! But before we go into the body to seek wisdoms, let us pour some afternoon tea into it.

They laugh, rise and walk out. Proverbius doesn't care for refined pleasures like afternoon tea. He remains standing, unperturbed.

Session 4: The Foundation (continued)

Actus and Spectus return from afternoon tea. Proverbius is still standing. On the wall, the holograph shows the foundation about half-filled with wisdom-stones. As Actus and Spectus sit down at their desks, the gong indicates the start of the session.

Actus. Look at that holograph: not too bad,. We made progress. We should be able to fill up the foundation by this evening if we keep going at this pace. - One thing worries me, though. You and me started this symposium. Then Proverbius joined us. But we have not heard much yet from these other characters sitting around here. There must be nearly a hundred of them.

Spectus. They will join us in due time, once we properly understood how to use them. - Let me see. We finished with the external parts of the body as a guide to wisdoms for the foundation. We now need to go inside the body. What is arguably the pre-eminent organ inside? The brain. I suggest, therefore, that we start discussing wisdoms closely associated with the brain.

Act. I can name one wisdom right away: *use* your brain. In other words: *think*! The brain needs exercise, just like the muscles do. Something as valuable as the brain must be kept fit. Few minds wear out, but many rust out for lack of exercise.

Spe. Then let us exercise ours. - What is the first activity that comes to your mind when we speak of exercising our brains?

Act. Learning.

To learn

Spe. All right: here we go. Proverbius, set us off, please. *(Spectus forgot to say the word "learning". But Proverbius reveals his capabilities by showing that he does not need such primitive instructions. He follows the conversation and knows what is expected of him.)*

Pro. We learn by doing.

Act. Ah, I fully agree with that. Learning requires action. It needs doing. He that does nothing, learns nothing - But let me extend Proverbius' statement a bit. We start by doing. By doing, we gain experience. By accumulating experience, we gain wisdom. We therefore have a chain with three links: action-experience-wisdom.

Spe. Yes: action quasi-automatically begets experience. But experience does not automatically beget wisdom. It does so only if we analyse and put to proper use what we have experienced. - And that brings me to an interesting question. What we experience can be good or bad. We have successes and failures. Do you think that we profit equally from both? In other words: can we derive as much wisdom from our successes as from our failures?

Act. I try to learn from both my good and my bad experiences. From failures as well as successes. I see no difference.

Spe. But is that generally so? What do you think, Proverbius?

Pro. Man learns little from success, but much from failure.

Spe. Aha. Popular wisdom is quite clear on the matter. Many others would agree. Among them Franklin.

Benjamin Franklin, *the "first civilized American", begins to glow. He holds a kite into the air, from which he appears to draw the electric power that makes him glow. He looks very much like his portrait by Duplessis.* Experience keeps a dear school, but fools will learn in no other. *(He sits down, and putting his kite under his desk seems to cut off his own power.)*

Spe. That man speaks from bitter personal experience: he had a very hard childhood, yet managed to turn his hardships into wisdoms.

Act. Let me point out, Spectus, that failures and hardships are different things. - A failure has didactic value; it can teach a lesson and make people wiser. But deriving wisdom from hardship is quite a different matter. Franklin could do it, but he was an exceptional man. I reckon that most people are not strong enough to do what he did. Hardship does not usually make people wise; on the contrary, it tends to make them pessimistic, defeatist, resigned. - And there is more. Some people overreact to bad experiences. They derive more lessons from a bad experience than that experience actually contains. We then have the burnt child who is afraid of a candle or the man bitten by a snake who will be scared by a rope. - So I repeat my thesis. I can see no proof that negative experiences are more conducive to wisdom than positive ones. To regard bad experiences as a more effective source of wisdom than good ones is a lopsided view. - But we said enough on this. Proverbius: lead us on.

Pro. Wise men learn from other men's harms.

Spe. An excellent trick.

Act. But a trick that applies, once again, to good experiences as well as bad ones.

Spe. *Smiles.* Of course.

Act. But let me point out something important. - While learning from the experiences of others is certainly beneficial, I think we can learn more from our own, direct experiences. My reasoning is simple. If we do something, we get feedback. Feedback shows us plainly the effects of our actions. If we just study what others have done, there is no feedback. Therefore, learning from personal experience tops learning from study.

Spe. Hmm. What do you think of Actus' claim, Proverbius?

Pro. Experience with little knowledge is better than knowledge with little experience.

Act. You see? Popular wisdom agrees with me. Mere study, knowledge without experience, is sterile. What is the merit of knowledge if you need to keep running to others for advice, because you lack the experience to apply it?

Spe. *After a brief pause.* Your points are well taken, Actus. But allow me to recall a definition you particularly liked when we went through the meaning of wisdom this morning: "Wisdom is the combination of experience *and* knowledge with the ability to apply them judiciously." This definition assumes that experience and study have equal value. Your action-experience-wisdom chain is certainly valid. But there is a second, parallel and equally valid chain: study-knowledge-wisdom. Knowledge alone, without experience, may not suffice. But I claim that experience alone, without the support of knowledge, leads only partially to wisdom. Study helps us to become more receptive to the lessons of our experiences, and so it broadens the spectrum of our wisdom. Experience and knowledge, action and study, go hand in hand. The wise will seek to combine them.

Act. *After a moment's reflection.* You have a good point there, Spectus. Still, I continue to maintain that experience tops knowledge. - There is an ancient adage: Knowledge makes a good man better, but an evil man worse. The adage is explicit: it does not say that *experience* can make an evil man worse, but *knowledge* can. It is knowledge, not experience, that is misused for evil purposes. That is the theme of all James Bond stories. The arch-villains are mad geniuses with a tremendous amount of technical knowledge. Yet this knowledge does not teach them wisdom; so, in the end, they get blown up. The lesson is: men of great knowledge are not necessarily also wise.

Spe. What you are saying is that experience is necessary to check knowledge and put it to responsible use.

Act. Correct.

Spe. In other words, what you claim is this. The first chain, action-experience-wisdom, is valid on its own. The second chain, study-knowledge-wisdom, is effective only in combination with the first.

Act. That's it in a nutshell. - And, Spectus, I have yet another argument to support my view. I have not come across silly people with a lot of experience. But I have come across silly people with a great amount of knowledge.

Spe. *Smiles.* True. Addison had a caustic remark about such people.

Joseph Addison. *Glows and rises, with an issue of "The Tatler" in one hand and of "The Spectator" in the other. Huge wig, as painted by Dahl.* The truth of it is, learning makes a silly man ten thousand times more insufferable, by supplying variety of matter to his impertinence, and giving him an opportunity of abounding in absurdities. *(Sits down and becomes indignant wax.)*

Act. Thank you for an excellent witness to support my point. - And Addison makes me think of something else: showing off. People rarely show off with their experiences; but many do with their knowledge. But since the wise will never show off, we have another argument in favour of experience. Have you, by any chance, also got a witness for this point of mine?

Spe. *Laughs.* I may. Provided Lord Chesterfield is with us.

Philip Dormer Stanhope Chesterfield. *Appears, at first, not to have heard that his name was mentioned, because, though wax, he is engaged in writing a letter to his son. After a short while he realises that he has been summoned, begins to glow, rises, and reads a text, apparently from the letter he has just been writing.* Wear your learning, my son, like your watch, in a private pocket, and do not merely pull it out to show you have one. If you are asked what o'clock it is, tell it; but do not proclaim it hourly, and unasked, like a watchman. *(He sits down and resumes writing.)*

Act. A wise, witty and gentlemanly advice. - But since we are discussing the pitfalls of mere knowledge unsupported by experience, let me point out another one. People who value experience usually know when their experience is deficient; so they go out to get more. It is not the same with knowledge. People with inadequate knowledge are often unaware of their deficiency. Though they only possess half-knowledge, they are convinced they know enough. - This time, let me summon a witness to support my point. Is Mr Pope with us? If he is, he will know which poetic lines of his I am thinking about.

Alexander Pope. *Begins to glow and attempts to rise, but fails, because of the curvature of his spine. Yet, even seated, he immediately commands attention through his marked profile and extraordinary eyes. He wears a headgear like in Hudson's portrait of him.* A little learning is a dangerous thing. / Drink deep, or taste not the Pierian spring. / There shallow draughts intoxicate the brain, / and drinking largely sobers us again. *(Turns back to somewhat distorted wax.)*

Act. Well written, isn't it?

Spe. It is. But beautiful as Pope's poetry is, let me qualify it. - I cannot accept the idea that little learning, or shallow knowledge, is in itself dangerous. All knowledge, even if limited, is valuable. - The trouble lies, as you pointed out, in human nature. It lies in the mental attitude of those who, though they only possess half-knowledge, attribute to themselves an authority as if they possessed full knowledge. It takes humility to avoid that. The wise are humble as far as their own knowledge is concerned. They realize that what they know is surrounded by an ocean of things they do not know. In fact, they realize that all their knowledge will, necessarily, always be half-knowledge. And they will revere what they have not explored.

Act. *Smiles.* Your poetic expression rivals that of Pope. - But answer me this. There is generalized knowledge and specialized knowledge. Which is more valuable?

Spe. Both taken together. The wise will know something about everything and everything about something. The latter will get him a good job, the first will make him a good leader.

Act. *Laughs.* An excellent answer. - But I think we have exhausted the themes of experience and knowledge. Let us revert to our original starting point: learning. *(Turns to Proverbius.)* What other wisdoms on learning have you got in your register, Proverbius?

Pro. The wise learn from every man.

Spe. Indeed they do. Everyone knows at least one thing well and it pays to learn that one thing from him. Let me illustrate that point by an interesting story. - In a colony of monkeys, the youngest, least experienced monkey was taught how to get bananas out of a machine, by pushing a certain button. His elders kept taking the bananas away from him; none of them ever hit upon the idea to observe and learn how to operate the machine. Then, the eldest monkey, the chief, was taught to handle the machine. Within 15 minutes every monkey in the colony knew how to get at the bananas. The old monkey was accepted as an authority from whom one can learn; the young monkey was simply dismissed as someone you couldn't possibly learn anything from.

Act. Does that mean that if we refuse to learn from people we consider too young or inferior, we act under the dictate of our simian inheritance?

Spe. *Smiles.* That may well be so.

Act. Well, then, I proudly claim to have overcome my atavistic roots. I firmly hold that learning works not only from the top down, but also from the bottom up. An engineer can learn from his foreman. A boss from his associates. A father from his son.

Spe. *Smiles.* You are an advanced human specimen, Actus. Many still need an effort to accept that they can learn from the young or from an underling. - What else on learning, Proverbius?

Pro. A moment's insight can be worth years of learning.

Spe. It can indeed. Some of the most valuable things I learned emerged from sudden insights. Often I suddenly grasped the true significance of certain words which, for years, have been nothing but words. - Go on, old fellow. You are doing well.

Pro. Most things are difficult before they become easy.

Spe. Yes. First comes drudgery. Then comes mastery.

Act. And then, for a selected few, comes perfection. Or will the wise not aim at perfection at all? What do you think, Spectus?

Spe. *Thoughtful.* A difficult question. Perfection is a function of the time available. There was a famous Japanese painter who set up a life-plan: he expected to reach perfection by the age of 115. Of course he knew he would fail. Leonardo sought perfection; he worked on some canvasses for decades but then let them unfinished. The wise may seek perfection, yes; but they know that they will most probably not have the time available to achieve it.

Act. Frankly, Spectus, I do not care much for perfection. It is something static, rigid, final. It can usually be achieved only if you keep doing the same one thing over and over again for years. But life is not about just one thing, it is about many things. Life is imperfect by definition, since it keeps continuously changing. I think it is futile to seek perfection in an imperfect world. - Instead, the wise should seek something else: excellence. Perfection can only be attained by a few, if ever. But excellence is attainable by many. Excellence is within reach. It means doing one's best in one's allotted time. Excellence will not make a perfect world, but it will make a better one. And that is sufficient.

Spe. Well said, Actus. - Proverbius, lead us on.

Pro. Never too old to learn.

Spe. An important message. Learning should be a never-ending process. Seneca thought so too.

Lucius Annaeus Seneca. *Glows and rises. Fat figure, bald, double chin, resembles the actor Charles Laughton. One has difficulty believing that he ever smiled, but also that he was ever angry. He speaks English with a cultivated accent, obviously translating himself from Latin.* We must go on learning as long as we are ignorant. And our ignorance lasts as long as we live. *(He sits down slowly and becomes poised wax again.)*

Act. Hmm. A discouraging prospect, remaining forever ignorant, despite a continuous effort to keep on learning. I have a more positive advice: remain curious, as long as you live. For it is curiosity that makes you diminish your ignorance and urges you to go on learning.

Spe. I agree. - Unfortunately, there is a snag. In youth, we learn easily. And we retain easily what we have learned. Quod nova testa capit, inveterate sapit.

Act. *Mumbles to himself.* Odd seminar, this. Seneca talks English, Spectus talks Latin. *(In a normal voice).* Go on. I am curious to hear what the snag is.

Spe. As we grow older, our *premises* to learn improve: we become less impressed by false truths; we are better able to judge what is right and what is not; we see more clearly what really matters. Unfortunately, at the same time, our biological *capacity* to learn decreases. We can no longer take in as many new lessons as when we are young. That is the snag.

Act. *After having briefly considered this.* But you overlook something, Spectus. In youth, as you correctly say, we mostly *add* learning, since everything is new to us. As we advance in age, we add less; we rather *correct* what we have learned, modify what is familiar. If we possess the open-mindedness to keep on correcting what we have learned, then our wisdom will keep increasing. And that is what really matters.

Spe. It is comforting what you say, Actus. Incidentally, it goes to show how important it is to learn the right things when young: we need to correct less later.

Act. So it is. And the right things to learn are, for me, the practical things. We can make use of those throughout our lives. It is highbrow speculations that need most of the correcting. - But let me add another comforting thought. Another argument against your snag. We can turn learning into a habit. And since habits get ingrained with age, those who make a habit of learning will keep on learning, whatever their age.

Spe. *Smiles.* Make good habits, and they will make you. - But another thought just occurs to me. We need more than correct our stock of learning as we grow older. We also need weeding. Discarding unnecessary ballast. Focusing on what really matters. This was taught, among others, by a Chinese gentleman I highly respect. The Chinese call him Meng K'e. We call him Mencius.

Mencius. *Sitting next to Confucius, as his best pupil, begins to glow and rises. Clad like Confucius, but he has less severe features than his master and looks almost benign.* Learn widely and then go into what you learned in detail, so that, towards the end, you can return to the essentials. *(Looks briefly at Confucius, who would nod in appreciation if his mechanism allowed it; then slowly sits down and joins his master in waxiness.)*

Act. Great sage; profound saying. - But let me add a warning. I agree that focusing on what really matters is wise. On the other hand, we must not overdo the weeding. Discard too much from our treasury of lessons. Define as ballast what is not ballast. Throw away too much of what we think is no longer essential. For if we do that, we may end up with a stock of lessons that is too narrow. The world, and life, are complex. So we must be careful not to narrow down what is not narrow, to oversimplify what is not simple.

Spe. *Smiles.* Your wisdom almost matches that of Mencius. - Have we done with the subject of learning?

Act. Almost. One last question. What is the relationship between learning and doubting?

Spe. *Thinks for a second.* The less we know, the less we doubt; and the less we doubt, the happier we are going to be. - The more we learn, the more doubts we are likely to encounter. We can turn those doubts into something negative, unfruitful: into mere denial. But we can also turn them into an urge to keep on looking for the truth. - Those who are certain, stop learning. Those who doubt, go on learning. The wise will, therefore, welcome doubt. They know that doubt can, ultimately, lead them to more wisdom than premature certainty can.

Act. A philosophical answer. But I wonder if it applies to the practical world around us. In a world where the ignorant are cocksure and the learned wise full of doubt, isn't there bound to be trouble?

Spe. The cocksure ignorant, Actus, will at one point begin to doubt. But the doubting wise will at one point reach certainty.

Act. *Smiles.* Be that as it may. - But let us end this topic and take up the next one. I suggest the opposite of learning: teaching. And an activity related to it: counselling, advising. - Proverbius: set us off, please.

To teach, to advise

Pro. Practice what you preach.

Act. Ah, that is a fundamental wisdom indeed. We can only convince through example. You can't expect people to follow your teaching if your behaviour is contrary to what you preach. You can't say: do as I say, not as I do. Like the proverbial priest who preaches water but drinks wine - or the other way around, I can never remember.

Spe. *Smiles.* But I can remember a sophisticated version of that metaphor. It is by Francis Bacon.

Francis Bacon, Baron Verulam, *the founder of Empiricism, glows and rises. He is clad like a lord chancellor of England in the early 17th Century and holds a book, "Novum Organum" in his hand.* He that gives good counsel builds with one hand. He that gives good counsel and good example builds with both hands. But he that gives good counsel but bad example builds with one hand and pulls down with the other. *(Sits down and returns to wax.)*

Act. Excellently put. Much more articulate than the adage about that silly priest. - Proverbius: tell us a few more articulate things on teaching.

Pro. He teaches ill who teaches everything.

Spe. He means the wise teacher will always leave something for his pupils to work out for themselves. In other words, he will teach them to think. How to think, not what to think.

Act. *Smirks.* Eclectus certainly follows that maxim. He makes us work out not just something, but practically everything, at this seminar.

Spe. Eclectus is like Socrates, who called himself a midwife, helping others to reach wisdoms on their own, without appearing to teach them.

Act. *Grumbles.* An invisible chairman playing the midwife helping two men give birth to wisdoms. Some aspects of this seminar are decidedly bizarre. - Go on, Proverbius.

Pro. Teaching others teaches the teacher.

Act. Now that I can confirm from personal experience. I understood a subject fully only after having had to teach it - first at college, later at seminars. Teaching cleared the last recesses of my mind, as Huxley put it. - What else, Proverbius?

Pro. Don't teach the fish to swim.

Act. Now what silly fool would want to do that?

Spe. *Laughs.* All those silly fools who imagine they know better and try to teach people who need no instruction. There is a funny alternative to Proverbius' adage: You will always find an Eskimo eager to teach a Nigerian how to cope with heat waves. I find such Eskimos tremendous bores. - But let us leave teaching and move on to counselling. What can you tell us on that topic, Proverbius?

Pro. Only the vulgar think they need no advice. Noble minds seek counsel.

Spe. A very fine maxim. Sounds oriental. - Go on, wise old fellow.

Pro. Steer not after every mariner's advice.

Act. And he who builds according to everyone's advice will have a crooked house. Two classics. But I see a difficulty. - We should, obviously, not change our course following every new advice that comes along. On the other hand, we should not ignore good counsels either. But how to judge which counsels are good and which ones are not? How to know which advice to follow and which one to reject? Can you answer that, all-knowing Proverbius?

Pro. Even if you have sixty counsellors, consult yourself.

Act. But if I do that, I will have sixty-one counsellors, instead of sixty. I have not solved the problem. All I did was to increase the number of counsellors. Try again, old chap.

Pro. *Seems for the first time to hesitate, evidently searching for the right answer in his databank. He finally seems to have found one.* Kommt Zeit, kommt Rat.

Act. You mean postpone the issue? That is no adequate answer either. Postponing an issue makes me lose time, without necessarily helping me to choose the right advice. Try again.

Pro. Night is the mother of counsel.

Act. You mean: sleep on it? Well, some decisions may be helped if we do that. But you still haven't convinced me.

Spe. *Cuts in.* Fascinating dialogue, you two. But aren't you playing games, Actus? I have the feeling you have the answer.

Act. I haven't got *the* answer. But I have got *one* answer.

Spe. Which is?

Act. Select the *advisor,* not the *advice*. Listen to the counsel of those you consider to be the most competent in the matter at hand. Take the advice of the expert, the one who has proven in the past to be able to solve issues similar to yours.

Spe. That is no doubt a sensible solution. But let me play the advocatus diaboli. - Is expertise really that reliable a criterion? Tell me, Actus: haven't you, in your business career, come across competent advisors who gave you not the right advice, but the advice they thought you wanted to hear?

Act. *Becomes thoughtful.* In fact yes, I did. Some professional advisors simply confirm their clients' preconceptions. But in such a case the fault lies with the advisees: though they ask for advice, all they want is approbation.

Spe. But this means that expertise, alone, is not a sufficient criterion to select the best advice. An expert may seek his own benefit, rather than that of the advisee.

Act. So how would *you* select the best advice, Spectus?

Spe. By extending your suggestion and listen to two different types of advisors. One will be the expert, competent in the matter at hand. The other will have another, a complementary qualification: he is an unselfish friend who wants the best for us. - In other words: the wise advisee will listen to advice that comes from the head, as well as to advice that comes from the heart. How he combines these two counsels, what he ultimately decides to do, remains his responsibility. But his decision will be based on a more solid foundation than if he listened to one of these advisors alone.

Act. An interesting suggestion.

Spe. And there is more, Actus. The professional advisor may be reluctant to give us advice that hurts. A true friend will have no such inhibition. He will not withhold counsel from us that may be bitter, but necessary.

Act. But bitter advice may be rebuked, and will then fail its purpose. Some wise man wrote: Harsh advice will be repulsed like the hammer by the anvil. *(That was Helvetius, who does not appear to be at the seminar.)*

Spe. We must not confuse harshness with bitterness, Actus. Bitterness has to do with the *content* of an advice, harshness with the *manner* it is delivered. No advice should be delivered harshly, especially not if it is bitter. Gracián said something to that effect. Is he with us?

Baltasar Gracián. *Glows and rises, clad as a Jesuit. He holds, half hidden in his robe, a huge book, which brought him some trouble: "El Criticón". Though he wrote in Latin, he speaks with the words of his English translator, courtesy of Eclectus.* When you counsel someone, you should appear to be reminding him of something he has forgotten or overlooked, rather than show him bluntly the light he is unable to see. *(He remains standing.)*

Spe. Yes: that, for me, is the correct approach. An advisor should be firm, but gentle. Forte in re, suaviter in modo. He will not try to force his advice on the advisee. Rather, he will help him arrive, on his own, at the decision that the advice is correct. Then it will be effective. - But Gracián is still standing. Have you got another wisdom for us, Padre?

Gracián. *Obviously waited to be asked.* Good advice is often transmitted successfully through a well placed joke, rather than through grave and serious teaching. *(Now he sits down and returns to wax.)*

Act. *Laughs.* He is right: some advices are indeed more effective if wrapped in jest. Wisdom should not be afraid of being playful. - Have we finished with teaching and counselling?

Spe. Let us decide that we have. - Now: what else can we use our brains for?

Act. To make judgments.

Spe. Excellent. - Set us off, Proverbius.

To make judgments

Pro. The good judge understands quickly but judges slowly.

Spe. I fully agree with the old chap. Quick judgments are usually no judgments at all: they tend to be prejudices. *Pre*-judices, that is opinions formed *prior* to having properly judged. The prejudiced are ill-informed, or half-informed, but believe that they possess all relevant facts for a judgment. But they do not really judge; they simply jump to conclusions.

Act. And jumping to conclusions is the only exercise some people give their brains.

Spe. *Laughs.* True. - And the prejudiced incur another error, even graver than jumping to conclusions. They condemn, rather than judge. But we have no right to judge, let alone condemn, what we have not properly understood. - By the way, all this reminds me of a famous saying quoted by Plinius. The elder one.

Plinius the Elder. *Glows and rises. Open, intelligent, cheerful, almost modern face. His white toga is covered over and over with black ashes from Mount Vesuvius, the eruption of which he watched, but he does not seem to care.* Ne supra crepidam sutor iudicaret. *(His Latin pronunciation is beautiful. He brushes a bit of ash from his toga and turns back to wax.)*

Act. Can you please translate, Spectus?

Spe. He said: a cobbler should not pass judgments about things that lie beyond his last. A last, in case you have forgotten, is the wooden form on which a shoe is fashioned or repaired. - But let me explain the origin of that maxim. A cobbler once criticised the way the famous painter Apelles painted a shoe in one of his pictures. Apelles gladly accepted the criticism. Thereupon the cobbler started to criticise the whole painting. Apelles cut him short with his famous sentence: cobbler, stick to your last. What he meant was that our judgments should not extend to things beyond our profession. Thanks to Plinius, who retold the story, the warning of Apelles to the cobbler became a proverb.

Act. *Thoughtful.* You know, Spectus, I have some difficulty with that proverb. Taken literally, it means that only cobblers are allowed to pass judgments on shoes and on other cobblers, since any judgment by a non-cobbler would be outside his profession. That seems to me too narrow a view. If I am a well-to-do non-cobbler and can afford to buy several shoes a year, then, necessarily, I will gather a lot of information about shoes. I end up with a certain knowledge about shoes, since I am able to compare the products of different cobblers.

Spe. So you want to modify Pliny?

Act. Yes. Slightly. - Not the limits of our profession should be the criterion that allows us to pass judgments, but the limits of our *competence.* If I do something frequently, I gain experience; with it I gain competence. My highest degree of competence will, of course, be in my profession, since it is there that I do things most frequently. But I may also do things frequently outside my profession; thus I can also gain competence outside it. And the more competence I build up, whether in my profession or outside it, the more I shall have a right to pass judgments connected with that competence.

Spe. *Smiles.* Actus the logician! - But answer me this: if one lacks competence in a certain matter, but has a great deal of common sense, does that also entitle one to pass judgment?

Act. No, I think common sense is not enough. We need to assess and evaluate a great deal of information in order to judge properly, and common sense does not replace that need. But common sense is certainly a co-ingredient when passing sound judgments. It is competence plus common sense that make the wise judge.

Spe. Another question. We said the wise should combine advice coming from the head with advice coming from the heart. Does something similar apply to judging?

Act. I think the wise judge should primarily listen to his head. He should bring light, but no heat, into the matter he judges. The wise judge is a cool judge. - Nevertheless, there are many situations where the one who judges should also listen to his heart. Sometimes, deep human motives play a major role in the matter we are judging. We must try to understand those motives, put ourselves into the others' shoes. If we do not, we run the risk of condemning rather than judging. - But don't get me wrong: the wise judge, though he may listen to his heart, will never become sentimental. The wise judge is not sentimental: he is humane.

Spe. Good comments. Let me round them up with a slightly cynical one of my own: the humane judge will not attribute a deed to malice if he can attribute it to mere stupidity. - What else have you got for us on judgment, Proverbius?

Pro. If you listen to just one bell, you will hear only one tune.

Act. Ah, this is one of my favourite maxims. If Proverbius knew Latin, he would have said: Audiatur et altera pars. Listen also to the other side. To pass a fair judgment, we need to listen to all parties involved. The wise judge is impartial. I presume this is one of the oldest wisdoms of mankind. - Go on, Proverbius.

Pro. Do not judge the wine by the barrel.

Spe. Or a book by its cover. The message is clear: try to see through appearances when passing judgments. - Unfortunately, this is often very difficult to do. A lot of effort in this world is directed at making things appear what they are not. A judge may have to cut through a maze of pretences, falsehoods, deceptions, half-truths. It is easy to say: stick to the facts, when it is almost impossible to distinguish fact from appearance. Often appearances are the only clue we have got.

Act. Have you a remedy?

Spe. Unfortunately, no. I can only stress, as you did earlier, the importance of competence. A competent judge is more likely to be able to distinguish fact from appearance than an incompetent one. There are two opposite poles. In the best case, competent persons make judgments on the basis of facts. In the worst case, incompetent persons judge on the basis of appearances. - But I think we said enough on this topic.

Act. Then I suggest we look at another activity of the brain, related to judging: decision-making. - I wonder what Proverbius can contribute to it.

To make decisions

Spe. *cuts in before Proverbius can say anything.* I fear Proverbius' contributions would be very limited in this case. To popular wisdom, decision-making takes the form of simple choices. Such as: You cannot have it both ways. Or: Of two evils choose the less. Or: No choice among rotten apples. Let us do without the help of the old fellow this time, and rely only on our own experiences. Or rather on yours, Actus. You are a businessman. You are confronted, more or less daily, with decisions to take. Let us hear what wisdoms you have reaped from all that decision-making over the years.

Act. *Smiles.* I will try to oblige. But let us forget the small, easy decisions and focus on the complex ones. It is when we face big, complicated issues that we need all the wisdoms we can summon to make the right decisions. - To begin with: two basic rules. Rule One: do not procrastinate. Even difficult decisions should be made within reasonable time-frames. Rule Two: do not leave for others to decide what falls clearly within your field of responsibility.

Spe. Can you describe the process, the steps you take, to reach important decisions?

Act. Yes. *(Smiles.)* You view me as a pragmatist, Spectus. So you may be somewhat surprised at what I am now going to tell you.

Spe. Hear, hear!

Act. When faced with a big decision to take, I rely on two things. One is rational analysis; the other is what I would call "gut feeling". But please do not get me wrong: this "gut feeling" is nothing esoteric. It has a rational explanation. - When we face an issue on which we need to take a decision, there are almost always similar cases we have dealt with in the past. But the relevant facts associated with those past cases may not all be consciously present in our brain. Some of them may have drifted down into our subconscious. It is that subconscious I call "gut". We may have highly relevant data stored in our "guts" that we do not consciously remember. That data manifest themselves as the "gut feeling". That feeling should by no means be given preference over rational considerations; but it can effectively supplement them. - What I claim, therefore, is this: if we let both our brain and our "gut feeling" act together, they will bring about a wiser decision than if the brain alone is let to do the task.

Spe. How does this work in practice?

Act. I begin by gathering all relevant facts; I sort them, qualify them. This is a purely rational activity. I avoid making judgments at this early point; if I do, they are entirely unbinding. - Next, when I have gathered enough facts, I sit down and look at them. It is at this point that my "guts" want to get heard: so I listen to them. If my "gut feeling" is negative, it is a warning that there are important facts I seem to have overlooked or forgotten. Or that something is wrong with my rationale. So I go back and do some more fact-finding. I repeat this procedure up to the point when both my reason and my "guts" are in agreement. At that point I make the decision: either for or against. - By using this procedure, I avoid two pitfalls, an early boss of mine called "paralysis by analysis" and "going extinct through instinct". I do not rely on analysis alone, studying ever more data, much of which tends to be irrelevant. Neither do I rely on instinct, or "guts", alone. My aim is to combine analysis and instinct, rationale and "guts", and keep the two in a correct balance.

Spe. Interesting exposé, Actus. - Tell me, what is worse: wrong decision or indecision?

Act. Indecision. Wrong decisions can be painful, but at least they have didactic value. But indecision is debilitating; it feeds upon itself; it is transmitted to others and becomes something like a contamination.

Spe. And what about changing one's decision? Will the wise stick to their decision, once made?

Act. By all means - except if the circumstances that led to their decision change substantially. If that happens, the wise will re-examine their decision in the light of the new situation. This does not necessarily mean that they will alter their original decision; but they might. The wise will not be reluctant, nor ashamed, to reverse a decision, if new facts clearly compel them to do so. To change a decision, if the change is well-founded, is not inconsistency.

Spe. Every big decision involves risks. How can the wise avoid them?

Act. Risks are a fact of life: one has got to live with them. The important thing is that the decision-maker remains objective about the risks that may ensue. We shall have to go into the subject of risk later in this seminar.

Spe. Am looking forward to it. - One last question: is it wise to delegate decision-making?

Act. The wise will know which decisions they have to take themselves, and which ones they can leave to others. They know that people who are being continuously deprived from making decisions end up dumb, sterile, dependent. But those who delegate must make it clear that decision-making means assuming responsibility.

Spe. Actus: these were interesting recommendations. But even if one follows them, one cannot exclude making wrong decisions. No man is wise at all times. So let our next topic be: making mistakes.

To make mistakes

Spe. Let me begin with a classic: Errare humanum est. To make mistakes is human. Mistakes are a part of life. Faultless is lifeless. I find this to be comforting.

Act. Yet, Spectus, we should not give general absolution for *all* mistakes, just because we recognize that making them is human. While there are excusable mistakes, we should not be too lenient towards every kind of error. I claim that there are different levels of mistakes: some are excusable; others less so; still others, hardly.

Spe. Can you develop this thought in some detail, Actus?

Act. Sure. - On the lowest level I would place small, insignificant errors. A stumble, rather than a fall. Such a slight stumble may in fact prevent a fall. - The wise will disregard such small mistakes. In ancient Persia, boys helped the master to weave rugs. If one of the boys made an error in the pattern, the master simply neutralized it by slightly altering the design, so that the error went unnoticed. - Of course: we must recognize that even small mistakes can be dangerous. Even a small leak can sink a ship, as Proverbius would say, if we let him.

Spe. *Smiles.* True. - The next level?

Act. The next level is what I would call an honest mistake. For instance, errors that we make because we were deliberately misinformed. Or if we try to attack a problem by trial and error, and make mistakes in the process. Such cases can even be beneficial, since they enlarge our experience.

Spe. Agreed. - What is your next level?

Act. That one is less excusable: keep repeating errors of the same kind. Falling more than once into the same trap. It is the case for which a famous adage has been coined: Fool me once, shame on you; fool me twice, shame on me. - But here, again, one has to be indulgent, up to a point. We may be fooled twice because we have failed to recognize the trap being the same as the one we fell into in the past. The same danger may appear in different guises.

Spe. What errors are next?

Act. Those that have their roots in prejudice. Errors that could have been avoided if we had made an effort to get rid of our prejudices, if we used our reason. We make such errors when we do not take time to judge, but condemn right away.

Spe. What level follows?

Act. Mistakes due to laziness, indulgence, inattention, lack of care. So many errors could be avoided if one only cared.

Spe. True. - I am curious about the next level.

Act. That one has to do with undertaking nothing to redress the consequences of a mistake we made. That level involves, in fact, a double mistake: the original error, and the failure to redress the consequences of it. Such errors have a tendency to swell. It is much easier to dam a brook than a river; it is a grave mistake not to correct an error while we are still dealing with the brook.

Spe. What is the next degree?

Act. It is the last one: the obstinate refusal to admit an error, though it is obvious to everyone, ourselves included, that we have made it. This level has to do with dishonesty, arrogance, stubbornness, fear of losing face. But one loses more face by refusing to admit an obvious error than by openly admitting it.

Spe. True. Someone wrote that we could learn much more from our errors if we weren't so busy denying them.

Act. So it is. We must turn back on the wrong road, no matter how far we have travelled on it.

Spe. Instructive, your levels of error, Actus. - But what always fascinated me is that great men, even geniuses, are not immune to making stupid mistakes. Take the case of Napoleon, who ordered the execution of the innocent Duke of Enghien, though he knew that his act would raise all Europe against him. It prompted one of Napoleon's counsellors to make a celebrated remark: C'est pire qu'un crime, sire: c'est une faute! *(Boulay de la Meurthe has not been invited; Napoleon, though present, does not budge; apparently he agrees posthumously that his mistake was indeed stupid.)* As a matter of fact, a successful strategy for the weak is simply to wait for the strong to make a stupid mistake. - Any final comment, Actus?

Act. Yes. The wise will not be afraid of making mistakes. That fear can paralyse. The wise know that mistakes can be salutary and instructive. It is like with failures: we can turn an error into experience and wisdom - provided we admit having made it.

Spe. And the graver our mistake, the deeper the wisdom we may derive from it. - Now: what else can we do with our brain?

Act. We can remember. And forget.

To remember, to forget

Spe. Let's take those two together. Proverbius: please give us one wisdom on remembering and another on forgetting.

Pro. Absence makes the heart go fonder. - Out of sight, out of mind.

Act. Ah. A case of "sic et non". Absence increases our affection for the absentee, says the first adage. Absence makes us forget the absentee, according to the second one. Now which one is it? For we can't remember and forget an absentee at the same time.

Spe. Nevertheless, both adages are valid. Because there is a difference. - Note that the first one talks of "heart", the second of "mind". What makes these two situations differ is emotional involvement. If we don't care for a person, absence will make us forget him or her. If we dearly love someone, his or her absence will increase our affection.

Act. Which means that there is a link between remembering and emotion.

Spe. A stronger one that most of us realise. Memory is choosy. We tend to remember things selectively, and there appears to be no rationale behind that selection. But there is a simple explanation. We easily forget things that were not linked to some emotion; we tend to remember things that were emotionally charged - linked to some joy, pleasure, shock, or a sudden insight. The more intense those emotions were, the more acutely we remember.

Act. Interesting. - Go on Proverbius, tell us more. This topic seems to be tinted with psychology.

Pro. It is often harder to forget than to remember.

Spe. Indeed, this subject can't be discussed without reference to psychology. Proverbius just uttered a profound statement with strong psychological undertones. - Nothing, psychologists tell us, tends to fix itself more strongly into our memory than something we are struggling to forget. There are people who were exposed to traumatic experiences that will forever haunt their memories. The more these people want to forget, the more clearly they seem to remember. - Wisdom is not enough to overcome such trauma. To achieve it, the will to forget must be stronger than the faculty to remember. This is very difficult. I have a profound respect for those who manage to do it.

Act. So do I. - Go on, Proverbius. Never mind if you to stay psychological.

Pro. Men who forget what they were taught are like women who conceive and abort.

Act. *Grimaces.* This is not psychology, but plain naturalism!

Spe. *Smiles.* But it is psychology. Let me comment on it. - Some wise man wrote: I tend to forget what I was taught but remember what I learned. What makes the difference? It is, once again, the link between memory and emotion. We tend to forget what we were taught, because being taught is rarely an emotional process: the teacher speaks, we listen. But when we learn something, there is often some emotion involved: we experience a feeling of success, or of failure, or joy at having understood. Those emotions fix what we have learned into our memory. Thus: what we are taught, we may abort; but what we have learned, stays put.

Act. Let me point out that what you just said is additional proof that experience is superior to knowledge. Experiences are emotionally charged, because they derive from successes or failures: thus well remembered. Acquiring knowledge is unemotional: thus easily forgotten.

Spe. Unless, Actus, we acquire knowledge from someone we dearly love or deeply respect. There are things I was taught that I remember clearly, because those who taught them to me played key emotional roles in my life.

Act. *Thoughtful.* Spectus, let us go a bit more into this interesting question linking emotions with the past. There are essentially three ways to consider the past. - One way is to see it through pink eyeglasses. To claim that most things were better than they are now. Laudator temporis acti. - The second way is to bedevil the past: most things were worse than they are today, we have made tremendous progress. - The third way is to try to be objective about the past, to resist any distortion through emotion. - Needless to say which of the three attitudes the wise should adopt: it is looking at the past without emotion.

Spe. *A bit dreamy.* You probably expect me to say, Actus, that you are right. Yet, I don't think we should always and necessarily deal with the past unemotionally. I must confess that, at times, I do get emotional about the past. You see: I believe in the importance of moods. I think they are an essential part of life. And nostalgia, though I agree that it lacks objectivity, is one of the most pleasant moods I know. Remembering the "good old times", chatting about them with a friend who was a part of those times, preferably in front of a blazing fireplace, with a drink in your hand. Such moods lack objectivity; but I wouldn't want to miss them. Nostalgic remembrances are a paradise from which we can't get expelled.

Act. *Smiles.* You have a warm soul, Spectus.

Spe. Warm souls have remembrances, Actus. Cold ones only have objective memories.

Act. But warm remembrances are not suited to learn from the past: they are biased. If we want to derive wisdoms from the past, we must be objective about it. This seminar would have no justification if it was based on warm remembrances. It has value only if based on objective memories.

Spe. That is certainly true. But in life I think we need both: nostalgic moods and strict objectivity. Of course: objectivity should predominate. After the fire went out in the fireplace and the drink is finished, the wise will shrug off romanticism and revert to objectivity. But they will do so with a relaxed, refreshed mind.

Act. *Smiles.* You have a talent for compromise. - One last question. Do you think an excellent memory favours wisdom?

Spe. No. Memory is like a dictionary. But a dictionary is not yet literature.

Act. *Laughs.* A snappy answer. Let us declare it to be the last wisdom on this topic. - We seem to have covered the brain. Our next essential internal organ downward is the heart.

There is a loud, short buzz from the screen, something like a warning.

Act. Goodness, Spectus. Look at that holograph. We have practically finished the foundation. There are just a few more stones missing. But there must be dozens of wisdoms associated with the heart. Are we supposed to ignore them?

Spe. By no means. But remember our plot, Actus. Wisdoms of the heart are associated with the soul, not with the body. They belong to the highest part our cathedral. We shall have to deal with them when we get to building the roof.

Act. But scores of wisdoms that have to do with the heart are fundamental. They belong to the foundation. Many are of the kind Proverbius could provide. And we said we shall use Proverbius only while we erect the foundation.

Spe. Oh, I have given up that restriction long ago. Pertinent proverbs fit everywhere into our cathedral, not just into the foundation. Proverbius will have many more chances to place wisdoms throughout the rest of this symposium.

Act. *Visibly relieved.* Good. I somehow got accustomed to have the taciturn old chap around. I got to like him, to tell the truth.

Watching closely, one could have remarked a very brief, fleeting smile on Proverbius' old, rustic face. But that must have been an illusion. After all, he is only a machine.

Act. But we still need a few wisdom-stones to complete the foundation. Eclectus obviously wants us to finish it tonight. It was a long day and I am getting tired. And, above all, hungry. My belly is starting to revolt.

Spe. Then let us finish the foundation with wisdoms about the belly.

Act. I doubt we shall find any.

Spe. Wait and see. *(Turns to Proverbius.)* Old friend, we need some wisdoms about the belly. Or the stomach. In fact: about eating and drinking.

To eat, to drink

Pro. He eats most who eats least.

Act. What kind of wisdom is that? Taoist?

Spe. *Laughs.* No. In fact it is very sound, down-to-earth logic. The one who eats sparingly lives longer. To lengthen thy life, shorten thine meals. The one who lengthens his life eating less, actually ends up eating more, since on the whole he has got more years to eat.

Act. Aha. That makes sense. - Go on, Proverbius.

Pro. Whatsoever was the father of disease, ill diet was the mother.

Act. Hear, hear. Proverbius reveals himself to be a nutritionist.

Spe. *Smiles.* Popular knowledge is full of medical wisdoms, Actus. Academic medicine is discovering that. - But the importance of diet makes me remember something. Or rather: someone. He could certainly provide us with a few wisdom-stones. *(Turns to the room.)* Has the greatest French expert on eating and drinking been invited to this seminar? I mean, of course, none other than Monsieur Brillat-Savarin?

Anthelme Brillat-Savarin. *Likeable old gentleman, dressed as a judge of the court of cassation of the time of the French revolution. He holds his famous book, "Physiologie du Goût",* *open at the chapter "Aphorismes". He turns some pages to find a suitable quote on diet and decides on this one:* Dis-moi ce que tu manges, et je te dirai ce que tu es.

Spe. Tell me what you eat, and I will tell you who you are. - Continuez, Monsieur.

Brillat-Savarin. *Encouraged by Spectus' invitation.* Ceux qui s'indigèrent et s'enivrent ne savent ni manger ni boire.

Spe. He is against overeating and getting drunk. The wise will do neither. - Et encore?

Brillat-Savarin. *By now highly enthusiastic.* La destinée des nations dépend de la manière dont elles se nourissent. *He begins turning the pages of his book, apparently to read many more of his delightful aphorisms, but his internal mechanism obliges him, with a regretful smile on his face, to return to wax.*

Spe. A pleasant gentleman, that. But his last aphorism goes a bit too far. The destiny of a nation is not necessarily linked to what they eat - though it cannot be fully excluded either. But his basic tenet is absolutely valid: choose your food with wisdom. - Proverbius: your turn.

Pro. No-one can worship Allah with an empty belly.

Spe. Indeed not.

Pro. Mount Fuji is without beauty to a hungry man.

Spe. Indeed it is. But have you got any Western wisdom on the subject? On hunger?

Pro. The guts uphold the heart, not the heart the guts.

Spe. *with a slight mock bow.* Your treasury of wisdoms is truly global, my friend.

Act. You know, Spectus, that last wisdom of the old chap sounds trivial, but actually it is not. I knew a highly successful executive who ate two huge steaks for breakfast before starting difficult negotiations. At midday, his opponents started to become hungry. But my friend pressed on, proposing to settle the last few remaining issues before lunch. For him, that was easy: he had a full belly. His opponents, driven by hunger, generally ended up agreeing to his terms. Their guts failed to uphold their hearts.

Spe. A good story. Though I would say your friend was clever, rather than wise.

Act. Where does cleverness end and wisdom begin, Spectus? - But go on, Proverbius.

Pro. Spread the table and contention will cease.

Act. Now that is very true. One of mankind's great achievements is to have turned eating, a purely physiological affair, into a civilised and socially meaningful act. I saw many conflicts getting settled during a good lunch or dinner. - But, Spectus, let us not leave all the work to Proverbius. You must have, in your literary treasure-box, quite a number of wisdoms on eating. Can we have a sample or two?

Spe. *Thinks for a second.* There is Rabelais: L'appétit vient en mangeant.

Act. That adage does not belong here. It is about greed, not about eating.

Spe. Then this one: At table one should eat wisely but not too well, and talk well but not too wisely.

Act. That is better. - Anything more?

Spe. *Ponders.* I can't think of anything else for the moment.

Act. Then let us switch to drinking. - Proverbius?

Pro. A glass of wine works more miracles than a church full of saints.

Act. Ah! A new side to Proverbius. Is there a hedonist behind that venerable white beard?

Spe. *Smiles.* He is a moralist, not a hedonist. In fact, he was paraphrasing a great moralist, Pestalozzi: To make people happy you either need a lot of wisdom, or a small glass of wine, he claimed. *(Pestalozzi has not been invited.)*

Act. If that is so, Spectus, then why on earth don't we go and have a bottle of "vino del paese", instead of torturing ourselves to find a few more wisdoms on drinking?

Spe. *Laughs.* Because we accepted a challenge. Let us finish our foundation first and have the wine afterwards. - Let me see: I am sure Proverbius has some more wisdoms on drinking.

Pro. The first glass for thirst, the second for nourishment, the third for pleasure, the fourth for madness.

Spe. He disapproves of drunkenness, like Brillat-Savarin. - Speaking of drunkenness: there is a story about Churchill. *(Churchill, though present, does not react; he probably knows what's coming.)* A lady once told Churchill in the face that he was drunk. Churchill replied: And you, Madam, are ugly; but *I* shall be sober in the morning.

Act. *Smiles.* Witty - but rude. It did not earn us a wisdom-stone. We have only two more to go. Help us, Proverbius, please!

Proverbius is silent.

Spe. We are on our own, Actus. We have to come up with two more wisdoms on drinking. Or on eating. We shall not be released before we found them.

They both think strenuously.

Act. What about: One glass of whisky is all right; two a bit much, but three too few?

No stone added.

Spe. Maybe this one, then: Adam and Eve ruined themselves for just an apple; what might they have done for a delicious truffled turkey?

No stone added.

Act. Try this one: A well balanced person has a drink in each hand?

No stone.

Act. Then this: There are two reasons for drinking. One is when you are thirsty, to cure it. The other, when you are not thirsty, to prevent thirst. Prevention is better than cure.

No stone.

Spe. Obviously, our minds no longer function properly at this advanced hour of the day.

Pause. Actus and Spectus look tired and lack inspiration.

Act. *Turns to face the seminar room.* Help, anyone? Two last wisdoms on drinking?

Surprisingly, without any names being mentioned, two figures come simultaneously to life.

Plinius the Elder. *Looks the same as before, only with a little less of Vesuvian ash on his toga.*

Erasmus of Rotterdam. *Looks like his portrait by Holbein. Long, pointed nose, strong chin, grey hair under a round hat. Clever eyes with a sleepy look, half hidden by lowered eyelids, as if slightly drunk, which of course he is not.*

Both of them say, synchronically, the famous words: In vino veritas.

Plinius makes a sweeping gesture brushing some more ash from his toga, then returns to wax. Erasmus continues to look strangely alive, though he, also, is nothing but wax.

There is an unusually loud "ping" from the wall. The last two foundation stones are simultaneously inserted. The foundation is finished. The holograph keeps revolving, with the completed foundation pulsating in an intense, golden light. Actus and Spectus look at it with some awe.

Act. What happened?

Spe. We completed the foundation.

Act. I can see that. But how did we manage to do it?

Spe. By discovering a completely new use of these automata, thanks to your initiative. It is obvious that we do not need to mention their names to bring them to life. They activate themselves, whenever they hear a subject on which they have got something to say, and are invited to do so. *(Rubs his hands.)* Excellent, excellent. This opens up a tremendous range of possibilities for the rest of this seminar. Finally we learned how to properly handle these automata.

Act. But electronic gimmicks apart: why did Plinius and Erasmus react synchronically?

Spe. Because that famous maxim is attributed to both; so both of them reacted. That earned us two stones, instead of one. - As to "in vino veritas", this is one of the oldest adages of mankind. Wine opens people up, reveals their true nature, their real character, their fears, aspirations and concerns. This effect of wine has been observed by all cultures, at all times, around the globe.

Act. Spectus: after this profound insight, basta! No more wisdoms, no more proverbs, please. All that counts for me now is that the foundation is finished. We should congratulate ourselves for that feat, since no-one else cares to do it.

Spe. Congratulations, my dear Actus.

Act. Cheers, my dear Spectus.

The gong is struck, marking the end of the last session of the first day.

Act. *Stands up and stretches.* I don't know about you, but despite of being tired, I have a tremendous appetite. I long for dinner and wine. And I will tell you something, Spectus: I am going to order and drink a full bottle of it. Even if I run the danger of becoming overly truthful by revealing all my secret aspirations to you.

Spe. *Laughs.* I shall have a bottle, too. So our revelations will be mutual.

Act. Up, then, to the pleasures of good food and the joys of civilized alcohol.

Spe. Good night, Proverbius, and thanks for your excellent contributions.

Act. Good night, everyone. Good night, Eclectus, in case you hear us.

Actus and Spectus leave for dinner. Proverbius remains standing, but goes into a kind of half-glow, presumably a sort of stand-by. As the door closes behind Actus and Spectus, the lights are dimmed, then go out completely. The holograph on the wall disappears. Except for Proverbius' half-glow, the huge seminar room is plunged into sleepy darkness.

End of the first day of the symposium

The second day

Session 5: The Pillars

It is eight o'clock in the morning of the second day of the seminar. Projected on the wall is the slowly revolving holograph of the previous day, with the foundation filled up. All over the surface of the foundation are circles indicating the bases for columns. As the holograph revolves, one can either see the foundation from above, with the bases for the pillars marked, or horizontally, at ground level. For the moment, since no pillar is standing, the horizontal view is empty.

All automats are seated, except Proverbius.

Actus and Spectus enter the room, obviously refreshed after a good night's sleep. The fatigue of the previous evening is forgotten. As they go to their usual places and sit down, the gong is struck. The second day of the seminar begins.

Spectus. Well, today we address ourselves to the pillars. We agreed that they are symbolic for individuals: both must stand upright on their own, with little or no support, refusing to get toppled. How do we proceed?

Actus. *Thinks briefly.* To stand upright, our hypothetic individual will have to possess certain qualities, adopt certain attitudes of mind, follow certain principles. We should see what those are, and find wisdoms that apply to them. - He will also have to be free of certain negative traits and damaging attitudes; we should concentrate on those next. - Finally, we should examine how the wise individual copes with the various tasks that he faces. - Having done all that, our pillars should stand, completed, by the end of the day.

Spe. A good plan. - And as we proceed, we should try to involve more of these dummies sitting around here. The performance of Plinius and Erasmus last evening gives me high expectations about their technical capabilities.

Act. All right, then, off we go: positive qualities and attitudes an individual needs in order to stand upright, and wisdoms associated with them. - I guess courage would be a good start.

Spe. An excellent one. - La séance est ouverte.

Courage

Act. We need courage in three situations: when taking risks, when facing dangers, and when coping with adversity. Let us discuss one after the other.

Spe. Agreed. Let us begin with courage to take risks. Introduce the subject, Actus.

Act. Risk, unlike danger, is avoidable. An individual is free to decide whether to expose himself to risk or not. You can live practically risk-free, if you want to. But life is a risky business. If you put up too many fences against risk, you end up shutting out life itself. The wise, therefore, will not shun risks; but they will take precautions against them.

Spe. I presume popular wisdom does not have your open-minded attitude to risk-taking. It is simply against taking risks, no matter what. Am I right, Proverbius?

Pro. The fly that plays with the candle singes its wings.

Spe. As I expected. He could also have said: Who handles thorns, will pick his fingers. Different words, same idea.

Act. It is not the same idea.

Spe. Ah?

Act. Note that Proverbius uses the word "play". By that he means irresponsible action. The fly, playing with the candle, exposes himself to unnecessary and probably fatal risk. But since it is unaware of that risk, it needs no courage. You don't need courage to play. - Now take the other proverb, the one about the thorns. That is not about play. The thorns symbolize the risks you incur when you pursue a worthy goal. The goal, in this particular case, is to get at the rose. In order to pick it, you must reckon with the thorns. If you fear to get wounded, forget the rose. But nothing risked, nothing gained. If you want the rose, you must be aware that you may get hurt. - So there is an essential difference between the two maxims. The fly does not expect to get burned, whereas the rose-picker reckons with getting wounded. But the rose-picker has an advantage over the fly. He can estimate the number of thorns he is likely to encounter, their size, their hardness. He can estimate the probability of getting cut and the gravity of the damage. In other words: he can *calculate* his risks. He still needs courage to face the risks he calculated, but he will fare much safer than the silly fly that simply plays with the candle.

Spe. Excellent logic. - Proverbius: try to find in your treasury other wisdoms pertaining to risk, so that we can enjoy Actus' sophisticated interpretations of them.

Pro. *Has fully understood what is required of him.* No safe wading in unknown waters. - Far from home, near thy harm.

Act. *Smiles.* It is not particularly difficult to interpret those. - As long as you stay at home, that is within your field of competence, you deal with the familiar. You are safe, since you retain control. - But there is a drawback to the safety of staying at home: you may start stagnating. So, at times, you must summon up courage and take the risk of moving into new territories. - However, when doing that, the wise risk-taker will follow an important rule: he will never move into fields totally unknown to him. He will only enter fields that are *adjacent* to his own, those that have a common frontier with his home territory. Several features of the new field he enters will then be familiar to him: he will have those under control. His risks will be confined to features he is not yet familiar with; but the number of those risks will be substantially lower than if he entered an entirely new field. For you can control what you know; but it is difficult, if not impossible, to control the unknown.

Spe. *Smiles.* You can hear the prudent businessman talking. - I think we have covered risk, and the courage to take it. Let us move on to danger, and the courage to face it. - What is the main difference between risk and danger?

Act. As I already pointed out, we are free to decide whether to take a risk or not. We are not free to decide whether to face a danger or not. We *must* face it, since it is imposed upon us from the outside. Thus, facing a danger requires more courage than deciding to take a risk.

Spe. Proverbius: what have you got to tell us on danger?

Pro. Far away drums have no sound.

Spe. He means distant dangers tend to be ignored. The mice dance when the cat is away. Frankly, I can't blame the mice. The poor creatures can't continuously think of the cat. Nothing is strong enough to last if it labours constantly under the weight of fear. *(A figure at the back briefly flares up as Spectus says this; the name-plate in front of him says Cicero.)*

Act. Yet, my advice to the mice would be not to become careless about the cat. He will not stay away forever. The wise mouse will distinguish between immediate and distant danger, but will not ignore the latter. - Go on, Proverbius.

Pro. Any port in a storm.

Spe. Agreed. The wise must not be choosy about the kind of protection they are being offered when in acute danger. - What else?

Pro. Don't halloo until you are out of the woods.

Spe. That is: do not relax until a danger has fully passed. - But we cannot discuss danger without also discussing fear. The two are linked. Have you any comments on fear, Actus?

Act. I do. - To begin with, we must make a distinction between fear and fright. Fright is a sudden, strong, but short-lived emotion. Nature copes with it by setting against it another emotion: anger. Humans and animals, when frightened, get angry at those who frightened them. Setting anger against fright is nature's defence-mechanism to assist the frightened. - Now fear is different. It is mental, rather than emotional. It often takes time to develop and to sink in, but then it has a tendency to last. However, therein lies an advantage: we are given time to confront fear rationally. And that is precisely what the wise will do. They will try to understand and analyse the causes of their fear. They will try to size up the thing they fear, establish the nature and the extent of the danger they face. Once they start doing all that, they begin to prevail over fear. - The gist of this is: since fear is mental, the best antidote against it is reason.

Spe. Allow me to be somewhat sceptical about that conclusion, Actus. Show me one who becomes fearless just because he tries to be rational about his fear.

Act. The point is not to become fearless, Spectus. A totally fearless man is probably a moron, who is fully unaware of the danger he faces. There is nothing as fearless as a blind mare. - The point of my argument is to *control* fear. To do that, we need two things: reasoning and courage. We need reasoning to tell us how to handle the danger we are facing. We need courage to implement the results of our reasoning. Courage without reasoning is foolhardiness. Reasoning without the courage to act is cowardice. It is reason and courage *combined* that will help us prevail over fear.

Spe. That was well put, Actus. - But now let me propose an experiment. Last night, remember, you did not call anyone by name, just launched a question, or rather an injunction, into the seminar-room. And we got the right answer. Let us try that trick again, and see what comes of it. *(Turns to the seminar room.)* Can we have contributions from the floor on the concepts of danger, courage and fear, please?

Act. *cuts in.* Hold it, Spectus! If you ask like that, we shall have a cacophony. Several of these dummies may rise and speak at the same time. I think you need to specify how many should speak, and in what order.

Spe. You are right. *(Turns back to the room.)* Let us have three contributions, please. The automaton seated nearer to me will speak first, the one furthest away will speak last.

A low buzz goes through the seminar room. The automata presumably check themselves for relevant data, compare them, and decide who should speak. Only Eclectus, and possibly God, know how they do it. Finally, three figures begin to glow and rise.

George Smith Patton. *The "old blood and guts" general. He is absorbed in examining the model of a new tank posed on top of his desk. Then looks up and speaks.* If courage means fearlessness, then I have not yet met a courageous man. Every man fears danger; the more intelligent he is, the more so. Courageous is the one who overcomes fear. *(He sits down and resumes his waxy interest in the tank model.)*

David Ben-Gurion. *Flying white hair, bald forehead, rugged features, no tie.* Courage is a special kind of knowledge: the knowledge of how to fear what ought to be feared and how not to fear what ought not to be feared. *(Sits down and returns to wise wax.)*

Napoleon Bonaparte. *Glows with particular intensity. He has one hand tucked in the front of his jacket, following an advice of his wife to keep him from gesticulating. He is surprisingly short, bald and pale. He speaks French with a strong southern accent, but somehow that adds to the fascination of his appearance.* La bravoure procède du sang. Mais le courage vient de la pensée. *(He surveys the seminar room as if it were a battlefield, but is then compelled by his mechanism to sit down and return to pale wax.)*

Spe. *Jubilant.* It works! My dear Actus, it works! We discovered a new way to use our co-participants. Just think of the possibilities this opens up. *(He is content like a child with a new toy.)*

Act. *Smiles at Spectus' enthusiasm.* Yeah. Great. But can we now comment on what we heard, please?

Spe. *Still radiant.* Certainly. Go ahead. Comment.

Act. Patton supports my thesis that courage is mastery of fear, not absence of fear. He does not say, though, how fear is to be controlled. But his reference to intelligence indicates that he thinks it should be done rationally.

Spe. Quite.

Act. Ben-Gurion made a very sensible distinction: justified versus unjustified fear. We need reason to distinguish between those two. Once we have done that, we need to summon up courage to overcome fears that are justified, since those arise from real dangers. But if reason tells us that a fear is unjustified, the danger imaginary, we need no courage; all we need then is determination to discard the unjustified fear and simply forget it.

Spe. Unfortunately, it is not always easy to distinguish between real and imaginary dangers, or between justified and unjustified fears.

Act. Of course. But still: I find Ben-Gurion's point is very well taken. It recalls what we said yesterday about seeing. The wise will be able to distinguish between fears that are justified and fears that are not, because they *see*. I could even re-formulate, or rather extend, Ben-Gurion's adage, linking it to seeing: We should learn to *see* what is there, and learn *not to see* what is not there.

Spe. *Smiles.* I guess Ben-Gurion would have appreciated that re-formulation. - What do you think of Napoleon's contribution?

Act. It confirms what we have been saying. He distinguishes between bravoure, or valour, that comes from the blood, and courage that comes from the head, a product of the intellect. He thus agrees, only using other words, that fear can and should be countered rationally.

Spe. Let me, though, raise a question about rationality in the face of danger. I am sometimes impressed by the courage shown by simple, but deeply religious people. They seem to be able to overcome fear without much reasoning. Isn't simple faith just as good a weapon against fear than reason is?

Act. Faith, call it trust in providence, can indeed be of great help in dangerous situations. But faith, to me, is an emotional thing. Being an emotion, it is vulnerable. If things do not work out as the faithful expect, then they may lose confidence. Their faith may then turn into doubt, the courage based on it shattered. My recommendation is: trust providence, but base your courage mainly on reason. You will fare surer.

Spe. *Smiles.* Actus the pragmatist. - Let me raise a final point. There is a view that in extreme situations the boldest measures are the most effective. But boldness, we said, has to do with foolhardiness, rather than with courage or reason.

Act. In extreme situations we need extreme courage, and that may appear to be foolhardiness. But it is not. It is the rational conclusion, arrived at under duress, that an extreme measure is the most likely to succeed.

Spe. Hmm. Let me put my point differently. - There is a famous dictum: Audentes fortuna juvat. The audacious are favoured by luck. Does that mean that the audacious, the foolhardy, the "bravoureux" guided by their blood, are more likely to be favoured by luck than the courageous, guided by rational insight?

Act. I think the real meaning of that dictum is: Luck favours those who show initiative. Both the audacious and the courageous have initiative. But there is a difference between them. The audacious will charge ahead without much prior reflection. The courageous, on the other hand, will develop a strategy before he charges. I claim that with that extra advantage the courageous will have luck more often on their side than the audacious.

Spe. I can accept that logic. - Now: we covered courage when facing risk and facing danger. Let us deal with the third case: courage when facing adversity. Risk and danger are only potentially harmful; adversity is real harm. How should the wise cope with it?

Act. One way is simply to bear it. Heroically supporting adversity can be admirable. But it makes people passive. It tends, often, to also make them caustic, resigned. Passivity perpetuates adversity. Thus, heroic bearing is not the solution of the wise.

Spe. Then what is?

Act. The wise will turn against adversity and fight it. They will not accept the status quo, but do everything in their power to change it. And that is where courage comes in. Certainly, you need courage to get resigned to adversity. But you need much more courage if you decide to fight it. And I am absolutely convinced that it is always worth to fight. Fighting adversity can even be greatly beneficial: doing it, we may discover potentials that slumbered within us, that we may never have discovered if we have not been subjected to adverse pressures. Never having to fight adversity means that some of our talents and abilities may remain forever dormant. Adversity is a teacher that can introduce us to ourselves.

Spe. *Thoughtful.* I subscribe to that, but with one proviso. To fight adversity, we need not only courage, but also hope. Courage must be nourished by hope. Without hope, fighting makes no sense.

Act. If there is no hope, Spectus, we no longer face adversity, but the inevitable. But even in the face of the inevitable we can either adopt an attitude of resignation, or an attitude of courage. Those who decide to face the inevitable with courage exhibit the highest form of courage there is. They deserve our deepest respect.

Spe. There is nothing to add to that. - Let me raise an interesting question. Is courage acquirable? Or is it an innate quality? In other words: are some people born courageous, while others are born cowards?

Act. *Thinks for a second.* My answer to your question is this. What is inborn is fear. It is implanted into us genetically for the purpose of self-preservation. What is not inborn is how we deal with fear. While we can't eradicate it, we can train our reactions to it. We can force ourselves to analyse and understand the reasons for our fear, to size up the true magnitude of the danger we face, to develop strategies to counter it. We can learn from the past where similar dangers have been successfully dealt with. We can tell ourselves that nothing can possibly happen that we shall not be able to handle in one way or another. If we do all that, we shall necessarily become courageous. Thus I claim that courage is a question of nurture rather than of nature.

Spe. An impressive answer. - But suppose we lack the time to do all those rational things you are recommending. Then, I think, your argument will not hold. Then we shall be courageous or not, depending on our genetic disposition.

Act. We are what we choose to be, Spectus. If we train ourselves to react to fear rationally, then we will be courageous when we need to be. The decisive moment then merely reveals what we have trained ourselves to become.

Spe. Perhaps you are right. - Now let me point out something else. Emerson once wrote: Courage comes from having successfully done the same thing before. *(Emerson is present but does not react.)* In other words: when a danger we are facing is familiar, and we have prevailed over a similar danger in the past, it is not too difficult to be courageous. But what if the danger we face is new and unfamiliar? If we have no help from past experience? Or, worse: what if we are confronted with a danger we have already encountered in the past, but failed to properly overcome?

Act. It is certainly easier to be courageous when we face a familiar danger, especially if we have mastered a similar one before. But I repeat: courage is a mental attitude, a quality of mind. Once we have developed it, we can face any danger, familiar or not.

Spe. And if we fail?

Act. For the courageous failure is but success postponed.

Spe. *Smiles.* Your optimism is commendable. - I suggest we bring this topic to an end by looking briefly at the opposite of courage: cowardice. It is generally understood as lack of courage. But is what appears to be lack of courage always cowardice?

Act. You expect "no" for an answer and you get it. Reason may tell us to refrain from doing certain things, and some will interpret that as lack of courage or plain cowardice. But what appears to be lack of courage is often just common sense, well-justified caution. Peter Ustinov once said: What in some cases appears to be cowardice is simply good information. *(Sir Peter is not present.)*

Spe. *Laughs.* Let's close the subject with that sound observation. - What is the next positive trait we should endow our hypothetic wise individual with?

Act. Honesty.

Spe. Here we go.

Honesty

Act. The topic is easy to start: Honesty is the best policy.

Spe. In most cases, yes.

Act. In all cases. Honesty is the best policy in all cases. In fact, honesty isn't a policy at all, it is a quality of mind, like courage.

Spe. Actus: remember our discussion, yesterday, on lying. We agreed that in some cases lying is acceptable for utilitarian reasons. Similarly, I think, there are cases where open, blue-eyed honesty is neither the best nor the wisest policy. - Policy means choosing a course of action among various alternatives. If we discard some of the alternatives open to us for rigid ethical or moral reasons, then we restrict our freedom of choice. Take someone who adopts a policy that is thoroughly honest but detrimental to himself and to others: he may be a stout moralist, but he is hardly wise. I claim that, if circumstances dictate it, the wise will allow to deviate from inflexible, naive honesty - provided they stay within morally acceptable limits.

Act. We fully disagree, Spectus. My experience tells me that honesty is the best policy no matter what the circumstances are. - My logic runs like this. To achieve what you want, you need to convince. In order to convince, you must be in agreement with yourself. To be in agreement with yourself, you must be honest. A dishonest person is not in agreement with himself; he forsakes a permanent advantage, that of being perceived as an honest person, for some temporary advantage dictated by circumstances. It is simply not worth it. - Furthermore, you are on slippery ground when you allow dishonesty within morally acceptable limits. Who sets those limits? They are fluid; it is tempting to overstep them. - No, Spectus, I am inflexible on this point: honesty should take no vacation.

Spe. You defend your point of view well, Actus. I would be interested to know who, in this seminar room, shares it, and who doesn't. This is an excellent opportunity to test the technical capabilities of these machines. *(He thinks for a moment, then turns to the seminar room.)* All those with important contributions to the subject of honesty, please let themselves be known. Proverbius, you keep out of this.

There is a busy buzzing going on among the automata, as they decide who should contribute;

after a moment eleven of them begin to glow, but remain seated.

Spe. Now, those who are for honesty in all cases and under all circumstances: please rise.

Four glowing dummies stand up.

Spe. *Visibly enjoys all this, as if he were a theatre director.* Now the four of you speak up, in alphabetical order, please.

Benjamin Franklin. *Same as he appeared the first day, but this time he leaves his kite under his desk.* Trickery and treachery are the practices of fools that have not enough wits to be honest.

Herbert Clark Hoover. *Round, energetic face, a mixture between engineer and Quaker.* You can't be a little crooked. There is no such thing as a no-man's-land between honesty and dishonesty.

John Ruskin. *Black hair, white beard, penetrating look, face marked by intellectual activity and internal controversies.* Your honesty is not to be based on policy. It is your policy that must be based on honesty. Your honesty, in turn, must be based, as the sun is, in vacant heaven; poised, as the lights in the firmament, ruling over day and night.

George Washington. *Elegant, impressive, looks like he just stepped out of the family picture painted by Savage.* I hope I shall always possess firmness and virtue enough to maintain what I consider the most enviable of all titles: an honest man.

Spe. Thank you, gentlemen. Please be seated. Now the counter-group: those who doubt that honesty is invariably the best policy, or who even doubt that absolute honesty exists at all. Also in alphabetical order, please.

The automata who have just spoken sit down and return to wax. The others rise. The whole performance is faultless.

Napoleon Bonaparte. *Same as before.* La voie la plus sûre de rester pauvre est d'être honnête.

Thomas Fuller. *Witty, but somewhat quaint face, tall, burly, dressed like a 17th century English preacher.* He that resolves to deal with none but honest men must leave off dealing.

Jean de La Bruyère. *Dressed in the green uniform of the Académie Francaise. Holds a book by Theophrastus in one hand, his own "Les Caractères", modelled on it, in the other.* L'honnête homme tient le milieu entre l'homme habile et l'homme de bien, quoique dans une distance inégale des ces deux extrêmes.

Gotthold Ephraim Lessing. *Looks like his portrait by Graff. Remarkably intense eyes. You can sense that he just loves polemics.* O, man ist verzweifelt wenig, wenn man weiter nichts ist als ehrlich.

O. Henry. *Calm, reserved face, without a trace of his bitter experiences in life. One has difficulty in believing that this man could create so many clown-like characters.* There is no well-defined boundary between honesty and dishonesty. The frontiers of one blend with the outside limits of the other, and he who attempts to tread this dangerous ground may be sometimes in one domain and sometimes in the other.

Arthur Schopenhauer. *Well-known grim old face, holds a copy of « Aphorismen zur Lebensweisheit » in one hand. Radiates a curious mixture of pessimism and compassion.* Ganz ehrlich meint ein jeder es am Ende doch nur mit sich selbst, und höchstens noch mit seinem Kinde.

Richard Whately. *Dressed as an archbishop, but looks rather like a politician.* Honesty is the best policy, but he who maintains that he is always governed by it is not an honest man.

All automata sit down, cease glowing and return to wax.

Spe. *Fully satisfied with his "mise en scène".* There you are, Actus. Seven out of eleven of these worthy gentlemen have doubts about the merits of absolute, uncompromising honesty. Aren't those who maintain the contrary simply unrealistic - and therefore unwise?

Act. I can't help it, Spectus, but I continue to be attached to the view of the first group, even though they are a minority. - And let me point out something you may have overlooked. Napoleon and Fuller spoke of honesty not in general terms, but only in connection with moneymaking. They doubt that you can make money if you are honest. I again disagree. Honesty and wealth do not exclude each other. I happen to know many examples personally.

Spe. *Looks sharply at Actus.* I lack your business experience, Actus, but allow me to be sceptical. Show me a successful businessman who freely reveals to a buyer all the drawbacks of a product he intends to sell. Or one who openly praises in front of a seller all the merits of the product he wants to purchase. If you can, I shall change my stance.

Act. *Ponders silently, but does not answer.*

Spe. To put it bluntly, Actus, I doubt that any successful businessman can allow himself to be fully honest at all times. He will necessarily have to exaggerate advantages a bit here, play down disadvantages there, pass over some things in silence. - Besides: you met your business acquaintances you claim to be both honest and wealthy when they were already wealthy. But can you be certain that they have always been fully honest on their way to wealth? Allow me to doubt that one can get wealthy without some dishonesties here and there along the way. There was a wise man, whose name I forget, who saw this issue very pragmatically. "Ah - he once said - you call Mr X an honest man? That means he can afford it."

Act. *Continues silently thoughtful.*

Spe. But let me come back to something I said earlier. I believe there can be, and should be, limits to dishonesty. One should be allowed, at times, to be a bit dishonest, in order to procure some advantage or deter some harm. But with one important proviso: you should never act dishonestly if the fortune, the happiness or the security of other people are substantially threatened by your action.

Act. *Still pondering.* What about conscience, Spectus? Dishonesties, even if moderate, will bother those with a healthy conscience. Honesty gives you peace of mind. No honest man ever repented that he chose to be honest.

Spe. But he may have regretted it.

Act. And what about the opinion that honesty begets honesty?

Spe. It doesn't. On the contrary, alas: honesty is often met with dishonesty. If you are always honest, you become calculable and then some people take advantage of you.

Act. You may be calculable if honest. But you are also dependable.

Spe. You are dependable if you can be trusted. But you cannot necessarily be trusted if you are naively honest. - But, Actus, let me add a final comment and then let us close this discussion. While I maintain that moderate dishonesty is at times necessary to get ahead in life, I also believe this: all of us need a few selected individuals towards whom we are always, entirely, unconditionally, unreservedly honest.

Act. No matter what?

Spe. No matter what.

Act. At least there is one of your questionable views on honesty I can fully support.

Spe. *Smiles.* I am glad. And, Actus, our views on honesty are, happily, still a far cry from those of Juvenal. Probitas laudatur et alget, he proclaimed. Let honesty be praised and then thrown out the window. *(No-one stirs in the audience.)* But that is not wisdom; it is plain cynicism. - May I suggest our next topic? Cunning.

Cunning

Act. Cunning? What has cunning got to do with wisdom?

Spe. It can help, even save, our hypothetic individual in precarious situations. Cunning is practical wisdom, cleverness. And yesterday, Actus, you claimed that the frontier between cleverness and wisdom is fluid.

Act. But cunning is about tricks. Deception. And deception is a form of dishonesty. We are back to our previous subject.

Spe. Deception is different from dishonesty, Actus. Deception is widely practiced in Nature. Nature is full of clever, deceptive tricks; they are in fact an essential part of Evolution. And popular wisdom, being close to Nature, knows this. It values, but also warns against, deception. Am I right, my shrewd friend Proverbius?

Pro. If you deal with the fox, think of his tricks.

Spe. There you are. Enter the fox, arch-symbol of cleverness and cunning. The expression “old fox” is by no means derogatory. On the contrary: it designates someone with a great deal of practical wisdom. To be called an “old fox” is rather a compliment. - Tell us more about the fox, Proverbius.

Pro. If the lion’s skin won’t do, the fox’s will.

Spe. What he means is that cunning is superior to force. Cunning helps where force fails. This, I reckon, is one of the oldest wisdoms of mankind.

Act. Doesn’t the fox also sometimes wear sheep’s skin?

Spe. You mix up your skins, Actus. Sewing a fox’s skin over the lion’s means giving priority to cunning over strength. Sewing a lion’s skin over any other skin is trying to appear stronger than we are. Sewing a sheep's skin over the wolf's skin is a dirty trick: the wolf wants to get at the sheep and parades as one of them. I never heard of the fox getting into a sheep's skin.

Act. *Sighs.* This is developing into a seminar on dermatology.

They both laugh.

Act. Nevertheless, Spectus, the fox, despite his cunning, usually ends up badly in popular fables.

Pro. *appears to support Actus' comment.* In the end, the fox is brought to the furrier.

Act. You see? Proverbius first praises the fox for being shrewd, then prognosticates a bad end for him. In other words, he expects that cunning will backfire.

Spe. That is one interpretation of Proverbius' adage. A more likely one is this: the hunter will bring the fox to the furrier because he is shrewder than the fox. In order to prevail, you must be cleverer than your antagonist.

Act. What you are saying, in effect, is that in order to catch the fox we must first learn to think like one, and then we must become even foxier than the fox himself.

Spe. That is the general idea.

Act. Hmm. It may work. But it is somewhat degrading for the hunter to lower himself to the level of the fox and adopt his mentality. Furthermore, it may also mean loss of control: the tricks the hunter may need can become so complex that he may have trouble handling them.

Spe. Have you a suggestion how to deal better with the fox?

Act. Perhaps. Maybe the hunter should simply unveil the fox's tricks. Unveil the guileful. Make the tricks public, bring them out into the open, publicize them. Chances are that this will deflate the fox, take the wind out of his sail and make him give up. I may be wrong, but I think this is a wiser policy than trying to outwit him with increasingly cleverer tricks.

Spe. Perhaps you are right. - Any more comments?

Act. An important one. - I think the wise must, above all, learn to see *through* all those skins, the fox's, the lion's, the wolf's. They must learn to see the real persons beyond appearances and deceptions. The wise will try to go deeper than the skins: they will attempt to go to the core. They will endeavour to understand what makes those foxes, lions and what not tick below their skins. That, I think, is real cleverness.

Spe. *Smiles.* Your comments are a fitting end to this short lesson on dermatology. - Let me suggest our next subject. I propose moderation.

Moderation

Act. I am for the subject, though not always for the thing itself.

Spe. Aha? We shall have to go into that remark later. - For the moment, let us hear what popular wisdom has to tell us about moderation. I presume it is all for it. Isn't it so, Proverbius?

Pro. Leave the table with appetite.

Spe. No, old fellow, that adage does not quite fit in here. If you leave the table with appetite, you are not moderate, but dissatisfied. Moderation should not be carried so far that it results in dissatisfaction. Try again.

Pro. Too much spoils; too little does not satisfy.

Spe. That is much better. Moderation, indeed, has to do with "too". And there are two kinds of "too": too much and too little. Moderation aims to eliminate both. In medio stat virtus, said the ancients - the virtue lies in the middle. And they saw the middle as golden: aurea mediocritas.

Act. I have some trouble with that famous golden middle. It may simply mean mediocrity. But moderation and mediocrity are different things. For the mediocre it is easy to be moderate; but it is often hard for the non-mediocre, for the outstanding, to be moderate. Besides: where lies that famous "middle"? And how do we define "too"? Both terms are subjective. What is adequate for some-one may be insufficient for another. I claim that there is no objective measure for moderation, nor, for that matter, an objective definition of the golden middle.

Spe. *Thoughtful.* Hmm. Help us out, Proverbius. How do you measure moderation?

Pro. Measure is treasure.

Spe. No puns! Definitions!

Pro. *After a brief search, that takes longer than usual.* The half is better than the whole.

Spe. Too vague. Lacks precision. Try again.

Pro. *Obviously tries to be helpful searching in his register, but finds nothing and ends in silence.*

Act. Give it up, Spectus. Not even Proverbius can help. You shall find no objective definition of "too", and consequently no objective measure for moderation. The golden middle lies somewhere between nothing and full, but where you locate it is highly subjective.

Spe. All right, let us give up trying to define moderation with precision. But I still maintain that the wise will always be moderate. It is one of their basic traits.

Act. Whereas I maintain that moderation is conditional. It depends on the circumstances.

Spe. All right, let us find out what the floor thinks about it. **(***Turns to the room, delighted to play his role of theatre director again.)* Those who believe in moderation please let themselves be known.

The usual buzzing goes through the room and several automata begin to glow.

Spe. *In a commanding tone.* Now, those who agree with Actus that moderation depends on the circumstances, in other words that it is not valid in each and every situation, please cease glowing.

Surprisingly, all automata cease to glow and return to wax.

Act. *Laughs.* The show is off, Spectus. All historic characters present in this room have been programmed to believe unconditionally in moderation. No "auditur et alia pars": we only hear one bell. There is no-one here, except me, who believes that moderation, though wise, is not valid in all situations.

Spe. *Somewhat irritated, since he was looking forward to a good performance.* I refuse to believe that Eclectus overlooked this difficulty. I expect pro and contra arguments whenever I ask the floor for contributions. That is what these dummies are here for.

Act. Nobody is perfect, Spectus. - Besides, Eclectus overlooked something else. We have dozens of famous historical characters sitting around here, and we can draw on their wisdoms. But you can't invite everybody. There are thousands of people who have said or written profound wisdoms, yet are not present. Including, I am sure, people who support my view that moderation is conditional. But that immense treasury of pertinent wisdoms is lost to us, because no-one here can remember and utter them. A pity. But we can't help it.

An automat suddenly switches into intensive glow and rises. It is a woman. She is something of a cross between a highly efficient executive secretary and an intellectual spinster managing some library. Dark hair, held together at the back in a bun. Thick spectacles on an energetic, protruding nose. Dressed plainly, but by no means cheaply. She is the type who always knows better, but is too well trained to show it. There is a name-plate in front of her desk: Citatia.

Actus and Spectus look at her for a moment in amazement.

Act. Well, chapeau. A huge plus point for Eclectus. He has a remarkable habit of coming up with solutions at the precise moment we need them. This lady, obviously, represents all those who did not have the honour of being invited to this symposium, yet are worth listening to.

Spe. *Very glad to have another, highly promising character added to his cast.* I told you not to underestimate Eclectus. Welcome to the show, Citatia, ambassador of the uninvited. And please show us right away what you can do. Give us some wisdom on moderation.

Citatia. *Speaks with an agreeable alto voice.* I believe in moderation in all things - including in moderation.

Actus and Spectus burst out laughing. Spectus applauds.

Spe. I wonder who the author of that delightful paradox is. But I guess Citatia is not programmed to reveal us that. She just gives us the contents, not the origins. No matter: she is exactly what we need. This woman will extend our possibilities enormously.

Citatia seems for a moment peeved at Spectus' reference to her as "this woman". But she remains standing, obviously waiting for further instructions.

Spe. Now, let us revert to your thesis, Actus, that moderation depends on the circumstances. Citatia: what can you tell us in support of Actus' claim?

Cit. Lack of moderation when defending a just cause is no vice, just as moderation in the defence of a just cause is no virtue.

Act. *Enthusiastic.* Bravo, Citatia! This is precisely the kind of conditionality I hoped to hear from the floor. If we want to attain a worthwhile goal, then we must, from time to time, leave moderation behind. We simply cannot stay forever in the cosy, safe, warm, golden middle.

There are times to be moderate, and times when we must go to extremes.

Spe. But extremes can't be sustained for long.

Act. Obviously not. No-one can function continuously at high gear without burning out. But that does not mean that we should shun extremes in the name of moderation, if and when extremes become necessary. - I tell you what the wise will do, Spectus. They will be moderate when they can afford to be. There is no use going to extremes when it is not necessary. Besides, being moderate spares their forces. Thus they will have the energies required to go to the extremes if and when their goal, or their purpose, or their conscience call for it. Wisdom lies not in moderation per se; it lies in knowing when to be moderate and when it is necessary to leave moderation behind.

Spe. That makes sense. But let me point out something, Actus. - You say the middle is subjective. Conceded. But I say extremes are subjective too. Furthermore, extremes can turn into excesses. While extremes may, indeed, become necessary at times, excesses must be avoided at all times. But how to determine whether an extreme is still an extreme, or whether it has turned into excess? On the temple at Delphi was written a warning: "Nothing in excess". Those who leave behind the safety of the golden middle, must, therefore, be able to distinguish between extreme and excess. But how are they to do that?

Act. *Thinks for a moment before he answers.* I think there are three different kinds of excess, so there are three different ways to answer your question. - One kind of excess is when we take upon ourselves more than we can bear. When we bite off more than we can chew. In other words when we overstep the limits of our capabilities. Extremes lie within our capabilities; excesses lie beyond them. One way to distinguish between extreme and excess, therefore, is to learn to assess clearly the limits of our own capabilities.

Spe. Not bad. - What is your second kind of excess?

Act. Requesting too much from others. Expecting from them more than they can deliver. Forcing them to go beyond their capabilities. The Romans said, wisely: Uti non abuti. Use, but do not *abuse.* Abusing others is excess.

Spe. Agreed. - And what is your third kind of excess?

Act. It has to do with a recurring theme: control. As long as we retain control, we have to do with extremes. When we lose control, it is a sign that we have become excessive. Control is the criterion by which we recognize the frontier between the extreme and the excessive.

Spe. Good arguments, Actus.

Act. And now that I come to think of it, there is even a fourth criterion.

Spe. Ah?

Act. We can recognize the difference between extreme and excess by the way we react to them. - We can become inspired, elated, awed by extremes. By a huge personal effort that results in a great and lasting achievement; by an opera or circus performance that requires the utmost ability of the performers; by an expedition to some inhospitable part of the Earth, carried out successfully despite great duress. There are many other such instances.

Spe. And what will our reaction be to excess?

Act. It produces a feeling of distaste, aversion. It does so because excess is exaggeration, and exaggeration debases, repels. In fact, exaggerating a thing creates a new thing. Overstepping the limit between extreme and excess turns a sublime thing into a ridiculous thing. The sublime and the ridiculous lie near each other, as Napoleon remarked when retreating from Russia. *(No reaction from the floor.)* Even a good thing, when excessive, can turn into its contrary: if a good thing is in excess it ceases to be good. The Arabs say: Do not wish your friend too much happiness, it may ruin him.

Spe. Good comments. Have you got some more, in the same vein?

Act. I do. In fact, I wish to introduce a concept that embodies all these things we have been discussing about moderation, extreme and excess. I call it "proportionality".

Spe. I am looking forward to hear about it.

Proportionality

Act. Proportionality is about finding the correct relationship between something that has to be done and the means needed to support it. In other words: finding the right proportion between what we want to achieve and what we must invest to achieve it. It means mobilizing just the right amount of resources that the situation demands. It calls for restraint when circumstances allow it, but for full engagement if and when the situation calls for it. Proportionality thus keeps us from squandering our resources, from using a musket to kill a butterfly. On the other hand, it incites us to draw all registers, throw in everything at our disposal, when our goal is in danger. It helps to keep us from losing ourselves in trifles, but urges us to give the necessary attention to important details. Proportionality thus helps us avoid two kinds of excess: too much and too little. For all excess is disproportional.

Spe. *Impressed.* I believe this concept of yours is one of the wisest we have formulated so far. I am itching to come up with cases to illustrate it.

Act. Then don't let it itch. Do it.

Spe. Take medicine. Some drugs heal in small doses, but kill in overdoses. Knowing the correct dose has to do with proportionality. If you respect proportion, you heal; if you do not, you kill. - Take politics. What we call political extremism is in reality political excess, since it lacks proportion to the cause. - And then another thought comes to my mind.

Act. Let's hear it.

Spe. Take an overloaded, over-decorated work of art: it is not pleasing, it is even repulsive, because it is excessive. Take a crude, incomplete work of art: again you will not be satisfied; you will have the feeling that more effort should have gone into making the thing. But now take a beautiful work of art to which nothing can be added nor taken away from. Such a work is bound to give you a feeling of deep satisfaction. - Take a business project that consumed more money, more effort, more energy than would have been necessary. It irritates you, since the investment was larger than the need. Take, on the other hand, a business project that failed, because you did not invest the effort it should have required. Again there is a feeling of dissatisfaction. But take a well-managed project, where the right amount of effort and means were invested to reach the goal. Once again you experience a feeling of satisfaction. - What is the common link between the good artist and the good manager? It is this: behind the work of both your proportionality is at work. From which I derive two conclusions. One is, that proportionality is a universal phenomenon, applicable to art, to business, and whatever. The other is: proportionality has to do with aesthetics. It is wisdom that appeals to our aesthetic feeling.

Act. *Smiles.* You may indeed go a bit too far there, Spectus. But your theory is interesting. - But we said enough on proportionality. It is clear what we mean by it. So let us move on. As to our next subject, I suggest patience.

Patience

Spe. Fine. Let us ask what Proverbius thinks of it. I presume he will be full of praise.

Pro. Everything comes to him that waits with patience.

Act. Sorry, but I disagree. To those who simply wait with patience things will either not come at all, or they will come too late. If you want milk and sit down on a stool in the middle of a field patiently waiting for a cow to walk up to you, chances are that you will be waiting for a long time. If you want something, you must do something to get it; you need more than just patiently wait.

Spe. We can interpret that proverb in two ways, Actus. - One is your interpretation: sit back, do nothing, be passively patient, expect time to work for you. Patientia vincit omnia. I can understand that a doer like you condemns this attitude. - But there is also another interpretation: don't get impatient if you do not get quick results. Accept that what needs time also needs patience. It is the old classic wisdom that an oak is not felled at one stroke, nor Rome built in one day. In other words: concentrate on your goal, work hard to achieve it, but be patient if you do not reach it as swiftly as you may wish.

Act. I do not condemn patience. What I condemn is inactivity, laissez-faire.

Spe. I know, Actus, and again we differ. I do not, like you, condemn laissez-faire - at least not in all cases. Sometimes, if you practice laissez-faire, if you just leave an issue alone, it tends to resolve itself. This is a very ancient wisdom that goes back to Tao. But I am not going to try to sell it to you, since I know you wouldn't buy it. - But you said that you do not condemn patience, only inactivity. That means that patience and activity are compatible. Can you name a few examples where the wise will need to be both active and patient?

Act. *Thinks for a moment.* To begin with: all complex tasks require hard work, intense activity, coupled with patience. But there are many other examples. - Only if we patiently learn to do simple things well, can we gradually acquire the skill to do difficult things with ease. We must, patiently, learn to walk before we can run. - We must also have patience while climbing the ladder of a hierarchy. We need to synchronise our climbing with the development of our abilities, and that requires patience. - We need patience when we search for the truth: uncovering the truth can sometimes be a long process. - And then: we must have patience with some natural processes, such as healing. A "patient" is called so because he patiently, though not passively, waits to get healthy.

Spe. That was a good list, Actus. - But I wonder what Citatia, our new acquisition, can add to the subject of patience. Citatia?

Cit. Patience is the virtue of an ass that resolves to trot quietly beneath a heavy burden.

Spe. *Bursts out laughing.* Looks like she does not appreciate patience.

Act. But she is right, Spectus. Patience ceases to be a virtue if it means to just stupidly "grin and bear it", like a silly ass. Not try to remove a burden that could be removed; accept a bad situation that could be improved. Patience must not be misused as an excuse for failing to make changes for the better. If it is, then patience becomes a handicap. In that case I would even go as far as to praise impatience: impatience can be creative, constructive.

Spe. *Smiles.* Looks like Citatia's wisdoms can trigger a lot of interesting comments. Have you got more on patience, Citatia?

Cit. Dear God, give me patience. And, God, I want it *now*!

Spe. *Laughs.* You are a master of paradoxes. But we want something more serious, please.

Cit. *After a moment's thought.* He who bears injury with patience invites new injury.

Act. That is certainly true. An injury that is born with patience emboldens the offender. That will make the situation even worse. Not reacting energetically to an offence is patience misplaced. - Give us one last wisdom on patience, Citatia.

Cit. Patience provoked can turn into fury.

Spe. Yes, that is also true. Patient men are slow to get angry. But if and when they do get angry, their anger can be very intense indeed. So beware the wrath of a patient man. - But I think we covered the main points on patience. Let us move on to another quality of our hypothetic wise individual. What do you suggest, Actus?

Act. A quality that both you and I, fortunately, possess. Curiosity.

Curiosity

Spe. *Smiles.* Yes, we both know how important curiosity is. It makes us understand how things work; and the more we understand, the more we can do something about them. Curiosity shaped our culture: had the ancient Greeks not been curious, we would not be as we are. - Incidentally: do you know where our word "school" comes from? From the Greek "scholà", meaning "leisure". While all Greeks were curious, it was only the privileged who could satisfy their curiosity, because only they had leisure to go to school.

Act. *Sighs.* A long haul from some of our modern schools, where drudgery often predominates over curiosity.

Spe. True. The wise teacher makes his pupils curious. - But I think we need to distinguish between different forms of curiosity. Curiosity for the sciences characterized the Greeks. But curiosity can also mean something else: sticking your nose into other people's affairs.

Pro. *Cuts in, prompted by his register.* Enquire not what boils in another man's pot.

Spe. Precisely. Mind your own business, says popular wisdom.

Act. Minding one's own business may be commendable from the point of view of popular wisdom, but not necessarily from that of a modern businessman. If a businessman followed Proverbius' advice and ignored what is boiling in other people's pots, especially in the pots of his competitors, he may get seriously hurt. At times it is simply a question of survival to know what others are cooking.

Spe. You mean we need to qualify Proverbius' adage?

Act. Yes. I would qualify it like this. - We should be curious about another's pot if it means protecting our own interests. - We may also want to look into another's pot if the boiler is a friend. Perhaps he is boiling something that is dangerous and he is not aware of it. We then look into his pot because we want to protect him from harm. - On the other hand, we should *not* look into another's pot if we have no reason at all to do so. The worst case is not only to look without justification into what another is boiling, but start meddling with the affairs of the boiler. - In other words: the wise will know why and when to pry into another's pot, and they will be selective about the pots they pry into.

Spe. There is definitely more finesse behind all these boiling pots than I imagined. Curiosity turns out to be a complex thing.

Act. Curiosity is above all a double-edged thing. On the one hand there is no progress without it. On the other hand it may lead us into dangerous waters, where we lose control. The wise will try to be cautiously curious. Unfortunately, that is not an easy mix.

Spe. True. - But now I am really curious to hear who, among our co-participants, share our positive view on curiosity. *(Turns to the room.)* Those who wish to defend curiosity please rise. Citatia, you may participate, of course.

The usual buzz, then five automata begin to glow and rise, joining Citatia who, like Proverbius, is on continuous alert.

Spe. *Slips into his theatre director's role and enjoys it tremendously, as usual.* Now speak up, starting from the back to the front.

The automata understand; there is no confusion.

Linus Pauling. *Open-faced, good natured professor. Before starting to speak he quickly swallows 5 grams of vitamin C.* One of the greatest sources of happiness in life is the satisfaction of one's curiosity.

Dr. Samuel Johnson. *Appears like his portrait by Joshua Reynolds, a bit unhealthy and unfriendly. He looks around searching for Boswell, who has not been invited.* A generous and elevated mind is distinguished by an eminent degree of curiosity.

Jean-Jacques Rousseau. *Looks like his portrait by Quentin de la Tour. Intelligent eyes, thin lips. Wears a wig, with a coloured Indian feather stuck into it, a discreet reference to his admiration of the noble savage.* On n'est curieux qu'à proportion qu'on est instruit.

Gilbert Keith Chesterton. *Rotund figure, exuberant personality. Disguised as Father Brown, the ever-curious detective-clergyman.* Inquisitiveness is rebuked as one of the weaknesses of humanity. But I think, on the contrary, that most people are not curious enough. However, they should have what I call clean curiosity - an appetite for truth.

Rudyard Kipling. *Holds his first jungle book in one hand and the second in the other. On his desk is a small replica of Baloo, the wise bear.* I had six honest serving men / they taught me all I knew / their names were: Where and What and When / and Why and How and Who.

Cit. One of the secrets of life is to keep our intellectual curiosity ever acute. Curiosity keeps us alive. Abandoning curiosity means turning one's back on life.

Citatia remains standing, the other five return to wax.

Spe. A broad range of praises. The one I like most is the one by Citatia: curiosity perceived as an elixir of life.

Act. I like the term coined by Chesterton: "clean curiosity". Defined as "appetite for truth". That is precisely the kind of curiosity our wise individual should possess.

Spe. Surprising, isn't it, that curiosity can be both clean and unclean, justified and unjustified. Maybe that is so because we have only one word, curiosity, to denote two rather different things: Chesterton's appetite for truth, and Proverbius' boiling pots.

Act. Yet the two are related. Father Brown's appetite for truth would not be effective if he did not stick his nose into other people's pots.

They laugh.

Spe. I suggest we now turn to a quality not far from curiosity: imagination.

Imagination

Act. A trait not to be confounded with fantasy.

Spe. Aha? And what is the difference between the two?

Act. Imagination is guided by facts. It is based on reality. It is creative. - Fantasy is disconnected from facts. It deals with things that do not exist. For that reason fantasy is often just bizarre, rather than creative. - I claim that our hypothetic individual needs imagination, but not fantasy.

Spe. Hmm. Tell me: is this seminar of ours a product of imagination or of fantasy?

Act. It is a mixture of both. The concept behind this seminar is a product of imagination. Citatia is a product of fantasy.

Citatia is totally unimpressed. She knows why she is at the seminar and how to do her job well, whatever she is the product of.

Spe. But I remember that, at the beginning of this symposium, you doubted that Eclectus had fantasy. Where, then, does the fantasy in this seminar come from?

Act. I must revise that early statement of mine. Eclectus obviously possesses both imagination and fantasy. But I insist on the difference between the two. This symposium is primarily guided not by fantasy, but by imagination. It is based on facts, taken from life. It pursues a concrete, worthy purpose. It is no tale told by an idiot.

Spe. *Smiles.* Then tell me more about the benefits of imagination, as distinct from fantasy.

Act. *After a moment's reflection.* Imagination, as I already said, is creative. It helps to open up new frontiers, to look at things with a fresh eye. There are thousands of things surrounding us in everyday life that no-one could have foreseen a few decades ago. Had they been products merely of fantasy, rather than of imagination, they would still not exist: it is imagination that made them become reality. Jules Verne, whom I still enjoy reading, had tremendous imagination: that is why many of the things he foretold have since been realised. *(Verne has not been invited and so cannot appreciate Actus' praise.)* - Imagination helps us formulate goals; fantasy doesn't. While imagination leads to exciting, yet feasible objectives, fantasy merely engenders vague desires. - Imagination is also of help when we face complex problems. Most advances in science have been made by people with a lot of imagination. Einstein, in fact, went so far as to maintain that imagination is more important than knowledge. *(Einstein, sitting at the back, acknowledges by a brief flare that this is indeed so.)*

Cit. *Cuts in, obviously inspired by Einstein's thought.* He who has knowledge but no imagination has feet but no wings.

Spe. *Smiles.* Thank you, Citatia. That was a very poetic rendering of Einstein. - But let me join you in praising imagination, Actus, though my reason for doing so is different from those you mentioned. I strongly believe in the value and the importance of empathy, the ability to place oneself into the situation of someone else. Empathy helps us to understand other people's problems, needs, feelings. I claim that this ability is badly needed in our present world. But empathy can only work in conjunction with imagination. Those without imagination simply do not know what empathy is. - But, Actus, I cannot follow you in belittling fantasy. For me, it is often highly welcome. It relaxes, entertains, because it makes possible what reality does not allow. I strongly believe that all of us, once in a while, need to shed the fetters of reality, forget about facts, and abandon ourselves to uninhibited, refreshing, playful fantasy.

Act. We obviously react differently, Spectus. I am refreshed and relaxed by products of imagination, whereas products of mere fantasy bore me. Besides, I see a danger. Those who abandon themselves too often and too intensely to fantasy may lose their capacity to distinguish between it and imagination. They risk ending up taking for imagination that is but fantasy, for real what does not exist.

Spe. I think that danger is minimal. But let us agree to disagree and move on. - Any suggestion as to the next positive trait our wise individual should possess?

Act. Optimism.

Spe. An excellent suggestion. And an excellent trait.

Optimism

Act. Yes: optimism is essential to help our individual stand upright. He will, in fact, live longer: experiments indicate that optimists tend to have a longer lifespan than pessimists. Optimism is a kind of healthy diet for the mind.

Spe. Though that diet may be administered in different forms, since optimism can be of different kinds.

Act. *Surprised.* Really? I never heard of that. Please explain.

Spe. To begin with, there is the so-called philosophical optimism. It is the belief that we live in the best of all possible worlds. Tout est pour le mieux dans le meilleur des mondes possibles, as Dr. Pangloss, alias Leibniz, told Candide, according to Voltaire. *(Leibniz and Voltaire are present, but do not react; they obviously do not want to reopen a discussion settled 250 years ago.)* Philosophical optimism ascertains something for which there is no evidence. Or, rather, it ascertains something despite evidence to the contrary.

Act. Your philosophical optimism is akin to fantasy. I cannot accept it.

Spe. I don't blame you. Neither can I. - Now: the second kind of optimism is religious optimism. It maintains that God is good and will, in the end, always triumph over Evil. It is the optimism of the faithful.

Act. May I suggest that we postpone discussing this point and revert to it when we erect our tower of religious wisdoms?

Spe. Agreed. - A third kind of optimism recommends that we always look at the sunny side of life, practically ignoring the dark one. It is more down-to-earth than the previous two kinds, but it is lopsided. It is optimism gained at the price of distorting realities.

Act. *Smiles.* I expect the last kind of optimism will be my kind.

Spe. Precisely. - Call it pragmatic, or realistic optimism. It is the conviction that most good things are here to stay, provided we take good care of them. Conversely, it claims that most bad things can be improved, provided we decide to do something about them. It is optimism based on confidence in our own abilities and in the abilities of others. It is the conviction that the right efforts will almost always yield positive results. This is the optimism of the wise.

Act. It is indeed. - But let me add a remark. I believe optimism, in order to be effective, must refer to the short-term future. Anyone can be optimistic about a vague distant future, but that is just pessimism in disguise. - Let me suggest our next topic. It is a trait without which the life of our hypothetic individual would be dreary. A trait that can save, and, despite appearances to the contrary, can be profoundly wise. Do you know what I am talking about?

Spe. *Smiles.* I presume you mean humour.

Act. Exactly. Humour, and its healthy by-product, laughter.

Humour

Spe. Did you know, Actus, that Dante relegated to Hell those who were gloomy, though they had reasons to laugh?

Act. No, I didn't. But I find the punishment justified.

Spe. Nevertheless, humour is a many-faceted thing. It means different things to different people. *(Seems to have a sudden thought.)* I have an idea, Actus. An exciting new experiment. Let us summon all those present in this room who have something to say on humour. Then you and I start a conversation on the subject and ask the others to comment on what we say, whenever they wish to do so. No more name-calling, no more instructions in what order they should speak. If the experiment doesn't work and ends in chaos, we shall have a good laugh. But if it does, then we have taken a major step forward in using these machines.

Act. *Sceptical.* I am afraid you expect too much from Eclectus and his products of imagination. But I don't want to keep you from experimenting. So go ahead.

Spe. *Happy to get another opportunity as theatre director, turns to the room.* You have heard and registered my proposal. Try to make the best of it. Let me repeat: I shall not determine at what time and in what order you place your contributions; you alone decide that. Have you understood? If you did, please make yourselves be known *now*!

The automata, obviously, have no problem dealing with Spectus' request. Seven of them begin to glow and rise, making eight together with Citatia. Proverbius goes into half glow, indicating that popular wisdom has not much to say on humour, except, perhaps, "laughter is the best medicine".

Spe. Great! - Let me, then, start our discussion by recalling my opening remark: humour is a many-faceted thing.

Cit. Humour can heal or wound. It can enlarge or diminish.

Spe. Indeed it can, Citatia. The effects of humour can be positive or negative according to the intention of the one who uses it. The wise, of course, will always use humour to heal and enlarge, never to wound or diminish. - But we have only just begun to list the things that humour can do. Another use of humour was already known to the Romans: Ridendo dicere verum. Use laughter to deliver the truth.

George Bernard Shaw. *Tall figure, white beard, straw hat, walking stick. Has a writing pad in front of him, on which he is scribbling paradoxes.* My idea of a joke is to tell the truth. Truth is the funniest joke in the world.

Spe. *Frowns.* That is not what I meant, Mr Shaw. The truth is no joke. But we can tell the truth packaged in a joke. Like caricaturists or comic poets do.

William Congreve. *Looks like his portrait by Godfrey Kneller. Huge wig, descending to the middle of his back. Intelligent face.* It is the business of the comic poet to paint with a laughter the follies of human kind.

Spe. Yes, that's it. Mr Congreve stands here as proxy for a long line of wise, humorous artists who jokingly told the truth. They held up comic mirrors and hoped that we will recognise ourselves in them. That by seeing our faults and deficiencies reflected in the mirror we shall start down the road to self-criticism - and therefore to more wisdom.

Act. The problem is that comic mirrors do not always achieve their purpose. Many don't recognise themselves in them. Others will resent them as unfounded criticism.

Cit. A person reveals his character by the jokes he resents.

Spe. That is very true, Citatia. Many reject the message in a joke meant to edify them. The wise, however, will understand the message. Because the wise can laugh at themselves. The humourless lack that ability. - But let us find additional facets to humour. I find that humour can ease, at times even save a strained situation. In fact, this could be one of its most important functions.

Quintus Horatius Flaccus (Horace). *Looks a bit conceited, but one senses that he also has a great deal of self-irony. He speaks English like a country gentleman of leisure educated at Oxford.* A well-placed joke often decides matters of importance more happily and more effectively than seriousness.

Act. Indeed it can, Quintus. I have experienced it at countless difficult meetings. A well-intentioned, well-placed, intelligent joke relaxes tensions and can indeed save delicate situations. - Unfortunately, the reverse is also true. An ill-placed, silly joke can create an atmosphere of resentment. Jokes can also be misunderstood and must then be painfully explained.

Spe. That happens sometimes because tastes for jokes differ.

George Eliot, alias Mary Ann Evans. *Looks like her portrait by D'Albert-Durade from the time she lived in Geneva.* I find that a difference of taste in jokes is a great strain upon the affections.

Spe. I find that also, madam. It is indeed very hard having to laugh courteously at a ludicrous joke that only the teller finds funny. And one of the greatest strains is having to endure the company of someone who tries to be funny about things that are not funny at all.

Pierre Augustin de Beaumarchais. *Dressed as Figaro, the Barber of Seville; holds Occam's razor in one hand.* Je me presse de rire de tout, de peur d'être obligé d'en pleurer.

Spe. Non monsieur, that goes too far. Something we should weep about is not funny. Gloominess must not parade as humour. Humour must be genuine, spontaneous, hearty, well-meant, refreshing. It can be salty, but not bitter. Forced humour is not humorous.

Act. *Thoughtful.* Yet there is an exception, Spectus. There is a kind of forced humour that deserves praise. Even high praise. It is humour in the face of hardship, adversity. Call it heroic humour. It is humour that can save. Somehow it has to do with keeping up human dignity.

Cit. Be fond of the man who jests with his scars.

Act. Yes, Citatia. Thank you for that quote; it is what I meant. And let me point out that it is by no means easy for a man with scars to joke about them. It requires willpower. Those who manage to do it deserve our respect - and our help.

Spe. A noble remark. - Can you think of other facets of humour, Citatia?

Cit. Humour reveals the earthly limits of those who pretend to be sublime.

Spe. An interesting comment. Let me illustrate it by something I once read. - In native American Indian cultures, and also, it seems, in Tibet, clowns were used to disturb holy processions. They poked fun at the priests as they marched by, made all sorts of jokes about them. The idea was to make it clear that the priests were just the earthly representatives of the divine, not the divine itself. It kept the priests from perceiving themselves as sublime. Similarly, the European court jester was originally meant to remind those in power of their earthly limits. And guess which Renaissance court had the greatest number of professional jesters? The Vatican! - Speaking of the Vatican, guess what John XXIII once wrote into his diary? "Giovanni, don't take yourself so seriously!" I find that statement remarkable; after all, he was the pope. But his note reveals that he was wise. For the wise do not take themselves too seriously; only the unwise do. - Now, who hasn't spoken yet? Ah, I see Lord Nelson standing there. What have you got to tell us on humour, admiral?

Horatio Viscount Nelson. *Elegant, good looking, impressive. Admiral's hat, breast full of decorations. One arm and one eye are missing. In his remaining hand he holds the telescope that he applied to his blind eye at the battle of Copenhagen.* I could not have tread many perilous paths in safety, if I did not keep a saving sense of humour.

Spe. Interesting: humour as saviour in perilous situations. But Nelson must know. - I think we should slowly come to the end of this topic, Actus. Will all those who already contributed to the subject please take their seats?

Except Citatia, Proverbius and one other automaton all others return to wax.

Spe. Who is that still standing, Actus?

Act. *Somewhat surprised as he reads the machine's name-plate.* It is Irving Berlin.

Spe. Is it? Well. Come on and hear! Come on and hear!

Irving Berlin. *Dressed as Father Christmas, sparkling white snow we used to know glistening on his cap and shoulders.* The world would not be in such a snarl, if Marx had been - Groucho, and not Karl! *(He grins, brushes some snow from his shoulders, then joins the others returning to wax.)*

Actus and Spectus laugh heartily.

Act. To which facet of humour does that pun belong to?

Spe. I cannot say. Perhaps the kind of joke that makes you laugh first, and ponder about later. - But let us come to an end. I found Citatia was particularly brilliant with her contributions to this subject. As a recompense, I suggest we give her the final word. - Citatia: the floor is yours. Tell us briefly what, in your opinion, are the main aspects of humour.

Cit. *Has a fleeting smile of pleasure, obviously appreciating Spectus' praise.* Humour, used wisely, is a tonic for the mind and the body. It is an antidote for anxiety and depression. It lightens burdens. It prompts tolerant views. It attracts and keeps friends. It is the shortest distance between two people and the most direct route to contentedness. Humour can protect us from harm, for those with no sense of humour are more open to evil.

Spe. Thank you, dear. Indeed: life is more enjoyable if we keep remembering that there is that healthy, praiseworthy thing called humour. Not to be confused, though, with irony and cynicism.

Act. No. Yet, behind those may also be wisdom. Irony draws attention to some incongruity, a difference between what is expected and what actually is; that can be salutary. Cynicism is negative; but at times it is just wisdom standing on its head to attract attention.

Spe. Whatever. - What is our next topic?

The gong is struck, marking the end of the session.

Spe. Well, it looks like Eclectus regards humour as the crowning quality of our hypothetic individual - whatever he may think of irony and cynicism. *(Stretches.)* This was an interesting and many-sided session, Actus. I enjoyed it. But now I long for coffee. - How are we doing with our columns, incidentally?

Most of the pillars have risen to considerable heights, though some are only beginning to rise.

But Actus and Spectus are satisfied with the results so far. They rise and leave contentedly for morning coffee. No-one else in the room is lured by the delicate aroma drifting into the seminar room.

Session 6: The Pillars (continued)

Actus and Spectus return from morning coffee. The revolving holograph on the wall shows the progress made with the pillars. The gong starts the second session of the day.

Spectus. Let's see. We discussed some of the positive features that should help our wise individual stand upright. Also, we discovered that these talking dummies are programmed to have greater autonomy than we initially thought; we can make use of that discovery in future sessions. - Next, we must examine what negative attitudes and traits our wise individual must avoid, since they might topple him. Any suggestions, Actus?

Actus. Worry.

Worry

Spe. Good. Here we go. - We discussed fear and how to deal with it. But worry is something different. While fear is a natural reaction to some concrete danger, worry is often vague, ill-defined. Because of this vagueness it debilitates, consumes. It often begins small, but then gradually comes to dominate all other thoughts. Someone compared worry to rust creeping slowly upon a blade.

Act. And some other wise fellow said worry is a stupid waste of time in unpleasantness. One of the first life-rules I coined for myself, when I was a kid, had to do with worry. Be a warrior, not a worrier, I told myself valiantly.

Spe. *Laughs.* A wise pun. - But worry needs to be taken seriously. Charles Mayo once claimed that he has never known anyone who died from overwork, but several who died from worry. *(Charles Mayo, founder of the famous clinic, has not been invited.)* - I reckon popular wisdom knows about the detrimental effects of worry, and so does Citatia. I suggest we listen to what they have to say. Proverbius first: age before beauty. *(Citatia ignores Spectus' oblique reference to her looks.)*

Pro. If a man harbours worry, he is landlord to a ghost.

Cit. Ignore those big black clouds that loom on the horizon - and usually end up looming, nothing more.

Spe. Interesting two similes. Both confirm that worry is something vague, undefined, like a cloud, or even unreal, like a ghost.

Act. But Citatia suggests a remedy: just ignore the cloud. If you do not, you are like the man who had a lot of trouble in his life - most of which never happened.

Spe. No, Actus, I don't think that simply ignoring worries is the right attitude. Not all worries are merely clouds. Furthermore, if we try to ignore a worry, we may just repress it, let it sink into our subconscious. There the worry becomes a ghost. And then, suddenly, when we least expect it, it re-surfaces.

Act. Then let us belittle worries, rather than ignore them.

Spe. That is Plato's advice. Nothing in the affairs of men is worthy of great worry, he wrote. *(Plato briefly glares.)* But there is a snag. While we try to convince ourselves that our worry is insignificant, we may not quite believe ourselves. And then, sneakily, our worry grows into something bigger than the thing that initially caused it.

Cit. Worry can give a large shadow to a small thing.

Spe. Precisely, Citatia. - Conclusion: we should neither ignore worry, nor belittle it.

Act. Then let me tell you what the wise will do.

Spe. Hear, hear!

Act. First, they will stop worrying about things that are utterly outside their control; things they can do nothing about whatever.

Spe. Such as?

Act. Getting involved in a plane crash; getting hit by an asteroid; getting buried under the ashes of a super-volcano. Such things are fatalities, fully outside our influence. In all such cases the wise will simply leave things to providence and turn to other matters. They will tell themselves that it seldom comes as good as many hope, but rarely as bad as some expect. Just think of all those books and reports with apocalyptic predictions, and you will realize how wrong the doomsday prophets were.

Spe. True. Go on.

Act. Then, there are potential calamities that may justly worry us, but against which we can make tiny contributions. Take climate change: we can use our cars a bit less, avoid squandering energy. Our own measures will only be a drop in the ocean - but if millions do the same, the drops will have huge effects. That will lessen worries: our own and those of others.

Spe. If I follow your logic, we are left with worries we can do a great deal about.

Act. Exactly. - Against those, the wise will adopt the same attitude I suggested when we discussed danger. They will not ignore, repress, nor belittle such worries, but face them, and do so rationally. The moment such a worry begins, the wise will pack it by its roots. They will not let a vague, undefined "ghost" take possession. They will make an effort to fully understand what causes their worry. Once they have identified those causes, they will undertake everything in their power to eliminate them. If they cannot eliminate them fully, they will estimate the harm that might ensue and draw up counter-measures to protect themselves. But once those measures are in place, they will forget about the worry. They will not have it constantly weighing on their minds.

Pro. *Has a relevant maxim.* Don't worry about having to cross the river till you get there.

Act. Precisely, wise old friend. We should reckon with the river, accept the possibility that we shall have to cross it, prepare measures to do the crossing. But once we have done all that, let us stop worrying about the river. It may never turn up, because it flows elsewhere than we thought. Or it may turn up, but it carries such low water that we can cross it without difficulty. Or we may find a bridge, so the whole problem simply implodes. We may even decide that we do not need to cross the river at all. - What I am driving at is this: be prepared for the river, reckon with the difficulties of crossing it, but then refuse to worry about them until they become real. Live in the present-tense; the worry concerns the future.

Spe. Commendable counsels. - Unfortunately, some people tend to forecast too many difficulties that lie ahead. Trying to get rid of worry by reckoning with future perils then backfires: people get paralysed into inaction by their own forecasting.

Act. There is nothing wrong with forecasting difficulties and perils: the more of them we prepare for, the surer we shall fare. And there is an excellent way of overcoming the danger of getting paralysed into inaction: estimate the *probabilities* of the perils ahead. Let me illustrate what I mean. - During my career I have set up hundreds of so-called "business scenarios". They show the various possible outcomes of expensive, complex projects. But I followed an iron rule: never present a scenario without a probability figure attached to it. The chances for the best scenario actually happening are usually small; but so are the chances for the worst scenario. The wise businessman will focus on scenarios with high probabilities. To worry about a bad scenario with low probability is like being impressed by Citatia's large shadows cast by insignificant things.

Spe. A clear exposé, Actus. I think it makes any further comments on worry superfluous.

Act. All right: may I then suggest our next topic? Anger.

Anger

Spe. A good suggestion. - We dealt briefly with anger when we discussed courage, and said it is a natural reflex against fright. But there is also anger not caused by fright, and that is what we have to discuss here. - Let me start with a proposition: anger, in whatever form and for whatever reason, is dangerous and detrimental, and should therefore be avoided under all circumstances. This was the view of the Stoics. *(Turns to the room.)* Can we please have some well-known Stoic confirm the proposition I just presented?

Marcus Aurelius Antoninus. *Glows and rises. Looks as if he just got off his horse at Capitol Hill in Rome. Serene and noble countenance, his arm raised in the Roman salute (later imitated by Mussolini and Hitler, who failed, though, to imitate his stoicism). Despite his Roman look, he speaks English with a highly cultivated accent.* Consider how much more you suffer from anger than from the very thing you are angry for; how much more grievous are the consequences of anger than the causes of it. *(He slowly sits down and returns to wax with his arm still raised.)*

Spe. I must say that I agree with Marcus. Anger can hurt an angry man more than the one his anger is directed against. An angry man refuses to listen to reason: he enters into a sort of craze; that is why the words "angry" and "mad" are synonymous. An angry man tends to insult his opponent; but insult invites insult. An angry man is vulnerable, because in his craze he thinks he can do more than he is actually capable of. This wisdom was expressed in beautiful Latin eight hundred years ago by Albertano di Brescia: Iratus semper plus putat posse facere quam possit. *(Albertano has not been invited.)*

Pro. When a cock bristles up his feathers, it is easy to plume him.

Spe. *Laughs.* And there we have good old Proverbius interpreting in plain English Albertano's thought. Don't get mad, get even, was the counsel of the father of a famous American president. Nothing can justify anger: that is what it boils down to.

Benjamin Franklin. *Discovers he has something to say on precisely this point and rises so suddenly that he forgets his kite under his desk.* Anger is never without a reason; but the reason is seldom or never a good one. *(Returns to kiteless wax.)*

Spe. You must admit, Actus, I am in good company: Marcus Aurelius, Franklin, Kennedy senior. And I can even add my wife to their company. She claims that when I get angry, I do so because I am in the wrong, but not prepared to admit it. In other words, I get angry *because* I know that I am not in the right.

Act. Your wife, who I am sure is beautiful and wise, may be right in some cases, but not in all cases. *(Turns to the seminar room.)* I call on a participant with authority to support my view that Marcus Aurelius, Franklin, Kennedy and Spectus' wife are only partly right, because there is, often, not only a good reason to become angry, but also a good reason to show it.

Aristotle. *Glows and rises. Looks exactly like his statue in the Vatican Museum. You can even see the bit where his nose was restored. He appears to be wanting to walk around the seminar room, as if it were the Peripatos, but is restrained by his mechanism.* That man be praised who gets angry on the right grounds, with the right people, in the right manner, at the right moment, and for the right length of time. *(He sits down with decorum and returns to wax.)*

Act. You must admit, Spectus: my view, also, gets support from high authority.

Spe. Aristotle's statement is impressive. But can we really follow all his precepts? Hardly. Consequently, it is wiser not to become angry in the first place.

Act. No, Spectus, it is not wiser. All of Aristotle's precepts, though they do require some effort, are feasible. And there is more: we meet once again one of our recurring themes, control. - The Stoics recommend a very simple kind of control: never get angry, no matter what. Aristotle recommends a much more subtle form of control. He allows us to get angry for the right reasons; but our anger must remain under control. We must direct it at the right person; never overdo it; show it at the right moment; not stay angry longer than necessary. Aristotle is not against anger per se; he condemns unjustified, uncontrolled, misplaced anger. I believe he is right. I just can't agree with the simple precept of the Stoics. - However, I concede one thing. There are moments where things menace to boil over, ready to explode. The wise know that such moments can be very dangerous. When such a moment comes, the wise may choose to stay calm and detached, like a Stoic. They know that in such extreme situations more can be achieved by calm than by anger. But even these situations were foreseen by Aristotle: be angry at the right moment, he writes. Sometimes, the moment is not right for anger.

Spe. *After a moment's thought.* All right, Actus, you convinced me. I concede that there can be good reasons for getting angry and good reasons for showing our anger. Nevertheless, let me add this: we should never get angry for insignificant, petty reasons, bagatelles. That only diminishes us.

A cigar begins to glow in the seminar room; cigar smoke fills the air. Following the example of the cigar, an imposing figure begins to glow and then rises with the cigar in his mouth.

Sir Winston Leonard Spencer Churchill. *Bow tie, dark suit, waistcoat, watch-chain, bulldog look, like his photograph by Karsh, except for the cigar, which is missing in the photo. He speaks with a surprisingly high-pitched voice.* A man is as big as the things that make him angry. *(He draws on his cigar with relish and sits down.)*

Spe. A deep wisdom, from a great man. - But we haven't heard Citatia yet. Have you got a pertinent remark on anger, my dear?

Cit. An angry man without power is merely ridiculous.

Spe. Hmm. Not necessarily. If a powerless man gets angry for the wrong reason, he is indeed ridiculous. But if he gets angry for a just reason, he is not ridiculous; merely pathetic. Furthermore: a powerful man, angry for a wrong reason, is dangerous. On the other hand: a powerful man, angry for the right reason, can make history.

Act. *Laughs.* That covers all possible combinations. *(Turns to the seminar room.)* An additional remark on anger, anyone?

William Blake. *Glows, rises. Bald head, penetrating eyes, arrogant mouth, looks like his portrait by Linnell. He has an aura of slight madness but also of sparkling genius about him.* I was angry with my friend; I told him my wrath, my wrath did end. I was angry with my foe; I told it not, my wrath did grow. *(He sits down and starts painting watercolours, but his mechanism returns him to wax after a few brushstrokes.)*

Spe. Blake is right. Being angry at someone behind his back will only increase our anger. When we are angry at someone, let us openly discuss with him the reasons why. - Let me make a final remark. If someone is angry at us, he may tell us things he would normally withhold. Let us never ignore what an angry man tells us: it is probably the truth. The wise will listen to an angry man's critique and turn what he says to their benefit.

Act. That wisdom deserves to close this topic with. - Any suggestion for our next one?

Spe. I suggest Pride.

Pride, Conceit, Vanity, Arrogance

Act. Hmm. Do you really consider pride to be a negative trait? I can be justifiably proud of a lot of good things: of a job well done; of the achievements of my son; of my country. Even of my new car.

Spe. None of those things you listed got to do with pride, Actus. A job well done should make you satisfied, not proud. Your sentiment about your son's achievements is appreciation mixed with affection. Being born in a great country is not your accomplishment; how can you be proud of a mere accident? And as for your new car, let me quote a Greek sage: If you boast about possessing a beautiful horse, you are priding yourself with a quality that belongs not to you, but to the horse.

Act. *Laughs.* Touché. - All right then, let us regard pride as an essentially negative trait. But why is pride a danger for our hypothetic individual?

Spe. For the simple reason that pride can easily turn into other, much more despicable traits. Into conceit, the exaggerated opinion about one's achievements or possessions. Into vanity, the desire for inordinate praise. Into arrogance, the overvaluing of one's own importance. Pride is dangerous because it is at the root of all these negative features. And because pride has a tendency to become exaggerated, ostentatious, misplaced. - But let us proceed in an orderly fashion. I suggest we first have a look at pride itself, then at conceit, vanity, and arrogance. *(Turns to the room.)* And I ask our co-seminarians to get actively involved in this discussion. You may want to confirm what Actus and I say, or disagree with us. Or you may want to point out that what we say is acceptable, even excusable, in some cases, but not in all cases. Citatia, Proverbius: you are invited to join the debate.

Spectus knows by now that he only needs to issue succinct orders, since all automata closely follow and register the discussions between him and Actus. They know what to do. There is some buzzing, then four figures rise, joining Proverbius and Citatia.

Spe. Here we go, then. We begin with pride. Citatia: you start the discussion.

Cit. I am proud and you are proud, but who will take the garbage out?

Spe. *Laughs.* This had to come from a woman! Some men, indeed, regard certain menial tasks as below their dignity and leave them to women. I call that misplaced pride. My wife calls it the pasha-attitude.

Act. I plead not guilty of this form of pride. Take an example: I have forced myself to learn all essential tasks of my secretary, so that, in case she became unavailable, I could do them myself. I see no debasement in doing secretarial work - occasionally.

Spe. *Grins.* And do you also take the garbage out? Occasionally?

Act. I do. I even handle the dishwasher. Regularly.

Spe. *Nods in approval.* Good boy. - Who else on pride?

Pro. Pride with pride will not abide.

Act. It will not, indeed. I know of a case where two companies were about to merge, then called it off, because the top two executives could not agree over the distribution of their competencies after the merger. Misplaced pride prevented a potentially huge benefit.

Spe. And I know of a pertinent example from History. There was an emperor of China who chose able, but proud men to advise him. These counsellors could work well with the emperor himself, but pride prevented them from working with each other. But this suited the emperor: he was safe from conspiracy. - Anything else on pride?

Pro. Pride prefers to go out of the way rather than go behind.

Spe. He means proud men have a tendency to refuse guidance. They insist on doing things their own way, rather than adopt the better methods of another. This is not only presumptuous: it is outright stupid. - More on pride, please?

Cit. Pride in one's work is a great motivator. It can turn work into art.

Act. Ah! Many thanks, Citatia. So, after all, I am not the only one in this room who believes that pride is not necessarily detrimental. Pride in one's work can be a motor, leading to success. It can transform a mere job into highly motivated work. We can justly be proud of a great effort that produced outstanding results. If we are not, we are hypocritical. I do not think that any great achiever can be free of a certain amount of pride in his accomplishments - nor should he be.

Spe. Perhaps you are right, Actus. There is such a thing as healthy, justified pride. - But let us switch to conceit, shall we? Who wishes to comment?

Cit. Conceit is God's present to the little man.

Spe. An interesting thought. What Citatia means, in effect, is that conceit is allowed if it gives comfort to the unimportant - to those who did not quite make it, but who are proud of the little power they wield. I have met such cases in the shape of condescending policemen and arrogant guardians of famous museums. - But what about the truly successful and important?

Benjamin Franklin. Every man has the right to be conceited - until he is successful.

Act. *Smiles.* There you have your answer, Spectus, in the form of an interesting paradox. While conceit may be allowed to the little man, it is no longer permitted to those who have become important and influential - despite the fact that they have more reasons to be conceited than the little man.

Spe. *Thoughtful.* This reminds me of something I have observed, as I am sure you did also. The half-educated tend to be more conceited than the highly educated. The half-educated are often under the illusion that they know an awful lot. The highly educated are more humble: they realize all the things they do *not* know. - What else on conceit?

John Ruskin. Conceit may puff up a man, but it can never prop him up.

Spe. Ah, this casts a doubt on the adage we heard from Citatia. Conceit may not really help the little man. On the contrary. Puffed up with conceit, overvaluing himself, he may become grandiose. Worse: he may induced to show his teeth without being able to bite - with possibly dramatic consequences. The wise will at times be emphatic; but they will never be grandiose. - Anything on conceit from you, Proverbius?

Pro. Every bird loves to hear himself sing.

Spe. *Laughs.* Frankly, I cannot blame the birds. I find great pleasure in singing - in other words in talking, since that is what Proverbius really means.

Act. *Smiles.* Do you mean talking, or, rather, hearing yourself talk? Because Proverbius really means the latter.

Spe. Now don't tell me, Actus, that you are not familiar with the pleasure of hearing yourself talk to an interested audience?

Act. Of course I am. But I follow certain rules. For instance this one. I said a moment ago that we can be justly proud of some of our accomplishments. But that does not mean we should go around publicizing them. Self-propaganda is a form of conceit. I think we should exercise restraint when we talk about our achievements.

Spe. Allow me to qualify that rule of yours, Actus. - We are not necessarily conceited when we talk of our achievements, provided two conditions are met. Condition number one: we should talk of our accomplishments only when asked to do so. Condition number two: we should remain objective about our achievements, avoiding overstatements as well as understatements. If those two conditions are met, we are free of conceit. We then simply communicate something others want to hear and are likely to find interesting, even rewarding. - And what applies to accomplishments, also applies to experience and knowledge. Take this seminar of ours. We keep presenting, examining, analysing wisdoms derived form experience and knowledge, much of it our own. We have been asked to do so, and we try to be objective about it. There is, therefore, nothing conceited about what we are doing here.

Pro. Don't hide your light under a bushel.

Spe. See? Even Proverbius confirms that we are not acting out of conceit. He even put his prophet's hat on to do so: he quoted Saint Matthew. The case is clear: we must not hold back knowledge, experience, or a description of our accomplishments, if they benefit others. People will turn away from the conceited who *think* they are better than others; but they will turn toward those who can *demonstrate* that they are good. - But enough on conceit. Let us turn to vanity. Who wishes to contribute?

Cit. La vanité fait plus d'heureux que l'orgeuil.

Spe. *Smiles.* That had to come from a woman. Women know that vanity is easily satisfied. They even accept flattering remarks from people they do not care for at all. So vanity makes more women happy than pride makes happy men, which is what Citatia meant. - What else, Citatia, dear? You are on your home territory. Most women are vain.

Cit. *Is silent. Either she has nothing else on vanity in her register, or she is cross with Spectus for continuously treating her as a woman rather than as a highly efficient automaton.*

Spe. What about you, Proverbius?

Proverbius is also silent, though surely not out of solidarity with Citatia; with him, it is Occam's razor at work. One of the other standing automata decides to place its wisdom.

Jonathan Swift. *Looks like his portrait by Charles Jervas. Before he speaks, he grabs a couple of noisy Lilliputians, who came alive at the same time he did and argue about something on his desk; he puts them angrily in his pocket and says "hush".* It is an old maxim, taught in schools, that vanity is the food of fools. Yet: now and then some men of wit will condescend to take a bit.

Act. Aha: Swift invalidates your thesis, Spectus, that vanity has mainly to do with women. Vanity is a trait of both sexes. In fact, History is full of great men who exhibited considerable vanity. I would guess that half of the historic figures sitting around in this room were more or less vain. I believe that vanity is very common. I further believe that it is not as pernicious as some moralists claim it is. Vanity can even be life-sustaining, because it maintains an interest in oneself and in life. My mother was quite vain, up to the end; she died aged 95.

Spe. *Smiles.* All right, Actus. Let us be indulgent toward vanity. - But we cannot be indulgent toward our last negative trait: arrogance. Who cares to begin condemning arrogance?

Frank Lloyd Wright. *The architect who erected more structures than any other of his time. Rather old gentleman, round white hat, odd tie, a flower in his buttonhole. He looks around with a critical eye, possibly to see if the seminar room conforms to his idea of "organic architecture".* Early in life I had to choose between honest arrogance and hypocritical humility. I chose honest arrogance, and have seen no occasion to change my choice.

Act. Some of the terms one hears at this symposium are truly amazing. "Honest arrogance!" Anyway, Wright does not seem to condemn arrogance, provided it is "honest".

Spe. Wright is wrong. Arrogance in whatever form is repulsive. And dangerous: it is often the threshold to decline and fall. Arrogance tumbled Lucifer from Heaven: it can also tumble our hypothetic individual. - Proverbius: what can you tell us on arrogance?

Pro. Some think they are giants because they sit on the hump of a camel.

Spe. Meaning that they attribute to themselves merits that actually belong to others. That, incidentally, reminds me of Newton, who said his achievements were possible only because he stood on the shoulders of giants. That is the exact reverse of arrogance. *(Newton is not at the seminar, an oversight of the organisers.)*

Act. Yes: the arrogant rarely acknowledge the help of those without whom they could not have succeeded. They find it sort of natural that others give them assistance, and then convince themselves that they have done it all on their own. Arrogance and ingratitude are closely linked. - Can you name other facets of arrogance, Spectus?

Spe. Snobbism. And name-dropping. Pretending to be on friendly terms with the famous and the powerful.

Pro. *has a relevant dictum.* The tsar's chamber pot is prouder than the cauldron of the peasant.

Spe. *Laughs.* That must have been coined before 1917. But Proverbius is right. "I know the tsar intimately", the imperial chamber-pot presumably, and justly, claimed, omitting the fact that this intimate acquaintance was restricted to the tsar's bottom. The arrogant feel great even though they stand only in the shadow of greatness. - Go on, Proverbius. Your metaphors are highly amusing.

Pro. The powerless glorifies the phallus of his father.

Act. Hey! Hey! First chamber-pots and bottoms, now phalluses. What's next? Is Proverbius turning Freudian? Is this seminar degenerating into obscenity?

Spe. *Laughs heartily.* Proverbius' adage is Arabic, not Freudian. He condemns, in a most picturesque way, the arrogant but weak epigones of famous forebears. Those who are haughty because of their birth. Who talk as if they had chosen their famous ancestors, rather than having been begotten by them. Such people ignore a basic wisdom: Value no-one for another's merit. - But let us come to the end of this topic. Proverbius: can you re-establish your good reputation and quote, for a change, something decent on arrogance?

Pro. Never be haughty toward the humble. Never be humble toward the haughty.

Spe. A clear and wise message. - Any concluding remark on arrogance from you, Citatia?

Cit. Don't feel superior when confronted with the deficiencies of others.

Spe. Do not, indeed. Perhaps the worst form of arrogance is to be haughty towards the lowly, the poor, the inferior, the struggling but unsuccessful. And there is a particularly ugly variant of this form of arrogance: racism. We know what havoc that can cause. - But enough of arrogance. My thanks to those who have contributed. *(The four automata who have spoken, apart from Proverbius and Citatia, return obligingly to wax.)* - For our next subject, I propose one that is not quite as controversial as pride: Envy.

Envy

Act. Envy may be less controversial than pride, but it is certainly more pernicious.

Spe. Above all, it is self-destructive. There is an ancient Greek image of Envy shooting arrows at others; but the arrows turn back and end up wounding Envy herself. The envious tend to hurt themselves rather than those they envy.

Act. What causes envy, Spectus?

Spe. It starts with comparison, that turns into discontent, that turns into envy.

Act. What do people envy most, do you think?

Spe. Wealth. Success. Talent. Merit. Possibly power.

Act. You put wealth first. But in modern societies wealth is not as difficult to attain as it used to be. And the easier something is achieved, the less it is envied.

Spe. That is not necessarily so, Actus. Take success. Some people work hard and for a long time to attain it. Others seem to achieve it with little effort. Those who have to work hard for success envy those to whom it comes easily.

Act. But then it may not be success itself that is being envied, but rather the ability, the talent that enable one to attain it. Envy is the resentment of the mediocre toward the capable. Success is just the outward sign; what is really envied is what makes it possible.

Pindar. *Glows and rises. He holds in his hand dozens of obscure, exalted, but lost poems.* Envy attaches itself to ability and talent. It has no quarrel with mediocrity. *(He looks around as if waiting for applause, but since there is none, returns to somewhat offended wax.)*

Spe. That fellow is out of place here. He should have made himself known when we discussed conceit: he considered his poetry to be the epitome of Greek literature. When he talks of envy attaching itself to talent, he means his own.

Act. Whatever Pindar's attitudes, his observation is valid. - Let's see: you had merit on your list of enviable things. I can see that wealth, success, talent can provoke envy. But merit?

Cit. *Cuts in, as if responding to Actus' doubt.* The envious refuse to accept merit in others, like the sick eye denies the brightness of the sun.

Spe. Merit can indeed be the object of envy, and Citatia knows it. Envying merit is the reaction of the pale moon when put in the presence of the bright sun. Who likes to feel like a pale moon? Certainly not the envious. So what will the envious do when confronted with merit? They will deny it. Pretend they don't see it. Admitting it would mean acknowledging the sun's superiority - and superiority in others is a thing the envious have difficulty to accept. So, they develop a strategy. They pass over in silence the achievements of the meritorious, but publicize widely the few misses or mistakes they make. They secretly hope that by doing this the meritorious will ultimately fail.

Cit. The dullard's envy of meritorious men is always assuaged by the expectation that they will come to a bad end.

Spe. So it is, Citatia. Envying merit is an ugly thing. And a stupid one, to boot. The wise will never feel like a pale moon, because they seek the brightness of the sun, rather than deny it.

Act. Well said. - What about power? Is it also an object of envy?

Spe. Power is probably less envied than wealth, success, talent or merit. Most people resent the power of others, but few envy it.

Act. You may be right. - But something is missing from your list, Spectus. Luck. The luck of others, of course.

Spe. Ah, you are absolutely right, Actus! Luck must of course be included in the list of enviable things. Maybe it should even head the list: possibly it is the most widely envied thing of all. Particularly the luck of those who do not seem to deserve it. That is perhaps the hardest thing for the envious to bear.

Act. And the most despicable form of it is to envy the luck of a friend. - Any final comment?

Spe. Yes. We said envy starts with comparison. But it arises only if comparison leads to a feeling of inferiority. People are envious when they feel inferior. But, as Eleanor Roosevelt proclaimed: No one can make me feel inferior without my consent. *(Wise Eleanor is not present.)*

Act. That is indeed a profound insight. - I think we completed our tour d'horizon of envy. Your next suggestion? What else should our hypothetic individual avoid?

Spe. Greed. The excessive desire to obtain wealth or power.

Greed, Avarice

Act. *Thoughtful.* I think the key word is your definition is "excessive". Most of us try to obtain wealth and power; some of us more, others less. I would regard that as a natural urge. Greed differs from that natural urge in that it has to do with excess. It is about wanting to obtain *ever more* wealth or power. The problem of the greedy is that they are unable to assess what is sufficient. Thus they are permanently dissatisfied with the status quo. Greed robs them of the pleasure to enjoy what they have, by forcing them to focus on what they do not have. They do not realize that the things we possess, but do not use and enjoy, is like not possessing them at all. And there is worse: the greedy often try to obtain what they cannot obtain, or want to become what they are unable to become. The greedy, therefore, are unhappy people.

Spe. And what characterizes the non-greedy? The wise free of greed?

Act. The non-greedy appreciate, enjoy and care for what they have already got. They may reach out for more, may want to improve, enlarge, but only if they are sure it is worthwhile to do so. They may well decide that they have got enough. They know that having enough is better than having much.

Spe. But what you are saying is that greed is a highly subjective concept. We face the same difficulty we had when we discussed moderation. Some may find that you are greedy, while in your own eyes you are simply attempting to enlarge and improve.

Act. That is perfectly true. Greed is one of those things that cannot be measured objectively. But there is a *subjective* measure for it. Where there is satisfaction, there is no greed. The more dissatisfaction there is, the more greed there is likely to be.

Pro. *is prompted by his mechanism.* He is not poor that has little, but he that desires too much.

Act. Indeed, friend Proverbius. Greed can make you feel poor; free of greed you may feel rich. A tub was large enough for Diogenes, the world too small for Alexander. It is as simple as that. - Have you got further wisdoms on greed, Proverbius?

Pro. Grasp all, lose all.

Act. Ah, two themes, excess and control get linked here. Since the greedy desire too much, they tend to go beyond what they can safely manage. As a result, they lose control. With control lost, they lose all they wanted to grasp. A deep wisdom, expressed in only four short words. Difficult to top the brevity of that one.

Plinius the Younger. *Nephew of Plinius the Elder, dressed as a Roman consul, glows and rises. Sitting next to his uncle and adoptive father, he reverently brushes a bit of Vesuvian ash from the latter's toga, then pronounces his famous adage.* Multum, non multa. *(He looks again affectionately at the other Plinius before returning to wax.)*

Spe. So we have both Pliniuses here, do we? This seminar is well attended.

Act. My Latin is not what it used to be, Spectus. What did Plinius Junior mean?

Spe. "Multa" means many; "multum" means much. Freely translated, what Plinius meant was this. Avoid "multa", or doing too many things at once. That is akin to greed: it scatters your forces and in the end you accomplish little. Rather: adopt "multum". That is: select and focus on a few important things. It is better to do fewer things well than many things badly. The basic message is the same as that of Proverbius. But Plinius tops Proverbius by using only three words, instead of four. Ah, the admirable conciseness of Latin!

Act. *Smiles.* Tell me something, Spectus. You have broad and varied interests. You said so when we presented ourselves on the first day of this seminar. Are you following Plinius' precept? Aren't you inclining more towards "multa", rather than towards "multum"?

Spe. *Thinks for a second.* I used to, Actus, but no longer. I now heed Plinius' advice. Let me illustrate it by an example. - When travelling in younger years, I wanted to see everything. Every museum, every sight, every church, every temple. I ended up with a heap of impressions, a profusion of details. Becoming mature, I became satisfied if I saw only the most important sights. I ceased to be a greedy traveller. I learned that the essential satisfies more than trying to take in every detail.

Cit. *who obviously follows the discussion.* By wanting the superfluous, one loses the essential.

Spe. That is indeed so, Citatia. - But what else on greed, anyone?

Pro. Catch not at the shadow and lose the bone.

Act. Hmm. A somewhat obscure adage.

Spe. Not if you know the context. This happens to be the moral of an old Chinese fable. A dog carries a small bone in his mouth and passes a pond. He sees the bone reflected in the water of the pond, where it appears much larger. The dog lets the small bone drop into the water and snaps after the large reflected image. The small but real bone sinks into the pool and is gone, and with it the large reflection. The poor dog loses everything. He was too greedy.

Act. Sad story. Greed, indeed, can make you chase a fata morgana. - More on greed, Proverbius, my friend?

Pro. I got the cheese, but let the calf die.

Act. He is getting increasingly obscure. Another enigma asking for explanation.

Spe. *Laughs.* But this one is not difficult to interpret at all. I took away the milk from the cow and made cheese out of it. But, by doing that, I let the calf die for want of milk. Wanting a small benefit, cheese, I forsook a much greater benefit, letting the calf become a cow. Moral: greed makes one impatient, and impatience leads to harm. - Any other wise message about dogs, cows, calves, or whatever, while we are at it, Proverbius?

Pro. Milk the cow, but do not tear off the udder.

Spe. Now this one even you can readily interpret, Actus. Do not destroy, by being greedy, the very source of your benefits. - But let us leave cows and dogs. Citatia: what more can you tell us on greed? *(Maliciously.)* Perhaps from a woman's point of view?

Cit. *Equally maliciously.* A woman with more than 365 pairs of shoes is a greedy pig.

Actus and Spectus burst out laughing.

Spe. This is the best illustration of how subjective greed is. But enough on that topic. - Let us look briefly at a trait closely linked to greed: avarice. Who wishes to contribute?

Citatia and Proverbius do not immediately react. Instead, a figure glows and rises at the back of the room.

Zeno the Stoic of Citium. *Dressed like a prominent Phoenician. He holds his biography by Diogenes Laertius in his hand.* The avaricious man is like the barren sandy ground of the desert, which sucks in all the rain and dew with greed, but yields no fruitful herbs or plants for the benefit of others. *(Sits down and becomes dignified wax.)*

Proverbius and Citatia, apparently inspired by the example of Zeno, now find the right contributions in their registers.

Pro. Hoarded wealth stinks like dung: spread it, and it will fertilise.

Cit. Knowledge gained but not forwarded to others is like lighting a torch and then closing your eyes.

Spe. Ah, we have three interesting adages with slightly different messages. Proverbius links avarice to material wealth, Citatia to spiritual wealth, Zeno to both. We tend, in fact, to think of avarice in connection with material things only; but it applies also to immaterial things. If we hoard knowledge but apply it only for our own benefit, we are avaricious. Spread your knowledge. Let others benefit.

Act. Speaking of spreading knowledge: the organisers of this symposium are certainly not avaricious. They must have spent a fortune building all these automata and feeding them with hundreds of adages, just for the intellectual benefit of the two of us.

Spe. Maybe, Actus, all this is not meant for our benefit alone. At some later stage, once we have finished this seminar, others may benefit from it also. Furthermore, we have been asked to do hard work during four days, giving our best to fulfil a difficult assignment. When you expect people to do that, you cannot leave them standing in the rain, refusing to supply them with adequate means to support their effort. That, indeed, would be avarice. - Now, as to our next topic, I suggest a rather controversial one. I am not sure if it supports our hypothetic individual, or whether it may topple him. Possibly it can do both. I am talking of selfishness.

Selfishness

Act. Indeed, selfishness is a Janus-faced trait. It can take on bad forms: egoism, egocentrism, disregard for others while seeking our own advantage. But it can also take on forms that are not only justifiable and commendable, but outright necessary: defending our own interests, ensuring our welfare, even assuring our survival. The trouble is that the frontier between the bad and good forms of selfishness is fluid.

Spe. Let us, then, deal with the bad forms first and then with the good ones. - Popular wisdom must have hundreds of adages condemning selfishness. Proverbius: let us just hear three of them. Go ahead and select the ones you prefer.

Proverbius takes only a second shifting through his entire material and establishing his preference. The memory of the bearded old fellow is formidable.

Pro. He is slave to the greatest slave who serves nothing but himself.

Spe. One.

Pro. If my heart is narrow, and sees only itself, what's the use of the world being so vast?

Spe. Two.

Pro. If you want to go to heaven alone, you will not get there.

Spe. And three.

Proverbius is silent.

Act. And now, to amortize the generous investment of the organizers, let us also ask the floor for contributions. *(Makes a mock sweeping gesture to the room.)* Let the wisdoms fed into you worthy machines fertilise and fructify this our symposium.

Three automata glow and rise, responding to Actus' somewhat tongue in cheek invitation; two of them have already spoken.

Francis Bacon, Baron Verulam. His own self is indeed an extremely poor centre of a man's action. *(He is returned to wax as he sets out to deliver empirical facts to demonstrate what he said.)*

Lucius Annaeus Seneca. No man can live happily who considers himself alone and attempts to turn everything to his own advantage. You must live for another if you wish to live for yourself. *(Returns to dignified wax.)*

Voltaire. *Looks like he just stepped out of his Berlin studio, painted by Monsian, leaving Frederick the Great behind in the painting. Ironic, highly intelligent face, eyes shining, as if lit by the Enlightenment.* C'est n'être bon à rien de n'être bon qu'à soi même. *(Returns to wax, probably happy to continue whatever he was saying to Frederick.)*

Spe. *Looks slightly amused.* Odd thing, Actus. All these venerable gentlemen who just condemned egoism with strong words were tremendous egoists. We just witnessed an illustration of the proverbial priest who preaches wine but drinks water - or the other way round. But let that pass. Their wisdoms are valid, even if they themselves hardly followed them. - Citatia: what have you got for us on egoism?

Cit. I am always ready to recognize that there can be two points of view: mine, and that of another who is probably wrong.

Act. *Thoughtful.* That sounds like a joke, but it isn't. If you study the history of science, you will read about famous scientists who continued to defend their theories after new facts proved them to be wrong. Those scientists, fearing to lose their reputation, put obstacles in the way of progress for purely egoistic motives.

Spe. Yet, up to a point, the behaviour of those scientists is understandable. Scientific theories are often the products of a lifetime. They are important things, worth fighting for. - For me, the small, petty, obnoxious egoisms are more condemnable. Take, for instance, some silly habit an inveterate egoist refuses to change, though it irritates all those living around him. We must strictly condemn all egoisms that make the everyday life of others miserable. - But let us leave the egoist and turn to the egocentric. Can you define the egocentric, Actus?

Act. He is one who believes his own behaviour to be the standard. He judges everything and everyone in relation to himself. A corrupt egocentric businessman is convinced that every other businessman is like him. The egocentric thief is convinced that everyone steals. - The egocentric is unable to see and grasp the needs of others. He believes that when he has eaten, everyone else must have been fed. If he slept well, he is certain everyone else has slept well. When a bad thing happens to him, the egocentric is convinced that his misfortune is greater and more terrible than that of everyone else. The egocentric loves himself only: he is unaware that those who only love themselves are hated by all.

Spe. An excellent profile of the egocentric. - What other bad forms of selfishness have we got?

Marquise de Pompadour. *Begins to glow, though the glow is hardly seen through the heavy white makeup covering her face. Clad with exquisite taste in a huge dress, looking very much like her portrait by Boucher. She charmingly pronounces the famous words:* Sire, après nous le déluge ! *(She winks at Voltaire sitting further back and returns to graceful wax.)*

Spe. *Delighted.* Ah, a most charming automaton.

Act. Indeed. - But why did she react to your question? And what was the occasion that prompted her remark?

Spe She said it to Louis XV, who was utterly dejected after he lost the useless battle of Rossbach. She reacted to my question because she knows that her saying came to represent a particularly nasty form of selfishness: total lack of responsibility for one's actions. Selfishness utterly unchecked by bad conscience. After us the deluge. - But I think we now covered the main negative aspects of selfishness, those our individual must avoid. Let us turn to the other face of Janus. What can we say in defence of selfishness, Actus?

Act. Quite a lot. A certain amount of healthy selfishness has been implanted into all of us by evolution. And since evolution knows what it is doing, there must be good reasons for evolution to have done it.

Spe. What is the most common form of positive selfishness?

Act. Self-help. One of the most famous wisdoms is: God helps them that help themselves. If self-help was bad, God would not offer his assistance, would He? It is perfectly legitimate to take our interests into our own hands. To be the architect of our own fortune. - And there are two more positive aspects that go with self-help. One is: only if you are able to help yourself will you also be able to help others. The other is: self-help brings self-respect. One who lacks self-respect will hardly be of use to anybody.

Spe. Good arguments, Actus. - Yet, I believe that self-help must have limits. There is a well-known adage: If everyone took care of himself, care would be taken of all. I doubt the validity of this adage. A world of uninhibited self-helpers would inevitably end up in intolerable inequalities and permanent instability.

Act. That may be so. But consider this: if you discourage people to help themselves, you encourage their dependency on others. And, finally, you end up having people perfectly capable of taking care of themselves, but who choose to let others, usually the State, to take care of them. Discourage self-help, and you encourage passivity and laziness. No, Spectus: we cannot do without a healthy amount of self-help. Anyone who claims the contrary is not wise.

Spe. *Smiles.* Then I will not claim it. - Tell me: do you think that total lack of selfishness is attainable at all?

Act. No. At the most by a few saints.

A piano begins to play "Oh, when the Saints...". Actus and Spectus swivel around to face the room in amazement. A black figure at the back has risen, but continues to play on his desk, which turns out to be a small piano. On the piano a name-card: Duke Ellington.

Duke Ellington. *Obviously relishes the surprise he has caused. But then his mechanism makes him stop playing and deliver the message he was programmed for.* Selfishness is actually a virtue. Why? Because it is essential to survival. And without survival we are not able to protect and help those whom we love. *(He plays a few more tunes of the famous song, then switches to a few improvisations, with obvious relish. But after a minute it's over; the Duke has been, regretfully, returned to wax.)*

Act. *Laughs.* Well: the very last person I expected to meet at this symposium is the Duke. But we have further proof for what we said at the outset: not the source of a wisdom counts, but where it fits into the cathedral structure. And the Duke's reasoning fits perfectly into our discussion. It is clear and convincing and goes like this. - We must first ensure that we survive. Next we must become strong, since we are of no use if we are weak. But we can only survive and become strong through a certain amount of selfishness. Once we have become strong, we are in a position to help and defend others, especially those we cherish and who need us. But defending and helping others is altruistic. So the process starts with selfishness and ends with altruism. While selfishness is implanted to benefit the individual, it ends by benefiting the group the individual is a part of. There is profound wisdom behind all this.

Spe. Then try to formulate a conclusion about positive and negative selfishness.

Act. We are positively selfish when we try to help ourselves. We are negatively selfish when we do not help others, though we are in a position to do so. Egoists and egocentrics are prisoners of their own horizon; they stay self-centred, unconcerned about others. Those who pursue a healthy self-interest in order to develop their strengths, will become capable of helping others. In helping others, they in fact break through their own horizon and leave selfishness behind.

Spe. Faultless reasoning, Actus. I have nothing to add.

The gong is struck. The session is over.

Act. Ah. Obviously Eclectus is satisfied and wants no more negative traits. That being so, I am looking forward to a thoroughly selfish action: I am going to calm my hunger with a hearty lunch.

Spe. *Laughs.* And that, in turn, will make you strong. Having become strong, you will be fit to help us during our challenging afternoon session, where I presume you will be the main contributor.

Act. Faultless reasoning, Spectus. Off we go.

They laugh, rise and leave for the dining room.

Session 7: The Pillars (continued)

The revolving holograph shows several of the pillars almost completed, but others only half-built. Proverbius and Citatia are standing. Actus and Spectus return from lunch and siesta and resume their seats.

Spectus. Let's see. This morning we discussed the personal qualities a wise individual should cultivate, and mental attitudes he should avoid. We now want to see him in action: define how he should handle the various tasks he faces. What will be his first move?

Actus. He will begin by setting priorities among his tasks. I have a method for that.

Spe. Let us hear it.

Setting priorities

Act. I begin by classifying the tasks I need to do in two categories: simple and complex. Simple tasks have chronological priority: I want them done and out of the way, in order to set my mind free for the complex ones. - Next, I examine which complex tasks I am facing benefit a lot of people and thus are important to many. Those are to be done next. - Finally, I am left with complex tasks benefiting just a few people, perhaps only myself. Those come last.

Spe. A logical system. - But assume you are facing several complex tasks important to many. How do you decide which one to do first? You can't chase several rabbits at the same time.

Act. In our modern world, my dear Spectus, we do, unfortunately, need to chase several rabbits at the same time, if we want to succeed. But we do not need to shoot them all at once. - Let's presume we are faced with two complex and equally important tasks. The thing to do is break down each task into manageable stages and distribute those over time. For instance, work on one stage of the first task in the morning, on another stage of the second task in the afternoon. Or do several stages of the first task for a few days in a row, then do the same with the second task. In other words: focus at any one time on only one stage of any given task. Do not try to shoot all your rabbits at once. Shoot them one after the other, one at a time. - Furthermore, it is hardly ever so that two complex tasks have the same deadline: so focus on the one whose deadline is imminent. - All these things are rather elementary.

Spe. *Smiles.* But they are more easily said then done. - Let us, then, focus on complex tasks, since those are the ones that require wisdom. How do complex tasks arise, Actus?

Act. There are two principal motives behind complex tasks. - One is the need for change. You want to improve a given situation and decide to launch a project to accomplish it. - The other is an opportunity that comes along and you decide to grab it.

Spe. I suggest we start by looking at the first motive: wanting change.

Developing the right attitude to change

Act. Fine. - Wanting change can be quite a challenge, because people react differently to suggestions to change something. We have the progressives battling the conservatives, each side believing it has the right attitude to change.

Spe. *Rubs his hands.* Since that is so, we have a fabulous opportunity to involve our fellow participants in a grand discussion. Actus: you lead the progressives, I shall lead the conservatives. - Ah, but we are forgetting a third group.

Act. Which group is that?

Spe. Those who neither seek nor resist change, but simply accept it as given. The view that individuals are powerless against currents of change. The school of Heraclitus with his "panta rhei", of Tolstoy and the Tao. Or of Lothar the First, Holy Roman Emperor, who proclaimed: Tempora mutantur, et nos mutamur in illis. Times change and we change with them. - Citatia, dear, let us hear a handful of maxims that illustrate the stance of this school. Or am I overstepping your technical capabilities?

Cit. *Does a fleeting grimace. Of course Spectus' request is not beyond her technical capabilities and of course she has the relevant adages.* There is nothing permanent, except change. - There is no permanence, because change itself is permanent. - Change is as old as time, and as unlikely to disappear.

Act. Spectus: we need to separate two things. Let me point out that what Citatia, Lothar and Heraclitus said fully agrees with the views of modern science. The universe is indeed a place of permanent change, full of events and processes we simply can't influence. But that is not our subject here. We want to examine changes we *can* influence, and people's attitudes to those changes. So let us focus on our subject and forget science and philosophy.

Spe. I was going to suggest that myself. Let us, then, open the debate on changes we can influence, that lie within our power to accept or reject. - I suggest we start by listening to popular wisdom. I expect it to be conservative, so Proverbius will be my witness. Am I correct, old friend?

Pro. Do not try to change what cannot be changed.

Spe. *Acting as leader of the conservatives.* Ah! We, the conservative camp, open the debate with a pragmatic statement.

Act. *Acting as head of the progressives.* Pragmatic? Ha! It is the attitude of the lazy. Of those afraid that the change proposed will require too much effort, so let's forget it. The view of those unable to see beyond the status quo, maintaining that there is nothing worthwhile beyond it. It is the stance of people with no imagination.

Spe. Nevertheless, I must defend the view of my witness. If, after due consideration, one arrives at the conclusion that something simply cannot be changed, then it is unwise and unreasonable to go on insisting. Leave such situations alone. Going on would only be a waste of time and energy.

Act. But then you risk giving up too early.

Spe. Conceded. That risk remains. - But go on, Proverbius, honourable pillar of the conservative faction.

Pro. Endure patiently what you cannot change.

Spe. The brave man's view.

Act. Or that of the stupid. Do you know the story of the four men back from Africa, Spectus?

Spe. *Smiles.* No. But the conservative camp would like to hear it.

Act. Four explorers return from an African expedition and go to a doctor for check-up. He tells them they have a fatal disease and only three more months to live. The first man goes home and begins putting his papers in order. The second goes to his club and orders a double whisky. The third goes to a brothel. And what does the fourth, the wise one do? He goes to another doctor!

Spe. *Laughs heartily.*

Act. The point of the story is, that before we bravely and patiently accept to endure a supposedly unchangeable situation, we ought to make sure that we are not simply making a damned stupid mistake.

Spe. I believe the conservative side should concede that as wise. - Go on, Proverbius.

Pro. Changing and improving are not the same.

Spe. I presume the progressives agree with that one.

Act. We agree with the premise. Changing and improving are indeed different things. Merely changing something does not yet mean improving it. I will even go further: if something functions well, think twice before changing it.

Spe. Hear, hear! Is the leader of the progressives changing sides?

Act. By no means. We progressives are wise enough to know that if something ain't broke we should not try to fix it. What we do advocate is fixing what is broken. We are against obstinate conservatism that freezes an unsatisfactory situation, on the grounds that a change will bring no improvement anyway. Change may not bring *all* the improvements you hope for. But you cannot improve unless you change.

Spe. But you can change without improving. Plus cela change, plus c'est la même chose. Incidentally: do you know the origin of that well-known phrase? It comes from a play by Aristophanes. He was referring to government. He meant each new government makes the same old mistakes the former ones did. Ecclesiastes put it another way, but meant the same thing: There is nothing new under the sun.

Act. The progressive camp strongly objects to the irony of Aristophanes and to the gloom of Ecclesiastes. We believe that there are, indeed, constantly new, improved things under the sun. And that is so because, fortunately, some people have the courage to initiate changes - if necessary, against the stolid resistance of dumb conservatives.

Spe. Before the honourable leader of the progressive camp allows himself any more nasty remarks about us conservatives, let me make one thing clear. We do not reject change. What we advocate is to make changes carefully, selectively. What we condemn are needless changes, and changes with dubious outcomes. We claim that the new is not necessarily better just because it is new, nor the old false just because it is old. You emphasize improvement at all costs. We refuse to endanger what is good and proven.

Act. But with that attitude you invite stagnation. You act upon the principle that the better is the enemy of good - and proceed to miss the boat. We progressives have another principle: there is always a better way to do almost anything. Past ways may be good, but not the best. If you refuse trying to improve, you will, sooner or later, cease to be good.

Spe. And yet, there were great minds in all ages who kept insisting that only tradition, doing things the proven way, can save us from calamities. I cannot help being sympathetic to that attitude. The very purpose of this symposium is conservative: searching for wisdoms that endure.

Act. No. The purpose of this symposium is to separate wisdoms that endure from those that no longer apply. This is a progressive seminar.

Spe. *Smiles.* Let us say that both purposes apply. - But let me put a question to the esteemed leader of the progressives. You applaud courageous people who initiate changes. But can't it be that such people promote changes primarily because they see benefits for themselves?

Act. The initiators of changes may profit from the changes they promote. But I refuse the innuendo that their primary motive is personal. The aim of us progressives is to improve conditions for an ever greater number of people.

Spe. I have some doubts about that. But let it be. - But let us now turn to the floor for support of our respective views. And once we have done that, let us attempt a synthesis. Perhaps we can reconcile the conservative with the progressive stance on change.

Act. Possibly.

Spe. By the way, I am really glad Eclectus provided us with these automata. We could not do half of what we are accomplishing here without the help from these machines. They are a tremendous improvement over books, I must say.

Act. I note with pleasure that the honourable leader of the conservative camp admits that there are new and improved things under the sun, thanks to creative change.

Spe. *Smiles.* I never denied it. - May I now call upon my conservative witnesses?

Act. *Waves.* Please do.

Spe. *Turns to the seminar room.* Will those with a conservative or sceptical attitude to change please rise and deliver their message? We shall not interrupt while you do it.

After some buzzing three automata glow and rise.

John Quincy Adams. *Looks like his photograph taken in 1848. Interesting, almost bald head, you can sense the able diplomat, but there is a certain coolness and reserve about him.* All great changes are irksome to the human mind, especially those attended with dangers and uncertainty.

Samuel Taylor Coleridge. *Stands uncertainly on his feet, as if he just smoked some opium. Clad like an ancient mariner.* Every reform will be carried to excess. And that excess will then itself need reforming.

Woodrow Wilson. *Looks like his photo from 1919. Pince-nez, spotless white collar. Holds a top hat in one hand and the covenant of the League of Nations in the other.* If you want to make enemies, try to change something.

All three sit down and return to wax.

Spe. Your comments on the opinions of my witnesses, esteemed leader of the progressives?

Act. Adams does not really condemn change; he just points to the difficulties when trying to implement it. - Coleridge exaggerates: thousands of reforms have been successful and were far from excessive. - Wilson realises that changes will be opposed by people who are disadvantaged by them. But this leads us to an important lesson concerning change: if you want the change you are proposing to be successful, know how to sell it to those affected by it. The wise changer creates a desire for the changes he proposes. There is a passage in the Koran: Allah will change the situation of a people only when the people themselves want the change. That is profound wisdom. - May I call upon my witnesses now?

Spe. Please do.

Act. *Turns to the room.* Will participants with a positive attitude to change let themselves be known?

Four automata glow and rise. Two, Chesterton and Churchill, have spoken before. Churchill's cigar is a bit shorter than last time.

Gilbert Keith Chesterton. All conservatism is based upon the idea that if you leave things alone, you leave them as they are. But you do not. If you leave a thing alone you leave it to a torrent of change.

Sir Winston Churchill. There is nothing wrong with change if it is in the right direction.

Benjamin Disraeli, Earl of Beaconsfield. *Narrow face, heavy eyelids, scanty hair brushed from back to front, curved nose.* In a progressive country, change is constant and inevitable.

Richard Wagner. *Looks like his portrait by Lenbach. Black cap, piercing eyes, set mouth, whiskers. Holds a lump of wet gold in his hand, presumably fished out of the river Rhine.* Wer lebt, liebt Wandel.

The four sit down and re-become wax.

Act. Your comments, leader of the conservatives?

Spe. Chesterton uttered a great truth: things do change when left alone. But let me point out that we conservatives do not passively leave things alone: we actively defend what is good. - Churchill's comment seems valid, yet there is a snag: who decides what is the right direction of change, and on what grounds? - Disraeli, as leader and creator of a modern conservative party, should, in principle, have been my witness: but, of course, he was a progressive conservative. What he said, though, reminds me of the school of Heraclitus: change is simply given. Inevitable forces are at work, pushing politicians to act as they do. - As to Wagner, being an artist, he liked change because he saw in it a manifestation of life. I doubt he cared much about the direction of change, as long as there was any change. - As a matter of fact, uncertainty, haziness about the right direction of change is my major criticism of the statements made by your witnesses. - But I suggest we now put down our hats as camp leaders and return to our good old selves, shall we?

Act. Before we do that, allow me to make a final comment you conservatives will applaud.

Spe. Oh? Hear! Hear!

Act. Though I fully support change, I raise two warnings. - Simple changes can be done quickly. But complex changes should be done at a careful pace. The wise will adapt the rate of the change they initiate to the capacity of acceptance of those affected by it. They may even decide to break down the process into several stages to ease the impact. They know that if a major change, with huge effects on many people, is carried out in an unduly short time, rather than gradually, it may create a counter-reaction. The initiator of the change may then have to go into reverse, and that is the worst thing that can happen if you want to change something. - We are back to our familiar theme of control. Those who initiate and implement changes must keep the effects of those changes under control. If the rate of change is too hasty, control can be lost.

Spe. Wise remarks. - What is your second caveat?

Act. Avoid doing too many changes at once. Too many parallel changes can bring indigestion, disorientation, chaos, an identity crisis, rather than the intended benefits. The wise will implement few changes at a time. Multum, non multa, as we heard from Pliny this morning.

Spe. I raise my non-existent hat as leader of the conservatives to acknowledge the practical and wise warnings of the leader of the opposition. But now I definitely put that hat down.

Act. *Smiles.* So do I. But who won the debate?

Spe. Let us say the score is one to one. There were wise arguments on both sides. - But now to the big question. Is it possible to reconcile the progressive and the conservative attitudes toward change? Can we build a bridge between the two views? *(Turns to the room.)* Anyone wishes to try a synthesis?

Ralph Waldo Emerson. *An old man, but with a fresh, youthful face. He apparently could not decide what to wear: he is clad partly as a clergyman, partly as a Hindu, partly as an American puritan, with hints of ancient Greek ornaments on his clothing.* We are all reformers in the spring and summer. But in autumn and winter we stand by the old. Reform goes for truth; conservatism goes for comfort. *(Returns to wax.)*

Spe. Emerson means our attitude to change is a question of age. We react to change differently at different periods of our lives. Is he right?

Act. No. I am not the youngest, but I still continue to strongly support reasonable changes, whenever they are necessary. Age has not turned me into a conservative.

Spe. *Smiles.* Perhaps we should modify Emerson's wisdom to mean *inner* age. You, Actus, seem to have remained young inside. You are fortunate. Others may be less so. - But is there no-one else to attempt a synthesis?

Cit. *Was obviously waiting for the right moment to place her wisdoms; she definitely has a sense for timing.* Have no fear of change as such; but, on the other hand, no liking for it merely for its own sake.

Spe. Ah! Very good, Citatia. The synthesis begins. The bridge is starting to be built. Go on.

Cit. The balanced man clings to the best of the old and appropriates the desirable in the new.

Spe. The bridge advances.

Cit. Give us the serenity to accept the things that cannot be changed, the courage to change things which should be changed, and the wisdom to know one from the other.

Spe. Bravo, Citatia. The bridge advances still more.

Cit. Part of human nature resents change and loves equilibrium. Another part welcomes novelty, loves excitement and unbalance. There is no formula for the resolution of this tug-of-war. But do not surrender to either side, because that invites disaster.

Spe. Excellent, Citatia. Is the bridge complete?

Citatia is silent.

Spe. Is the bridge complete, Actus?

Act. *Smiles.* I think it is. But to be sure, let me attempt to formulate a synthesis of my own, following in the footsteps of Citatia. - The wise will avoid both reckless change and blind conservatism. While they will endeavour to improve, they will take care to safeguard what is good and proven. They will actively promote change only if it is in the right direction. They must be convinced that the direction chosen is right. That will be the case if the change they propose benefits the largest possible number of people, and clearly promises to improve what everyone agrees is imperfect.

Spe. Congratulations, Actus, Citatia. The bridge is definitely completed. There is nothing more to add. - Let us return to our complex tasks and their motives. One motive, the desire for change, we just finished discussing. The other motive, we said, has to do with grabbing opportunities. - Actus: lead the discussion, please.

Grabbing opportunities and chances

Act. To begin with: I believe that opportunities are more frequent than most people presume.

Spe. Yet many people complain about the lack of opportunities.

Act. Those with a positive mental attitude never do. I claim that life is a long row of opportunities constantly being presented to each one of us. Not only that: all of us get presented, during our lives, with a few really great opportunities. With chances of a lifetime. The wise will be particularly receptive to those.

Spe. So what will our wise individual do to become receptive to opportunities?

Act. To begin with, he will develop a strategy, a framework, into which a broad range of opportunities will fit. He then watches closely what each day brings. He will not disdain opportunities that appear insignificant: he will examine whether they are not the seed of bigger ones. In other words: he will keep alert and be prepared - like the boy scouts. An opportunity brought to someone who is not prepared is like an unfertilised egg. But for those who are prepared even a cock may lay an egg. This sounds like a joke, but is not: the phenomenon is known as serendipity.

Spe. But you may get overwhelmed by all those eggs. How to decide which eggs to keep and which ones to throw away?

Act. The wise will give preference to opportunities that best fit their strategy and are closest to their own field of competence. They will resist being lured by fanciful chances in distant fields, however fascinating they may appear.

Spe. That sounds sensible. - Once you have recognized an opportunity, what do you do?

Act. Take the initiative and grab it. Initiative is to opportunity what a lighted match is to a candle. Put the match to the candle and do it right away. Opportunities do not last; swift action, therefore, is of paramount importance. In business we talk of "opportunity windows"; we know that the windows are open for just a short period of time.

Spe. *Smiles.* Much before the term "opportunity window" was coined by businessmen, popular wisdom said the same thing, only it sounded less sophisticated. Am I right, Proverbius?

Pro. Strike the iron while it is hot. - Make hay while the sun shines. - Hoist your sail while the wind is fair. - Il faut tourner le moulin lorsque souffle le vent.

Spe. There you are. The smith, the peasant, the sailor, the miller, they all agree with the modern businessman. Even Citatia, I reckon, has a simple version of the same idea.

Cit. It may chance in an hour what happens not in seven years.

Spe. It may, indeed. - But there is a snag. The chance may come at an inconvenient hour. What if opportunity knocks at an inopportune moment?

Act. Grab it nevertheless. It may not knock again. - The Greeks had a god of opportunity, Kairos. He had a forelock, but was bald at the back of his head. You could grab his lock when he was flying towards you; but once he flew away there was nothing more to grab. A lost opportunity can seldom be redeemed. So take the goods when the gods provide them.

Spe. But even if you grab the lock of Kairos, it may slip out of your hand. What then?

Act. Be angry for a moment, then forget it. Start looking for new opportunities.

Alexander Graham Bell. *Rises, holding a model of the first telephone. He delivers his message speaking into the mouthpiece.* When one door shuts, another one opens. But we often look so long and so regretfully upon the door that closed, that we do not see the new ones that open for us. *(He listens through the earphone if there is a reply, but since there is none, he returns to wax.)*

Act. Bell's message could not be clearer. - But let me go a step further. Not only can opportunities be recognized. They can, in fact, be generated.

Spe. Surely the chances for that are low?

Act. On the contrary. The wise may actually generate more opportunities than they can find. It is not difficult to see why. - If an opportunity is brought to you, you must be the right man, on the right spot, at the right time, equipped with the right strategy, to make use of it. The opportunity is then like a door that suddenly, unexpectedly, opens. - But our wise hypothetic individual will not wait for doors to open by themselves. He will identify doors for which he is the right man, on the right spot, with a fitting strategy. He will then force those doors to open. If he fails with one door, he will move on to the next. He will try to open as many doors as he can. That is what I call generating opportunities.

Spe. *Smiles.* This is unmistakeably Actus the doer talking. - But tell me: if generating and grabbing opportunities is so commendable, why does the word "opportunist" have such a bad flavour?

Act. As I pointed out, Spectus, our wise individual will first develop a strategy and only then look for opportunities. Thus he knows what kind of opportunities he is looking for, and why. - The opportunist does it the other way around. He sees some opportunity, and then formulates a strategy to justify it. Thus he keeps changing his strategies with every new opportunity that comes along. Therefore he is unpredictable, inconsistent - a weathercock. That is why he has a questionable reputation.

Spe. Maybe he is just clever.

Act. All opportunists are clever. But, for me, an opportunity is a means to implement a pre-existing strategy. The right sequence is: get ready, aim, fire. The opportunist lacks this rationale. He fires, then gets ready, then pretends he has been aiming all along.

Spe. That is a clever simile, but I am still not quite convinced. Assume an attractive opportunity is brought to you, but you have no corresponding strategy in your drawer into which it fits. It would be silly to let that opportunity pass, just because you have not done your homework properly.

Act. Let me repeat: for me, an opportunity is attractive only if it fits into a pre-established strategy. If we respond to opportunities without strategic justification, we scatter our forces and end up in confusion. That, at least, is what my experience tells me.

Spe. I guess you know what you are talking about. - But I think we covered opportunities. Where do we go from here?

Act. We identified the two main motives behind complex tasks: the will to change something and the decision to grab a promising opportunity. Both motives have what I call "push-effect". They push us to act. - But motives are not enough. The "push effect" must be supplemented by a "pull-effect": in other words by a well-defined goal. Motives tell us why we want to do something. Goals tell us where we want to end up by doing it. A well-managed task, therefore, has "push", a motive sanctioned by strategy, and "pull", a clearly defined goal. Together, motive and goal define the purpose of the task. If a task lacks either motive or goal, forget it; if you went on with it you would not be doing work: you would merely keep busy.

Spe. Our next topic, then, is goals. How should our wise individual go about setting them?

Setting goals

Act. To begin with, he will not simply cry "forward", but will specify in what direction "forward" lies. He will then specify in sufficient detail the final state of the task he intends to attain. If that final state is only vaguely described, then those involved will be uncertain whether the task is finished or not. To attain your goal you must see it clearly.

Spe. What are the characteristics of a good goal?

Act. A good goal is feasible, achievable. It is not enough to aim; you must also have good chances to hit. So when you set a goal, don't ask for the moon. - A good goal is understandable, not only to the one who formulates it, but to all concerned. - A good goal is concise:

verbosity obscures it.

Spe. *Thoughtful.* Actus: those are really excellent criteria for setting goals from a practical businessman's point of view. But let me raise a question: are such realistic goals sufficient? Many great men maintained that we also need something else: vision. Visions often have a much more intensive "pull-effect", to employ your term, than pragmatic goals have. *(Turns to the seminar room.)* Can I please have a few illustrations of what I mean?

A rather large number of automata begin to glow and rise. Two of them, Emerson and Chesterton, spoke before.

Spe. *Surprised.* Ah? There seem to be quite a number of idealists attending this seminar. Let us hear what they have to say.

Marcus Tullius Cicero. *Elegant in spotless toga, looks like his bust in the Capitol Museum in Rome. Serious face, but there is a slight bitterness about the mouth, perhaps because he did not achieve all his ideals.* If you aspire to the highest place, it is no disgrace to stop at the second, or even the third place below it.

Johann Wolfgang von Goethe. *Looks as if he just stepped out of the picture by Schmeller, portraying him when dictating his memoirs to Eckermann. This is Goethe at 83, old and wise, yet vain.* Den liebe ich, der Unmögliches begehrt.

Ralph Waldo Emerson. Hitch your wagon to a star. Let us not fag in paltry works which serve our pot and bag alone.

Henry David Thoreau. *Clad in outdoor clothes he used to wear at Walden, but there is a Harvard University pin in his buttonhole. He winks at Emerson, his mentor.* In the long run, you hit only what you aim at. Therefore, though you should fail at first, you better aim at something high.

Sir Philip Sydney. *The perfect gentleman of the English Renaissance, beautifully dressed as a courtier of Elizabeth I, plissé collar, holds his book "Arcadia" in one hand.* Who shoots at the midday sun, though he will never hit the mark, will yet shoot higher than who aims but at a bush.

Gilbert Keith Chesterton. Heights are made to look at, not to look from.

Theodore Herzl. *The advocate of the Jewish State. Huge black beard. Holds the Balfour-Declaration in his hand.* If we will it, it is no dream.

All automata cease to glow and return to wax.

Spe. What do you say to all this, Actus?

Act. I warn against a confusion of terms. - When we face a task, our goal is an objective. Objectives can be challenging, but must be feasible; an unfeasible objective is a contradiction in terms. - When we talk of life-goals, we deal with aspirations; those, also, must have reasonable chances to be attained. - But when we start talking of visions, we must be careful. No doubt, much of what is good in our world today has been created by men of vision. Faceless functionaries can merely manage the present, and that is not enough. We continue to need strong men with vision to create our future. But even visions must have chances to be realized. - That is no longer the case when we start talking of shooting at stars and the like. We then leave feasibility and reasonableness behind. We deal with dreams. Visions have potential; dreams do not. They will forever remain poetic fantasy. - My point is that the wise will recognize and keep these domains clearly separate.

Spe. *Thoughtful.* Have you heard the parable of the three men laying bricks, Actus?

Act. No.

Spe. Three men are laying bricks. Someone comes along and asks each of them what he is doing. The first one answers that he is laying bricks. The second, that he is working to earn money. The third says: I am building a great cathedral. The first is a drudger; the second a pragmatists; the third an idealist. They all live under the same sky, but have different horizons. Which one is wise?

Act. My answer may surprise you. I claim that the wise will combine all three attitudes. - To build anything, you need, nolens volens, to lay brick upon brick; you simply cannot get around drudgery. You also need to make a living: if you can't survive, you can't build. But while you lay bricks and earn money doing it, you should keep in mind that what you are doing is part of something worthwhile, even something great. - Yet, even a great cathedral must not be so huge that it cannot be finished. Even this our cathedral of wisdoms must be completed on time. So even great goals must not be hung up so high that they become out of reach. We must not let the impossible ruin the possible.

Spe. Wise remarks.

Act. And there is yet another reason why I insist on achievable goals. It has to do with proportionality, the wise principle we discussed this morning. Our aims must be in the right proportion to our capabilities. If our goal is out of proportion to our capacity to achieve it, we breach the rule of proportionality and are likely to end in frustration. That is why dreamers tend to be unhappy people.

Spe. What you say reminds me of Anaxarchus, who told Alexander the Great that there is an infinity of worlds. Alexander burst into tears, lamenting that he has not even entirely conquered one, let alone such a great number. *(Neither Anaxarchus nor Alexander are at the seminar.)*

Act. Alexander was clearly no adept of proportionality. And that obviously prevented him to have peace of mind. You can hardly achieve peace of mind while you have the urge to become a great historic figure.

Juvenal, *the sombre satiric poet, begins to glow and rises. He puts on a face expressing strong indignation, but one can sense that it is partly theatre. He speaks with the words of his English translator.* Go climb the Alps, ambitious fool, to please the boys and be a theme in school. *(He returns to indignant wax.)*

Act. Precisely. Would you prefer to be a theme at school, Spectus, or rather have peace of mind?

Spe. *Laughs.* Since there is no chance of me ever becoming a theme at school, the question settles itself. - This was an interesting topic, Actus. What is the next step?

Act. We talked of motives and goals. The next step is to link them. That link is the plan.

Planning means mapping the road that leads from motive to goal.

Planning

Spe. Isn't planning primarily a technical matter, little to do with wisdom?

Act. It is, so we should not spend too much time on it. But there are two wisdoms connected with planning that must be mentioned.

Spe. The first?

Act. It has to do with a well-known warning: Show me not the aim without the means. Before actually starting a task, our wise individual will examine the means at his disposal. If they are inadequate to reach his goal, he must ascertain that he can develop, or acquire, the missing means as he goes along. If he doubts that he is able to do that, he will reconsider or reformulate his goal.

Spe. *Thoughtful.* Einstein said something interesting about goals and means.

Albert Einstein. *Glows and rises. As he does so he quickly retracts his tongue, that was hanging out. The well-known face from his Princeton years. He is in slacks and wears no socks.* In my opinion, perfection of means and confusion of goals seem to characterize our age. *(Returns to wax with his tongue politely in his mouth.)*

Spe. Interesting observation, isn't it? Our means may at times be inadequate to reach our goals. But Einstein thought our goals are often inadequate in view of the means we have.

Act. Einstein was talking of social and economic issues and of things that concern humanity as a whole. We are talking of individuals who are facing complex tasks. Let us not bring confusion into our discussion.

Spe. You are right. Mea culpa. - What is your other wisdom in connection with planning?

Act. It has to do with my favourite recurring theme: control. Complex tasks cannot be carried out in one big leap. To be manageable, they must be broken down into reasonable steps. A good plan clearly specifies those steps and gives estimates of the time needed for each step to be completed. Considered in its entirety, a complex task may appear awesome. Broken down by a good plan into manageable, controllable stages, the awe disappears.

Spe. How comforting. - We drew up the plan. What's next?

Act. We start to implement it, endeavouring to bring our task to a successful conclusion. We need to examine what it takes to do that.

Spe. One thing we will certainly need is perseverance.

Act. Precisely.

Persevering despite obstacles and setbacks

Spe. And what do we need to persevere?

Act. Determination.

Spe. Maybe also - dedication? Or even devotion?

Act. No. Let me explain why not. - Determination proceeds from the mind. It has to do with the rational conviction that the goal we pursue is worthwhile, our means adequate, our strategy sound. - Dedication, and even more so devotion, are not rational qualities. They have to do with emotions, beliefs; consequently, they are less stable, less certain, more vulnerable than determination. Devotion can even be dangerous, since it focuses not on the task, but on some individual behind it.

Spe. With due respect, Actus: I disagree. I challenge your thesis that all we need to persevere is rational determination. The more difficult and challenging our task, the more we require emotional factors that supplement the rationale. A great effort needs the support of both the head and the heart. Reason alone is not enough to sustain it. Perhaps a better word for what we need to persevere is enthusiasm; it combines determination and dedication. - And then, I think, we also need hope.

Act. I can't agree. Hope is something vague. We cannot set a goal and then say we hope to attain it. We would lose credibility. We must be convinced that we are going to attain the goal. Hope is wishbone. Determination is backbone.

Spe. What about courage? We certainly need that to persevere.

Act. There I agree. Courage and determination are closely linked. Both are mental things. Courage helps us to face risk and danger. Determination helps to overcome difficulties, obstacles, setbacks.

Spe. I am glad we agree at least on one thing. - What else do we need to persevere?

Act. Exertion. It may be required at the beginning of the task, in the middle, towards the end, or practically all through. But we agreed on our first day that the wise will seek the right pace for everything they do. They will, therefore, know when they need to exert themselves and when they can afford to economize their forces. They will need exertion above all when deadlines are moving close or when serious problems or obstacles arise.

Spe. And how should we deal with those?

Act. We should start by defining what the problem is. An undefined problem cannot be dealt with. A French general, whenever a problem was brought to him, used to ask: "De quoi s'agit-il?" What is it about? This is one of the wisest questions I know.

Spe. Once defined, how do we proceed? How should we deal with an obstacle?

Act. To begin with, find out if it really keeps you from attaining your goal. You should not bother too much about an obstacle if you can walk around it. - If the obstacle does lie in your way, assess its correct size. Belittling it brings the danger of committing inadequate means to deal with it. Exaggerating it will unnecessarily bind means and effort. This is where the wisdom of proportionality comes in once again. - Find out where the obstacle offers the least resistance. The cattle will spring over the hedge where it is lowest, as Proverbius would wisely remark. - If you need to remove the obstacle, do it as soon as you can. Obstacles tend to grow bigger if left unattended. Be sure to remove the obstacle fully: if you do not, it may become a constant drag on your road to the goal. - And let me add a last suggestion. If you have the choice between removing an obstacle brutally or diplomatically, choose diplomacy. Do not shatter where you can untie.

Spe. Very sensible prescriptions, indeed, Actus. Congratulations. Have you got any more?

Act. Yes. Do not fear obstacles. I would even go one step further: rejoice at having to overcome obstacles. Where there are obstacles to deal with, there is life. You may remember an amiable P.G. Wodehouse character called Uncle Fred: he regards obstacles as entertainment.

Spe. *Smiles.* Hail to good old Uncle Fred. - But let me ask you this. Should we modify our goal if a particularly severe obstacle happens to lie on our road?

Act. No. We should be inflexible about our goal. But we can be flexible about our plan. We may modify the road, but not the destination. We should stick to our plan, but not obstinately. The one who successfully perseveres often does so because he is flexible enough to follow alternative routes. There is usually more than one way to arrive at our goal.

Spe. Reminds me of Black Sam.

Act. *Surprised.* Who is Black Sam?

Spe. A character in "Uncle Tom's Cabin". He wants to get to the top of a hay stack. He puts his ladder to one side of the hay, but it doesn't reach to the top. So he walks around the stack and puts his ladder to the other side. He perseveres because he wants to get to the top. It doesn't matter which side he climbs.

Act. *Smiles.* A simple, yet wise story.

Spe. Actus: we talked of obstacles. What about setbacks? How should our hypothetic wise individual deal with those?

Act. He will refuse to get bogged down by them. Setbacks are stumbles, not falls. They are perils; but what is imperilled is not lost. When experiencing a setback, the wise may decide to let things rest for a while. But then they will resume the fight. There have been some brilliant moves inspired by setbacks.

Spe. Most setbacks have external causes. But can we also produce setbacks by our own fault?

Act. We can. Let me mention two mistakes that can lead to setbacks. - One is to become anxious in the wrong moment. Putting the brakes on when you should not have done it. Pulling back your horse when it is about to leap. - Another mistake is to slacken your effort because you think, wrongly, that you have practically reached your goal. Determination and exertion must be kept up all the way, even when your goal seems in easy reach. Nothing is sillier than to choke on the tail, after having swallowed the ox.

Spe. Actus: you gave us an excellent tour d'horizon. I am convinced that we have covered the essentials on the subject of perseverance. But, in order to be sure, let me ask the floor whether we have omitted anything. *(Turns to the room.)* Is there anyone who wants to round off what Actus and I have just discussed?

Laurence Sterne. *Glows, rises. Dressed like an English clergyman of the 18. Century. He coughs, obviously in need of another sentimental journey to the south of France to ease his lung trouble.* What is known by the name of perseverance in a good cause, is known as obstinacy in a bad one. *(Coughs some more, but is then silent wax.)*

Spe. A valid distinction. Suppose, Actus, we are on our way to a goal and then realize that it is not what we believed it to be. What then?

Act. I can recognize a worthy goal when I see one, and I am sure so do you, Spectus. A bad goal is evident from the start. However: turn back on the wrong road, no matter how far you have advanced. We learned that wisdom on our first day.

Spe. That takes care of obstinacy. - Now: what else do we need to reach our goal?

Act. The right abilities and methods.

Developing and using the right abilities and methods

Spe. Can you specify what you mean?

Act. Abilities are inborn or acquired. Inborn abilities are talents, acquired abilities are skills. A method is a particular way of doing a task, combining talents and skills.

Spe. Let us then start with talent. A thing some people have, others lack.

Act. Nobody is without any talent, Spectus. No man is an empty drawer, even though the drawer may contain just a single talent.

George Eliot. *Begins spontaneously to glow, then rises.* To have just one talent is a sort of clever stupidity.

Cit. *Looks sharply at Eliot as she returns to wax, speaking with a certain irritation in her voice.* Having just one talent is no tragedy. The tragedy is failure to use that single talent.

Spe. *Laughs.* Well, well. Our co-participants begin to exchange opposite views among themselves. We are discovering a new dimension of their abilities. - But what do you think of Eliot's remark and Citatia's rebuttal?

Act. I would advise someone with just one talent to make the best of that talent, as Citatia correctly suggested. Find tasks that suit that one talent.

Spe. Sensible. - What other wise things can we say in connection with talents?

Act. I must insist on what Citatia said: use your talents. Do not leave them lying fallow. Talents grow with use. One well-cultivated talent is worth more than a hundred undeveloped potentials. - And then: publicize your talents. A talent is no good unless it is recognized by others. Hidden talents count for nothing. Make your talents known, and they will create opportunities for you.

Spe. What about intelligence? It is a kind of innate talent.

Act. Intelligence has many advantages, certainly. An intelligent person can handle difficult tasks more easily. He is likely to spot shorter routes to a goal. He will quickly see through the intentions of others. He will be less credulous, more difficult to deceive, less subjected to fate and circumstances. He is likely to turn mistakes and failures into useful experience. - But while intelligence is serviceable for many things, it should not be confused with wisdom. It is merely conducive to wisdom.

Spe. Does intelligence also have drawbacks?

Act. Yes. An intelligent man is more likely to turn into a cynic than an unintelligent one. He may also become conceited; the brains of an intelligent man can go to his head.

Spe. *Laughs.* True. - But let us turn to skills. Suppose, Actus, that you have listed the skills required to attain a certain goal, and then discover that you lack some of them. What do you do then?

Act. Go and get them.

Spe. Hmm. Let me get the logic straight. - You are a defender of feasibility. Feasibility requires that our goals be consistent with our means. In other words, we should only pursue goals for which we possess the necessary skills. If we lack those skill and have first to go out and get them, we should not attempt handling the task. That, at least, is how I would reason.

Act. Your reasoning is clear, but false, Spectus. Feasibility does not mean that we must possess, right from the start, *all* skills necessary to accomplish the task. There is a widely practiced thing called learning on the job. - Feasibility, in practice, means this. We start by listing all the skills we need to do our task. We know which skills we have already got. We identify those we must acquire en route, and make sure they are acquirable. They usually are. Remember: even the skills we already got were acquired at one time or other. - With the skills we already possess we are on firm ground. With the skills we need to acquire we enter new land. But there is usually no reason why that new land should not be conquered. - There are two caveats, though. One: avoid tackling tasks where the skills you need to acquire vastly outnumber the skills you already possess. Two: do not take on tasks where the acquisition of a new, key skill would take an inordinately long time.

Spe. But assume that I have doubts that I can acquire a certain skill I need. Or if I feel that some skills are beyond my capacity to acquire them.

Act. *Smiles.* Why don't you ask our fellow participants what they think about that problem?

Spe. I will. *(Turns to the room.)* Can we please have contributions to the issue I just raised?

Short buzzing, three automata rise.

Publius Vergilius Maro (Virgil). *Looks like he just stepped out of the famous mosaic in the Bardo-Museum in Tunis. Elegant toga; surprisingly modern, sunburnt face, due to his rural lifestyle in Sicily.* Hos successus alit: possunt, quia posse videntur. *(There is an audible click, and Virgil is forced to translate his own wisdom.)* Success comes to those who are convinced they are able.

Marcus Aurelius Antoninus. *His arm still raised, evidently feeling no fatigue. He seems to have learned a lesson from Virgil, since he dispenses with Latin and starts translating himself right away.* Just because your own abilities seem not to be equal to a task, do not assume that they are beyond your power. If the task is within the powers of any man, believe that it can also become one within your own capabilities.

Horace Walpole. *Holds a few of his entertaining letters in his hand and wears a helmet with golden feathers, like the one in his story about the castle of Otranto.* Men are often capable of greater things than they perform. They are sent to the world with bills of credit that are seldom drawn to their full extent.

Cit. I have gone through life believing in the abilities of others, but never in my own. Then, dazzled, I discovered that my own abilities were real. It was like finding a fortune in the lining of an old coat.

Virgil, Marcus and Walpole return to wax.

Act. *Smiles contentedly.* There you have your answer, Spectus. And I could add many more adages with a similar message. He can, who believes he can. One can, if one must. If it is indispensable, it will become possible. To believe a thing is possible is to make it so. - It all boils down to this: have confidence in yourself and you will discover that you can acquire skills you thought were beyond your reach.

Spe. That is indeed encouraging. - But let us not neglect Proverbius. Select three popular adages on skills, old friend, and let us hear them.

Pro. It takes rough seas to form a skilled mariner.

Act. Smooth seas certainly do not. Moreover, smooth seas are boring. There is no thrill in easy sailing on smooth seas. I like a strong wind blowing in my face - unless it is a gale.

Pro. Work in clay, before you work in gold.

Act. A sensible suggestion. Exercise a newly acquired skill on minor tasks first. Apply it to important tasks only after you have achieved mastery. - Your last adage, Proverbius?

Pro. The best carpenter makes the fewest chips.

Act. He means the more perfected a skill becomes, the less waste there will be. That is certainly so. Highly skilled workers are simply more proficient. Not because they have better tools. It is the other way around: tools become good in the hands of proficient workmen. Bad workmen blame their tools, whereas they should blame themselves.

Spe. Actus: I think we said enough on skills.

Act. Not yet. Let me add an important remark. - It is, in fact, not necessary to try to acquire *all* the skills we need to do a task. We may then risk becoming a jack of all trades but a master of none. Instead, we may acquire *people* who possess the skills we lack. But that has to do with co-operation and teamwork, and those will be subjects for the walls.

Spe. I am looking forward to discussing them. - Let us move on to method. We defined method as the combination of talents, skills, and a particular way of doing things. We certainly need method to handle complex tasks. In fact, we even need method to handle simple tasks. My wife claims that even a charwoman needs method.

Act. *Smiles.* A charwoman especially needs method. Over 90% of her total cost have to do with way she works. Less than 10% with the machines and cleaning products she uses. Just think of the extra costs if her cleaning method is inefficient. Cleaning is a classic example of a task that needs method.

Spe. *Grins.* I was only trying to be funny, but it looks like I hit on a profound practical wisdom. - But I have an important question concerning method. Assume we have been very successful with a method we applied when handling a difficult task. I guess we would then want to use it again and again in future tasks. Or shouldn't we?

Cit. *Cuts in, before Actus can reply.* Do not face tomorrow with the methods of yesterday. That would be standstill. After you have done a thing the same way for two years, look it over carefully. After five years, look at it with suspicion. After ten years, throw it out and start all over.

Spe. Do you agree with Citatia, Actus?

Act. I agree with her basic message: we must regularly review the adequacy of the methods we use. As I said earlier: there are easier, better, quicker, more efficient ways to do almost anything. - But I do not agree with Citatia's recommendations on timing. We should re-examine our methods not after two years, as she suggests, but in fact each time we begin a new task. And we should not throw out a method just because it is ten years old; it may still be perfectly useful. In other words, my criterion for a method is not age, but suitability.

Spe. What you are saying, in fact, is that methods should be tailor-made for each new task.

Act. Precisely. Let me try to summarize how I see one should proceed. - Before you begin a new task, look at your existing stock of abilities and determine which of them are relevant to the present case. Next, identify abilities you lack, but will be needing. Draw up a plan on how to get them: either acquiring them yourself or seeking the collaboration of someone who possesses them. Combine all these abilities in a way that best suits the task at hand. To achieve an optimal combination, look at methods used in the past and make use of the experience gained with those methods. - If you do all this, you will almost certainly reach your goal.

Spe. I think there is nothing more to add to that. - What else then, Actus, do we need to have, or to do, to ensure that we reach our goal?

Act. Keep order.

Keeping order

Spe. You mean keep things at their proper places.

Act. No, I do not mean that. Keeping things at their proper places is static order. That is useful, but elementary. - What I *do* mean is dynamic order. Keeping the task flowing in an orderly manner. Avoiding procrastination. Doing one step after the other. Finishing each step in the allotted time. Keeping deadlines. Being punctual. Setting priorities when faced with obstacles, rather than dealing with them at random. If you do not keep such dynamic order, you have a mess. And a mess is debilitating, to say the least.

Spe. I see. And what do we need to ensure that we keep dynamic order?

Act. Discipline. This morning, we should have listed discipline among the positive qualities our hypothetic individual should possess; but better late than never. Discipline is a key quality of the successful individual. A disciplined, self-possessed person helps not only himself, but also others. He induces order into his surroundings - because discipline radiates outward.

Spe. And what do you need, in turn, to become a disciplined individual?

Act. Willpower. If we achieve discipline through willpower, we are in command, we choose our own order. If we lack discipline, then order will be imposed upon us from the outside. We will then cease to be in command, being forced into an order that is not ours, but that of someone else. Discipline, in other words, brings freedom.

Spe. A compelling chain of thought. But let me play the advocatus diaboli. - I believe that over-emphasis on order kills creativity. We need a certain amount of disorder to be creative. Order appeals to reason; but it may cripple the imagination. And we said imagination was a key quality of the wise. We certainly need it to set and to attain challenging goals.

Act. *Thinks for a moment.* I agree that creativity itself needs freedom from strict order. But the *products* of creativity, the fresh ideas, the fresh approaches, must be subjected to order. Those products will not survive, nor become effective, in an atmosphere of disorder. To implement the results of creative action, order must follow upon creative disorder. Order brings focus; and nothing can grow great unless it is focused.

Spe. I think we met halfway. - Tell me, Actus: is routine part of your concept of order?

Act. Routine is a kind of automatic order. The more of our actions we can delegate to an effortless automatism, the freer our mind will be to cope with the truly difficult parts of our task. But mind: things done automatically have no didactic value. Only things that are done consciously, with concentration, can bring new experiences.

Spe. One last question. Order means following rules. But is it wise to always keep strictly to the rules?

Act. *Smiles.* You probably expect me to say yes, just like I said that honesty should apply in all cases, no matter what. But, surprise: this time I say that the wise will not always blindly follow rules. They will recognize exceptions to the rules. They know when to deviate from the rules, should that become necessary. That is why they are wise.

Spe. *Smiles.* Let that wisdom conclude this topic. - Actus: you have been an excellent guide so far on our road to the goal. But there is yet another thing we often need to reach it. A factor that is irrational, uncontrollable, and that usually works only if we believe in it. But if and when it works, it can be of tremendous help. I speak of luck.

Courting luck

Act. You call luck an irrational and uncontrollable factor. I don't agree.

Spe. Ah?

Act. I believe that luck is very often simply the consequence of a positive mental attitude. It belongs more to the domain of the rational than to that of the irrational. I would go as far as saying that being lucky might be a character trait. Napoleon, before naming a new general, used to ask: "Is he lucky?" *(Napoleon briefly glows in appreciation.)*

Spe. But what, then, is bad luck? A fault in one's character?

Act. Not necessarily. But it can be insufficient belief in luck. - The central question, Spectus, is this: does luck entirely depend on external circumstances we cannot influence? You maintain it is. I claim it is not. Shall we have a debate on our respective views?

Spe. Gladly.

Act. Then please go ahead and define your viewpoint.

Spe. For me, luck is Tyche, the goddess of fortune, walking among us, distributing her kisses at random. The one kissed by her needs to have no special merit whatever; he may even be a fool. Tyche's eyes are blindfolded. Fortuna caeca est.

Act. Let me point out, Spectus, that we are discussing luck, not good fortune.

Spe. But they are synonymous.

Act. No, they are not. Fortune depends, as you say, fully on chance. Luck also depends on chance, but by no means entirely. To a very considerable extent, luck is the result of good qualities like diligence, perseverance, skills, efficiency.

Spe. There are many who possess those qualities, yet are not particularly lucky.

Act. That is correct. I was going to point that out. We need three more ingredients to be lucky, and we discussed them already at some length. They are: preparedness, opportunity, initiative. The good qualities I mentioned can be developed. Being prepared is not particularly difficult. Taking initiative can be trained. Opportunities, we saw, can be created. Thus, all ingredients of luck can be relatively easily assembled. Luck, in fact, is something quite straightforward.

Spe. So our debate vanishes into thin air, since we have been talking of two different things.

Act. Exactly. Fortune may favour anyone, but it is rare. Winning the first price at a state lottery is less likely than being hit by lightning. Luck, on the other hand, is quite frequent, because it comes to those who use their heads to bring it about. Go and wake up your luck, said the ancient Persians.

Spe. Your logic is compelling, Actus. - But answer me one more thing. There is an old saying: The more wicked, the more lucky. There is another version of the same idea: The devil's children have the devil's luck. How do you explain those adages?

Act. Rationally. The wicked are usually very good at strategy. They are also particularly receptive to opportunities that suit them. When chance brings them such opportunities, they grab them. The wicked are also talented at creating opportunities and situations that help their evil purposes. All these things combined makes them lucky. But their luck has nothing to do with the devil; it has to do with using their brains.

Spe. A convincing explanation. - Any final comment on luck?

Act. Just a footnote. - Some say that life on Earth originated by pure chance, so it is the result of good fortune. I disagree. Life is a great grabber of opportunities brought to it by chance. In view of what we just said, life is much more than merely fortunate: it is lucky.

Spe. This is more than a footnote, Actus. It is an insight worth pondering about. - But now, I fear, we must deal with a disagreeable subject. Assume that, despite having good motives, a clear goal, the right method, despite having persevered and kept good order, we fail at our task. How should our wise hypothetic individual deal with failure?

Dealing with failure

Act. First of all, he will ascertain if it is really failure he is facing, or just a setback. Failure is permanent; a setback is only temporary. He will not make the stupid mistake of taking a setback for a failure.

Spe. But if the failure is genuine? Definitive?

Act. Above all, our wise individual should refuse to be depressed by it. At least not for long. If he allowed himself to be discouraged, dejected, down-hearted, he will attract even more misfortune. To a broken ship all winds are contrary, Proverbius would say. So: avoid lamenting, feeling sorry for yourself; it will only make you miserable. Failure, in fact, is as heavy as you take it to be.

Spe. *Smiles.* I wish I had your positive attitude to things. - What else is to do when we have failed?

Act. Learn from your failure. If you fall, stand up - but pick up something as you get up. All failures are full of experiences gained. Use them when you embark upon your next task. If you know why you have failed, you have excellent chances to win next time. Someone even claimed that unless a man has mastered several failures, he is neither experienced nor dependable.

Spe. *Smiles.* You make it sound as if failures were a good thing. - What else should our wise individual do, or rather not do, when facing a failure?

Act. Search for excuses. Blame bad luck. Blame someone else. Look for a scapegoat. If you fail, you must accept responsibility, and accountability, for your failure. If you do not, you will never learn from it.

Spe. Actus: I think we covered failure. Let us turn to the contrary outcome. - Our hypothetic individual surmounted all obstacles, defied all difficulties, and arrived at his goal. His task is successfully completed. So now we need to discuss success and wisdoms associated with it. You start.

Dealing with success

Act. My first wisdom is a familiar one, but it cannot be repeated too often. Our successful individual must know why he was successful. He should analyse the reasons for his success. He must make sure that he understands the factors that led to it. We can only stay successful in the long run if we know why we succeed.

Spe. What are the most important benefits of being successful?

Act. We are judged not by what we do, but by what we accomplish. People gain confidence in an individual who successfully accomplishes things. That confidence generates goodwill. Goodwill, in turn, opens up new opportunities. So the ultimate reward for success is simply the chance to do more.

Spe. In other words: nothing succeeds like success. - Nevertheless: there is a widespread belief that success can spoil people. Make them conceited.

William Somerset Maugham. *Glows and rises. Dark suit, white shirt, dark tie, a cigarette in his left hand. He examines Actus and Spectus through half-closed eyelids, like a psychiatrist sizing up a patient.* The common idea that success spoils people by making them vain, egoistic and self-complacent, is erroneous. On the contrary: it makes them for the most part tolerant and kind. *(He draws on his cigarette and returns to wax without exhaling the smoke.)*

Act. I fully agree with Maugham. In my experience the effects of success are overwhelmingly positive.

Spe. What other comments can you think of, concerning success?

Act. There is a dimension to success that has to do with *how* we attained our goal. If our means are plenty and our goal easy, it is not that difficult to succeed; but our success, then, is really just mediocre. If our means are not plentiful and our goal relatively difficult, our success will be more substantial. Then, in a few cases, our means are scarce and our goal very difficult: yet we succeed. I would think twice before embarking on tasks like these; but I respect the courage of those who do not shy away from them. - But what I just said points to a general idea. There is not *one* kind of success, but *several*. I can think of at least three. You may think of others.

Spe. What would be your first kind of success?

Act. It has to do with having successfully completed a difficult step of a complex task. Though only intermediary, such successes boost confidence. They are like the rungs of a ladder we need to climb: the rungs are not meant to rest upon, but only to hold your foot long enough to heave you up to the next rung. But it feels good if success has made a solid rung beneath your feet.

Spe. The next kind of success?

Act. That is the big, final one, that comes with the successful completion of a task. But this success hides a danger. Someone likened it to a plateau, on which you rest and look back down upon the difficult path you have travelled. But you cannot climb further on a plateau; you can merely sit on it. And if you sit on it for too long, it gets boring. Moreover, people will gradually turn away from someone who, sitting on his plateau, expects continued praise for some past achievement. Laurels will wither if you sit on them, as everyone knows. So: our wise individual should not sit too long on his plateau of success. After having rested on it for a while, enjoying the benefits the plateau brings, he will descend from it. And he will start climbing another mountain.

Spe. A healthy thing to do. - What is your third kind of success?

Act. That one has to do with prevailing at critical moments. There are moments in our lives when we simply have to succeed, otherwise we lose something very important. Let me illustrate what I mean. - Such critical moments may suddenly appear while you are working at a complex task; they may decide the fate of the task. When young, such a moment can be an important exam: your degree may depend on it. Later, it can be a job-interview: it may decide your future. Still later it can be a critical business meeting: your career may depend on it. - I would call such critical moments "historic". The wise will anticipate them, prepare for them with particular diligence, and recognize them when they arrive. - But, Spectus, I said enough. It is now your turn to try to define other kinds of successes, and wisdoms around them.

Spe. *Thinks for a moment.* The kind of successes you presented, Actus, are what I would call *external* successes. But I think our wise hypothetical individual will also need other kinds. Let me call them *internal* successes. They are measured by different criteria than those you have mentioned.

Act. And what would those criteria be?

Spe. Contentedness. Serenity. Peace of mind. Deep inner satisfaction. Some people go as far as to claim that those who achieve internal successes based on such criteria no longer need external ones.

Act. I am no saint, Spectus. Nor a hermit, nor a yogi. For me, contentedness and peace of mind are the results of external successes. But since we are at it: how do you propose to go about achieving what you call internal success?

Spe. The answer is really quite simple. By avoiding the negative attitudes of mind we discussed this morning, and by cultivating the positive ones we also reviewed this morning. Our discussion, so to speak, has come full circle.

Act. I see. But tell me: if you had to pick out some of those mental attitudes as particularly relevant to what you call internal success, which ones would you choose?

Spe. *Thinks for a moment.* I would choose two negative ones: greed and envy. But let me go into all this a bit more, if I may. - I think there are several routes to internal success, but two of those are particularly relevant. One is being grateful for what we have and not wanting more than we can get. We touched upon this wisdom briefly when we discussed greed. It can be found all over the world in proverbs that always show the same structure: If you cannot have "this", be content with "that". Give us an example, Proverbius.

Prov. If you can't have an elephant, be content with a buffalo.

Actus and Spectus burst out laughing.

Spe. I guess a car owner would say: If you can't have a Jaguar, be happy with a Beetle.

They laugh again. But Spectus seems to have opened up a fruitful subject. Several automata begin to glow and rise spontaneously, evidently finding it necessary to deliver their wisdoms. Among them is Franklin, holding his kite again.

Daniel Defoe. *Disguised as Robinson Crusoe, clad in animal furs, with a gun hanging on his back and a telescope in his hand. For a shipwrecked, he is indeed well provided with instruments of civilisation.* All our discontents spring from the want of thankfulness for what we already have.

Benjamin Franklin. Content makes poor men rich; discontent makes rich men poor.

Epicurus. *Exudes kindness. He has a watering-can in one hand, with which he obviously intends to water his "kepos", the garden of his house in Athens, where he taught his students.* One is not rich through possessions, but through that which one can with dignity do without.

Plutarch. *Clad like a priest of the oracle of Delphi. Before he speaks he looks around to see if there is anyone present whose biography he has written, and is visibly glad to discover Julius Caesar, Cicero and Cato.* Contentedness is when superfluities are not required and necessities are not wanting.

Cit. I was discontented because I had no shoes. Then I met a man who had no feet. Now I am contented with my state.

After this spontaneous manifestation, all except Citatia return to wax.

Spe. Thank you, gentlemen and lady, for so forcefully and unexpectedly supporting my point. Any comments, Actus?

Act. In my opinion, in all these wisdoms we heard three things were rolled into one, which need to be separated. We should, of course, be grateful for what we have already got. Also, we should not crave what is entirely out of our reach. On the other hand, I believe we should not give up trying to get something we always wanted. Personally, trying to obtain something I always wished to have is an effort that makes me feel particularly alive.

Spe. It is a question of motives, Actus. If you strongly wish for something because you find it valuable, interesting, beautiful, rewarding, it is understandable if you don't give up wanting to obtain it. But there are other, base motives. For instance, there are those who want something only because others have got it too. You cannot be content if you labour under that motive, for you can't be envious and content at the same time.

Act. I have no quarrel with that statement. - What is your second route to internal success?

Spe. It has to do with being good friend with oneself. Contentedness coming from having developed a talent one was born with. Satisfaction out of having deepened a good character trait. Peace of mind coming from abandoning a bad habit, or taking on a good one. Leading a life surrounded by things made by oneself, rather than by others. To actually be what you want to appear, or, even better: be more than you appear to be.

Act. Spectus: allow me to attempt a synthesis of all these clever things we have been saying. - I see no contradiction between your wisdoms on success and mine. Let our hypothetic individual strive for external successes and let him try to get the things he always wanted to have: after all, he was created for action. At the same time, let him seek contentedness and peace of mind by being grateful for what he already achieved, and by not craving things for the wrong reasons. For me, external and internal successes complement each other. I think it is their combination that produces the truly successful individual.

Spe. *Smiles.* A wise synthesis indeed - though not easy to achieve. *(Looks at the holograph.)* But our pillars are almost finished. I wonder what is still missing? There must be something that our hypothetic individual needs, but we have so far overlooked.

Act. I think I know what is missing. In fact it is not missing at all. It has been with us ever since we started. It keeps us standing upright, like our pillars, and will continue to do so till the end of this seminar.

Spe. You intrigue me, Actus.

Act. We are having fun, Spectus.

Having pleasure

Spe. Ah, but you are absolutely right! We are having fun, aren't we? Well then: let us have a closer look at fun. And let us involve our co-seminarians.

Act. I am all for it. But do you think they understand what "fun" is?

Spe. Maybe they don't. But they certainly understand the term "pleasure". So let us discuss pleasure. - What is your attitude to pleasure, Actus?

Act. Normal, I guess. My work gives me a great deal of pleasure; it is like a hobby. I know I am lucky: most people consider work and hobby to be different things. I don't. - From what do you derive pleasure, Spectus?

Spe. Being with people I like. Talking with them about interesting subjects. Attending a good theatre performance. Travelling to places I haven't been before. Having a good meal and tasting a good wine. Reading a good book.

Act. So pleasure is the normal consequence of pursuing things one likes to do. That takes care of this topic.

Spe. *Laughs.* Easy, my dear Actus. There is more to pleasure than that. In fact, it is quite a controversial subject. Some see it as the highest good. Others condemn it.

Act. So what do you suggest we do?

Spe. I suggest we listen to what our fellow participants have got to say on the subject, and then draw our own conclusions. *(Turns to the audience, once more the authoritative theatre director.)* Contributions, please, on pleasure. Form three groups: condemning, permitting, and openly recommending pleasure. We shall hear one group after the other. Proverbius and Citatia may join any of the groups, as they please. Actus and I will comment only after all three groups have finished talking. I would, furthermore, appreciate if Latin and Greek contributors translated themselves right away into English. Each contributor will sit down after he or she delivered his or her message, except Proverbius and Citatia. Limit the number of contributions to maximum five per group. The first group, condemning pleasure, please start delivering - now!

These were the most complex instruction issued by Spectus so far. Obviously, he wants to test how far the artificial intelligence of the automata reaches. There is more than the usual buzzing from the room, several automata begin to glow but then cut themselves off, indicating that some sort of competition is going on. Finally, 13 automata rise, the largest number yet seen standing. It makes a colourful lot. Proverbius is the first speaker, as a member of the group condemning pleasure. He quotes the Bible.

Pro. All pleasure is followed by remorse.

Marcus Tullius Cicero. It is not virtuous to perform our duty for pleasure as its main purpose.

Sir Richard Steele. *Round baby face, has a copy of "The Tatler" in one hand and "The Spectator" in the other.* Pleasure disappoints itself, because constant application to it palls our faculty of enjoying it.

William Paley. *Dressed as a clergyman, with a thick volume before him on his desk entitled "Natural Theology", with the words "compulsory reading" stuck on them.* Pleasure is always the same; pleasures differ in nothing but intensity.

John Davison Rockefeller. *Top hat, set features, rather humourless face; holds several oil company shares in one hand and the statutes of the Rockefeller Foundation in the other.* I can think of nothing less pleasurable than a life devoted to pleasure.

There is a small pause, indicating the end of the contributions of the first group. The second group, the "permissives", gets into action.

Cit. A sip is the most that should be permitted from the goblet of pleasure.

Baruch Spinoza. *Jewish features, large dark eyes, prominent nose, broad white collar spread over a dark coat. On his name plate the first name "Baruch" has been crossed out and replaced by "Benedictus".* Indulge yourself in pleasures only so far they are necessary for the preservation of health.

Dr. Samuel Johnson. The liberty of pursuing harmless pleasures will not be disputed; but it is still to be examined what pleasures are indeed harmless.

Thomas Jefferson. *Clad like he appears in the painting of the Yale University Gallery. He holds in his hand the original, uncorrected version of the Declaration of Independence.* Do not bite at the bait of pleasure, till you know there is no hook beneath it.

Albert Camus. *Open, intelligent face, penetrating eyes. In his left hand he holds an injection needle against the plague.* Soit ami des plaisirs normaux, sans en être l'esclave.

Short pause, marking the end of the contributions of the "permissive" school. The last group, those unrestrainedly recommending pleasure, gets into action.

Epicurus. Pleasure is the first good. It means absence of pain and of trouble in the soul.

Jeremy Bentham. *The founder of utilitarianism, appears as if he just stepped out of the glass case, set up at the University College in London, in which his waxed skeleton is preserved; has a happy expression on his face.* Pleasure is itself a good; excepting immunity from pain, it is even the only good.

Phaedrus. *The first Latin fabulist, holds his own fables in one hand and those of Aesop in the other.* The mind must be amused by pleasure, so that afterwards it can better return to serious thought, to duty, and to self.

Martin Luther. *Looks like his portrait by Lucas Cranach. Black cap, curly hair, round, somewhat peasant-looking face. He stands there and cannot do otherwise.* Wer nicht liebt Wein, Weib und Gesang, der bleibt ein Narr sein Leben lang.

Lord Chesterfield. I am advising you as a friend, as a man of the world: take all the pleasure that reason points out and that decency warrants.

The third group has finished. All automata, except Proverbius and Citatia, have reverted to wax, according to Spectus' instructions. Due to their contributions, and despite the fact that their wisdoms widely differed, most pillars have been completed. Only a few capitals are still missing.

Act. *Impressed.* I commend you on your mastery over these machines, Spectus.

Spe. *Smiles.* The merit is not mine. It is Eclectus' technical ingenuity. - Would you like to comment on what we just heard, Actus? Starting with the statements of the first group?

Act. I disagree with Cicero. He claims that duty and work should not be mixed with pleasure. That is too severely republican Roman. I believe the contrary: if we manage to combine work with pleasure our work will improve.

Spe. I fully agree with you. - I think Steele is right that pleasure disappoints itself. The same pleasure, repeated over and over, will gradually erode. It must then be intensified to remain effective. But intensifying pleasures brings dangers. - Nonetheless, I think that all those who categorically condemn pleasure are wrong. They equate pleasure with immorality. But most pleasures do not offend morality at all. So let us discard, in toto, the stance of the first group. - What about the permissives?

Act. In that group the one I preferred was Camus. Be a friend of normal pleasures, without becoming their slave. A clear, wise statement. - Spinoza's suggestion that we restrict our pleasures to things that promote health I find a bit too narrow. All others in this group uttered some sort of warning against pleasure, despite their apparent permissiveness.

Spe. What about the third group, those who openly recommend that we have pleasure?

Act. I was surprised to find Martin Luther in that group. I would not have expected a religious authority like him recommending wine and women.

Spe. *Smiles.* Luther does not recommend debauchery. He simply urges us to have a normal and healthy attitude to life. I think his recommendation is profoundly wise. - Chesterfield's stance is similar to that of Luther: though he recommends pleasures, he specifies that they should be limited by decency. - I cannot accept the views of Epicurus and Bentham. Pleasure is too controversial a thing to be regarded as the highest good, the "summum bonum", of humanity. There is nothing wrong with seeking decent pleasures; but we go too far if we declare that seeking pleasure is the principal aim in life.

Act. So what is your conclusion, Spectus, after having listened to all these statements? Can you formulate your own stance on pleasure?

Spe. *Thinks briefly.* I believe the attitude of the wise to pleasure should be a question of degree. As far as I see there are three levels of pleasure. The wise will have different attitudes to each level. - On the lowest level we have the utterly harmless little pleasures, with no hook hidden underneath. Pleasures derived from small things, things that cost little or nothing. Such pleasures help us to relax, to recuperate. They further our health. The wise will have no problem with that level at all. - Next, there are the sophisticated pleasures, those that bring us substantial moral and cultural enrichments. The wise will be a bit more careful about those. They will not indulge in them too frequently, nor for too long. They know that if they do, they risk eroding the effectiveness of such pleasures. - Finally, we have the highest level, the extreme forms of pleasure. The wise will decidedly avoid them. They know that such pleasures risk turning into addictions. "Caveat principiam". Do not venture into the domain of dangerous pleasures.

Act. *Grins.* Into which category would you put drinking amaro, a pleasure you obviously indulge in?

Spe. Since I never drink more than one, or maximum two glasses a day: into the first category, that of harmless pleasures. If I would gulp down half a bottle a day, which I do not: into the third, that of dangerous addictions. But, happily, my pleasure has measure.

Act. You mean you keep your pleasures under control. We are back to my favourite theme: control. We need no control with small, innocent pleasures. We need some control when indulging in sophisticated ones. We need strong control to avoid the lure of dangerous pleasures. But, happily, you and I seem not to be lured by those at all.

Spe. Happily. - But let me point out another aspect of pleasure none has mentioned so far. I believe that the purest form of pleasure is not having it, but giving it to others.

Act. A profound wisdom, indeed. - But look at our holograph, Spectus. There is just one capital missing. We need only one more wisdom-stone, and our pillars are finished. We have the same situation as at the end of our first day. Come on, search your intellectual treasury-bag for a last wisdom on pleasure.

Spe. *Scratches his chin, then grins.* What about: To scratch is nature's sweetest pleasure and the one nearest at hand. After all: it was Montaigne who said it.

No wisdom-stone.

Spe. *Continues to think.* Life's greatest pleasures are either immoral, illegal or fattening.

No stone.

Act. *Laughs.* Cut it out, Spectus. We shall never finish our pillars with that kind of stuff. Let us ask Citatia; perhaps she can help.

Cit. *Seems to have caught Spectus' playful mood.* An abstainer is a weak person who yields to the temptation of denying himself a pleasure.

Citatia also fails to earn a wisdom-stone.

Act. Spectus, Citatia, I am deeply disappointed in you.

Spe. *Had his fun, turns serious.* In fact, Actus, I do have a famous piece of wisdom that should fit. - You claim that work gives you pleasure. But I am sure this is primarily so because your work is diverse, many-sided. No task you face is probably quite the same as any of the previous ones. - It is the same with me. I seek variety in my intellectual activities. I read about one subject, then about another. When I have read enough, I listen to music. - Or take playing bridge: it is fascinating because no game is quite like any of the previous ones. - Or take this seminar. We keep discussing one subject after the other, but they are all different; and before a subject risks to become boring, we switch to the next. - What I am driving at is this. One of the greatest sources of pleasure lies in variety. Particularly in the variety of the challenges we face. There is a famous Latin adage that expresses this truth succinctly, but forcefully. It is…

Act. *Cuts in.* Variatio delectat!

Spe. *Speaks at the same time as Actus.* Varietas delectat!

There is a loud "ping" from the projection wall. The last capital has been put in place. The pillars are finished. The holograph, with the completed foundation and a beautiful row of gothic pillars glows in a golden light. Actus and Spectus look at it with satisfaction.

Spe. We made it, Actus.

Act. But which one of us did? Which is the one that delights: is it variatio or is it varietas?

Spe. Both do. Variatio means change, varietas means diversity. But both refer to the same general concept: variety. So both formulations are valid. Variety is the soul of pleasure, the spice of life. The wise know it. But let me add a footnote. The wise also know that there must be moderation, restraint in variety. Variety overdone, carried to excess, will turn into its opposite: monotony. And there is no pleasure in monotony.

Act. A very wise footnote, indeed, Spectus.

The gong indicates the end of the session.

Spe. *Stretches.* Ah. This was a highly interesting, but a rather long and exacting session.

Act. *Smiles.* But in the hour of success no fatigue is felt.

Spe. I must confess that I do feel a bit of fatigue. I am looking forward to tea before attacking the walls in this evening's session.

Act. *Takes out a piece of paper.* Really, Spectus, you should look at the programme more often. There is no evening session today. It says here: "Following the first afternoon session of the second day, the rest of the day is at the free disposal of the participants. We suggest taking a walk in the beautiful forest surrounding the Piavello Hotel, or visit the nearby churches with their world-famous frescoes."

Spe. *Happy.* Well, I say, that is good news. You are going for a walk in the forest, I presume?

Act. Yes. I have seen the frescoes.

Spe. So did I. But I keep discovering new aspects each time I see them. They are the same pictures, yet the pleasure they give is always different. - Well then, bonne promenade.

Act. My greetings to Giotto, Gozzoli, Martini and their worthy followers.

Spe. Actus! You are more of an art connoisseur than you care to admit!

They laugh and leave the seminar room together. The room plunges into silence. Proverbius and Citatia go into half-glow, but occasional "bips" of light emanate from them. Are they exchanging opinions on the progress of the seminar? Or do they check their registers, preparing themselves for tomorrow's challenging sessions?

End of the second day of the symposium

The third day

Session 8: The Walls

It is eight o'clock on the morning of the third day of the symposium. The revolving holograph on the wall shows the finished foundation and pillars. The view from the top shows the bases of the walls, that now need to be erected. All automata are seated, except Citatia and Proverbius. Actus and Spectus, entering, say a resounding "good morning", but the automata are not programmed to react to such formalities. The gong is struck. The day begins.

Spectus. Our assignment today: build the walls. Can you remind us what the walls stand for, Actus?

Actus. For wisdoms that apply to social behaviour.

Spe. Can you suggest a plan for our work?

Act. I propose that in the morning sessions we keep to generalities. Let us examine what attitudes the wise should adopt, or avoid, when dealing with their fellow beings. We should also discuss what the wise can do, in a general way, to enhance the effectiveness and efficiency of the group they are a part of. - Then, in the afternoon, we should become a bit more specific. Let us look at wisdoms that apply in particular to married couples, families, friends, and, finally, to societies as a whole. - Two general subjects for the morning, two more specific ones for the afternoon. Our walls should stand by the end of the day.

Spe. Hopefully. We face a difficult task. We are not sociologists.

Act. We are observers of and co-players in the social game. That should be enough.

Spe. Well then, set us off, Actus. Suggest a general social attitude you believe the wise should adopt.

Act. Courtesy. I happen to strongly believe in the merit of it.

Courtesy, Manners

Spe. So do I. But let me raise a question. The word "courtesy" comes from "court". Historically, therefore, courtesy was the attitude of courtiers. It was a product of breeding, of having been taught manners. How can the behaviour practiced by a small segment of society be regarded as valid for everyone?

Act. Courtesy is not limited to any one segment of society. I have met simple, lower class people who were courteous, and members of the elite who were unbearably rude.

Spe. But those high class rude must have had breeding, while the courteous lower class people had none. There is a contradiction in all this.

Act. Only if you assume that courtesy and manners are synonymous. They are not. - Manners are a social code, a convention, a set of rules that a segment of society imposes upon itself. Manners need to be taught; they are, indeed, a product of breeding. - Courtesy, on the other hand, is not a code. It is not imposed from the outside, and is therefore independent of social levels. It emerges from an inner attitude, namely from respect towards our fellow beings.

Spe. But why do we speak of good and bad manners, but not of good and bad courtesy?

Act. Because manners are good or bad according to whether you follow certain social codes or not. But no code regulates courtesy. A discourteous man does not have bad courtesy; he simply lacks courtesy - because he lacks respect.

Spe. *Smiles.* Inscribed over the gate of Winchester College, Oxford, is the motto "Manners maketh men". In the light of what you are saying, Actus, the word "manners" should be erased and replaced by "courtesy". - But, before we go into details on courtesy, I wonder what our co-participants think about breeding and manners, good and bad. *(Turns to the room.)* May we hear some wisdoms on the two subjects I just mentioned, please?

Four automata rise. A funny pantomime begins. Inspired by the subject being discussed, each machine politely signals to the others to begin. They all seem to say "after you, please". As a result, no one speaks. Spectus is at first amused, then, as nothing happens, gradually looses patience. His somewhat rude reaction is at odds with the subject.

Spe. Stop this monkey business! You are at the Hotel Piavello, not at the royal court of the Escorial. Say what you have got to say, and do it without further chichi!

A slightly offended murmur goes through the room. The machines, apparently, enjoyed being civil to each other. But their mechanisms finally override their playfulness.

Thomas Carlyle. *Looks like in his portrait by Millais. He musters the audience, apparently to see if there are any heroes present he forgot to write about. His mechanism forces him speak before he can complete the survey.* High breeding differs from good breeding. The first insists on its own rights. The second remembers the rights of others.

George Bernard Shaw. The test of good breeding is how you behave in a quarrel.

Ralph Waldo Emerson. Good manners are small sacrifices.

Charles Dawes. *Energetic face. Holds his plan to manage Germany's war reparation payments in one hand, the Nobel Peace Prize in the other.* I never met a really great man who was not natural and simple.

The automata bow to each other as if to show appreciation of each others' wisdoms, then return to wax.

Act. *With a short courteous gesture.* Go ahead, Spectus, start commenting.

Spe. I liked Carlyle's distinction between high breeding and good breeding. I interpret it like this. Someone with high breeding tends to respect only the other members of his class. Someone with good breeding respects all those who deserve it, independently of class. I equate high breeding with arrogance, good breeding with courtesy.

Act. I liked Shaw's observation. If you do not forget your manners during a quarrel, it shows that you are in control. Those in control will remain courteous even toward opponents who are not. - I also liked Emerson's remark. Good manners do indeed often mean small sacrifices. Fortunately, they are not difficult to bear.

Spe. I was impressed by Dawes' statement that all truly great men behave naturally and simply. Affectation is certainly not a character trait of such men. - But let us not forget Citatia, our ambassador of the uninvited. *(Makes a mock bow.)* Citatia, dear, if you have a wisdom on manners or breeding in petto - or should I say in your delicate feminine bosom - please let us hear it.

Cit. *knows that Spectus is clowning and decides to respond in the same vein. She puts her hands to her bosom, waggles her buttocks and assumes a haughty expression.* This woman is so refined, she has no bosom and no behind!

Actus and Spectus burst out laughing.

Spe. Touché, Citatia. I forgot my manners. I solemnly promise that from now on I will not tease you again. - But, seriously: what contributions can you make to our topic?

Cit. *Again her serious self.* The best test of good manners is to be able to put up with bad ones.

Spe. True. It recalls Shaw's control during a quarrel.

Cit. Do on the hill as you would in the hall.

Spe. Indeed. Some people keep up manners while in good society, but discard them, like a cloak, when in less prominent surroundings. The well-bred are so everywhere. - One last wisdom, Citatia?

Cit. Some are polite by telling lies. Others are polite by telling the truth.

Spe. Ah. Citatia, as usual, tells us something full of potential for our discussion. - Take her use of the word "polite". Does politeness mean manners, or does it mean courtesy? And, while we are at it, Actus: where would you place civility?

Act. Without going too deeply into semantics, Spectus, I would say this. Manners are formal, since they come from breeding. Civility is also formal, but maybe a bit less so than manners. Politeness is even less formal. The least formal is courtesy, since it does not emerge out of external factors, but out of an inner mental view. The two antipodes are manners and courtesy; civility and politeness lie somewhere in between.

Spe. Good. That settles the question of definitions. Now to another theme that Citatia's adage opens up. - We talked on our first day of lies, and whether they can be, under certain circumstances, justified. Citatia's adage brings a new dimension to that debate. There are those who lie out of politeness; men tend to do that when flattering women. Others, I would say it is a minority, equate telling the truth with being polite. So: are we allowed to lie out of politeness? I say yes. Are we polite when we tell the truth? I doubt it. - But there is still more to Citatia's observation. You claim, Actus, that courtesy proceeds from an inner attitude, namely respect towards others. That sounds fine. But is it really so? Cannot courtesy also be used not out of respect, but as a mere façade behind which we hide our true intentions? Cannot courtesy be used simply to obtain something we want? Or, even worse: can courtesy be a screen to hide the fact that we actually despise those we are being courteous to?

Mark Twain. *Glows and rises. Clad all in white. White moustache, white goatee. Remarkably, he has a burning pipe in his hand.* Courtesy consists in concealing how much we think of ourselves and how little of others. *(Draws on his pipe, but is returned to wax without having time to exhale the smoke.)*

Spe. A rather sinister statement, isn't it? Courtesy, it seems, can be a trait of the hypocrite. Shouldn't we, therefore, qualify our praise of courtesy?

Act. I see no reason to do that, Spectus. - In accordance with my definitions, courtesy, since it is a product of an inner attitude based on respect, can never be misused. - What can be misused, though, is politeness. But let me remind you what we said yesterday: excess changes the nature of a thing. The hypocrites who use politeness as a means of deception usually make a capital mistake: they are excessively polite. They overdo it. And by overdoing it they reveal themselves to be liars, hypocrites. The wise will never be exaggeratedly polite. Their restraint is the sign that they are sincere.

Spe. *Thoughtful.* That was not only clear, but also good psychology, Actus.

Act. Thank you. And I am sure that there are many who not only radically disagree with Twain's cynical remark, but who also share my view that the root of courtesy is respect. *(Turns to the seminar room.)* But since we lack the time to hear those many, can we have just one participant speak for all? Someone with great moral authority?

Marcus Porcius Cato the Elder. *Glows and rises. He has the most beautiful toga of all Romans present at the seminar, similar to the one he wears on his statue in the Lateran. He fixes Mark Twain with a hard, censorial stare.* Courtesy is the art of showing a man, by external signs, the internal appreciation we have for him. *(He rearranges his toga and returns to grave wax.)*

Act. Thank you, Marcus Porcius. For me it is clear: Cato holds the correct view on courtesy, Mr Twain does not. And while we are at it, let me try to list a few of the social benefits courtesy can bring. - The most important effect is that it provides lubrication where people are forced to rub together. It is a buffer that eases the jolts and bumps that tend to disrupt the dealings people have with each other. Some claim that courtesy has become outdated, superfluous, having no longer a place in the modern world. Those who say this do not realize what they are jeopardizing. If we discard courtesy, we degrade interpersonal relations. We throw sand into the machinery of collective effort. I am convinced that a group of people who face a difficult situation, but remain courteous towards each another, will master the challenge more easily. - There is an interesting fact that supports what I just said. In some cities, people in the streets are discourteous, unhelpful, rather rude. In other cities they are courteous, helpful. Invariably, these latter cities turn out to be more striving, more successful, more fun to live in. They receive high ratings for the quality of living they offer. Are people in such cities polite because those cities are well-off? No. Those cities are well off because its inhabitants are polite. - In other words: courtesy is simply a social necessity.

Spe. *Smiles.* You are indeed an eloquent defender of courtesy. Can you list other, minor effects?

Act. Courtesy can help you win acquaintances and keep friendships intact. It promotes a healthy family life: familiarity should be no licence for discourtesy towards those you are familiar with. Difficult arguments are more readily accepted when tempered by courtesy. I have seen furious opponents being disarmed by quiet courtesy. Indeed: courtesy costs nothing, but can bring a great deal. - But enough on courtesy. I claimed it emerges out of respect for our fellow beings: let respect be our next subject. And its opposite: contempt.

Respect, Contempt

Spe. And I suggest we add yet another topic, related to respect: admiration.

Act. Sorry, but I have strong reservations about admiration.

Spe. Why?

Act. For the same reason I distrusted devotion, remember? Respect proceeds from the mind. Admiration is an emotion. And, as you know by now, I trust more something that is rational than something that is emotional.

Spe. Let us not exclude admiration, anyhow. - You start with comments on respect, Actus.

Act. As I just said, respect is the product of a rational process. It comes from having identified, weighed, acknowledged and experienced excellency in another person. It is based on objective analysis and lasts as long as the objective reasons last that led to it. Respect, therefore, is a concrete, enduring, rational social value.

Spe. Makes sense. Go on.

Act. We may also respect someone not for being particularly eminent, but simply because he or she is a human being. Anyone who is shown respect is likely to react positively. He or she will tend to live up to the respect shown.

Spe. But I think this works only if our respect is genuine. Simulated respect will be answered by hypocrisy. - What other effects can respect be expected to have?

Act. It can support and strengthen other social values. - One such value is loyalty. We tend to be loyal to those we respect. Both values taken together stabilize human relations. - Another such value is solidarity. We cannot feel solidarity towards a group we are a part of but whose members we do not respect. - Then there is a link between respect and praise. We may be almost indifferent to praise by someone we do not respect; but we are motivated by praise coming from one we do respect.

Cit. *Obviously keen to support Actus' interesting comments.* Praise by those we respect is worth more than the applause of a multitude.

Act. So it is, Citatia. But let me go on. - I maintain that respecting others is not a question of age. Some old people expect respect simply because they are old; but if they lack the qualities that justify respect, then age alone is not sufficient. Conversely, the wise will not withhold respect from a young person if that respect is justified.

Spe. I would even go a bit further. Respect shown to a young person may not necessarily be for his or her fully developed qualities, but for those that are emerging. We may respect a young person for what he or she is likely to become. That will be an incitement for the young to realize their potential. - How about self-respect, Actus?

Act. It is a thing we most definitely need. Without self-respect we cannot respect others. And, in turn, no-one will respect us if we have a low opinion of ourselves.

Spe. Actus: I think that concludes our tour d'horizon of respect. - Let's turn to admiration.

Act. As I said, I am suspicious of it. Admiration is an emotion. Being an emotion, it has two weaknesses. One is that it can be manipulated: it can be the result of misinformation, propaganda. Often, admiration is nothing but prejudice. The other weakness is that, being an emotion, it tends not to last. Admiration is volatile. Therefore I do not regard it as a stabilising social factor.

Spe. Sorry, but I can't agree. Admiration can be a noble, uplifting emotion. For me, it is a far cry from your image of it as volatile prejudice. *(Turns to the seminar room.)* Am I not right, gentlemen?

Two automata respond to Spectus' appeal. Carlyle has spoken before.

Thomas Carlyle. No nobler feeling than admiration for one higher than himself dwells in the breast of man.

Paul Claudel. *Holds a pair of satin shoes in one hand; from the other dangles a long, unrhymed poetry-line called a "verset claudelien".* Quelqu'un qui admire a toujours raison.

Both return to wax.

Spe. You see, Actus? I am not alone with my positive view on admiration. Don't you want to reconsider your negative opinion of it?

Act. No. Neither Carlyle, nor Claudel, nor yourself convinced me. I continue to regard admiration as dangerous. It can lead to youngsters idolizing third rate pop-stars, or being manipulated into unconditional obedience to an admired fanatic leader. Pop idols are harmless; fanatic leaders are not.

Spe. But life would be drab and shallow if we always just respected, but never admired. You talk of the dangers of admiration; all right, I concede those. But there are dozens of healthy reasons for admiration, with no dangers attached. We can admire great artists, great historic figures, or a person for a noble gesture. Admiring, I claim, enriches us. If we only respected but never admired, we risk becoming emotionally poor.

Act. Spectus: let us agree to disagree. However, I can offer some sort of compromise. There are indeed cases where mere respect may not be sufficient. In such cases I would go as far as to concede *deep* respect. But I stop short of admiration.

Spe. *Smiles.* Well, you stick to your rationality. As for me, I will not desist from admiring people who clearly deserve it. I am not afraid of emotions. - But we have another topic still to cover: contempt. It is intimately linked to a trait we discussed yesterday: arrogance. Both contempt and arrogance come from overvaluing ourselves and undervaluing others. The root of both is an unjustified feeling of superiority. But no-one is superior just because he looks at others with contempt. - Oddly enough, though, contempt is also linked with familiarity. The latter is said to breed contempt. Why is that, Actus?

Act. I do not agree with that famous adage. In my experience, familiarity breeds warmth, connectedness, trust. But since nobody is perfect, familiarity also reveals negative traits. Yet only those who by nature like to focus on the negative will overemphasize those traits.

Spe. But let us face it: some people do deserve contempt.

Act. No-one deserves contempt, Spectus. At most, some deserve pity.

Spe. But assume that you have been gravely offended. There is an age-old advice how to deal with an offender: treat him with contempt.

Act. If you do, he is likely to offend you again, for people cannot bear contempt. No, Spectus, do not show contempt for an offender. Instead, calmly and rationally criticize his *act.* This makes your standpoint clear, without offending the offender. Contempt blurs your vision; if you are free of it, you remain clear-sighted.

Spe. You have some strong arguments there.

Act. Then let us conclude that the wise will avoid contempt under all circumstances and move on to our next topic. - I suggest gratitude and its contrary, ingratitude.

Gratitude, Ingratitude

Spe. Fine. I reckon gratitude is valued highly by popular wisdom. Am I right, Proverbius?

Pro. When you drink from the stream, remember the spring.

Spe. Very poetic. Have you got more?

Provebius is silent.

Spe. *Surprised.* What! Only one single adage on gratitude?

Act. *Smiles.* I think popular wisdom understands ingratitude more than it does gratitude. Remember: it learns more from failure than from success. Isn't it so, old friend?

Pro. *Reacts promptly and generously to Actus' cue.* Once the house is finished, the carpenter is forgotten. - When the rain stops, the umbrella is thrown away. - When the danger has passed, the saint is mocked. - Do not push away the boat that helped you cross the river.

Act. You see? Popular wisdom experiences ingratitude more keenly than it does gratitude. So there are much more proverbs on ingratitude than on gratitude. But the message is the same in both cases: if you enjoy a benefit, do not forget the one who made it possible.

Spe. You understand the psychology of proverbs better than I do. - But let me raise an issue that is beyond old Proverbius' horizon. On the first day of this seminar we discussed charity and reciprocity. Charity, we said, is a one way street. It goes from giver to receiver. The receiver should, of course, be grateful to the giver. - But now take reciprocity. That is a two-way street. The giver gives something to the receiver, but expects, in due course, to get back from him something more or less equivalent. In this case there is nothing, really, to be grateful about. Giver and receiver are quit. I ask you: do we need gratitude at all in cases where reciprocity applies?

Act. You ask a complicated question; let me try to give a simple answer. I think reciprocity functions more effectively when supported by gratitude. If I am grateful, I will think of repayment; if I am ungrateful, I may forget to repay. Gratitude makes me remember that I must reciprocate. The ungrateful, lacking such a reminder, may simply forget to do so. They may get away with this once, perhaps twice, but not repeatedly. I doubt, therefore, that reciprocity can function à la longue without gratitude. Neither can society as a whole.

Spe. Yet lack of gratitude seems to be all around us in our societies. There are even people who turn against their former benefactors. Literature and the film industry produce scores of plots based on this ugly phenomenon.

Pro. *Cuts in to illustrate this.* Save a thief from the gallows and he will cut your throat. - Warm a frozen serpent and it will sting you.

Cit. *Does not want to leave the terrain entirely to Proverbius.* Do good to a pig, and it will come and shit at your doorstep.

Actus and Spectus burst out laughing.

Spe. Citatia gets the palm. As usual.

Act. But she presents a case that is rather rare. I continue to uphold that gratitude is necessary if a society is to function. The ungrateful will ultimately get isolated. And if they continue to be ungrateful, then, finally, they will eliminate themselves.

Spe. It serves them right. - Any final comment, Actus?

Act. Yes. A very important one. The wise will not simply feel gratitude, they will show it. Gratitude is worthless unless it is expressed.

Spe. A profound wisdom. - What is our next subject?

Act. I suggest reliability. A quality without which interpersonal relations can hardly function.

Reliability

Spe. How do you propose to go about discussing the subject?

Act. By breaking it down into its three logical components. Let me explain. - A asks B to do something for him. That can happen only if A trusts B. Trust is the first component of reliability. - B accepts the assignment and promises to carry it out. Promise is the second component. - B accomplishes the assignment to A's satisfaction. He acted responsibly. Responsibility is the third component. - Trust, promise, responsibility. They are the three ingredients of reliability. I propose we discuss one after the other.

Spe. *Smiles.* What would we do without your logic, Actus? - All right, then, let us start with ingredient number one: Trust.

Act. There are actually three kinds of trust. You have the blue-eyed simpleton who trusts everyone. You have the sceptic who trusts no-one, apart from himself. In between those extremes lies the attitude of the wise.

Spe. The Romans knew about that middle attitude. Vitium est omnia credere, vitium nihil credere. He that trusts everyone, misses; he that trusts none, hits not. - I wonder which attitude popular wisdom is nearer to. Proverbius, can you tell us that?

Pro. Trust is the mother of betrayal, distrust the mother of security. If you mistrust you avoid injury.

Spe. I expected that. Old peasants, like Proverbius, are notoriously distrustful. They lack subtlety, so distrust is the safest attitude they can adopt.

Pro. *There is a fleeting, cunning smile behind the white beard.* Trust not a great weight to a slender thread.

Spe. *Surprised.* How was that?

Act. *Laughs.* My dear Spectus, I am afraid you have to revise your somewhat contemptuous opinion of popular wisdom. Proverbius is more subtle than you assume. If I interpret correctly what he said, he warns against entrusting a task to someone who is not up to it. That is precisely what I, as a businessman, would do - or, rather, not do. We need to strike a balance between the job we ask someone to do, and his capabilities for doing it. We are back to proportionality, our ever recurring wisdom. - But I am sure Proverbius has other practical wisdoms on trust. Don't you, cunning old jester?

Pro. *Once again a fleeting smile.* From a cow, expect a calf; from a chicken, only an egg.

Act. *Laughs.* Exactly, my wise old friend. Not only trust another in proportion to his or her capabilities, but, also, do not expect more than he or she can deliver. This has nothing to do with distrust; it is plain common sense. - Go on, let us hear more.

Pro. Who trusts to a rotten bough, will fall.

Act. The rotten bough, I presume, stands for a questionable person. Do not trust someone who showed himself untrustworthy in the past. At least not with important things. Again, I fully agree. - One more adage on trust, Proverbius?

Pro. First test, then trust.

Cit. *Obviously somewhat jealous of Proverbius' continued success.* First think, then trust.

Act. Aha. Together, the two of you arrived at what I consider the core of our subject. - Let us take Citatia's wisdom first. If you trust without thinking, you may have to face disagreeable consequences. So the wise will do a little mental exercise before trusting anyone. They know that they can trust some people fully, some partly, and that there are a few they cannot trust at all. They also know that they can trust some people fully with one kind of job, but not with another kind. They will consider all this before they decide whom to trust with what. - Now let us take Proverbius' wisdom. The wise will, whenever they can, test a person by giving him a minor assignment before giving him a major one. Thus they will have secured themselves against surprises. - The full, combined formula for trusting is therefore this: Think; test; think again; trust. The Germans formulated this whole process in a brief wisdom: Trau, schau wem. Trust, but see whom you trust.

Spe. A lot of practical wisdoms there. - But tell me something. During yesterday's discussion I doubted that honesty can beget honesty. Maybe it is different with trust. Do you think that trust can beget trust, Actus?

Act. I do. And let me tell you an anecdote to illustrate it. - I once took a taxi-cab in a Middle American country, got excellent service, and had the feeling that I could trust the driver. So I asked him if I could rent him for two full days to show my wife and me the sights. He said yes. We agreed on the price, and I paid him immediately the whole sum. He was totally astounded: his clients obviously never paid in advance. He could have gone off with the money. But he didn't. He was always there waiting for us. He turned out to be a charming guide from whom we learned a lot, and at the end we parted almost as friends. I know I can depend on that man any time I went back to that country. Trust was answered by trust.

Spe. But your taxi driver was obviously a trustworthy man to begin with. What I meant with my question was something different. Can you turn someone untrustworthy into someone you can trust, simply by treating him as if he were trustworthy?

Act. *Thinks for a moment.* Certainly not overnight. But showing trust may initiate an internal process with the untrustworthy. They may realize that it is in their interest, to their advantage, to live up to the trust shown. This discovery may bring about a change. But, just as well, it may not. Many who are untrustworthy will remain so forever. So heed the advice of Citatia and Proverbius: think and test before you trust.

Spe. That is certainly the safe thing to do. - But let us move on to your second component of reliability. Assume A has done his homework thinking and testing, B has passed the test, he is asked to do something for A. We now switch our attention to B, who promises that he will do what he is asked to do. Proverbius: what have you got to say on promises?

Pro. A promise made is a promise kept. - A hundred "noes" hurt less than one "yes" that is not kept. - Mieux vaut donner sans promettre, que promettre sans tenir. - Gebrochenes Versprechen, gesprochenes Verbrechen.

Spe. The old fellow seems to feel very strongly about the subject. He rarely breaks his one-proverb-at-a-time rule. And I must say he is right: we simply must keep what we have promised. So what can a wise man do to avoid having to breach a promise?

Act. First of all he will promise only what lies within his capabilities to accomplish. It is usually those who promise the moon that deliver small results or none at all. - He will assess the degree of probability of keeping his promise. If that probability is low, he will turn down the job. Or, if he decides to accept it after all, he will make it clear that his promise is conditional on certain odds, and he will specify what those odds are. If he succeeds despite those odds, so much the better: he will gain goodwill. If he fails, he can point out that he warned at the outset that he might not be able to deliver. - Furthermore, a wise man will avoid having to make a promise under pressure. Such promises are rarely objective and often not feasible.

Spe. A lot of common sense, there. I have nothing to add. So let us move on to the third component of reliability: B, who promised to do the job, now has to deliver. Do his duty.

Act. May I point out, Spectus, that doing one's duty is not the same thing as acting responsibly. Our third component is not duty, but responsibility.

Spe. Can you clarify the difference between the two?

Act. If you are part of a hierarchy and someone above you orders you to do something, specifying how he wants it to be done, then you carry out a duty. Performing a duty means acting under some-one else's authority. Responsibility, then, lies with the one who commands, not with you. The military are organized this way; that is why soldiers accused of wrong-doings plead, rightly, that since they were acting under orders they were not responsible for what they did.

Spe. But aren't modern corporations organized the same way? If A is the boss of B, then A will rarely ask if B is willing or not to do a job. He simply tells him to do it.

Act. That is true up to a point. Early corporations were a bit military; but modern ones have moved away from the military model. It is rare, nowadays, that a sensible boss simply commands an associate to do a job. He will give him an assignment, which is not the same thing. By giving him an assignment, the boss delegates part of his own responsibility to his associate. Thus, within his field of competence, the associate is granted freedom of action. Having been given that freedom, the associate must assume responsibility for the assignment he agreed to do. - Besides, Spectus, when we talk of responsibility and reliability we must also include cases where there is no hierarchic relationship whatever between A and B. This is the case with this seminar. We were asked by Eclectus, who is not our boss, but merely the elusive chairman of this seminar, to do a job. We could have declined it; but we accepted. Now we have to carry it out to the best of all abilities, otherwise we would be called not only irresponsible, but above all unreliable.

Spe. I must fully agree with all you said, Actus. Can you make some final statement to crown your logic about responsibility?

Act. Yes, and I must underline it, because it is an important wisdom: there can only be responsibility where there is also freedom of action.

Spe. That is the gist of it, indeed. - But tell me: how does accountability fit into all this?

Act. If you assume responsibility, you become accountable, that is answerable for your actions. Someone without responsibility cannot be held accountable; but anyone who accepted responsibility must be held accountable. Accountability is the price you pay for your freedom of action. There is no responsibility without accountability and no accountability without responsibility. The two go hand in hand.

Spe. Actus: thanks for these excellent comments. We arrived at the end of this topic. We covered all three ingredients of reliability: trust, promise, responsibility. We even added a fourth: accountability. So let us assume that both A and B are happy and leave them to their happiness by moving on to another topic. - I suggest that topic should be tolerance.

Tolerance

Act. And a remarkable topic it is. Tolerance seems to be the only thing that does not turn into something else when it becomes excessive. We have no word for excessive tolerance. Tolerance remains tolerance, no matter how far it goes.

Spe. It is also a highly controversial thing. On the one hand, society can hardly function without it. On the other hand, it may lead to disastrous consequences if it is not checked by wisdom. - But let us begin by defining what we mean by tolerance. To me, it is an effort to understand and accept other people's tastes, opinions, motives, beliefs, without necessarily sharing them. Tolerance also means that we excuse people if they misbehave or make mistakes - at least when they are minor.

Act. For me, tolerance has mainly to do with endurance. The tolerant must endure something undesirable or something they don't agree with. Difficulties with tolerance always begin when our endurance nears unacceptable levels.

Spe. Right. And since we endure some things more easily than other things, we are more tolerant toward certain things than towards others. Tolerance, in other words, is a question of degrees.

Act. Spectus: I suggest you try to define those degrees and comment on them. I talked a lot on our previous subject: allow me to mainly be a listener on this one.

Spe. *Smiles.* I hope, though, that you will also occasionally comment, Actus. - All right, let me begin at the bottom of the scale, where we have nothing to endure, because the impact on us is practically nil. Who cares, for instance, about what happens to the inhabitants of Lapland or the Fiji Islands? We can be generously tolerant about what they say or do: they are too far away and too insignificant. We simply don't care. And it is easy to be tolerant if you don't have to care. - But let us move from Lapland or Fiji nearer to home. There is a point where we do begin to care, because we start to feel an impact. The nearer the source, the greater the impact.

Act. But distance to the source is just one criterion. We also have to consider the nature of the impact. I even believe that the nature is more important than the distance to the source.

Spe. Precisely. It is the nature of the impact, in fact, that determines the degrees on our scale of tolerances. - The lowest degree, where we need the least effort to be tolerant, has to do with other people's tastes. Having to endure tastes different from ours is annoying, but by no means critical. We do not have to adopt the taste of others, and we can avoid discussing the subject. De gustibus et coloribus non est disputandum. A wisdom coined in the Middle Ages by the Scholastics, of which there is a well-known modern French version ...

Cit. *Cuts in, to show how much she knows.* Chacun à son goût !

Spe. *Smiles.* Voilà! - The next thing we can still be relatively tolerant about is other people's habits. The wise will, as a matter of fact, examine the causes of those habits: there may be good reasons behind certain customs we perceive as odd. But a certain amount of tolerance will be needed when those habits clash with our own. The wise will then try to reduce the interface where the clash occurs. And they will mind an ancient German adage...

Cit. *Cuts in again.* Leben und leben lassen.

Spe. Jawohl! Live and let live. A most profound wisdom. *(To Citatia.)* It is a pleasure, incidentally, to work with such a widely read and polyglot automaton as you, Citatia. We highly appreciate your comments.

It is difficult to penetrate Citatia's impassibility to find out if she appreciated the compliment, but there seems to be a hint of satisfaction crossing her severe face. At last Spectus treats her not as a woman, but as what she is: a highly efficient machine. And, happily, he seems to have stopped calling her "my dear".

Spe. We now come to the next degree of tolerance. It has to do with other people's views. There is nothing wrong with people having different opinions. Quod homines, tot sententiae. The wise will respect the opinions of others: they know how drab the world would be if everyone thought alike. But difficulties start when those different views are not simply expressed, but when their holders try to force them upon us. If that happens, then our endurance can be put to a severe test.

Act. What will the wise man do in such a case?

Spe. He will, first of all, re-examine his own view, to see if the opinion held by his opponent is not, in fact, preferable to his own. If he concludes that this is not the case, he will attempt to reason with his opponent. Seek a dialog. He will attempt to find common grounds and be tolerant about the differences that remain. If this fails, he will politely, but determinedly, cut short any further discussion. He and his opponent will agree to disagree.

Act. Sensible. - What is the next degree on your scale?

Spe. Opinions can harden into mindsets, into uncompromising patterns of thinking. Opinions can change. But anyone who tries to change a mindset will have the feeling of talking to a wall. - But the danger lies elsewhere. People with uncompromising mindsets tend to become fanatics. They will try to force their mindsets on their surroundings. The impact on us of such militant people can be very serious indeed. The wise will then have to decide among several options. They can continue to be tolerant, detachedly analysing the motives of the militants. They can seek a dialog. Or they can take action and stop the militants; do it to them, before they do it to us. The decision is not easy.

Act. We have obviously arrived at the limit of tolerance.

Spe. Not yet. There is a last degree. It is the case where an individual, or a small group of individuals, seize power and use it brutally for their own personal advantage, oppressing the majority, behaving without any moral restraint. Such a case can only be met with zero tolerance.

Act. Even if the case you just described happens far away from us, so that we feel no direct impact?

Spe. There should be zero tolerance towards brutally ill-used power wherever it occurs. Even if we feel no direct impact, we must not ignore it: we must support those who are in a position to do something about it. Being tolerant of ill-used power stabilizes that power, and that may one day harm us. Because in today's world everything connects.

Act. This was a convincing exposé, Spectus. - But perhaps some of our co-participants have additional things to say on the subject. Can we find out whether they do?

Spe. Of course. *(Turns to the seminar room.)* We shall now listen to those who have something interesting to say on tolerance. Those who are unconditionally in favour of it, please speak first. Those who think it should have limits, speak last. Actus and I will not interrupt. After you have delivered your statement, please - ah - sit down. *(Spectus was about to say "please return to wax", but on second thought found that expression somewhat insulting.)*

After the usual buzzing, six automata rise, joining Citatia. Among them Erasmus and Goethe, who have spoken before.

Germaine Baronne de Stael. *Clad in empire clothes, youthful locks, round face, like in her portrait by Isabey. She looks around with a friendly, welcoming attitude, as if the participants of the seminar would be her guests in her salon at Coppet.* Tout comprendre rend très indulgent. Tout savoir, c'est tout pardonner.

Erasmus of Rotterdam. Sustine et abstine.

Johann Wolfgang von Goethe. *Wants obviously to show his excellent command of English, vain as he is.* Tolerance comes with age. I see no faults that I myself could not have committed at some time or other.

Donatien Marquis de Sade. *Clad in expensive clothes in complete disorder. He struggles with some buttons on his trousers, but is compelled to talk before he succeeds.* La tolerance est la vertu du faible.

Cit. Nothing is more difficult than trying to achieve results when we are full of tolerance.

Edmund Burke. *Dressed as an 18th century member of British parliament, looks around to see if there are any other Whigs present. Holds a book in his hand: "Reflections on the Revolution in France".* There is a limit at which tolerance ceases to be a virtue.

Anthony Trollope. *Holds his Palliser-novels in one hand and an old-fashioned camera in the other, a hint at his role as "literary photographer" of the Victorian era.* It is because we put up with bad things that people continue to give them to us.

Cit. We are in favour of tolerance. But it is difficult to tolerate the intolerant, and impossible to tolerate the intolerable.

By now all automats are seated, except Citatia.

Spe. An interesting range of opinions. Let me start with comments. - I disagree with Madame de Stael, though I respect her intellect. While we must try to understand people's motives, we should not pardon everything they do. If we strictly followed the lady's view, we would have to excuse terrorism, even murder.

Act. If my translation of Erasmus' Latin is correct, "sustine et abstine" means "bear and forbear". In other words, endure patiently what is being imposed upon us. I strongly disagree. We condemned that kind of passivity when we discussed the right attitude to change. Besides, a moment ago we concluded that there are things we simply cannot tolerate. If we strictly followed Erasmus' advice, we should patiently bear brutal tyranny. He cannot have meant that.

Spe. Goethe may be right when he says that tolerance increases with experience and age. Nevertheless, I have met some stubborn old gentlemen whose intolerant views were solidly set, once and for all.

Act. Sade, in my opinion, is gravely mistaken. Tolerance is by no means the virtue of the weak, as he claims. Quite the contrary. Often we have to be strong to keep on being tolerant. - Citatia deserves praise for her first statement. Too much tolerance can indeed lead to lack of discipline and endanger our goal. A firm leader will not tolerate laxities.

Spe. I fully agree with Burke. Tolerance is a virtue only where it is not out of place.

Act. And I agree with Trollope. We must not tolerate the activities of people who mean to harm us. If we do, we only invite them to do more.

Spe. That leaves Citatia's second statement, that I find the best of all. It summarizes our entire discussion. Tolerance is a question of degrees and it must have limits. That is the gist of it. It should be the stance of the wise.

Act. Agreed. And so we covered tolerance. - What's next?

Spe. What about - kindness? It is akin to courtesy, yet it is something different.

Act. *Smiles.* Go ahead. I leave that subject to you. Show me the link between kindness and wisdom, Spectus.

Kindness

Spe. There is an old adage: The hardest thing to resist is kindness. Kindness is a noble weapon. With it you can disarm bossy secretaries, grubby taxi drivers, arrogant door-keepers, stubborn children. It is surprising how many things you can achieve just by being kind. - The wise will be particularly kind to unkind people, to those who do not seem to deserve it. The wise know that such people are often unkind because they are treated badly, or because they are fighting some inner battle that makes them grumpy. - But kindness should never be submissive, servile. The wise are firmly kind. Kindness must proceed from a position of strength, not out of weakness. Furthermore, the wise are genuinely kind; they know that hypocritical kindness is not effective. - Let me conclude by quoting an advice given by a don of a Cambridge college: "It is no use being clever, gentlemen. We are all clever here. Just try to be kind; a little kind."

Act. Bravo, Spectus. This was almost like a Sunday sermon. Do you want to summon someone who supports your exposé?

Spe. Yes. I call Albert Schweitzer into the witness stand.

Albert Schweitzer. *Glows and rises. Tall figure, forceful but compassionate face, large moustache. Clad in a tropical suit, but holds the score of an organ work by Bach in one hand.* Kindness works simply and perseveringly. It relaxes strained relations. It puts to flight mistrust and misunderstanding. It strengthens itself by calling forth answering kindness. Hence it is the furthest reaching, the most effective of all forces. *(Sits down and turns a waxy attention to the Bach score.)*

Act. Let me raise just one objection to all this, Spectus. You said the wise will be kind out of a position of strength. But I have met many who were strong but unkind. Many, also, who were weak and kind. But not as many who were both strong and kind. Kindness, it seems to me, is not a frequent ally of strength.

Spe. That may be so. But the wise should not abandon seeking that alliance.

Act. Agreed. He should not. - This was a short but edifying topic. What's next?

The gong is struck, marking the end of the first morning session.

Spe. Ah. Our next topic is coffee.

Act. I think I shall have tea this morning.

Spe. Tastes differ, Actus. And that is good, since those selling coffee and those selling tea will both prosper. We hit on an additional wisdom: tolerance in tastes is good for commerce.

They laugh and leave for morning coffee and tea respectively, chacun à son goût.

Session 9: The Walls (continued)

Actus and Spectus return from morning coffee and tea respectively. The gong is struck, the second session of the morning begins.

Spectus. Well, we continue erecting the walls. Our next topic: actions that further collective effectiveness and efficiency, and wisdoms around such actions. But let me point out that, when we built our foundation, we already discussed several collective actions: giving, receiving, teaching, advising, judging. We now have to extend that list. - Can you suggest an extension, Actus?

Actus. Communicating? Finding wisdoms about things like the mass media, the world-wide-web, advertising, interconnectedness? Should be interesting.

Spe. I think we can skip communicating. Let me tell you why. - I believe that communication can be reduced to six basic actions: speaking, hearing, listening, looking, seeing, lying. We dealt with all of these on our first day. Communication is about what we tell or not tell, hear but fail to listen to, look at but do not see. It is about whether what we communicate is true, half-true, or a lie, and about our ability to distinguish one from the other. Those things apply whether we communicate electronically or otherwise. The technical sophistication behind modern communication is undeniable. But the media are not the message: they are just vehicles that convey the message. And we seek wisdoms about the message, not the vehicle.

Act. *Thoughtful.* You have a good point there. But somehow I find it hard to swallow. Modern media of communication have radically changed our lives. There must be many new insights and wisdoms associated with that change.

Spe. Let me suggest a solution. We shall re-introduce the subject of mass media when we erect our science-tower. At that point we shall have to discuss anyhow the changes brought to us by applied science, and wisdoms surrounding those changes.

Act. Agreed. I am looking forward to that discussion.

Spe. So do I. But for the moment, let us find collective actions that fit our walls. - There is trading. But we covered that when we discussed giving, receiving and reciprocity.

Act. *Laughs.* You seem to enjoy reducing complex actions we have not yet discussed to a few simple ones we already did. You are a reductionist, Spectus.

Spe. By no means. Reductionism is passé. I am simply trying to follow Occam's principle: when you want to clarify a subject, do not introduce more features than are necessary. - But why don't you, Actus, make a suggestion?

Act. Co-operating.

To co-operate

Spe. *After briefly thinking.* Ah, yes. We certainly cannot reduce co-operation to simpler actions we already dealt with. All right then, we have our first topic. Since it was your invention, go ahead and present it, Actus.

Act. Let me start by pointing out that co-operation is not something invented by Man. Life invented it on this planet over three billion years ago, possibly even earlier in other parts of the universe. - The bodies of most living beings are aggregates of organs, and those organs co-operate. They do so for a simple reason: each organ has a specific function that other organs lack. Living bodies, particularly those of the more evolved animals, are superbly organized co-operative teams, made up of specialists that depend on each other. Behind those teams are two basic concepts at work: specialisation and division of labour. These two concepts emerged together with the very first forms of life; thus they are practically the most ancient wisdoms of Nature. They existed much before Man was even thought of. - But let me also point out that not only organs in the body co-operate. We can see many other forms of co-operation in Nature. The so-called law of the jungle, meaning that eating each other is all that counts, no longer holds. According to newest observations the jungle functions primarily on the bases of co-operation and communication: between individuals of the same species, between different species, between animals and plants. The jungle is a huge co-operating body. Species that refuse to co-operate tend not to survive.

Spe. Fascinating. - But let us not forget that our assignment is to discuss co-operation in human societies, not in Nature. And there, it seems to me, co-operation is a relatively new concept. Historically speaking, humans tended to fight each other, rather than co-operate. I see a simple reason for that. The organs in our bodies co-operate because they are different from each other; consequently dependent on each other. But this principle is no longer dominant on the level of human society, because despite minor differences human individuals are quite alike. Thus, at the level of human society, co-operation is supplanted by another principle that becomes dominant: self-preservation, selfishness of the individual. We discussed it yesterday. Individuals will seek their own advantage, even if it is to the detriment of their fellows. Thus, at the level of society, we tend to encounter more competition than co-operation. - I therefore repeat my thesis: wherever we do see co-operation in human society, we must conclude that it is a relatively recent phenomenon.

.**Act.** You are right and wrong at the same time, Spectus. It all depends on how you define “recent”. - From our own human perspective, co-operation is by no means recent. Already our distant humanoid ancestors discovered the advantages of it. They could not have survived otherwise. You can’t catch a deer or destroy a mammoth single-handedly, if all you have are primitive weapons. You need co-operation to do it. So our early ancestors either evolved such techniques themselves, or they learned them from species older than themselves, such as wolves or lions. Predators, including man, are quite clever at such techniques. Many of our modern forms of co-operation may simply be improvements upon a few basic techniques invented or copied by our mammoth-hunting forebears. So, considered from a human point of view, you are wrong, Spectus, to call co-operation a recent phenomenon. - But you are right to call it a recent one if your perspective is that of evolutionary time.

Spe. Aha?

Act. We encounter co-operation among individuals of the same species mainly in the case of recently evolved, higher animals, not among the primitive species. And that points to a clear conclusion: co-operation, as we understand the word, is a product not of instinct, but of the brain. Co-operation is a triumph of the intellect over instinct. You need brains to discover that co-operation can bring more benefits than competition can. In order to achieve co-operation, the innate aggressiveness among individuals of the same species must be neutralized, controlled, superseded by the brain. And the highly sophisticated forms of human co-operation we now experience all around us in the world is the exclusive achievement of the brain of homo sapiens sapiens. I think we should be proud of it.

Spe. *Makes a mock bow to Actus.* Fascinating exposé, ô thou proud specimen of a highly evolved species.

Act. *Bows back.* Thank you in the name of my species.

Spe. But now let us descend from Olympian heights, and turn to more prosaic and practical aspects of co-operation. What comes to your mind, Actus, when you, as a businessman, think of co-operation?

Act. To begin with: team-work.

Spe. Fine. Let's go into that in some detail. - What makes a good team, Actus?

Act. A good team is where all members agree on and support a common goal. Team-work needs a shared purpose, just like organs share the common purpose of keeping the body healthy.

Spe. Describe a well-designed team, please.

Act. In a well-designed team each member has his or her specific sphere of responsibility - like the organs in the body. Any specific job within the collective effort of the team will be assigned to just one person, who will be responsible and accountable for it. Ideally, no single team member will be an expert in the field of any other member. Thus each member has something unique to contribute: an expertise the team needs, but the other members lack. In this way there will be no overlap of responsibilities, and no internal competition. - The analogy between a good team and the body can even be carried further. Take away an organ, the body it was a part of may die. Take away a member of a well-designed team, the team is no longer effective. Allow a person with a weak sense of responsibility, like a defective organ, become part of the team: the team will become inefficient. - And let me add something else a good team needs. It is mutual trust and respect among its members. Without them, a team will not be effective.

Spe. Aren't you describing a rather idealized team, Actus?

Act. No. I have led dozens of teams that functioned the way I described. But even if not all teams are ideal, we need to define what the ideal is, if we want an approximation to it in practice.

Spe. Yet, allow me to doubt that team-work is in all cases desirable. There are certain advantages when you work alone. One of them is that you can make quicker decisions.

Act. That is true. A team needs consensus, and that can take time. However, in my experience, decisions taken by teams tend to be more informed and better founded than decisions taken by single individuals.

Spe. But take scientific discoveries: they are predominantly made by single individuals, not by teams.

Act. It used to be that way, Spectus, but no longer. Scientific discoveries are increasingly the result of co-operation. Scientific issues have become too complex to be handled by just one person. Nobel Prizes in the sciences, as you may have noticed, are nowadays shared by co-operating individuals. Those individuals work like a team: each has some expertise the other needs, but lacks. And not only do we see individuals of the same scientific discipline, but of different expertises, co-operating with each other. Scientific progress is increasingly the result of different *sciences* co-operating. For instance medicine and mathematics are now co-operating to develop extremely precise laser therapies. Putting a man on the moon could never have been done without a huge team of co-operating experts, coming from different scientific disciplines, each with a specific sphere of responsibility, but all of them sharing an exciting common goal. No, Spectus: the time of the lone genius is definitely passé.

Cit. *Cannot restrain herself from adding a relevant observation.* Two men working as a team will produce more results than four men working as separate individuals.

Act. Precisely, Citatia. Your mathematics are absolutely correct.

Spe. Can you also tell us what the principal sign of a bad team is, Actus?

Act. Overstaffing. It leads to internal jalousies. There is much wisdom in the old adage that too many cooks spoil the broth. I repeat: only one person should be assigned to any one area of expertise. Then you will have one cook specializing in soups, another in hors d'oeuvres, still another in entrées, and one in desserts, each doing his utmost. The result will be a four-star meal.

Spe. *Laughs.* You make my mouth water! - But now another question: besides team-work, what other instances of co-operation can we find in the business world? And what wisdoms can we associate with them?

Act. You can have companies co-operating, forming joint ventures. The wisdoms that apply here are the same as for teams. There must be a shared purpose that the companies agree on. The partners forming the venture should have different expertises, complementing each other. If the partners in a joint venture have similar competencies, then, after a while, each will think it can do the job better than the other. This leads first to critiques, then to irritations, and finally either the joint venture breaks up, or one of the partners swallows the other. In my experience, all co-operations between partners of similar expertise are potentially unstable.

Spe. And cases where the expertises are similar, but there is no common purpose?

Act. Those are not co-operations, but simply a pooling of resources. This happens when partners with similar competencies join together, because they realize that they can more easily reach their individual, separate goals than if they acted alone. Lawyers and doctors often adopt this model. Yet even in such cases there is at least one common purpose: cut costs.

Spe. Political parties, though they pursue different political aims, may also join together.

Act. Those cases, again, are not co-operations, but coalitions. And coalitions are a far cry from co-operations. Coalitions need to get along by a process of continuous bargaining and sacrifices. And even coalition-partners must find some common ground, some shared purpose. But even if they do, they will always give priority to their own political aims. Therefore all coalitions are essentially unstable.

Spe. So what is the gist of our discussion on co-operation?

Act. The gist is, that successful co-operations must comply with two essential criteria: a shared purpose, and complementary competencies of the members. If those conditions are not met, we will not have co-operation: we will have competition.

Spe. Then, my dear Actus, let us look at competition.

To compete

Act. Competition is a fight for something in limited supply: food, space, a natural resource, a market segment, a managerial position, a beautiful female. Competition is a universal phenomenon: where there is life, there is bound to be competition. It is a trick to enable superior individuals to hand down their strong genes to future generations. Competition is therefore the very motor of evolution.

Spe. By selecting the fittest.

Act. Correct. - But we need to understand what we mean by "fittest". Today's fittest have an advantage, but that advantage may only be temporary. Change the environment, and the hitherto fittest may no longer be able to cope with it. Another may then become the fittest.

Spe. So what lessons will the wise competitor draw from this?

Act. He must strive to secure a lasting, not just a temporary advantage over his competitors. In order to achieve that, he must learn not only how to respond to competitors, but also how best to deal with changes in the environment. He must realize that he competes not only against other competitors, but also against an environment that is forever changing.

Spe. Actus: let us draw on your experience and look into these things in a bit more detail. Tell us what a modern company must do to compete successfully.

Act. That will, necessarily, have to involve some technicalities.

Spe. I am aware of that. But this symposium is supposed to deal with every kind of wisdoms. And I am sure the organizers would not be happy if we left out those that guide the modern business world. So tell us: how does the successful modern company best secure an advantage over its competitors?

Act. It will, first of all, know its customers and study their needs in great detail. It will offer them not only products that are of good quality, but products that fit their needs. The customer is the real boss. - It will provide not only products, but also excellent service to its clients. - It will keep improving both its product range and its service through continuous innovation. - It will be in full control of every stage of what is called the supply chain, ranging from raw materials through production to finished products. - It will continuously enhance its strengths, since it is the strengths that provide it with a competitive edge. But it is aware that the strengths it possesses today may not be the ones it will need tomorrow.

Spe. Because environments change.

Act. Exactly. - If you are strong and fit today, fine. But if you want to stay strong and fit tomorrow, watch out for changes in the external conditions in which you operate. The successful company has an antenna for changes in the environment. It is ready and willing to adapt to those changes, by developing strengths it does not yet possess. It will adapt to external changes before its competitors do. Business is full of case histories of once-glorious but arrogant and now defunct enterprises, that lacked the flexibility to adapt, and were surpassed by newcomers. If you don't adapt, you break.

Spe. Indeed. - What else will the wise competitor do? Or not do?

Act. It will respect its competitors. It will speak well of them, so that they speak well of it. It will not belittle nor look down on competitors. Above all, it will not attempt to annihilate them. Though it will endeavour to stay ahead of its competitors, it will not treat them in an unfair or uncivilized way.

Spe. *Smiles, somewhat doubtfully.* Will the customers of such a civilized and fair competitor appreciate that wise attitude?

Act. Perhaps not all of them will. But those who matter are likely to do so. And fairness brings an excellent reputation. And an excellent reputation is of great advantage, as every wise competitor knows.

Spe. *Smiles.* And every wise individual also knows. - Competition can be excluded by decree. We then have a monopoly. I presume you are against monopolies, Actus?

Act. Definitely. Competition spurs responses. But monopolists have no need to respond, since they lack the pressure of competition. Therefore they tend to stagnate, let their products become obsolete, neglect their service, become increasingly inefficient. Often, on top of all this, they become arrogant. Nothing is more destructive in the long run than the dominance by a monopolist. Wise societies should forbid them.

Spe. Let me, to round up this interesting discussion, ask a philosophical question. Competition is a fact of life, you said. But does competition always make sense?

Act. Let me give you a philosophical answer: no. Competition can indeed be senseless. Take, for instance, new tanks being developed parallel to new anti-tank missiles to knock them out. Isn't that rather stupid? The wise realize when a competition is senseless and will refuse to be drawn into it.

Spe. Actus: you painted a healthy world based on fair competition. I may be wrong, but I see signs of another world coming upon us. One where fierce and unfair competition rages to secure dwindling resources and limited markets. Where you will have to abide by the old law of the jungle, otherwise you risk not to survive. A world where you either have lunch, or be lunch.

Act. Spectus, you read too many pessimistic books. That view is too sombre. My own scenario is much brighter. I see ahead of us an increasingly intelligent world, where competition and co-operation are in balance. Where people have learned to compete fairly, whenever competition is healthy and desirable, and to co-operate effectively, whenever co-operation is beneficial and necessary. A world where there is room for compromise. One that brings increasing benefits, if not to all, at least to many. Possibly to most.

Spe. *Sighs.* Well, I hope you are right. Time will tell. - Anyhow: let us close this topic on that optimistic note of yours. Help us find the next one.

Act. You just gave the cue: helping.

To help

Spe. Good. - Help is a subject popular wisdom must be familiar with. Give us a helping hand,

Proverbius.

Pro. If you are looking for a helping hand, best take the one at the end of your arm.

Act. *Laughs.* Excellent pun, old friend, but this is the wrong place for that wisdom. You are praising self-help; but that was a subject for the pillars, and we dealt with it already. What we mean here is not helping oneself, but helping others. So try again.

Pro. A little active help is better than a huge amount of pity.

Act. That is much better. Indeed, help should be action, not words.

Spe. *Raises a hand.* I would not exclude words as categorically as you do, Actus. Help often takes the form of the right words, uttered at the right time. They can have huge beneficial effects. - But go on, Proverbius.

Pro. Help often rides a snail.

Act. Alas, it does. Help that arrives too late is generally no help at all. If you want to help, do it when it is needed. - Incidentally, one of the silliest questions I know is: "Can I help"? Of course you can. Don't ask: do it. - Proceed, Proverbius.

Pro. A mouse may help a lion.

Spe. He took that one from Aesop.

Act. Wherever he took it from, he is right. No-one is so unimportant that he could not, at one time or other, be of help. So never disdain a mouse: you may need him in the future. - What else?

Pro. He that helps the evil hurts the good.

Act. I think he means this as a warning against indiscriminate help. Know whom you are helping, why you do it, and what the consequences of your help might be. - Proverbius: you are full of sensible wisdoms on this topic. Go on.

Pro. Give a man a fish, and you feed him for a day. Teach a man to fish, and you feed him for a lifetime.

Act. Now this is the most pragmatic adage of the old boy so far. Help so that those whom you help learn to help themselves. This should be the motto of all those who want to assist emerging nations. Give them food, if they badly need it. But above all give them tools and know-how to work their own land. - One more of your sensible wisdoms, Proverbius?

Pro. Many hands make light work.

Act. *Scratches his head.* Hmm. I miss the point of that one.

Spe. This wisdom, as far as I know, goes back to Hesiod. Then Erasmus re-formulated it: multae manus onus levius reddunt. *(Hesiod is not present, Erasmus briefly glares his thanks for being quoted.)* Then Erasmus' Latin was translated into English and we just heard it quoted by Proverbius.

Act. Your erudition is absolutely astounding, professor. But answer me a simple question: what the hell does it mean?

Spe. *Laughs.* But it is quite simple. If you engage many people to help you do a task, it will be easily done, since distributing the work among many helpers will make it a light job for each.

Act. Hmm. I now see the point. But I have doubts about its implementation. It requires extensive organisation and many willing helpers.

Spe. But there are examples to prove that it is feasible. Let me tell an anecdote, since we haven't had one for some time. - Recently, a group of women in South Africa, living in dilapidated huts in a slum, got fed up with the sluggishness of the administration and resolved to take matters into their own hands. They decided to follow the famous motto of the French musketeers: one for all, all for one. They pooled their money, bought cement and a brick-making machine, and started, together, to build houses for each one of their group. The first house turned out a bit slanted, but the next one was much better, and the women finally ended up as qualified masons. Whose house was to be built next was decided by drawing lots; but the entire group of women built just one house at any one time, following Erasmus' wisdom. So, work on each house was not particularly onerous. The husbands of the women at first laughed the whole thing off; but then they became hugely impressed and at the end humbly asked to be allowed to join the women and help.

Act. Excellent story, Spectus. It is, in fact, more than a story: it is an example for the world. It shows what potentials can be released by mutual help. Let us stay a bit longer with this theme, shall we? What more can you tell us on mutual help, Proverbius?

Pro. Scratch my back and I'll scratch yours.

Act. Ah. Every child knows that one.

Spe. But not every child knows who first formulated it. It was Epicharmos, who lived many hundred years before Plato. This, in fact, is one of the oldest extant proverbs of mankind.

Act. If is that old, there must be other ways to express the idea of mutual help than scratching each others' backs. I find that version a bit vulgar for such a venerable old wisdom.

Spe. The Romans had a more civilized formulation: Manus manum lavat. One hand washes the other.

Act. That is somewhat better. But it has a slightly suspicious ring to it. It has often been used to illustrate mutual help in somewhat shady businesses.

Pro. *Understands that Actus is looking for a dignified wisdom on mutual help. He finds one in his oriental treasury.* Help thy brother's boat across, and lo! thine own boat has reached the shore.

Act. Ah. Thank you, old friend. That is a formulation that befits this ancient wisdom. *(Turns to the seminar room.)* Now: does anyone wish to make a statement on help beyond what Spectus, Proverbius and I have already said?

Henry Ford. *Glows and rises. Clad in an elegant suit and wears a bowler hat, but his hands are full of grease, as if he had just been tinkering with a new car model in his barn. Tries to* *wipe the grease off as he speaks.* To help is better than to give. *(Goes on rubbing grease from his hands, but is returned to wax while still in the process.)*

Act. *Thoughtful.* Let me comment on that short statement. - There are those who look away so that they can avoid having to help. Their motto is: what the eyes do not see, the heart does not grieve at. - Then there are those who equate help with giving. Their form of help is transferring money to some charitable organisation. This is commendable. But such people are not helpers, only donors. - And then, finally, there are those who set up charities, go out and do field work, distribute medicine, give local assistance, show the needy how to help themselves. They very often do all this in some remote country, accepting risks, exposing themselves to illnesses, dangers, duress. These, and only these, really help. Only these deserve our deep respect. - That is, I gather, what Ford meant.

Spe. Actus: let us end this topic with your noble remarks.

Act. I propose, then, that we examine one of the most widespread and most typical social actions: working.

To work

Spe. Hmm. You call work a typical social action. I wonder if you are right. I am sorry if I again sound as a reductionist, but it seems to me that we sufficiently covered work on our second day, when we discussed wisdoms that help an individual master a task. Work on the level of society is but the aggregate of tasks done by individuals. In other words, work has primarily to do with individuals. The social aspects of it are, I believe, secondary.

Act. I can't agree. Most work, though carried out by individuals, is embedded in a social context. Work is predominantly a social action. Take team-work, that we discussed earlier today. I tried to point out the mutual dependence of the individuals that form a team. Team-work is collective action, thus a social one.

Spe. But you also pointed out that each member of a team has its own well-defined, individual sphere of responsibility and accountability. It is the individuals' expertise and performance that makes the team function. - Actus: I propose an interesting duel. Since you regard work primarily as a social activity, you maintain that work belongs to our walls. I regard work as something that essentially concerns the individual, allowing him to stand upright, refusing to get toppled; thus I maintain that work belongs to our pillars. Let each of us defend his position - and let the best man win!

Act. *Enthusiastic.* I accept the challenge, sir. Draw!

Spe. I maintain that a cobbler mends and sells shoes to make a living for himself, not to serve society. This applies, mutatis mutandis, to all work.

Act. The cobbler could not survive without his customers. The people who wear shoes have as much need for the cobbler as the cobbler needs his clients. Thus, mending and selling shoes is a social action, based on mutual need.

Spe. But if the cobbler got rich enough through mending and selling shoes, he will stop mending and selling them. He will not go on toiling for mere love of his customers. Which is clear proof that his priority is personal, not social.

Act. Forget the cobbler. Take medical doctors. They work to keep their fellow human beings healthy.

Spe. They heal for money. And they revolt against the lawgiver if their incomes are curtailed.

Act. Then take business executives who regard their work as a contribution to the success of the companies that employ them. Clearly a thing for the walls.

Spe. The primary concern of executives is the level of their incomes and how to secure and improve their position within the organisation they work for. They complain if their work is not adequately compensated, and resent bitterly if they are not promoted. They resent even more if someone else gets promoted instead of themselves. The executive world is one of personal interests. We are back at the pillars.

Act. But the very raison d'être of a modern company is to serve its customers. Most companies express their goals in social terms: develop products and services that make people's lives easier, better, healthier. We are back at the walls.

Spe. They do these things primarily to make a profit. Companies act as individuals, which in legal terms they are. As legal individuals, companies strive to overtake competitors and to ensure that they remain standing firmly upright. We are clearly back at the pillars.

Act. Of course companies are there to make a profit. But they do it for their owners. And the owners are often a large number of small shareholders. Producing financial benefits for a large number of people is definitely a social action. We are decidedly back at the walls.

Spe. A company strives to produce financial benefits for shareholders mainly to strengthen its financial position. High dividends mean high share prices, better ratings, more credit. This in turn helps the company, as legal individual, to succeed. We are back at the pillars.

Act. But you cannot deny that most people prefer to work in groups and teams, rather than in isolation. Work brings people together, promotes contacts. It even promotes friendships.

Spe. What promotes friendships is not work, but meeting your colleagues in the bar at the corner after work is over.

Act. But we agreed how important a shared purpose is. Work is a common effort to reach a shared goal. Thus work is fundamentally social.

Spe. Up to a point, that is true. A shared purpose is important. But behind it there is another motive, and that one is selfish: help the team succeed, so that you, as a member of the group, can partake in the team's success. The team is but a vehicle to achieve individual benefits. - Come on, Actus, fight back.

Act. *Smiles.* Spectus, we can go on fighting, but it seems that neither of us will draw blood. I suggest we push our swords back into their sheaths, and try to find out, instead of fighting each other, what our co-participants think of work in general, and of our opposite views on it in particular.

Spe. Fine.

Act. Let us begin by asking popular wisdom. *(Turns to Proverbius.)* Old friend: you are a peasant, a labourer. Work is your element, your home territory. What wisdoms can you tell us on work? Select three in your register.

Pro. If you won't work, you shan't eat. - You must blacken your hands if you want white bread. - Sweat decorates your hand better than a golden ring.

Spe. *Smiles.* Rather trivial wisdoms, aren't they? They sound like leftist party slogans. But mind you, Actus: even leftist parties and trade unions live off the self-interest of the individual worker. Their aim is to improve his working conditions, raise his wages, procure him extra benefits. They care little about the effects their demands will have on the economy; thus they often overdraw them. Socialists and trade-unions are definitely my witnesses. It is, essentially, all about the individual worker's self-interest. We are back at the pillars, old boy.

Act. Let me, then, call Citatia into the witness stand. Citatia, I am sure you can come up with wisdoms on work that support my view. You are an intelligent machine. I am sure you think, like I do, that work must be seen predominantly as a social activity.

Cit. *With an odd expression on her face.* The sly live off the stupid, and the stupid work. - The working class can kiss my arse: I've got the boss'es job at last.

Actus looks perplexed. Spectus burst out laughing.

Spe. I am afraid Citatia refuses to support you, Actus.

Act. *Mumbles.* Traitor.

Spe. But now let *me* ask her to be *my* witness. And, Citatia, I want you to collaborate on a new experiment we haven't yet tried. Listen carefully. - I want to hear from you adages and maxims that support my thesis that work has primarily to do with the self-interest of individuals. And I want adages not only from you, but from everyone else in this room who agrees with me. However, you alone are to deliver all those adages. So please search your own register first, then communicate with all other participants in this room, collect their contributions, and then deliver what you have collected. *(Whispers to Actus.)* I wonder if this works.

Citatia glows more intensely than usual and there is a lot of buzzing going on in the room. It ceases after a time, the experiment having obviously succeeded. Citatia seems to have had no trouble with Spectus' request and starts delivering her collected wisdoms.

Cit. If you are burdened, disappointed, sorrowful, threatened, shattered: work. - If I were to suggest a general rule for happiness, I would say: work a little harder. - Honest work is a grand cure for all our maladies and miseries. It spares us from three great evils: boredom, vice and need. - Give me love and work: these two only. - Find some work you love to do and you will never again will have to work. - Set me a task into which I can put my very self, and it is a task no longer: it is joy. - To make a man happy, fill his hands with work and his mind with a purpose. - Keep working, and you will keep being alive. - The highest reward for a person's work is not what he gets for it, but what he becomes by it.

Spe. *Highly satisfied.* Thank you, Citatia. Excellent work. You are a truly amazing machine. - There you are, Actus. Praises, even hymns, offered at the altar of work, but all with a simple basic message: the purpose of work is to give joy and satisfaction to the *individual.* No hint whatever about work's social aspects. Work helps and benefits individuals: that is the gist of it. Quod erat demonstrandum.

Act. *Raises a finger.* Audiatur et altera pars, Spectus. You had your view supported by Citatia because you specifically asked her to be on your side. Now let *me* do a counter-experiment. *(Turns to the seminar room.)* I ask you for contributions supporting my thesis that work is primarily a social activity, though there are, of course, benefits to the individual. Please do not transfer your wisdoms to Citatia: stand up, show who you are and speak for yourselves. Citatia: you may participate. I generously forgive that you supported my antagonist a moment ago, provided you support me now.

Five automata glow and rise, joining Citatia. Einstein, Franklin and Wilson have spoken before. Citatia is obviously now keen to help Actus.

Cit. No matter how much work a man can do, he will not advance far if he cannot work with and through others.

Andrew Carnegie. *Has the statutes of all his foundations in one hand and "The Gospel of Wealth" in the other. On his desk is the model of the first railway sleeping car, which he invented.* It marks a big step in a man's development when he realizes that other men can be called in to help him do a better job than he can do alone.

Cit. It is the men behind who make the man ahead. Behind each able man are other able men.

Albert Einstein. Many times a day I realize how my own work is built upon the labours of my fellow men, both living and dead.

Cit. A man becomes valuable when he recognizes that his work is related to that of others.

Benjamin Franklin. I found that when I worked for myself, I was alone. But when I worked for others also, others worked also for me.

Cit. Only he who through his work adds to the wealth and knowledge of society is a true labourer. And only then will he honestly earn his wages.

Sigmund Freud. *Familiar bearded face and profound eyes. Behind his desk in not a chair, but a couch.* Work has a greater effect than any other technique to securely attach an individual to reality and the human community.

Cit. Even the smallest job has its place, like a piece in a jigsaw puzzle. The puzzle would be incomplete without it.

Woodrow Wilson. No task, done rightly, is private; it is always part of the world's work.

All automata, except Citatia, return to wax.

Act. *Very satisfied.* There you are, my dear Spectus. You can't deny that my witnesses are highly convincing. Work is beneficial to the individual worker, no doubt. But society could not function without it. Work is simply a part of the fabric of society.

Spe. *Smiles.* All, right, Actus. Let us end our debate and say that we are both right. Work belongs to the pillars as well as to the walls. It benefits the individual worker as well as society. There is a old mariner's adage: One hand for oneself and one for the ship.

Act. *Thoughtful.* You know, Spectus, I think we hit on a fundamental wisdom, without really having planned to do so. Now that I come to think of it, we met with it already when we discussed selfishness. It is this: self-interest and altruism seemingly compete against each other, but in fact they complement each other. They are two equivalent natural laws, planted into us by evolution. Self-interest is necessary to support the individual, altruism is necessary for the survival of the group or species he is a part of. Consequently, man has two duties: one is toward himself, the other toward society. Thus a part of him belongs to the pillars, another part to the walls. The two parts are fully equivalent, equally important. Where these two parts harmonize, there is wisdom.

Spe. An excellent conclusion indeed, my dear Actus. - I enjoyed this debate. Disputes can bring a lot of pleasure.

Act. Disputes: yes. Quarrels: no. - Why don't we have a look at those two?

To dispute, to quarrel

Spe. Let's do that. - Can you explain the difference between a dispute and a quarrel?

Act. A dispute means arguing, debating; it is generally civilized, often sophisticated. A quarrel is always associated with anger, and it lacks the sophistication of a dispute.

Spe. Then let us begin with the unsophisticated: quarrel. - Proverbius: what can you tell us about quarrelling?

Pro. It makes two to quarrel.

Act. At least two. Often more.

Spe. You didn't get his point, Actus. He does not mean the number of parties. He means that if one of two parties does not want to quarrel, there will be no quarrel.

Act. I see. Frankly, my experience shows the opposite. If one of two parties wants a quarrel, there will be a quarrel. But let that pass.

Pro. If two dogs quarrel about a bone, a third will run away with it.

Spe. Ah, this is a classic! Duobus litigantibus tertius gaudet. The reason is obvious: quarrel weakens the two quarrelling parties, enabling a third party to exploit the situation. Some countries used to turn this into foreign policy: they incited a quarrel, then sided first with one adversary, then with the other, weakening both. If the quarrelling parties wanted peace, their quarrel was artificially rekindled. A policy that combined "divide et impera" with "pouring oil on fire". A dirty trick. But, happily, it seems to be largely a thing of the past. Quarrelling parties no longer fall easily into that trap. They tend to realize what is going on, cease to quarrel, and unite against the inciter, who is then the one who ultimately gets hurt. - But let us hear more from Proverbius on quarrel.

Pro. There can't be two captains on the same ship.

Act. Indeed not, since they will inevitably quarrel. The same applies to the army: the wise military say it is better to have one bad general on the battlefield than two good ones. And what applies to ships and armies, also applies to business. There was once a fashionable corporate model called "double-peak management": two chief executives at the top, instead of one. It never worked. You can't have two suns in one sphere. - What else, Proverbius?

Pro. When buffalos fight, the grass gets trampled.

Act. That is to be expected. But where is the wisdom?

Spe. The wisdom is that whenever the powerful quarrel, it is the powerless who get hurt. Think of the multitudes who died because a few at the top wanted quarrel. The trampled grass usually has no idea what the quarrel of the buffalos above it is all about. There are no warlike peoples, only warlike leaders, some wise man said. Though, at times, I wonder if that is really true. - Anyhow. Go on, Proverbius.

Pro. If the quarrel lasts, truth is lost.

Spe. Yes: if a quarrel goes on and on, the quarrelling parties may end up forgetting what the quarrel was originally about. - But let me briefly qualify this. Where one quarrelling party is obviously right and the other obviously wrong, the truth will soon appear, and the quarrel will end. It is when both parties are partly right and partly wrong that a quarrel tends to drag on.

Act. Yes. It is particularly unwise to quarrel for ill-defined, hazy reasons.

Spe. It is unwise to quarrel for any reason. It is so much easier to restrain oneself from quarrel than try to end it. Think of a wisdom we learned on the first day: anything is easier to get into than out of. - One last wisdom, Proverbius, and then let us finish with quarrel.

Pro. To finish a quarrel, be the first to become silent.

Act. Hmm. Is falling silent in a quarrel really that wise? It may just be the easy way out. Once we did start a quarrel, it may be preferable to carry it to its end, rather than cut if off midway. One has to settle a quarrel by clearing the atmosphere, and that cannot be done if one of the parties retreats into silence.

Spe. You have a point there, Actus. Happily, sooner or later every quarrel ends. Toujours ne dure ni orage, ni guerre. - So let us leave quarrel on that optimistic note and turn to dispute. At the outset, you formulated briefly the difference between quarrel and dispute. Can you go into that in a bit more detail?

Act. In a dispute you argue. You put forward objective reasons that support your position. You want to convince, to persuade, but do so civilly. But the really important thing is this: in a dispute you listen to your opponent. You endeavour to understand his arguments. And your opponent, in turn, listens to your arguments. This mutual readiness to listen is the key feature of a dispute. When the parties cease to really listen to each other, then the dispute degenerates into a quarrel. - In fact, we meet again my favourite theme: control. If there is control, we stay civil and continue to listen to the arguments of our opponent. We then have a dispute. A dispute becomes a quarrel when we lose control. - But let us not neglect Citatia. Select one wisdom on dispute, Citatia, and let us hear it.

Cit. Before you start a dispute, make sure that it is not about mere words, and that it is not about trifles unworthy disputing about.

Spe. Ah, I fully agree! History abounds with disputes about mere words, definitions, unclear formulations, bagatelles. Many disputes are utterly superfluous.

Act. But disputing per se is not. It is necessary and beneficial. The wise will welcome, even actively seek constructive disputes. - You know, Spectus, there is an interesting theory why

Asians receive fewer Nobel Prices in the sciences than Westerners, despite the high levels of intelligence and learning of Asian scientists. The reason, it seems, is that in the East disputes are considered to be uncivil. Thus, new scientific ideas that clash with the tenets of the establishment tend not to be debated. In the West there are no such scruples: on the contrary. Scientific disputes are not only sought, but carried out openly, since they are expected to contribute to the advancement of knowledge. The stance in the West is that progress is hardly possible without disputes.

Spe. Interesting comments. - Let me formulate a conclusion. The wise will seek disputes if the subject matter is important and promises to be fertile, but will always keep the disputes civilized and under control. That's it in a nutshell, I believe. - What should be our next topic?

Act. I suggest criticising. Possibly also: blaming.

To criticise, to blame

Spe. Good. - Criticising is related to judging. We dealt with judging on our first day. In what way does criticising differ from judging?

Act. To judge means pointing out the truth. Criticism also points out the truth, but goes beyond judging. The well-intentioned criticiser not only judges: he wants to help, to improve, to be constructive.

Spe. But criticisms can be constructive only if certain rules are followed, both by the criticiser and by the criticised.

Act. So it is. Let us try to spell out what those rules are. You try to formulate them for the criticiser, Spectus. I will do so for the criticised.

Spe. *After having thought for a moment.* To begin with, the wise criticiser will differentiate between critique and faultfinding. He is no faultfinding grouch. He knows that faultfinding dejects, whereas well-meant criticism elevates. - He will allow himself to criticise only in matters where he has competence. He will not criticize where he lacks competence. This is the only way to ensure that his criticism carries weight. - He will start by pointing out mistakes and deficiencies, but immediately following that he will suggest better ways of doing the same thing. He wants not to demolish, but to improve. - He will, if possible, try to introduce a touch of humour. This will take the edge off his criticism, without diminishing its effectiveness. That is why caricatures are such effective forms of criticism. - But he will not confuse humour with cynicism. The wise criticiser is never cynical, because he knows that cynicism is not constructive. - He will always criticise face to face, never behind the back of the one being criticised. - Finally: whenever he can, he will criticise privately, not publicly. Right criticism seldom hurts; but loud criticism does.

Act. Very good, Spectus. - May I add a comments? The wise criticiser should not only suggest improvements, but end his criticism with encouragements. He must appear to be convinced that the one he just criticised can and will do better next time.

Spe. A valid comment.

Act. But now it's my turn. Let me try to paint the profile of the wise criticised. - To begin with: the more prominent one is, the more criticisms one is likely to get. The only way to avoid being criticised is to live in obscurity: do nothing, say nothing, be nothing. The wise criticised will welcome criticism, for he knows that it is a sign that he counts. - He will know how to distinguish between well-intentioned and malicious criticism. He will accept the former, since he knows it is meant to be constructive. If the cap fits, the criticised will wear it. On the other hand, malicious and unjust criticism will bounce off him; he will simply consider it irrelevant. - He will not show bad humour when listening to well-meant criticisms, even if they taste bitter. He will swallow them like good medicine, with a smile on his face. - He will not ruminate over criticisms for ages, turning them over and over in his mind. He will try, as soon as possible, to implement the improvements suggested by his constructive criticiser. If he cannot do that, he will store the critique in his mind for future use and go on to other matters. - And let me add a last point. Often, one does not get constructive criticism unless one asks for it. The wise, therefore, will not only welcome constructive criticisms: they will actually invite them.

Spe. An excellent review, Actus. I think between the two of us we covered the main wisdoms on criticising. There is hardly anything to add. - So let us look briefly at blaming. I have got an anecdote for you on the subject. - A priest had a man watching out for sleepers in his church while he preached. As soon as the watchman saw a faithful dozing off, he was instructed to - hasten to the pulpit and shake the priest!

Act. *Laughs.* A very wise priest, indeed. It is tempting to blame others where we should blame ourselves.

Pro. *Has the right proverb ready, as always.* If you point a finger at someone, remember that three other fingers of your hand point back to yourself.

Spe. Exactly, old friend. - So what attitudes should the wise adopt toward blame, Actus?

Act. I think I can answer that question rather concisely. If something goes wrong, we tend to look for a culprit and get involved in long discussions about who is to blame. But the wise will do something else. They will look for the *reasons* why things went wrong, why there could be culprits in the first place. Rather than blame, the wise will endeavour to understand. And after they have understood, they will focus on what is to be done to redress the situation.

Spe. I think that covers blame. - What's next?

Act. Let us now look at something closely linked to criticising: praising. And at its exaggerated form: flattery.

To praise, to flatter

Spe. Good. - But we have neglected our fellow participants lately. And this new topic is a good opportunity to get them involved again. So, this time, let these worthy machines do most of the work. *(Turns to the seminar room.)* Those who have contributions on praise and flattery, please rise.

18 automata rise, making 20 in all with Citatia and Proverbius. This is the largest number seen standing so far. Several automata are new, others have spoken before.

Act. Goodness me! A crowd. You will have to orchestrate this very carefully, Spectus.

Spe. *Obviously relishes the massive response from the floor and seems to be inspired by an idea.* Excellent cue, Actus. Orchestrate. Yes: that is exactly what we are going to do. We shall introduce a new technique, inspired by music.

Act. What the deuce do you mean?

Spe. I mean the technique of proposing a simple melody, then have it followed by a polyphony that develops it. The original melody is called the point. In our case, this will be some short statement delivered by you or me. Counter-points will then be supplied by our friends here, in the form of statements complementary to, and harmonizing with, our points. Point, counterpoint. If we do this right, we shall have a symphony composed of wisdoms on the theme of praise. Whether we can also do it with flattery, we shall see; I doubt it.

Act. *Highly sceptical.* I think this time you really overestimate the capabilities of these automata, Spectus. We risk having an awful ear-spitting cacophony.

Spe. I don't think so. I have full confidence in the technical abilities of Eclectus. *(Turns to the standing automata.)* All of you have heard my proposal. Any objections? *(No-one reacts.)* I take that as consent. - You will first wait for a statement by Actus or myself. That will be the "point". Then you will follow with statements of your own, the "counterpoints". Take care that "point" and "counterpoint" harmonize. If one of you has more than one statement to make, do not deliver them all at once, but mix them with those of your colleagues. Understood? *(A slight, courteous buzzing apparently means "yes".)* - Then here we go. Actus: let us hear your first "point" on praise. That will be our overture. Tata-ta-taa, tata-ta-taa!

Act. *Slightly dazed with Spectus' complicated arrangements, takes a few seconds to think about what his first "point" should be. Then he is ready to formulate it.* I believe in the positive effects of praise. Praise encourages and motivates those who receive it.

Pro. True praise roots and spreads.

Cit. Praise youth and it will prosper.

Pindar. Do not let an exploit pass in silence.

Cit. I have yet to find a man, whatever his situation in life, who did not do better work and put forth greater effort under the effect of praise.

They stop speaking.

Spe. Hurrah, Actus, it works! I told you it would. They are truly fantastic, these machines. - Now it's my turn. Here is my "point". It is in opposition to yours, Actus, but never mind: we want polyphony. I claim that the worthy and wise do not need praise at all. They do not depend on praise to encourage and motivate them: what they do carries its own recompense.

Confucius. The superior man does not mind if he does not get praise. He is too busy doing those things that entitle him to receive praise.

Publilius Syrus. *Clad in first century Roman clothes, holds a collection of his "sententiae" in his hand. Winks to Cicero and Seneca, his contemporaries.* To be worthy of praise is better than being praised.

Marcus Aurelius Antoninus. *His arm raised, indefatigably, in the Roman salute.* The emerald does not loose its value if it is not praised.

Aristotle. The high-minded man confers praises on others, but it shames him to receive them himself.

There are no more "counter-points".

Act. *Warms to the game, realizing it is fun.* Here is my next "point", also in opposition to yours, Spectus. Those who claim that they are indifferent to praise are hypocrites. All of us without exception, including the worthy and the wise, like to be praised.

Cicero. We are all imbued with a desire for praise.

Xenophon. *Clad as a Greek mercenary. He looks several times behind him, perhaps to see if the 10.000 he led from Babylon to Trebizond are still following.* The sweetest sound of all is praise.

Cit. Applause is the only appreciated interruption.

Pro. Those who do not value praise, will not do anything worthy of praise.

No more "counter-points".

Spe. I think I can reconcile your "point" with mine, Actus. All of us *like* praise; but the worthy and the wise do not *depend* on it for their performance. - But here is my next "point". The wise, though they may welcome praise, will always remain objective about it. Praise will not inflate their self-esteem, nor lead to a false perception of their own worth. Though they may be highly praised, the wise will always stay critical toward themselves.

Pro. Even if you are praised, do not forget to judge yourself.

Cit. Praise should show us not what we are, but what we ought to be.

The "counter-points" are getting fewer.

Act. My next "point" follows from yours, Spectus. The wise will not actively seek praise. They will never do things with the primary purpose of inviting praise. Such behaviour would be unworthy of the wise.

Plutarch. Those greedy of praise are often poor in merit.

Antoine Comte de Rivarol. *Clad partly as a poor clergyman, partly in expensive clothes of the time of Louis XVI. He speaks English, to show he is an "émigré".* It is not he that searches for praise who will necessarily find it.

Spe. Great, Actus. A rich harvest! - Now comes the second movement of our symphony. In the first we dealt with those who *receive* praise. We now turn to those who *give* praise. Like we have done when we discussed criticisms. - Here is my first "point" for the second movement: the value of praise depends on who gives it.

Sir Philip Sydney. It is great happiness to be praised by one who is himself praiseworthy.

Cit. Beware of the man who praises you because he wants some benefit for himself. At the first opportunity he will accuse you unjustly.

Spe. *Joins, surprisingly, the "counter-point"-group.* It is disgraceful to be praised by someone who deserves no praise. Turpe est laudari ab illaudatis.

Act. *Laughs.* You are a musical multi-talent, Spectus. You can handle "points" and "counter-points" equally well. - But here is my next "point". The wise will not lavish praise.

John Gay. *Clad like a beggar, holding the notes of his "Beggar's Opera" in one hand and Berthold Brecht's "Dreigroschenoper" in the other.* Praising all is like praising none.

Dr. Samuel Johnson. Praise owes its value to its scarcity.

Voltaire. Celui-là seul sait louer, qui loue avec restriction.

Spe. But while the wise will not lavish praise, they will not be avaricious with it either. That, incidentally, was my next "point".

Luc Marquis de Vauvenargues. *Poorly clad, disfigured by smallpox. Exchanges a smile with Voltaire, who shows him respect by a short bow.* C'est un grand signe de médiocrité de louer toujours modérément.

Act. Spectus: a brief comment before I formulate my next "point". - You may be aware that a recurring wisdom, proportionality, has popped up again. The wise, several of us just claimed, will neither lavish nor be avaricious with praise. But that does not mean that the wise will adopt some middle way between lavishing and avarice; only the mediocre do that, as was pointed out by Monsieur le Marquis who spoke last. It rather means that the wise will *adapt* their praise to what is being praised. They will praise restrainedly where much praise is not justified. But they will praise highly where the object of praise clearly demands it. In other words: the correct amount and intensity of praise is a question of proportionality. - Now to my next "point". What or whom you praise reveals who you are.

Cit. What a person praises is a surer sign of his character than what he condemns.

Johann Wolfgang von Goethe. Propria laus sordet in ore. *(He immediately adds his own famous translation into German.)* Eigenlob stinkt! *(And then, to show he is a polyglot:)* Self-praise stinks.

Pro. If you want others to praise you, never praise yourself.

Cit. Neither praise nor dispraise yourself. Let your actions speak for themselves.

Spe. *Smiles.* You surely agree with Citatia's last wisdom, Actus. - But our symphony is unfinished. It should have three movements, we only got two. We need some more stuff, out of which we could compose movement number three.

Act. I do have several "points" of importance that no-one yet mentioned.

Spe. Let's hear them. *(Turns to the automata still standing.)* No counterpoints this time. The third movement of our symphony will be a solo performance by Actus. Maestro: please!

Act. The wise will not praise vaguely, in a general way. He will be specific, indicating clearly the object and the reason for their praise. - Since the wise know that praise motivates, and also that well-intended criticism can be very constructive, they will often use a mixture of the two. They will praise as well as criticise. They know how fruitful that mixture can be. - We said earlier that the wise will criticise privately, not publicly. It is the opposite with praise. Whenever they can, the wise will praise publicly. Private praise is agreeable, but to be praised publicly can work wonders. - And now my last "point". The wise will not hold back justified praise from someone they happen to dislike. They will even praise an opponent if the praise is justified.

Spe. *Applauds.* Thank you, Maestro. Your solo performance finished our symphony. I think we all played well. It was a good performance. I thank the orchestra. *(He applauds into the room.)* - Now briefly to flattery. No "points" and "counterpoints": the subject isn't fertile enough to orchestrate. What is flattery? It is unjustified praise. Flattery aims to deceive, whereas praise aims to motivate. Flattery is meant to benefit the flatterer, while praise is meant to benefit those who are being praised. - Let's see: we have a Roman, two Frenchmen, and an Englishman still standing. Let us hear what they have got to say on flattery. *(Makes a sweeping gesture inviting the four automata to speak.)* Please, gentlemen.

Publilius Syrus. All flattery conceals poison.

Jean de La Fontaine. *Appears in a fantastic costume, a combination of various animals he described in his fables.* Tout flatteur vit au dépens de celui qui l'écoute.

Francois Duc de La Rochefoucauld. *Dressed as a rebel of the Fronde. He surveys the participants through a wounded eye but with a penetrating gaze.* La flatterie est une fausse monaie qui n'a de cours que par notre vanité.

George Bernard Shaw. What really flatters a man is that you think him worth flattering.

Spe. Thank you, gentlemen. What you said boils down to this: flattery is always insincere and appeals only to the vain. To those who have no vanity flattery is almost an offence.

Act. Yet, Spectus, there exists one sincere form of flattery.

Spe. Ah? What is it?

Act. Imitation.

Spe. *Laughs.* The exception confirms the rule. - Citatia: have you got some wisdom about flattery with which we can conclude this topic?

Cit. The only benefit of flattery is that, hearing what we are not, we are instructed as to what we should be.

Spe. *Smiles at her.* You get the palm. As so often before. - But let us consider praise and flattery as sufficiently covered and move on to another topic.

Act. *Stands up and assumes a solemn air.* Before we do that, I wish to say a few words. *(Turns to the wall with the revolving holograph.)* Let me praise you, Eclectus, though you choose to stay hidden and elusive, for an excellently organised seminar, which is turning out to be much more instructive than I expected. *(Turns to the seminar room.)* Let me thank you, ladies and gentlemen, for your wise contributions, and commend you on the faultless way in which you follow our instructions, no matter how complicated they may be. It is a pleasure to work with you. *(Turns to Spectus.)* Last, but not least, my dear Spectus, let me tell you that it is a privilege to be with you at this symposium. I value greatly the work you do and the effort you put into it, despite our disagreements from time to time.

Spe. *Is a bit moved.* Well thank you, Actus. This is a nice gesture. I must say it is also a great pleasure and privilege to work with you. I sincerely mean it. I highly appreciate the work you are doing. The effort you put into our seminar is often bigger than mine.

The revolving holograph disappears from the wall and is replaced by a message, reaching from one end of the screen to the other. It reads: THANK YOU, ACTUS. I APPRECIATE IT. BOTH OF YOU ARE DOING FINE. ECLECTUS, CHAIRMAN.

In the seminar room, all automata have risen; their eerie glow fills the room, as if illuminated by dozens of crystal chandeliers. They all bow, silently, to Actus and Spectus. It is a truly fantastic sight.

Short pause. Then all automata, except Proverbius and Citatia, cease to glow and return to wax. The holograph of the cathedral re-appears on the screen and starts slowly revolving again. Normality is back.

Spe. Well, well. Amazing what a little praise can do, isn't it? - But we still have not earned our laurels for the day. Our walls are unfinished. We need to go on. So I ask again: what is our next topic?

The gong is struck. The session is over.

Spe. Ah. Looks like the organisers have been flattered and release us for the rest of the morning. So much the better. The afternoon will be packed full of difficult subjects.

Act. No reason to fear them, Spectus, since Eclectus claims we are doing fine. - But I am really looking forward to lunch today. I saw succulent things on the menu…

As they rise, Actus goes on praising the lunch menu of the Grand Hotel Piavello. The morning session ends with everyone being praised and happy.

Session 10: The Walls (continued)

Lunch, so highly praised by Actus, is over; so is the siesta, needed to digest it. Actus and Spectus return to the seminar room. The revolving holograph shows the walls of the cathedral half-completed. The walls have a U-shape; there is nothing yet in the front. That space is obviously reserved for the towers and the façade, to be erected after the walls are finished.

The gong marks the beginning of the first afternoon session.

Spectus. Actus: remind us what the theme of this session is to be.

Actus. Wisdoms that apply to small groups of individuals interacting. Man and woman. Parents and children. Friends. Opponents.

Spe. Here we go, then. First topic: man and woman. - Hmm. I see a slight problem.

Man and Woman

Act. What problem?

Spe. If you asked me what comes spontaneously to my mind when I think of man and woman, in other words the couple, I would list love, affection, sex, mutual help, quarrel. Love and affection we decided to deal with when we build our roof. I vetoed sex on the first day, pointing out that adages about it are either vulgar or cynical or medical, and I am not prepared to change my view. Help and quarrel we discussed this morning. What, pray, remains to be discussed?

Act. To begin with, you left out a feature that comes to *my* mind when I think of the couple: partnership. Man and woman, the couple, are generally supposed to be partners for life. There should be plenty of wisdoms on how to make that partnership work. - Then there is an age-old controversy whether men and women are essentially different or essentially similar. Some insist on similarities, others on differences; we will need wisdoms on that issue. - As you see, we already have two new subjects to deal with here. There will be others, I am sure.

Spe. But how should we tackle these subjects? Playing roles? You play the man, I play the woman?

Act. No, that wouldn't do. We are not a couple, nor a pair. We are two sides of a coin.

Spe. Hmm. *(Scratches his ear.)* It would be best to delegate this whole man and woman business to some experts. But where do we get those from?

Two figures begin to glow at the back of the seminar room. They rise, holding hands. It is a man and a woman. The man resembles Rex Harrison in "My Fair Lady", but looks at least thirty years older. The woman is reminiscent of Audrey Hepburn in the same film, but also looks thirty years older. In front of the man's desk is a name plate: Professor Henry Higgins. On her desk the name plate says: Eliza Higgins, née Doolittle.

Actus looks a bit puzzled, but Spectus grins broadly, rubbing his hands.

Spe. Excellent. Simply excellent. Eclectus, though he insists on remaining invisible, is of tremendous help. He provides us exactly with what we need: the wise couple. You see, he asks us to assume that Eliza Doolittle and Henry Higgins, despite their obvious differences when the play about them ends, have married, and made a success of it. Something Shaw certainly never anticipated. *(Shaw briefly flares up at the back of the seminar room, as if to confirm that no, he certainly did not.)* So these two are going to tell us how they did it. - Besides: they are quite revolutionary.

Act. Revolutionary? They look like harmless old folk.

Spe. It is not their looks; it is what they are able to do. We reached a new level of sophistication at this symposium, Actus. Up to now we only met two kinds of machines. One type represent famous personages; they quote what these said or wrote in their lifetime. Then we have Proverbius and Citatia, of a higher status, because they can quote not only one individual, but hundreds. But their quotes are still verbatim. Now, these two here surpass even Proverbius and Citatia. I presume that they have been fed with entire libraries on marital issues and marital success. But rather than say the words fed into them, they are programmed to give us abstracts. They will not repeat the original texts, but only the gist, the salient points. I even assume that conversational skills were built into them electronically, to make it all look like a dialog. So the illusion is perfect: we have Higgins, the wise old husband, and Eliza, the wise old wife, married successfully for decades, telling us all about it.

Act. If what you say is true, maybe there are other machines sitting around here with similar capabilities.

Spe. Or even greater ones. We just haven't discovered them yet. But we will. As we get into more complex subjects, we need more sophisticated helpers. They will make themselves known in due time, rest assured.

Act. But aren't these two here rather old-fashioned? Do their marital wisdoms still apply to our present world?

Spe. If there is one domain where the elderly still surpass the young, it is in marital wisdoms. Just look at those soaring divorce rates. *(Waves to Higgins and Eliza.)* Wise husband and wise wife, the floor is yours. We are listening.

Actus and Spectus, for the first time since the start of the symposium, lean back and need to do nothing.

Eliza. 'enry, I mean Henry, dear, you once said you would equally be willing for a dentist to be drilling than to ever let a woman in your life. You have changed your mind since, haven't you?

Higgins. I certainly did, dear. I was a damn conceited fool to say a thing like that. Besides, with advancing age, I came to hate my dentist and his drilling.

Eliza. That is good to hear, Henry. I mean about your change of mind, not your dentist. You certainly did learn a lot in the past decades. But then, so did I. *(Sighs.)* Well, no wonder. We have grown old.

Higgins. Nonsense, dear. Every man is as old as he feels, and every woman as old as she looks. I feel fine, and you still look youthful and charming.

Eliza. *Blushes, a remarkable feat for a machine.* Well, thank you, dear. - But, Henry, you used to say something else too, for which I was rather cross at the time. You said: why can't a woman be more like a man? I thought that was injurious to us women.

Higgins. That was another silly statement I now regret, Eliza. At the time I had no experience with marriage, you see. If a woman was like a man, a marriage would be a comradeship. But marriage is not a comradeship: it is a partnership. And partnerships work best when the partners are different, each with his and her special roles and capabilities, complementing one another. Of course, the partners must also have similarities, common interests, shared values: otherwise there can be no mutual understanding between them. So you see, Eliza, things are more subtle than I used to think they were.

Eliza. Henry: why do men and women differ?

Higgins. *Becomes a bit professorial.* There are three main reasons for that, Eliza. One is biological, two are environmental. The first, the biological one, has to do with hormones. Did you know that a woman and a female chimpanzee have more sexual hormones in common than men and women do?

Eliza. *Grimaces.* Oh? No, I didn't know that. Still, I much prefer your company to that of a female chimpanzee. - But go on, dear.

Higgins. Hormones influence, of course, what males and females do or think. But let us not go into that in detail: it would lead us too far into genetics. - The second reason for the difference is embodied in a famous statement by Simone de Beauvoir: On ne naît pas femme, on le devient. *(Beauvoir is either not at the seminar, or Higgins has no power to activate other machines.)* What she meant was that there are strong social pressures at work that turn, psychologically, a woman into a woman and a man into a man. This factor, though, is becoming less relevant, as women get increasingly equal chances in society to those of men.

Eliza. It is high time they did, if you ask me. - But what is the third reason for the difference?

Higgins. That one has to do with evolution. You see, dear, for tens of thousands of years men used to be hunters, while women gathered herbs, sat in the ancestral cave and cared for the children. Thus men and women were exposed, for millennia, to different situations. This led to differences in their mental make-up, in their brain structures, that are still operational today.

Eliza. Now that's interesting, Henry. Can you give an example?

Higgins. For example, women's brains seem to be programmed for chats, because chatting creates a friendly atmosphere, and women needed that to avoid conflicts while sitting together all day in their cave.

Eliza. But we no longer sit around in caves.

Higgins. *Smiles.* No. But you replaced chatting in the cave by the telephone, because the old chatting instinct is still there. That is why I had two telephone lines installed and got us each a mobile phone. Now you can chat as much as you like with your friends: my phone is free when I need it. One potential motive for friction has been eliminated.

Eliza. *Smiles.* Yes, that was a clever idea, Henry. But tell me one thing. If we women are so fond of chatting, how come that you men are better at formulating? At least that is generally so, isn't it?

Higgins. We are not necessarily better at formulating, dear, but we are better at formulating *briefly.* And that has again to do with our prehistoric environment. When out hunting, the last thing we men needed was long conversations: that would have shied the prey away. On the other hand, we needed to communicate with our fellow hunters in order to co-ordinate the catching of the prey. So it became necessary that men thought before they spoke, select the right words, and then communicate those words briefly, sharply, directly, to the others. Thus men got trained, over tens of thousand of years, to be brief and to the point. Most modern men kept the habit.

Eliza. You certainly kept it, dear. In the early years of our marriage, you just sat behind your newspaper and spoke to me in monosyllables, while I was trying to converse with you. Happily, you got less taciturn as you grew older. You probably realized that being taciturn is being rude. And you also realized, happily, that often I simply need to converse with you.

Higgins. And you, dear, realized that we men simply must, at times, retreat into silence behind our paper or book. So we both understood each others' needs and met half-way.

Eliza. Meeting the other half-way is one of the most important trips a husband and a wife can make, isn't it, Henry? Each has to yield to the other once in a while. Make little concessions, bring little sacrifices. This is one of the major lessons we have learned. - But you said something interesting just now: that man's hunting ancestors first thought, then spoke. I have the feeling it is different with us women: it seems that we can think best while we speak.

Higgins. A clever observation, Eliza. Incidentally, Shakespeare observed the same thing: "Do you not know I am a woman? When I think, I must speak." It seems, indeed, that women develop their thoughts better while speaking, whereas men prefer to think silently before they formulate what they think. Nevertheless, there are many men who get their best thoughts while engaged in an interesting conversation. *(Grins.)* And some women seem unable to develop good thoughts despite continuously chatting.

Eliza. *Laughs.* I am sure such women are rare. - But let me say something in defence of us chatting women. Chatting makes friends. It is I, with my chatting and telephoning, who have created and kept our circle of faithful friends. If the task of making friends were left to you, Henry, we would hardly know anyone besides the Pickerings.

Higgins. *Smiles.* I realize that, dear, and am grateful for it. - Of course, there are some drawbacks to this urge of women to chat. One is they find it difficult to keep secrets.

Eliza. *Sighs.* That is true. You men are better at that. Secrets wear trousers, as a wise saying goes. But I did get better at keeping secrets, as I grew older, didn't I? I even kept some from close friends for a while, which is terribly hard.

Higgins. *Smiles.* I appreciate that sacrifice, dear. - But this urge of women to communicate does have other advantages. One is: it makes you good teachers. We men are not quite as keen on teaching, least of all where it matters most: teaching children. When we do teach, we prefer to teach grown-ups.

Eliza. But women also like to teach grown-ups. We love to correct the shortcomings of our husbands. Though, God knows, we need patience to do it.

Higgins. *Smiles.* You need patience, dear, because we men strongly resent women correcting us. I certainly did, at the beginning of our marriage. Later, happily, I learned not to. No wise man should resent the well-meant corrections of his wife. Goethe said women are the source of right behaviour in men.

Eliza. Yet, it seems to me, that all through history men warned other men against listening to the counsels of women.

Higgins. They warned against those counsels, and then proceeded to follow them. There is an old wisdom: A woman's advice is no great thing; but he who won't take it is a fool. And recently it became evident why that is so.

Eliza. Oh really? Why?

Higgins. It is because of something that may surprise you, Eliza: women are, on average, more intelligent than men. IQ tests confirm that. The brains of men, you see, are built rather like a cupboard with drawers. When men think, they open one drawer and focus on what is in it: but they usually have to close a drawer before opening another. Men tend to have what has been called a one-track mind. This helps us to concentrate on the contents of a drawer, but makes it difficult for us to discover connections between different drawers. Women, on the other hand, have little difficulty dealing with several open drawers at the same time. Thus they are apt to see connections among them that men may fail to see. But seeing connections is, precisely, what we call intelligence.

Eliza. But I thought women have smaller brains than men do.

Higgins. That is true. But you women have more interconnections in your brains. Women's brains are more extensively wired than male brains. And it is the wiring that counts, not the size. In other words, let us face it: you women are cleverer.

Eliza. But it has always been maintained that women have intuition, rather than reason.

Higgins. What is called feminine intuition, dear, is simply women's intelligence at work. Intuition is extremely quick reasoning. Women, because of the extensive wirings in their brains, can make the right connections very quickly. Give the same problem, with the same amount of information, to men and to women, and the women are likely to see the solution in a flash. In other words: a woman's instinct can be truer than a man's reasoning. Wise men always knew that. They sensed the truth about the superior wirings in the female brain before brain scanning confirmed it.

Eliza. Why, then, is the world dominated by men and not by us women?

Higgins. *Laughs.* Is it really so, Eliza? - But let me try to answer your question. Those superior wirings in your feminine brains have a drawback. Your minds tend to go off in different directions. You see too many alternatives, too many possibilities, and you are tempted to try them all. The less-wired male mind can better concentrate on a single purpose. This works in our favour, because it makes us more determined leaders.

Eliza. Aha. But how does all this relate to marriage?

Higgins. I would say it relates to it like this. When a couple is faced with an important problem, let the husband attentively listen to the counsels of his wife; she is likely to see things he has overlooked. Then let both of them together decide what to do. Once the decision is taken, let the husband implement it. He is usually better at focusing on what needs to be done.

Eliza. What you are saying makes me remember an old proverb: Man is the head - but woman the neck that turns it.

Higgins. *Laughs.* That is most certainly true. - But, Eliza, I think these people here have now heard enough on the differences between men and women. They expect us to tell them why good marriages are successful. We told them already some of the reasons why; but we need to tell them more.

Eliza. You are right, dear. How do you suggest we go about it?

Higgins. I said that marriage is a partnership. So let us talk first about choosing the right partner. Then let us tell them what it takes to keep the partnership happily going.

Eliza. Are there rules about choosing the right partner, Henry?

Higgins. *Becomes a bit professorial again.* In former times, there were. One of them had to do with age. In Europe, it was maintained that at the time when the wife was in the cradle, the husband should start to learn to ride. In China, the rule was that the age of the wife should be half that of the husband, plus seven years. - Other rules concerned geography. One of them was: choose your servant from afar, but your wife from the neighbourhood. - Then there were rules about social status. Solon advised men to marry women who are socially their equals. The ancient Jews, on the other hand, recommended men to ascend a degree when choosing a friend, but descend a degree when choosing a wife. - Frankly, I consider such rules to be too rigid and not particularly wise.

Eliza. Are there rules you do consider wise?

Higgins. Oh yes. One of them is: First strive, then wive. In other words, ensure a solid financial basis before you start choosing a partner. One may, of course, marry a rich woman. But, as the saying goes: Never marry for money; borrowing is cheaper.

Eliza. *Giggles.* You certainly followed that rule, dear. I was poor like a church mouse.

Higgins. *Smiles.* But I also followed another wise rule, dear: better a good cow, than a cow from a good cowshed. That is: character and good qualities in a partner are better than distinguished ancestry without those qualities.

Eliza. *Giggles again.* My ancestors were certainly not distinguished.

Higgins. *Smiles.* But your qualities were, dear. A woman is her own dowry, Eliza. *(Eliza gets slightly pink again.)* - But let me mention other rules I consider wise. Choose a partner whom *you* like, not one that *others* like. Do not marry too young. Do not marry in haste. And then there is an ancient wisdom: choose your partner not at a dance in the moonlight, but during the day at the harvest. The implication is that not a romantic atmosphere, a pretty face, or a stormy love-night should determine the choice of a partner, but how that potential partner behaves in everyday life. After all, you are supposed to choose a partner that lasts all your life, not just a few romantic moments.

Eliza. Because your choice is your destiny.

Higgins. *Looks at her with appreciation.* That was profound, Eliza. Your choice of a partner is indeed your destiny. So choose a partner who complements you, brings you what you lack. Then there will be mutual dependency, and that, in turn, will stabilize the partnership. Also, choose a partner with whom you share a great number of interests, tastes, values. That will promote harmony, deepen and intensify your enjoyment of the things around you.

Eliza. But it seems to me, Henry, that you and I had more differences than shared interests when we got married.

Higgins. I know we did, dear. But we also had something else, something extremely important: potential to evolve together, to converge toward each other. That potential is one of the most important pre-requisites of a happy marriage.

Eliza. *Dreamy.* We were also intensively in love, Henry. I think that was the main reason why we chose each other, wasn't it?

Higgins. *A bit embarrassed.* Eliza, you know we were told not to speak of love. These people here want to discuss love later, when they build some kind of roof.

Eliza. Pity. I could have told them a lot of wisdoms about love.

Higgins. *Tenderly.* I know, dear.

Eliza. *Stubborn.* And I am going to tell them one, whether they care to hear it or not. Though I was madly in love with you when we married, Henry, I always saw you as you really are. I did not deceive myself with an idealized image of you. Many marriages fail because the real partner no longer fits the first idealized image. Someone said it doesn't matter whom you marry, since your partner will turn out to be someone different anyway. But that is cynical. My simple wisdom is this: accept your partner, from the beginning, with his or her good qualities, as well as with his or her flaws. If you do that, you will be on solid ground. You will continue to be happy even after the first phase of pure adoration is over.

Higgins. A deep wisdom, Eliza.

Eliza. But I will even go a step further, Henry. We should not only see and accept our partner as he or she is. Marriage must be a platform for mutual improvement. Each partner should help the other to improve. Each should try to progressively turn the other into a better person. Only then can they converge.

Higgins. I certainly turned into a better person, thanks to your affection, dear.

Eliza. Affection and diplomacy, Henry. Both are needed if you want to improve your partner without hurting him. Our efforts to improve our partner must never be perceived as chicanery.

Higgins. True. Yet, despite all your affection and diplomacy, some of your efforts to improve me ended in quarrels.

Eliza. *Smiles lovingly at Higgins.* If you care, darling, you sometimes quarrel.

Higgins. *Smiles back.* That is correct, Eliza. - But we seem to have left the subject of choosing the right partner and are already discussing what makes a happy marriage going. So go on, dear, tell these people more about the things that help a marriage become a permanent success.

Eliza. A successfully married couple does not live in a house, but in a home. And, though I may sound old-fashioned, I believe that creating a happy home is mainly the task of the wife. Of course, the husband must agree with her taste; otherwise there might be trouble.

Higgins. *Smirks.* It is also the wife's task to set the rules to run the home. And at times it is damn difficult for us poor husbands to follow all the rules our wives have set.

Eliza. *Conciliatory.* Wives must keep discipline in the home, dear, otherwise it does not function. We wives know, of course, that husbands are reluctant to submit to domestic discipline.

Higgins. *Grins.* You bet we are. There was a widely circulated manifesto about that recently. I think I even got it somewhere here. *(Fumbles in his pockets and pulls out a piece of paper.)* Ah, here it is. Rule 1: The wife makes the rules. Rule 2: The rules are subject to change at any time. Rule 3: No husband can possibly remember all the rules. But in case he does, the wife will immediately change some of them. Rule 4: The wife is never wrong.; if she is, it is because the husband misunderstood a rule. Rule 5: …

Eliza. *Laughs.* Enough, Henry. You make it sound as if the home were some kind of prison.

Higgins. *Puts the paper away, smiling.* I was just joking, Eliza. Of course I appreciate what you do in our home. I have always admired the way you manage to be two things at once: a hard-working wife and an attractive lady.

Eliza. *Gets pink once more.* It is good of you to say that, Henry. Indeed, many husbands do not appreciate the work their wives do in the home. They take it for granted. There is a wise old saying: the man who simply swallows the paste does not realize that the woman who ground it may be tired.

Higgins. Yes, men can be unappreciative. Good husbands are grateful husbands. - Incidentally, Eliza, do you know what is written into the constitution of Ireland, the only one in the world, to my knowledge, that contains such a passage? It says there: "The State recognizes that by her life within the home, woman gives to the State a support without which the common good could not be achieved. "

Eliza. *Pleased.* That passage must have been written by some wise husband.

Higgins. But the world is changing, Eliza. Nowadays wives, not only husbands, work outside the home. So a new rule applies: husband and wife, together, must share the burden of homework. The wise husband will do more than just carry out the dustbin. - What else, do you think, will keep a marriage successfully going, Eliza?

Eliza. Someone said marriage is a book where the first chapter is poetry, and the rest is prose. But that need and must not be so. A bit of romance should never disappear from a marriage. It does not need to be grandiose or expensive: wives can be made happy with little, if it comes from the heart. An occasional dinner at candle-light, a small gift from time to time, given with affection. It is so easy, and it can achieve so much. Women are a bit like fire: we go out if we are left unattended.

Higgins. *Thoughtful.* That is an excellent simile, Eliza. Keeping a marriage happy is indeed like keeping a good fire burning. The logs must be kept near enough, otherwise the fire will go out. But there also needs to be space between the logs for air to circulate, otherwise the fire will go out also. A good marriage needs closeness for warmth. But it also needs privacy, enough space between the partners; for without it the partners would choke each other. Good fire, good marriage, same rule.

Eliza. You said that very nicely, Henry. - Now, let me think. What other wise things can we say on marriage?

Higgins. You already said a lot of wise things, dear. Which proves that wisdom is by no means a monopoly of men. Chaucer knew it: What is better than wisdom? Woman. And what is better than a good woman? Nothing.

Eliza. *Laughs.* I think Chaucer exaggerated a bit, dear. - But there is so much more we could tell each other and these good people here. I could go on and on talking with you. I think a happy marriage, like ours, is like a lifelong intensive but tender conversation.

Higgins. *Tenderly.* It is indeed, dear. But I fear we are overstepping our time limit. Our creator asked us to be brief.

Eliza. Our creator? You mean that certain - Mr Shaw?

Higgins. No. A certain Dr Erdely.

Eliza. Ah? It's all a bit confusing.

Higgins. Forget Mr Shaw and Dr Erdely, dear. You have got me. I have got you. That is all that matters.

Higgins and Eliza smile at each other, then sit down, hand in hand. As they return to wax, the smiles remain.

Act. *After a short pause.* That was touching.

Spe. And wise. - Any comments, Actus?

Act. They covered a lot of ground. Yet, I can think of three more wisdoms behind successful marriages they did not mention.

Spe. Let us hear them.

Act. These Higginses are obviously strong personalities, both of them. The best marriages are those were the partners are more or less of equal strength; that, then, is a true partnership. Marriages where one partner is strong and the other weak, may also turn out well. But marriages between two weak partners are doomed to failure; each partner will be forever demanding from the other what the other cannot give.

Spe. Good psychology. - Your second wisdom?

Act. In a good marriage, giving and taking between the partners must be kept in balance. No one partner can always give, and the other always take. If that happens, the partnership will sooner or later run into trouble. A good marriage is based on reciprocity. We said so on the first day.

Spe. Yes, I remember. - What is your third wisdom?

Act. If you want to keep on being happily married: have frequent laughs together.

Spe. *Smiles.* I would even extend that counsel: dance, occasionally, together. You know, Actus, there are cultures where only men are allowed to dance: the women sit around and watch. In other cultures both men and women may dance, but separately, each sex in its own group. And then there are cultures, like our own, that allow men and women to dance together, in each other's arms. I think our way of dancing expresses the correct relationship between man and woman. It symbolizes their equivalence, their complementariness. It may sound odd, but I believe there is wisdom behind the waltz.

Act. *Smiles.* And even more behind the tango. I don't find your comment odd at all, Spectus. - But tell me something: who is this fellow Erdely, mentioned by Higgins?

Spe. No idea. Probably some technician, who helped Eclectus construct the Higginses. We need not bother about him. - Now let me see. The natural outcome of marriage is the child. Man becomes daddy, woman becomes mummy. So next on our agenda should be wisdoms about the relationships between parents and children. I suggest we focus first on the mother, then on the father, then on both of them together.

Parents and Children

Act. With the subdivisions mother and son, mother and daughter, father and son, father and daughter?

Spe. *Laughs.* No. We don't want to split hairs. - I suggest we make this an ad hoc, open discussion. *(Turns to the room.)* If anyone has any pertinent remark to make, please feel free to do so at any time.

Act. Go ahead, Spectus, start the discussion. I am sure you have read a lot about this subject. So let us profit from your knowledge - and from your direct experience, of course.

Spe. *Smiles.* We shall need both to handle this topic. - The most basic family unit is the mother and child. A human baby is born prematurely, because the human mother's birth-canal is too narrow to give birth to a large baby. Perhaps Nature did not act too wisely when this was settled. Anyhow, the human baby depends at first fully on the mother, and the wise mother will actively respond to this need.

Act. How?

Spe. By being an affectionate, caring, tender mother. By not simply picking up her baby, but caressing it, fondling it, hugging it. By not only giving her baby milk, but allowing it to play with her nipples; the mother is a baby's first playmate. The more the mother does these things, the more emotionally secure her baby will be, the more it will want to explore the world around it, the more it will develop a sense of independence. Children without a strong emotional base provided early by their mothers tend later to isolate themselves, will be unable to create deep attachments, will tend to have frequent bouts of anger, and may even develop psychopathic personalities.

Act. In other words, the future of a child is in the hands of its mother.

Spe. Precisely.

Napoleon Bonaparte. *Glows and rises to deliver a famous sentence.* L'avenir d'un enfant est l'oeuvre de sa mère. (*He looks around, presumably hoping to see his mother, Letizia, who has not been invited. Disappointed, he returns to motherless wax.)*

Spe. Napoleon knows what he is talking about. He had an affectionate mother with a strong personality. Most of History's great men did.

Act. But doesn't a mother with a strong personality tend to attach her child, making it less self-dependent?

Spe. Not if she is wise. We are now talking about young children, rather than babies. In that phase, the wise mother, even if strong, will not bind a child to herself more than needed. She will encourage independency. At times she will even make herself unavailable, so that the child learns to do things without her help. Children often take their mother's help for granted; the wise mother will arrange things so that she is not always taken for granted.

Act. What else will the wise mother do?

Spe. She will allow freedom, but will set clear limits. She will show how far the child is allowed to go, explain why there must be limits, and punishes the child if it oversteps them.

Act. Can you also formulate the profile of the unwise mother, to round up the picture?

Spe. The unwise mother exaggerates the qualities of her child: its looks, its merits, its talents. The result is that the child becomes conceited and overestimates its capabilities. - Conversely, she is blind to the flaws of her child; or, if not blind, she will try to hide them, rather than correct them. The flaws thus get ingrained in the personality of the child. - She will give constantly, accustoming the child to receive constantly. This spoils the child for a lifetime.

Act. Spectus: Let us turn to the father. What is his main role?

Spe. He is the protector. That role gives him authority; thus a strong word from the father usually has a greater effect than the same word coming from a caring mother. - But the wise father will use his authority only for educational purposes, not for commanding the child around. He will not use words alone, but actions that provide examples to be followed. Children are often not too good at listening; but they are good at imitating. Imitating the actions of a wise father is one of the best things that can happen to a child. There was once a Greek sage who met a child who swore: he walked up to the father of the child and struck him in the face. He considered the father, not the child, to be responsible.

Act. *Grins.* And then there was a boy who was wondering why he is not allowed to tell words his father uses all the time.

They both laugh.

Act. Indeed: becoming a father is easy, but being one is much less so. - What other things will the wise father do?

Spe. He will praise his child whenever it does something praiseworthy. There is hardly anything a child hears with more delight than praise from an authority like the father. Praising by the father creates self-esteem, and that will help the child enormously in later years.

Act. Yet, fatherly authority tends to fade when a child arrives in his or her teens. The child then prefers to take counsel from its peers. The father may even appear to be ignorant.

Mark Twain. *Rises, appearing in spotless white as before.* When I was fifteen, my father was so ignorant I could hardly stand him around. But when I got to be twenty, I was astonished how much the old man had learned in just five years. *(Grins and returns to wax.)*

Spe. *Smiles.* A story that fits millions of cases around the world. But the wise father will not be bothered by it. He knows that teen-age rebellion is an innate natural reaction, programmed into us by evolution. He will continue to tell wise things to his rebellious teen-age children, though they may question those things. Some-one wrote: what a father tells his children is not heard outside the family - but it may be heard later by posterity.

Act. What if the father is exceptional? It is difficult for an ordinary man to have an extraordinary father.

Sophocles. *Glows and rises spontaneously. Full beard, proud head, erect bearing. Holds the Oedipus tragedies in his hand.* There is no higher joy for a good son than the glory of his father, and no higher joy for a good father than the exploits of his son. *(Begins to look in his desk for his 123 lost tragedies but is returned to wax before he can find them.)*

Spe. There is the answer, Actus. The right attitude between father and son is appreciation, never jealousy.

Act. Nevertheless, Spectus, I doubt that a son can develop all his potential if he stays in the shadow of a mighty father. Only mushrooms grow in the shadow of a mighty tree. If the son realizes that his father is a mighty tree, I would strongly advise him to move out of its shadow and follow his own ways. He that walks in another's tracks will not leave footprints of his own. - But please describe the unwise father, as you did with the unwise mother.

Spe. The unwise father is too permissive, overly merciful, exaggeratedly mild. He makes life too easy for his children. For instance by giving them money when they ask for it, without questioning what they want it for; such a father keeps his children from learning how to dispense with, how to renounce. - The unwise father is more interested in his work than in what his children are doing. He will be punished for this negligence: he loses the companionship, the chumminess of his children, things that are among the finest in life.

Act. Very true. - Now: let us turn to the last part of our discussion. Parents. Mother and father taken together. You did excellently on mothers and fathers, Spectus, so I am sure you will do equally well on parenthood.

Spe. *Smiles.* At least I can try. - Wise parents live an active family life: they are ready to do all sorts of things together with their children. Parents who sit in front of the television set, telling their children to go to their rooms and play or read a book, are not my idea of wise parenthood. Children who rarely do things together with their parents are prone to have trouble later. Some may even turn to drugs as a late surrogate for active parental care. - Wise parents will mind the old wisdom: as the twig is bent, so will the tree grow. This means observing closely the development of their children, trying to discover and to encourage talents from an early age onward. They will ensure that nature and nurture reinforce each other. However, they will encourage only real talents, not illusory ones that they imagine the children to have.

Act. *Smiles.* Reminds me of a delightful song of Noel Coward. *(Sings.)* Don't put your daughter on the stage, Mrs Worthington, don't put your daughter on the stage....Obviously, the daughter has no talent and Mrs Worthington is an ambitious, unwise mother. - But sorry for this silly interruption. Please proceed.

Spe. Needless to say, wise parents will not only promote real talents, but cut short with determination any development that pushes a child in the wrong direction. - Wise parents will impose a certain daily routine, in order to teach their children discipline. - Wise parents will keep their children busy. Not only with play. They will give them small assignments to do, thus helping them to develop a sense of responsibility. Some will even dare to expose their children to moderate dangers, teaching them not to fear difficult situations. Unwise parents do the opposite: they are overprotective, they bind their children to themselves too closely for too long, until it is too late for them to learn how to succeed on their own.

Act. I read somewhere that lionesses push their cubs down steep slopes and let them struggle back on their own, refusing to help.

Spe. Precisely. And there is no reason why lions should be wiser than humans.

Act. What else, Spectus?

Spe. Nothing unsettles a child more than when parents start behaving strangely. The behaviour of parents must be reliable, dependable. The familiar must be consistent. - Children often provoke their parents, not out of malice, but because they want to learn how far they can go. Wise parents will not get offended when provoked: they will calmly, but decisively, make the limits clear. They are kind, but not soft. - Wise parents will not treat their children as if they were irresponsible, unreasonable creatures. When things are calmly explained to a child, it will usually see the point. It may sound surprising, but children appreciate being regarded as rational beings. - And then there is another, very important thing. Children can put amazingly profound philosophical questions to grown-ups. Whenever they do that, the wise parents will not evade trying to answer such questions. They will not use phrases such as "you are too young to understand that" or "we shall talk about that when you are older". Wise parents will not leave their children standing in the rain when they are suddenly confronted with deep, disquieting issues. They will try to give answers as best they can.

Act. Spectus: you are an amazing fountain of parental wisdoms. But we must come to an end. Have you got one last wisdom on the topic?

Spe. Yes. A rather complex one. - Wise parents will try to teach their children how to cope with the world of today. That world is different from that in which they, the parents, grew up. If parents teach things that were valid when they were children, but are no longer, it will be like attempting to put old heads on young shoulders. Parents must read the signs of the times, understand the changes happening around them, see where those changes are leading, and prepare their children, the best they can, to fit into that new, changed world. This is the most difficult challenge wise and responsible parents need to face.

Act. But parents are supposed to be transmitters of tradition. They are expected to hand down timeless, unchanging values to their children.

Spe. Indeed, and that is what makes their task so difficult. What may appear to be timeless truth to parents, may seem dusty backwardness to youngsters. We then have the famous clash of generations. - Try to guess, Actus, where the following text comes from: "Today's young are rotten to the core. They are lazy, criminal, and lack purpose in life. They will never be like their parents and forbears."

Act. It sounds modern, but is probably old. I guess that is what you are driving at.

Spe. The text is engraved on a piece of stone found in Babylon, dating from about the year 3000 before the birth of Christ. That shows how far the clash of generations reaches back in human history.

Act. But how can wise parents avoid that clash?

Spe. I have only one answer: with intelligence. Wise parents will select wisdoms and values they consider to be perennial, and will keep repeating those to their children. But they will also tell them things that help them adapt to and cope with a changing world. In other words, they will attempt to find the right mix, the right combination between the traditional and the progressive, hand that mix over to their children, and then let youth have its course.

Act. Parenthood is a difficult task, indeed. Do you think children appreciate what wise parents are trying to do for them? Someone wrote that the most common ingratitude is that of children towards their parents.

Spe. I can't agree with that. It is normal that children, beyond a certain age, start to criticize their parents. It is a part of their natural development and should not be mistaken for ingratitude. If parents heed those wisdoms we just discussed, then affection, appreciation and gratitude will circulate freely, down from the parents, up from the children. The happy family is known by this two-way flow.

Act. Let us end this subject with that positive image. - Now to our next topic. Logically that should be relatives: the extended family. But relatives are either sort of neutral to us, so that no wisdoms about them apply. Or they are not merely relatives, but also friends. So let us skip relatives and go right on to friendship.

Spe. Agreed.

Friends

Act. Have you many friends, Spectus? Real ones? Good ones?

Spe. I do.

Act. So do I. Since we have experience with this topic, we can surely handle it on our own. No need to involve co-participants. - I suggest we start by trying to paint the picture of the ideal, wise friend. Go ahead, Spectus.

Spe. *After briefly thinking.* I shall talk of "he", but what I say applies equally to "her". He is a person to whom we can openly impart fears, hopes, suspicions. He is someone in the presence of whom we may think aloud; he will listen to us willingly, patiently, and will advise us justly. He likes us despite our shortcomings. He will not turn away and deny his friendship when we made a fool of ourselves. He has an understanding heart and a helping hand: helpfulness is perhaps his main feature. He will defend us if need be. He is a sort of shock-absorber, who reduces the bumps we meet with on the road of life. He is someone from whom we can draw strength.

Act. Not bad, Spectus. But I think you put too much emphasis on friendship in adversity. As if friendship mainly consisted of good offices in bad times. No doubt, friends are necessary when we are in trouble; but troubles are rather exceptional situations. For me, therefore, a friend is above all someone I can share joys with, so that those joys become more intense. A friend is one with whom I have common tastes, similar interests, who reacts to things like I do. Our opinions may at times differ, but then we shall openly discuss the difference and our discussion will enrich us, rather than divide us. A friend is someone from whom I can willingly accept criticisms, without any danger of harm to our relationship. A friend is one who can even tell me disagreeable truths about myself, without me minding it. My mother used to say that a true friend is one who tells me when I have bad breath.

Spe. *Smiles.* An example taken from life. - But let me raise an issue. You described friendship in trouble-free times. I focused on friendship in troubled times. Are we talking of the same thing? Aren't there two different kinds of friendship? Aren't there good-weather and bad-weather friends?

Act. No. Friendship is just one kind, with two different sides to it.

Spe. Yet, it seems to be a fact that when we are prosperous and successful we appear to have more friends than when we get into trouble. When all is going well, it is difficult to tell on whose friendship we can depend. Riche homme ne sait qui ami lui est. The acid test of friendship, I think, is adversity. Amicus certus in re incerta cernitur: only a friend in need is a friend indeed.

Act. I am convinced that most of my friends would help me if it became necessary. Maybe some would do so more intensively than others, but none would refuse.

Spe. Well, I will not insist. But a shade of doubt remains. - Now: we have painted the picture - or rather two pictures - of the ideal friend. What must we do to gain his or her friendship?

Act. To gain a friend we must offer friendship. Friends do not appear out of nowhere. One who passively waits for people to turn up and automatically become friends, will never have a friend. You must get interested in other people, and show it, rather than assume that they will get interested in you.

Spe. Nevertheless, we must be selective. We must not offer friendship to questionable people. If you call one wolf, you invite the pack. And if you frequent the company of wolves, you will end up howling like one. It is better to be alone than in bad company.

Act. But it is better to be in good company than to be alone.

Spe. Of course. - Let me proceed. We should not try to gain the friendship of people with defects similar to our own. They will only reinforce our shortcomings.

Act. Conversely, we should seek the friendship of those with whom we not only share good traits, but who counteract, help reduce our deficiencies.

Spe. *After a short pause.* I think, Actus, we said enough on how to select friends and how to gain them. Let us now look at how to keep them. - You start.

Act. To keep a friend, we must accept him with his merits, but also with his faults.

Spe. But never speak of his faults behind his back.

Act. We should react at once if a friend asks us for a favour. Between friends there should be no delays.

Spe. We should never fall out with a friend for mere trifles.

Act. Give him little presents, once in a while.

Spe. Never overburden him. - I think this is particularly important. We should never demand too much from a friend. Friends are like strings of a violin: if you stretch them too far, they snap. Remember what Higgins said about keeping the fire burning in a good marriage: the logs should be close, but there must be space between them. The same applies to friendships. There is an old adage: A low hedge between friends will keep the friendship green. - But now let me ask you this, Actus. Can lending money to a friend endanger the friendship?

Act. *Thinks for a moment.* I would not hesitate to lend to a friend if it really helps; otherwise our image of the friend as a helper in adversity would not hold. But we must reckon with dangers. Asking the money back, or insisting on giving advice to the friend on how to use it, may lead to irritation. The Germans say: eat and drink with your friends, but never do business with them. Perhaps friendships and money matters should be kept apart.

Spe. Maybe they should. - Do you think that friendships grow stronger with time?

Act. They generally do, since we share more common remembrances. But at times they do not. Some friends may evolve in different directions than we do. While such friendships never entirely disappear, they grow less intense.

Spe. Now here is an entirely different kind of question for you. There is an old adage: It is good to have a friend not only in heaven, but also in the house of the devil. What do you think of that?

Act. I would not call the one in the house of the devil a friend, but an ally. Alliances fulfil some strategic purpose. They arise out of calculation. But calculation can never be the basis for true friendship.

Spe. Excellent response. - What else can we say on friendship?

Act. I have a rather delicate issue. Some claim that true friendship is possible only among socially equals. They deny that it can develop between persons of different social status and background. Do you think that this is true? Can friendship really exist only between socially equals, or can it also happen between socially un-equals?

Spe. *Thoughtful.* A delicate question, indeed. - Pythagoras and Confucius were among those who believed friendship is possible only among equals; I presume they meant social equality, though they may have meant intellectual equality. I tend to think that their view is valid. Friendship requires a certain community of thought, a parallelism of lives, a sharing of similar tastes and aims; all that is possible mainly among those who are socially equal. Nevertheless, I hasten to add, there are many examples to the contrary. History knows of strong friendships between men who came from entirely different social backgrounds. Henry Ford, for example, maintained that he had close friends who wore blue overalls. *(There is a "bip" from Ford, sitting at the back.)*

Act. I believe, though, that we should not include in the term "friendship" relationships that have little or nothing to do with it. Let me quote from my own personal experience. - Early in my career, I was helped along by persons in high places, who pulled me upward. To these pullers I was useful; but I would never call them friends. Later, many of these early pullers did become my friends; but that happened long after I reached a hierarchic level similar to theirs. Then I became a puller myself; but those I pulled I would not call friends, nor would they call me so.

Spe. Interesting comments. Right from the horse's mouth. Indeed, we should not use the term "friendship" too broadly: we then risk devaluing it. True friendship, as a matter of fact, is a rather rare thing.

Act. Not necessarily. I consider scores of persons, in many countries, as close and true friends.

Spe. You may be an exception.

Act. Perhaps. But I think not. You see, I was always keen to turn mere acquaintances into true friends. *(Smiles.)* And, happily, I have a wife who cultivates and maintains them.

Spe. *Smiles.* You fortunate man. - That was it on friendship. Now: the last topic we settled on at the start of this session was adversaries. They range from opponent to foe.

Adversaries

Act. Should we manage this subject also on our own, with no-one to help?

Spe. I suggest we begin doing so, but then invite others to speak, to make sure nothing important was left out. - I presume, Actus, that in the course of your work you must often face opponents. I guess you were well trained how to deal with them. Can we have the benefit of your experience, please?

Act. Gladly. - There are seven basic rules on how to deal with opponents.

Spe. Let us hear them.

Act. The first one is: collect all the information you can get on your opponent. The more you know about him, the easier you can develop a strategy to deal with him. A famous German general said: surprise is lack of information. Don't let yourself be surprised by things you should have known about your opponent, but didn't. - Rule two: be sure to correctly gauge the strengths of your adversary. Discover what his advantages are. The wise will never be blind to the strengths of his opponent. Nor will he consider himself to be stronger than him, unless very thorough analysis clearly indicates otherwise.

Pro. *Reports back, after a long period of silence.* Though your enemy seems like a mouse, watch him as if he were a lion.

Act. Precisely. For the wise, there is no such thing as an insignificant adversary. If we underestimate an opponent, or, worse, believe him to be harmless, we may end up not reckoning with him. And then he can hit us when he sees fit. Only the arrogant and the stupid belittle their adversaries. And, incidentally, only they believe that their opponents do not think.

Spe. Would the wise ever fight an adversary stronger than themselves?

Act. Not if they can avoid it. They will first build up their strengths and look for allies. Nevertheless, there are some who are capable of using the strength of an adversary to their own advantage - like in Judo. But you have to be very smart to do that.

Spe. Rule three?

Act. Analyse the weaknesses of your adversary. The analysis of his strengths will tell you how to defend yourself against him. The analysis of his weaknesses will tell you how and where to attack him.

Spe. What are the next two rules?

Act. Four: Be certain that you gauge correctly your own strengths. If you overestimate yourself, you become vulnerable. - Five: Know your own weaknesses. You cannot be strong without knowing where your weaknesses lie.

Spe. And the remaining two rules?

Act. Rule six: Do not reveal all your strengths right from the outset. Hide some until you can put them to use. Nothing demoralizes an opponent more than when he is suddenly confronted by a strength he has not reckoned with. - Rule seven: Dissimulate your weaknesses as long as possible. Hide them as long as you can. - Let me add something to these rules six and seven. There is a frequently quoted maxim: When dealing with an opponent, focus on your strengths and forget your weaknesses. Focusing on your strengths is fine. But if you do not follow rule seven and dissimulate your weaknesses, you may become vulnerable despite your strengths.

Spe. You speak of hiding strengths and dissimulating weaknesses. That is deception. But deception is akin to dishonesty and lying, and you strongly condemned both of these on our first day. So how can you defend deception now?

Act. *Smiles.* You got me there, Spectus. I can only say, to my defence, that temporarily hiding strengths and weaknesses from an adversary is not the same thing as deliberately lying or being dishonest. You find deception in Nature; but Nature cannot be called dishonest.

Spe. *Smiles.* Let us not deepen this issue. - Any other rules, basic or not, on how to deal with opponents?

Act. Perhaps we should add a rule eight. Never give your opponent grounds to suspect that you do not strongly believe in your own cause. Self-doubt will immediately be exploited by your adversary. He will sense it and turn it to his advantage. If you have doubts about your own cause, you better not begin fighting.

Spe. Actus: I remember a few famous maxims that fit into our discussion. Let us have your comments on them. - Here is the first one: The adversary of my adversary is my friend.

Act. That has to do with tactics, not wisdom. A common foe unites. But once that common foe is gone, the alliance against him is likely to break up. I would modify that maxim: The adversary of my adversary is my ally.

Spe. Then take a famous passage from the Bible: Who is not with me, is against me.

Act. I have reservations about that statement, with due respect to the source. My reservations are purely rational and have nothing to do with religion. My objection is this: why should I consider anyone who is not actively against me as my enemy? Why should I push the neutral fence-sitters over into the enemy's camp? Why create more adversaries than necessary? It is much wiser to accept that there are some who are neither for nor against me, and who wish to remain so. Let them be a no-force, rather than a counter-force.

Spe. What about this one: Reply to the devil in the devil's own tongue. In other words, use the same methods against an adversary that he is using against you. The devil's own tongue may be the only one the devil understands.

Act. This is not easy to answer. At times we may be forced to employ methods we dislike, but which are the only ones our adversary seems to understand. But the wise will limit the use of such methods. I tend to think that descending to the low levels of an opponent's dubious methods is more likely to harm us than to help us.

Spe. Richelieu thought otherwise.

Cardinal Duc de Richelieu. *Glows and rises. Clad in purple church clothes. Narrow face, moustache pointed upwards, goatee, piercing, intelligent eyes, radiating willpower.* On peut tout employer contre ses ennemis. *(Returns to purple wax.)*

Spe. There you have one who disagrees with you, Actus. He successfully defeated his adversaries on all fronts, because he used any method that promised success. For him, defeating the adversary was what alone mattered. He was of the same opinion as Machiavelli or Lenin: the end justifies the means; he who wills the end must also will the means.

Act. You open up a moral question I suggest we leave out of our discussion, since it would take us too far. I can only say this. Let us not confuse dirty politics with strategy. Aims do not justify all methods; far from it. This applies to all those in power, including Richelieu.

Spe. *Smiles.* D'Artagnan would agree. So do I. - We talked about rules on strategy. Can you also name some wise rules on tactics?

Act. There are many; I can only mention a few. - When you attack an opponent, minimize the dangers to yourself. - If an attack fails, do not renew it along the same lines. - Put yourself into the shoes of your opponent before you attack him. And then attack where and when he least expects it. - Try to wear out your opponent through patience. Let him tire himself. This is the wisdom of the torero: it is surprising how often it works.

Spe. Assume that your strategies and tactics worked, and you have succeeded in defeating your opponent. What wisdoms apply to the winner?

Act. It is enough that the adversary lost; he does not need to be humbled, much less annihilated.

Spe. *Thoughtful.* I wonder if that is really wise. History teaches us what can happen if a defeated adversary is spared. He may turn against us with renewed hatred, once he has regained his strength. Vae victis, woe to the vanquished, was the advice of Titus Livius.

Act. But History also teaches us the contrary. The magnanimity of winners has often turned adversaries into friends. An adversary may become a friend if treated magnanimously; but never if he is debased. Give the adversary a chance. Humble him only if he turns against you a second time.

Spe. But aren't you drawing the profile of a highly idealized adversary? One who does not use dirty tricks; who takes defeat chivalrously; who turns into a friend once he is defeated. Does such an adversary exist at all?

Act. I certainly prefer to fight against an adversary who has those qualities, rather than against one that lacks them.

Spe. But that implies that you can choose your opponents. Like you choose your friends.

Act. *Poker-faced.* A man, Spectus, cannot be too careful in the choice of his enemies. *(Oscar Wilde, author of the adage, glows briefly, appreciating.)*

Spe. *Laughs.* No comment! - I have a last question. Are we allowed to hate our adversaries?

Act. It is allowed, but is not wise. Do you know what the Godfather, the famous literary mafia-boss, advised his collaborators? Do not hate your enemies: it dims your judgment.

Spe. *Laughs.* Chapeau to the wise Godfather. - Actus: we arrived at a point where I suggest we ask our fellow-participants if they have anything to add. We may have left out something important on this subject of adversaries. *(Turns to the room.)* If you have any points Actus and I overlooked when discussing opponents, adversaries, or foes, please let yourself be known.

Three automata rise, among them Burke and La Fontaine, who have spoken before.

Spe. Go ahead, please. We are listening.

Aristides the Just. *Dignified appearance in 6th century B.C. Greek clothes. Holds the statutes of the Delian league, which he authored, in his hand.* For an enemy that is retreating, build a golden bridge.

Jean de La Fontaine. Notre ennemi, c'est notre maître.

Edmund Burke. Our adversary is our helper. He that wrestles with us strengthens our nerves and sharpens our skills.

Cit. A wide-awake, persistent, tireless adversary is one of the most important ingredients of our success.

Aristides, Burke and La Fontaine return to wax.

Spe. Now, that is interesting. Three out of four said essentially the same thing, only using different words. Only Aristides the Just said something different.

Act. Who was Aristides the Just?

Spe. A Greek general. He warned Themistocles, a fellow general, not to destroy a bridge of boats Xerxes built across the Hellespont. Thus, when the Greeks began winning, Xerxes could leave the battlefield. - The wise lesson is this. If an adversary is losing and ready to retreat, help him do it. Leave him a bridge so that he can escape. Do not force him into a corner, where all he can do is turn around and fight you in desperation. - The wisdom of Aristides, incidentally, was reformulated by Erasmus; only he spoke of a silver bridge instead of a golden one. *(Erasmus glows, but faintly; he knows Aristides has precedence.)*

Act. A pragmatic wisdom, indeed. - But now we come to the last wisdom on this topic. As you rightly observed, La Fontaine, Burke and Citatia each expressed the same idea, only they were using different words. I think that idea is of paramount importance: our adversaries are, in fact, our teachers.

Spe. They are, indeed. And do you know, Actus, who was the first to express that wisdom? The Buddha. He insisted on it in dozens of sermons. Our adversaries are our masters. They correct us. They perfect us. They help us to recognize our shortcomings and weaknesses. Let us listen to our adversaries, for they reveal our faults. A great idea - and a deep wisdom.

The gong is struck. It is the end of the session.

Act. The Buddha's noble thought ends the topic and the session. - A particularly outstanding event of this session were the two Higginses. I hope that, in the future, at least some of our work will be taken over by such sophisticated machines. Heavy burdens lie ahead..

Spe. I told you, Actus, those machines will turn up. I expect they will do so pretty soon.

Act. They will be welcome.

Actus and Spectus rise and leave for afternoon tea, forgetting to look at the holograph. That is a pity, because they could have had the satisfaction to see that the walls of the cathedral of wisdoms have made considerable progress.

Session 11: The Walls (continued)

Actus and Spectus return from afternoon tea. The gong marks the beginning of the last session of day three.

Spectus. Up to the last battle of the day. Can you formulate, Actus, what the battle is about?

Actus. Essentially about wisdoms that apply to large groups such as teams, corporations, political parties, states.

Spe. A broad range. Too broad.

Act. Yes. Therefore we must simplify. In fact, we can reduce our task to three major subjects. - We should focus first on the man at the top of a large group. He has power, and he must have leadership qualities. So let us discuss wisdoms that have to do with leadership and power. These will be our first two subjects. - Then we should look at the various models that large groups, especially societies, have adopted over the centuries to organize themselves. We should discuss the pros and contras of such models, and whether they are wise or not. This analysis would be our third subject. - Together, the three subjects should be more than enough to fill the rest of this day with highly interesting insights.

Spe. *Smiles.* As I already said: what would we do without your logic? - All right, here we go. Our first subject: leadership. This is your terrain, Actus. Let us profit from your personal experience.

Leadership

Act. My experience is with business leadership. I am only an observer of political leaders.

Spe. But what you tell us on leadership in business will also apply, to a large extent, to all other forms of leadership. So, unless specified otherwise, our subject is leadership in general.

Act. As you wish. - As I experienced it, there are essentially two types of leaders. The first inspires and guides; the second rules. I was lucky to have had leaders pertaining to both types early in my career, so I could see how they fared. Under leaders who ruled, but failed to inspire, work was more like drudgery, but there was order and discipline. Under those who mainly inspired and guided, but neglected to rule, work was fun, but things tended to be somewhat chaotic. So I learned an important lesson: the good leader is a blend of the two types. He inspires, guides *and* rules.

Spe. What do you mean when you say a leader must inspire and guide?

Act. A leader must be able to set goals that are both exciting and achievable. He motivates his group not only to accept and support those goals, but to work enthusiastically to achieve them. By that, he inspires. - He must explain clearly how he intends to reach the goals he set, and what he expects the various group members to do. By this, he guides. - If he fails in any of these things, he is not a leader - only a boss.

Spe. And what about ruling?

Act. To rule means two things: to organize and to control. - To organise means to assign responsibilities. It means blending disparate parts into a well-structured whole, oriented toward the goal. It also means eradicating overlaps of responsibilities, double-work, clashes of competencies, all things that weaken the common effort. It also means enforcing that all members of the group co-operate; a boat will not advance if some of the rowers try to row their own way. - To control means essentially to impose discipline. It means ensuring that the plan is followed, deadlines are kept, tasks finished on time. At times a good leader will even get a bit tough to enforce these things. - And yet another thing belongs to ruling. Both the leader and his associates learn from successes, failures and mistakes; but it is above all the leader who must ensure that the lessons are applied.

Spe. There is an old maxim: No man can become a good leader unless he has been well led. What do you think of that?

Act. Someone who has been well led has learned the principles of good leadership from the one who led him. But knowing those principles is not enough. To become a good leader you need ambition, more than average determination, and the desire to build things that last.

Spe. What other qualities should a good leader possess?

Act. He must be an accomplished judge of people. He must be able to select the right persons for the right positions. Show me a leader, and I will know his men. Show me the men, and I will know their leader. - He must know how to delegate. Once he delegated, he will not interfere; a constantly meddling leader is not a wise one, since by interfering he shows lack of confidence in those to whom he delegated. But the good leader also knows what he cannot delegate: there are certain things only the chief can do.

Spe. Should the leader himself be capable of doing what he delegates?

Act. No. He should know enough about the tasks he delegates to be able to judge the performance of his associates. But he need not be, and indeed cannot be, an expert in everything. He is rather like the conductor of an orchestra: he knows how to play a few instruments, but his main role is to make sure that his musicians harmonize.

Spe. Must a good leader be particularly clever? Intelligent?

Act. He must not necessarily have a brilliant mind; but intelligence helps. A leader must see the essential behind complexity. He often needs to make lonely decisions. It is good if he can rely on his own intellectual faculties to do these things. But a leader must, above all, be able to co-ordinate brains. It doesn't matter if some of those brains are superior to his own.

Spe. You are truly a fountain of wisdoms, Actus. Go on. I am listening.

Act. A propos listening. The wise leader will listen carefully to news and rumours coming up through his organisation. Even what a junior clerk tells him can be of importance. - Conversely, he will keep those who work for him well informed. Nothing demoralizes associates more than being kept in the dark. The worst thing is when they learn about important developments or decisions not from the boss, but reading the morning newspaper.

Spe. How will the good leader deal with situations where he needs to reverse a decision he made earlier?

Act. He will communicate his new decision to his associates at once, explain the reasons for the change, and have them endorse it. A good leader is a convincing one: this extends to changes in policy he needs to make.

Spe. Evidently, the ability to convince is a major trait of the good leader. What other traits does he need to possess?

Act. Self-confidence: only the persuaded can persuade. - Composure at times of crises. Ability to deal with them. Determination to deal with them at once. A leader who hesitates in a crisis is an unsettling leader. - A good leader is something of a protector. He looks out for dangers that may hurt his associates and takes measures to forestall the harm. A lazy shepherd is the wolf's friend, as old Proverbius would say. - And let me add something else. To the young, a leader should be someone to look up to, to respect, to emulate. For the young, a leader may be perceived as something of a mentor. Leaders who ignore or neglect this role, and do things that are unethical, do not realize the psychological damage they may cause.

Spe. Apart from unethical actions, what other things will the wise leader *not* do?

Act. He will never show weakness, no matter how serious the situation; he knows how demoralizing that can be. He will not complain publicly of the shortcomings of an associate. He will not take credit for himself alone for work done by his group. He will not try to dissimulate mistakes he is responsible for. He will not talk down to, much less intimidate his associates; he knows that if threatened or scared his associates will not perform. He will not shuffle his associates about too frequently. And he will never change the members of a winning team.

Spe. Actus: you covered a lot of ground in just a few minutes. I think that much, even most of what you said applies not only to business leaders, but to leadership in general. Nevertheless, for the sake of completeness, let us ask our fellow seminarians for additional comments. And since we covered business leadership, let those additional comments be on military and political leadership. We should then have practically the complete view. - First, therefore, the military. *(Turns to the seminar room.)* Can we please have wisdoms on leadership from top military men present at this seminar?

Three figures glow and rise.

Napoleon Bonaparte. La froideur est la plus grande qualité d'un homme destiné à commander.

Charles de Gaulle. *Wears the uniform he wore when he entered Paris in 1944, plus a Saint-Cyr cap. Holds the model of a small bomb under his arm, with "force de frappe" written on it.* Les hommes sont sans importance; ce qui compte est celui qui commande.

Dwight David Eisenhower. *Wears the uniform he wore on the eve of D-Day. Smiling, fatherly figure, somehow unlike one's image of a soldier.* You do not lead by hitting people over the head - that's assault, not leadership.

All three make a military salute to each other and return to wax.

Act. Start commenting, Spectus.

Spe. I am surprised at what Napoleon said. His soldiers adored him. How can "froideur", coldness, achieve that kind of adoration? Besides, Napoleon also wrote that a leader is a dealer in hope. How can a "cold" leader inspire the emotion of hope?

Act. I don't think Napoleon meant "coldness". He rather meant "coolness". Composure. A prime quality for a commander on a battlefield, as it is for a business leader in a crisis. A leader who loses his head is no leader.

Spe. Yes, that must be what Napoleon meant. - But I also find de Gaulle's statement somewhat surprising. How can he say that men count for nothing? It sounds contemptuous.

Act. I, too, find de Gaulle's choice of words odd. Yet I see the wisdom behind them. There is a saying that an army of stags led by a lion would be more formidable than an army of lions led by a stag. History is full of victories by weak or numerically inferior armies led by an inspiring military genius. De Gaulle is right: when it comes to a battle, it is the leader who counts, the men must follow. This, incidentally, is also valid in business: when there is a crisis, it is the leader, not the group he leads, who is expected to deal with it.

Spe. Now to Eisenhower. His remark is surprisingly humane, coming from a top general. But then, Eisenhower oscillated between toughness and humaneness. Let me tell an interesting anecdote about him. - When he ceased to be a soldier and became American president, he started his term by practically abolishing executive presidential leadership. He was obviously afraid of being perceived as too much of a commanding general. He defined his presidential duties as developing ideas, formulating them, putting them before congress, and leaving the implementation to others. This attitude of his was a complete failure. People expected firm leadership and didn't get it. After a while, Eisenhower realised his mistake. Suddenly, a "new" President Eisenhower emerged: he was once more the general, making use of all the powers that his office granted him.

Act. Your anecdote underlines a point I made earlier: the wise leader is a firm leader.

Spe. Indeed. I think our three military men did not bring anything essentially new over and above what you already said, Actus. Maybe the political leaders will. *(To the seminar room.)* May we have comments on leadership from top politicians present, please?

Six automata begin to glow, including Disraeli, who spoke before. But only five of them rise, one of them remains sitting.

Harry S. Truman. *The familiar bespectacled face with the prominent nose and a smile resembling a grin. Before him, on the desk, are several ties he failed to sell when running a men's clothing store during the depression, and a sign reading "the buck stops here".* Leadership is the ability to get men to do what they don't want to do, and like it.

Niccolo Machiavelli. *Short-cut hair, highly intelligent eyes, thin lips, expensive but simple clothes. Surprisingly, he does not hold his infamous "Il Principe" in his hand, just a pair of gloves; this is supposed to convey that he has written other, quite different books than the one he is best known for. He speaks excellent English, rather than beautiful but antiquated Florentine.* There is nothing more difficult to take in hand, more perilous to conduct, or more uncertain in its success, than to take the lead in the introduction of a new order of things.

Franklin Delano Roosevelt. *He is the one who cannot rise, due to his polio. Flashes a broad smile with a cigarette-holder clenched between his teeth. He exudes energy, which contradicts what he says.* It is a terrible thing to look back over your shoulder when you are trying to lead – and find no one standing there.

Benjamin Disraeli, Earl of Beaconsfield. I must follow the people. Am I not their leader?

Lao-tsu. *Figure with sparse beard and hair, dressed in what seem like rags, not unlike some old hippie in a modern city. But serene, mildly smiling, fascinating face. Desists from looking at Confucius, his rival.* He who wants to lead men must position himself behind or below them.

Joseph Arthur Comte de Gobineau. *The arch-racist, stout supporter of individualism in politics, holds a copy of his book « Essai sur l'inégalité des races humaines ». Winks to his idol Richard Wagner, who, being wax, ignores him.* Un peuple a toujours besoin d'un homme qui comprenne sa volonté, la résume, l'explique, et le mène où il doit aller.

All six nod to the others in appreciation of their respective wisdoms, then return to wax.

Act. How did Lao-tsu get into this group? He was no politician.

Spe. Obviously by courtesy of Eclectus, who did not want Lao-tsu's contribution to be overlooked. - But start commenting on what these people said, Actus.

Act. Truman knew that some of the measures a leader must take will be unpopular. But he also knew that a leader must not shy away from such measures. Instead, he must try to persuade the recalcitrant. That is not easy. Machiavelli also knew that, as we just heard.

Spe. And persuasion can fail; that is the situation Roosevelt described. - Now to Disraeli. His point, I think, is this. A political leader is unlikely to succeed if he tries to act against the will of the people. Conversely, nothing guarantees the success of a politician more than if he gets identified with a broad popular movement the time of which has come.

Act. I must qualify that, Spectus. - Popular will can be in the people's interest, but not necessarily. A wise political leader will not spearhead a popular movement he clearly perceives as detrimental to the people. He will rather risk unpopularity by imposing his own well-thought-through policy. So I cannot agree with Disraeli. Nor with Lao-tsu, for that matter. A leader is not there to follow the people, he is there to lead it.

Spe. But, Actus, you advocate shared goals. If the people want one thing and their leader something else, there are no shared goals. No common purpose. Your logic collapses.

Act. It does not, Spectus. In business, it is not the team or the corporation that formulate goals: the team-leader and the corporate head do it. In politics, it is not the electorate that sets goals: political leaders must do that. The wishes of the people are generally hazy, diffuse, unspecific. Their leaders must give contour to what is hazy, condense what is diffuse, clarify what is unspecific. And if the leaders are able and wise, they will know how to persuade the people to share their convictions and accept the measures and goals they defined for them.

Spe. Yet, in politics, I see a danger that is largely absent in business. And that is where Gobineau comes in, the participant who spoke last. - At first sight, Gobineau's position is sensible. He calls for leaders who can perceive what the people want, formulate those wants, set aims in accordance with those wants, and then lead the people to reach those aims. There are many examples in History for such a successful symbiosis between leaders and their people.

Act. I agree with that view. History is not shaped by impersonal forces. It is individuals that cause and shape events. There are undercurrents, but they will be expressed only if and when individuals act to bring them out in the open and give them form.

Spe. Yet, Actus, there is also a sinister side to this. There were, and still are, political leaders who call themselves interpreters of the will of the people, and for that reason get support from the people. But once in power, they further not the aims of the people, but their own. Not seldom they precipitate their people, whose aims they purportedly embodied, into catastrophe. So Gobineau's tenet is ambiguous, because political leadership can be misused.

Act. That is not quite right. What can be misused is power, not leadership.

Spe. All right, then: this is the right moment to leave the topic of leadership and enter the topic of power. - Can you spell out the main links between leadership and power, Actus?

Power

Act. Leadership can only be exercised from a position of power. There can hardly be leadership if it is not supported by power. But power can be beneficial only when coupled with wise leadership. Power without wise leadership tends to hurt those subjected to that power.

Spe. Can you name just a few of the benefits that accrue when power is linked with wise leadership?

Act. In business or in politics?

Spe. In both.

Act. Business first. You may remember, Spectus, that I said a good business leader inspires, guides and rules. We may attribute inspiring and guiding to wise leadership, ruling to power. A business leader will use his power above all to ensure control, efficiency and discipline. - In politics, wise leadership will ensure that the law is respected, power will ensure that the law is enforced. The people will then have the right and the possibility to do whatever the law permits; their lives will be improved, without them being run. Someone once condensed all this in a well-put formula: When those in power are just, then what is just will have power.

Spe. And what happens when there is power but no wise leadership?

Act. Then only those who have power will benefit.

Spe. Actus: I can think of a certain number of theses in connection with power. Let me try to formulate them. May I ask you, after I have put forth each of my theses, to comment on them. Accept them, reject them, modify them, as you wish. In other words, let us try to have a hopefully constructive dialog on the subject.

Act. Excellent idea.

Spe. Here, then, is my first thesis. - Power, concentrated in the hands of one man, is advantageous and desirable, because it ensures stability and order, and avoids chaos. Consequently, the one in power should be allowed to rule as he sees fit.

Act. This thesis will be fully supported by dictators, tyrants, absolute monarchs and unscrupulous businessmen. It has its best known expression in the famous declaration of Louis XIV: "L'état, c'est moi!" I reject this thesis. No-one should be allowed to exercise power as he sees fit, without any checks on what he is doing. No-one should have absolute, unchecked power.

Spe. I agree with you. All right, then, here is my second thesis, introducing such a check on power. My thesis is this: Power should only be given to a man who is reputed and proven to be virtuous. His virtue will restrain him from abusing the power he has been invested with.

Act. What you mean, in fact, is that power should be given only to those who can be trusted. Fine. I agree with that. A trustworthy man, given power over others, is not likely to lose it over himself. Yet, one cannot really be certain about that. So your thesis has a weak point. It is difficult to tell whether a man, even if he has the reputation of being virtuous, will remain so *after* he has become powerful. Often the real test of a man's character comes after he has been invested with power. And he may fail the test. But by then it may be too late to retrieve the power he has been given. So: I agree with your thesis up to a point. But checks on power in the form of internal virtues alone appear to me to be insufficient.

Spe. A valid objection. Well, then, here is my third thesis. - Power in the hands of one man has definite advantages, such as ensuring stability and order; it is therefore desirable. However, power should be given to a man only if accompanied by external checks on that power. Those external checks must be based on mechanisms that are activated as soon as there is suspicion of abuse of power. Thus not the internal values of the incumbent, but external mechanisms will keep him from abuse.

Act. This is your best thesis yet, Spectus, and the one closest to reality. Power, indeed, needs external checks. Abuse can only be avoided if the one invested with power is constantly being checked by an external counter-power. That counter-power must be strong enough, if need be, to impede the abuse. I fully agree with this thesis of yours. - But may I suggest that you combine thesis number two and number three into one single thesis. Let power be given to men who have proven themselves to be virtuous, but let even such men be submitted to constant external checks. This, in fact, is what the world should be evolving to.

Spe. It should. But does it? And that question leads me to my next thesis. A radical one, but one that has been repeated time and again by different observers. The simplest version of it is: Power corrupts. Maybe you, Citatia, can give us a brief overview of other versions of the same idea.

Cit. Power changes profoundly the one who has it. - Power changes the character of a man who was virtuous before he became powerful. - Power tends to corrupt the minds of those who possess it. - Powerful men are almost always bad men. - The greater the power, the more likely its abuse. - Power corrupts, and absolute power corrupts absolutely. - The powerful do not care in which direction the car is travelling, so long as they remain in the driver's seat.

Spe. Thank you, Citatia. Those who agree that power corrupts are obviously legion. They all reached the sober conclusion that few of those in power can resist the temptation to abuse it. The greater the power, the greater that temptation.

Act. I cannot completely reject this thesis of yours, Spectus. There is a lot of truth in it. I can only claim that I personally know many cases where your thesis does not apply. There are still a lot of uncorrupted men in powerful positions. Of course I cannot tell whether their number increases or diminishes; let us hope it is the former. - But let me point out something. According to your thesis, the worst case is unchecked, totally unlimited power: no internal virtues of the incumbent, no powerful external checks to restrain him, no fear of punishments, no fear of consequences. That kind of unlimited power can become a kind of aphrodisiac. It may, at the end, overshadow reason. Thus those who reach that stage tend to eliminate themselves.

Spe. *Smiles.* Actus, the optimist. - But let me end with two more theses. They are well known adages. One is: Money is power. The other is: Knowledge is power. What are your comments on these, Actus?

Act. *Thinks briefly.* It all depends on how you spend the money or how you use your knowledge. - If you spend the money on a cruise around the world, I can see no connection with power whatever. If you use it to support a political party whose aims you find reasonable, or use it as a bribe to secure a business deal, you exercise power; in a good sense in the first case, in a questionable sense in the second case. - The same with knowledge. Like in the case of money, it depends on how you put your knowledge to use. Some amass knowledge without wanting to convert it into power. Others amass knowledge in order to gain power. Knowledge per se is neutral; but combined with the urge for power it can turn into an instrument that serves power. And whether the combination of knowledge and power will have beneficial or evil effects fully depends on who uses that combination.

Spe. *Thoughtful.* You know, Actus, this last remark of yours triggers a thought in me. There is something missing at this symposium. Up to now we assumed that wisdom is ethically clean, something that has to do with good people. We never connected wisdom with evil people. But, let us face it, there are evil people for whom the wisdoms of the good guys do not apply. Remember our definition of wisdom: it is the "ability to act and think utilizing knowledge, experience, understanding and insight". That definition is completely free of ethical considerations. It holds for good guys as well as for bad guys. - Just once, therefore, I would welcome a look at the other side, the dark side, that of the bad guys. The subject we are discussing, power, would be the ideal topic for such an experiment. It would enlarge the scope of this symposium, because it would help us understand the mentality of those who seek power in order to abuse it.

Act. Exciting idea, Spectus. But we would need a bad guy. A representative of the wisdoms of darkness. Who could that be? What about Machiavelli, present at this seminar?

Spe. He wouldn't do. He would just quote passages from his "Principe". He has not been programmed to abstract. No: what we would need is not a historic figure, but someone programmed like the Higginses. A machine that was fed with dirty tricks, with moral-free wisdoms on power, capable of giving us an abstract of what he was fed with.

Act. I reckon Eclectus forgot to create such a one. Pity.

Actus is mistaken. A hitherto unseen trap-door opens just in front of Actus' and Spectus' desks. A faint red glow issues from it, and a figure slowly emerges from below. As soon as he is at room level, the trap door closes. The figure is clad all in black, in a tightly fitting costume somewhat reminiscent of deep sea divers. There is a slight hint of two small red horns on the figure's forehead. He is tall, bears himself with grace and elegance, despite his simple costume. His face is dark, his features hard and smooth, intelligent and repulsive at the same time. Since there is no desk, there is no name plate. But written on the left side of the figure's costume, like on uniforms of army men, is a name in red characters: "Mephisto".

Actus and Spectus burst out laughing, delighted by the theatricality of the scene and by Eclectus' prompt fulfilment of their wish.

Mephisto. *Fixes Actus and Spectus with a chilly regard.* You laugh. But you will not laugh for long. You want something from me, and I can give it to you. But you will have to pay. Do you presume that I reveal my secrets without any payment in return? *(Takes a parchment* *from some hidden pocket, together with an old-fashioned red feather-pen.)* Before we start, you will have to sign this. Only then shall I attend to your wish. *(He begins to approach Actus and Spectus, holding the parchment and the red pen in front of him.)*

A voice. *It issues from behind the wall with the holograph, vibrant with authority.* Cut it out, Mephisto. Do your job and get gone.

Mephisto jerks, bends, and suddenly looks like Laurence Olivier interpreting Richard the Third. But almost immediately he resumes his former self; he is once again the elegant, fascinating black figure. He puts parchment and pen away and starts to walk slowly along the aisles of the seminar room, beginning to speak like a schoolmaster addressing a class. His voice is deep, pleasant, persuading, almost hypnotic.

Meph. You all possess powers you never dreamed of. You can do things you never thought you could do. There are no limits, except those in your own mind. I shall introduce you to the keys to power. I normally request a counter-payment, but I doubt that anyone in this room would profit from my wisdoms anyway. I see two souls here who would refuse to do so, and a lot of persons with no souls at all who would not be capable to do so. I see some of my former disciples sitting here, but I miss others, some of the really successful ones. I regret that those are not present. But it is your seminar, not mine.

Act. *Whispers to Spectus.* The first part of his introduction, the one about the power in us, could have been made by some Indian guru. This goes to show how ambiguous power is: it depends, indeed, who uses it.

Mephisto has heard, and turns slightly to Actus.

Meph. I know that you regard me as evil, Mr Actus. But what is evil? Evil is what springs of weakness. And what is good? Good is what augments the feeling of power, the will to attain power. Life is nothing but an instinct for power.

There is a slight commotion as Nietzsche, sitting in the audience, briefly but angrily glows in protest. Mephisto has borrowed his definitions of good and evil, without reference to authorship. But maybe Mephisto was the original author?

Meph. *Ignores Nietzsche.* So I will start by telling you how to grab power. - An aspirant to power will endeavour to win people, so that he can later manipulate them. He will never offend those who matter. He will never outshine his superiors, but flatter them; subtly, not obviously. He will make his bosses feel clever, even if this involves making himself appear less smart than he really is. At all times he will stay visible to his superiors; he will be conspicuous, ubiquitous, helpful, never lost in the crowd. - To his peers, he will pose as a loyal friend, but will carefully catalogue their weaknesses and vanities, so that he can use these later to apply pressure on them. He will never let himself be seen in the company of the unfortunate or the unlucky. He will use without scruples the know-how and the expertise of others, but will arrange things so that the credit is attributed to himself. - Gradually, he will make others depend on him. Making himself necessary to them will be the key to achieve this. When he, himself, needs help, he will not ask for it as a favour, nor will he remind his potential helper of services he has rendered him in the past. He will, instead, appeal to the helper's self-interest, point out the advantages the helper will gain through helping him. Thus he never enters into a moral obligation towards anyone. - He will covertly create dissent, and then arrange to appear as the peacemaker, in order to increase his prestige. - He will never reveal all his talents, nor everything he knows. He will meticulously plan his actions all the way to his goal, but will carefully hide his true purpose.

Mephisto makes a pause, to allow to sink in all he said. He then continues with his lecture, still walking up and down the aisles.

Meph. If the aspirant to power follows these precepts, he will, slowly but surely, attain his first goal: a position of power. He now has to enlarge that position. His second and final goal is *unlimited* power. - To attain it, he must discard all moral restraint. He will acknowledge just one principle: utter selfishness. He will seek for himself, and for himself alone, the highest possible advantages. Only if he adheres to the principle of utter selfishness will he be able to attain the highest, most enjoyable degree of power: that of absolute, unrestricted rule. Nothing is comparable to the enjoyment of unchecked, arbitrary power. Those silly fools who possess power but remain decent, restrained, ethical, will never know what real joys power can bring. - The absolutely powerful will, of course, provoke odium. But to endure odium is one of the most important lessons to be learned by the one who possesses unlimited power.

This time it is Seneca who shows anger by briefly glowing, for the same reason as Nietzsche. Decidedly, Mephisto is either a great plagiariser or a great original author.

Meph. And now: here are my precepts for consolidating and keeping unlimited power. - The powerful will assemble around himself a circle of collaborators; he rules through this circle. The collaborators will be fully dependent on him, being his creation. They will be devoted, not too clever, not too strong, neither of them too sure that he will still be in favour tomorrow. The most loyal will be put in key positions. But that does not protect them: if any collaborator makes a mistake, be he ever so close, he will be dealt with ruthlessly. Anyone who makes a serious mistake tarnishes the reputation of the one in power, his image of strength and infallibility, and must therefore be eliminated. - The one in power will destroy all opponents. Not just subdue them: annihilate them. Fully, mercilessly. He knows that a half-defeated adversary will seek revenge. At first, though, he will appear conciliating, open, even generous to his opponents, thereby gradually loosening their defences. At other times he will anger them, provoke them, causing them to make mistakes. Then, unexpectedly, he attacks. - But the one in power never dirties his own hands with the blood of his adversaries. He leaves the crushing of his victims to his collaborators. Should it become necessary, he will even sacrifice the one who did the dirty job on his behalf. - The one in power will not commit himself to anything. He will readily change sides, betray his allies, if he sees an advantage for himself. He will build an image of being unpredictable, incalculable, so that no-one can foresee his next moves. Thus he will retain control over all his options. - He will never concede a mistake, a setback, a defeat; he will make them look as calculation and tarn them as victories. - He will not be familiar with anyone, not even with his closest collaborators. He will appear remote, difficult to access. One who has absolute power is often lonely, but he does not mind. He has compensations enough. He suffices to himself.

Mephisto walks down towards the front of the seminar room and stands directly over the trap door. He fixes Actus and Spectus.

Meph. I know that you two disagree with what I said. I even know that you abhor my precepts. But I also know that you will spend the rest of this evening trying to find models of society which restrict the powers of the powerful. But you will not succeed. You cannot devise foolproof methods to check the rise of the ones with a will for power, nor fully control them once they have obtained power. There will always be successful disciples of mine acting in this world, gentlemen. I, Mephisto, shall see to that.

The trap door opens, red light pouring from it. Mephisto sinks into the floor, with a haughty look, elegant as ever. Before the door closes after him, a deep, ironic laughter is heard from below.

Actus and Spectus remain thoughtful for a moment, without speaking.

Spe. A sinister fellow. But an unhappy one. He personifies absolute evil. And absolute evil not only disregards moral frontiers; it also dries up all capacity for experiencing pleasure. Despite Mephisto's claims to the contrary.

Act. *Preoccupied.* He made an eerie prophesy: that we shall spend the rest of the evening discussing society models, but shall find none where power abuse is brought entirely under control.

Spe. *Sighs.* He is probably right. Human societies are far from perfect. But they can be improved. And so we arrive at the last topic of the day: society models. Or, rather, wisdoms behind various models of society that have been developed and tried over the course of History.

Act. But how should we go about examining such models? We are neither sociologists nor politicians, and the subject is huge. If we let our fellow participants loose on it, it would probably end in chaos.

Spe. *Scratches his head.* Aye, there is the rub.

Models for Society

Act. Time for another machine like the Higginses, I believe. *(Addresses the wall with the revolving holograph.)* Eclectus, you have helped us before. Help us again, please.

A figure begins to glow and rises from behind its desk. He looks smooth and frail and is clad in nothing but underpants. He is reminiscent of a shop-window dummy displaying boxer shorts. But, to compensate that oddity, he has a huge forehead, wears heavy gold-rimmed spectacles, and has a decidedly intellectual appearance. On the desk before him is a name-plate: "Politicus".

Politicus. Good evening, gentlemen. Please do not take offence at my clothes, or rather at the lack of them: it is to facilitate my work, as you will presently see. My name is "Politicus". However, I shall adopt other names as we proceed. I have been created by order of Mr Eclectus, who anticipated that you will be needing me. I am an expert in political theory. I have been fed with all political theories in existence, therefore with all models for human societies devised since early civilization. I have also been programmed to summarize, for your benefit, the major traits of each model. *(He takes off his glasses, breathes on them, then wipes them on his underpants.)* Of course, I know much more than my summaries will reveal; but I have been asked to be brief. So, I am sorry to say, you will benefit only from a tiny fraction of what I know. *(He puts his glasses back with a somewhat self-satisfied look on his face.)* I am at your disposal, gentlemen. We may begin whenever you wish.

Actus and Spectus cannot help smiling at this presentation, coming as it did from a technically astounding, half-naked, intellectual-looking shop-window dummy. However, they are happy. Once again a difficult situation was resolved, thanks to Eclectus' foresight.

Spe. Welcome in our midst, Politicus. I suggest we proceed as follows. We shall look at the society models fed into you in chronological order. We shall start with the Greeks and end up with the 20th Century. Please leave out minor models, concentrate on the really prominent ones. Present all major features of each model, but not longer than for two to three minutes. Then leave Actus and me time for comments on the wisdoms behind the model you have just presented. You may, of course, comment on those wisdoms yourself. Understood?

Pol. *Looks slightly offended.* Of course I have understood, sir. Please note that I am a highly evolved machine. You, in contrast, are merely human.

Spe. *In a low voice to Actus.* This fellow is more conceited than Citatia. Ah, the conceit that comes from too much knowledge!

Act. *Also in a low voice.* Proverbius also knows a lot, yet he is not conceited. I wonder how it comes that these automata develop such specific personalities.

Spe. *Whispers back.* I presume Eclectus himself did not foresee the side-effects of artificial intelligence. *(In a normal voice.)* Here we go, Politicus. Kindly present your first model.

Politicus dives behind his desk, but re-emerges after a few seconds, revealing himself to be an accomplished actor. He is clad in a toga, with a broad but slightly damaged nose, thick, curly beard, square, imperious face. He quickly exchanges the name plate on his desk: it now reads "Plato".

Politicus as Plato. Man has a lowly self that seeks gratification, an active self that seeks distinction, and a philosophical self that seeks wisdom. Society must be organized to reflect this tripartite nature of man. Peasants, craftsmen and salesmen provide for the gratification of natural appetites; police and army protect society; the wise govern. - Society would best be ruled by a god. But since this is not possible, the god is replaced by law, based on moral precepts handed down by tradition. Everyone is subordinated to the law, including the wise who govern. - The wise reach governing positions by accumulating knowledge and insights, obtained through hard intellectual discipline and a thorough study of the sciences. Thus those who govern are philosophers. - All members of society must understand and support the moral precepts upon which the law is based. Therefore, these precepts must be taught to the young from an early age. Everyone must realize that he has a moral obligation to contribute to the society he is a member of, each according to his aptitude and social position and to the best of his ability. - Given these considerations, the preferred model for society is either oligarchy, meaning the rule of a spiritual elite guided by law and justice, or monarchy, the rule of a philosopher-king. Democracy is to be discarded, except in societies where there is no law, and where, therefore, the common will of the people must replace the law. Tyranny is the worst model of all, since it is the rule of a fallible and selfish man guided neither by law, nor by justice, nor by moral tradition.

Politicus shoves the name-plate "Plato" under his desk, rips off his false beard and toga, disappears behind his desk, and emerges a few seconds later clad only in his boxer shorts.

Spe. Good summary of Plato's political ideas; I must praise you, Politicus. - Let us retain the essential in Plato's model. He is against democracy; he is for the rule of a philosopher-king or an elite, guided by law; the law, in turn, is based on traditional ethics. The people have no part in government, but a moral obligation to contribute to society the best they can. - Is all this wise?

Act. Partly. But mostly not. I think it is impracticable.

Spe. So do I. Plato's model lacks wisdom in one essential respect: it has an idealized conception of human nature. Plato assumes that the people are willing to get classified into categories and then contribute, unselfishly, to the benefit of all. Like ants or bees. But people are not ants nor bees. They want to work primarily for their own benefit, as I pointed out when we discussed work. - And then there is another idealized feature in Plato's model. I know of no philosopher-king in History. There is a simple reason for that. Those who want to rule are ambitious doers, not philosophers. Those who are philosophers, have no disposition to rule. Thus the philosopher-king is a theoretical figure with an internal contradiction: it is two opposite personalities united in one man, which is absurd.

Act. There is a further idealization in Plato. The philosopher-king, or the wise oligarchy, are supposed to respect the law. But if they decide not to respect it, there is no counter-force to deter them. Mere written words will not check a king who decides to abuse his power. For Plato's model to function, we must assume that those who govern are guided and checked by inner virtue alone. This was your second thesis, Spectus, when we discussed power; we doubted that it would function.

Spe. Let us, then, discard most of Plato's model as ideal, rather than realistic. Nevertheless, there are some features in his model that were handed down over the centuries, and surfaced later in other society models. I guess we shall meet those features again. *(Turns to Politicus.)* But tell me, Politicus: were there any significant theoretical models of society before Plato?

Politicus. No. In ancient times it was taken for granted that there is a ruler and there are the ruled. If improvements were suggested, they were not attempts to improve society, but to improve the ruler. Confucius, among others, tried to make the rulers wiser. *(Politicus disappears behind his desk, then re-*emerges *looking like an exact copy of the "real" Confucius sitting in the seminar room. But Politicus is a tick too late. The "real" Confucius has started to glow, has risen, and has begun talking.)*

Confucius. To rule means to do things right: if a ruler does right, who will dare to do wrong? So the ruler will be decent, as to be an example to his people. If the ruler wishes good, so will the ruled. The wise ruler will use the natural wealth of his people to make the people even wealthier. He will select carefully the tasks he imposes upon the ruled and will not ask for work to be finished before it can be easily accomplished. He will never belittle those he rules, nor be arrogant towards them. He will not kill; but if he must, he will tell the reason for it. He will not give unconsidered commands. He will not be miserly where praise and recompense are due. *(He bows his head briefly to his "alter ego" Politicus and returns to wax.)*

Politicus. *Seems at first to be somewhat peeved that he missed an opportunity to show what he knows, but then reveals his good nature by disappearing behind his desk and re-emerging again as his half-naked self.*

Act. Quite down-to-earth, Confucius, compared to Plato, isn't he? No philosopher-king there. Just a pragmatic ruler. Yet, our main objection remains: the only check on Confucius' ruler is his inner virtue. - But let me revert briefly to Plato. Politicus told us he discarded democracy. But I thought democracy was invented by the Greeks.

Spe. Democracy, in Plato's time, meant that assemblies of citizens were called upon to decide on issues of general interest. Plato saw a danger in this system. He realized how easily mass-emotions could play a role in popular decisions; how easily those assemblies of citizens could get under the influence of demagogues. Plato simply did not believe that the people were wise enough to make the right decisions. His pupil, Aristotle, didn't either. Aristotle even asserted that democracy is but an attempt of the poor to rule over the rich. He condemned it as unjust and saw in it an offence against social harmony.

Act. There are some, in fact many, who still think along those lines. - But tell me: how did all these ideas fare during the Roman Empire?

Spe. In the days of the Republic, the senate represented the patricians, the tribunes represented the people. They were supposed to rule jointly, guided by moral tradition. However, this was rarely so. Many senators and tribunes were corrupt and sought their own advantage. Only when in great danger did they remember that they were jointly responsible for the welfare of Rome. - Then the Republic was replaced by the Caesars. That shows, in fact, that the republican model was not strong enough to survive. What followed were many hundred years of unchecked ruling by one man. - Nevertheless, the Romans did make progress in one respect: they formulated some excellent laws. They realized, like Plato did, that Law is an essential feature of a well-functioning society. Even though some claim that in Rome there was much law but little justice.

Act. What happened after the Romans were gone? How did society models look like in the Middle Ages? Were they wiser than their predecessors?

Spe. Let us ask Politicus.

This time Politicus does not make an attempt to disguise himself. He represents no-one. This is Politicus the scholar.

Politicus. You correctly observed, gentlemen, that it is wiser to restrain those in power by external forces, rather than to expect that their internal virtues will guide them. In the Middle Ages, a model of society emerged that attempted to put this wisdom into practice. The emperor had the power; the restraining counter-force was meant to be the Church. - At first, this model seemed to work. The Church played, indeed, the role of the moral and spiritual controller of the worldly power. But slowly, under ambitious popes, the model became corrupted. Two worldly powers emerged instead of one; Emperor and Church were fighting each other to gain influence. - Some people got fed up with this state of affairs, left society and founded separate societies of their own. The Church condemned them as heretics. But I will not go into a discussion of such heretic society models, fascinating though they are; they were designed for a minority of puritan souls, not for society as a whole. - The lesson we should draw from these medieval calamities is that the State and the Church must have their own, clearly defined, separate roles: it is detrimental if those roles get confounded.

Spe. A wise lesson, indeed. - Can we move on to the Renaissance, Politicus?

Politicus. The Renaissance was more interested in the individual than in society. Machiavelli advised his prince to practice “realpolitik”. He did not give him advice on how to improve society. Francis Bacon, a pupil of Machiavelli, supported absolutism and criticised democracy. - Other thinkers did come up with new society models, but they went too far. Their suggestions were impossible to implement. Thomas Morus, for example, set up a model that was even more idealistic than that of Plato: private property abolished, money abolished, the difference between manual and intellectual labour cancelled, general tolerance reigns, people are ready and willing to sacrifice themselves for the community. Tommaso Campanella, a Platonist in Christian garb, suggested a society model based on metaphysical laws and ruled by a priest. - All such models are nothing but utopia.

Spe. Indeed. - But let us move on to times after the Renaissance. And when, Politicus, are we going to have the pleasure to see one of your fascinating impersonations again?

Politicus. Now!

He disappears behind his desk and re-emerges after five seconds as an old man. Bald head, hair hanging down loosely from each side, narrow eyes with a distrustful look, pinched lips, white collar, the attire of a 17th Century Puritan. He holds a book: "Leviathan". He puts a name-plate on the desk: "Thomas Hobbes".

Politicus as Hobbes. Unlike animals, man can anticipate future wants. If he stilled his hunger, he knows he will become hungry again. So he attempts to secure his future needs. He does that by trying to subdue everything he encounters. Thus, left to himself, man will fight all other men: "bellum omnium contra omnes". The consequence: each man fears all other men. Thus the two basic human passions are fear and the desire for power. Man seeks security for himself through power, but fears all other men who try to do the same. - All this plunges man into a crisis, the outcome of which is that reason comes to dominate passion. Man decides to give up his urge for power against a guarantee that he may live without fear. Men thus enter into a covenant with each other, promising to give up their individual wills to a central and sovereign power, that ensures peace, calm and order. They transfer their own individual wills upon this central power. The covenant gives legitimacy to this power and a mandate to subdue individual ambitions, the principal danger to peace. - The central power must be made as strong as possible, since only then can it be effective. Once constituted, the central power is no longer accountable for its actions to the individuals whose social contract brought it about. - The central power can be a monarchy, an aristocracy, or a commonwealth. Democracy is rejected, because it weakens the central power in the exercise of its functions. The best form is monarchy, since in that model the central power, the guarantor of order, is concentrated in just one person. Even tyranny is acceptable, provided the members of the society agree to have it.

Politicus has finished. He grabs the name-plate and sinks out of view behind his desk.

Act. I object to the basic premise of this model. The image of man as an aggressive egoist, constantly fearing his fellow beings, is false, or at least grossly exaggerated. Furthermore, the model opens the door to arbitrary, unchecked central power, authorized to decide who is dangerous and who must be eliminated. Individual freedom is non-existent. This is a sad, gloomy model.

Spe. Valid objections, Actus. Though let me point out that, according to Hobbes, the central power is not supposed to regulate every action of the individuals who enter the covenant. There are a few unregulated domains left, where citizens may act as they please. However, I agree that the model is essentially gloomy. It sacrifices individual will to the hope of living in peace. But that peace resembles a dungeon.

Act. So we need alternatives to Hobbes. What, or who, are they?

Spe. Politicus will tell.

A respectable figure emerges from behind Politicus' desk, dressed in 17th Century clothes. He radiates intelligence and honesty. He could be a doctor (he actually is) or a philosopher (he is) or a man of letters (which he also is). One cannot help feeling respect. He puts a name-plate on the desk: "John Locke".

Politicus as Locke. Man is not a purely egoistic creature; he is also governed by many positive sentiments, including love and a desire for justice. Above all, he is an individual, with individual rights; he is not to lose those rights when he enters into society. Thus the foremost duty of the state is to protect the rights and freedoms of individuals. - These rights and freedoms are, among others: to build and keep property; to think as one wishes; to worship as one wishes; to speak one's mind openly; to freely assemble; to be physically protected. In fact, the only freedom an individual gives up when entering into society is to judge and punish his fellow men. - All individuals are equal before the law. The state must protect this equality. - Freedom and individual rights do not, however, mean unchecked liberty or licence. Freedom and rights are limited by the necessity to honour the freedom and rights of others. - The state must not have absolute power; society models that advocate this are to be rejected. In order to avoid absolute power and its abuse, the central power must be divided. This is to be achieved by separating it into a power to legislate and a power to execute. The legislative power must be transferred to an elected assembly. The executive power is best held by a government headed by a monarch. - Since the legislative assembly itself may be in a position to abuse power, it is to be partitioned further. It will have two chambers: the representatives of the people (house of commons) and the representatives of the nobility (house of lords). Both chambers have perfectly equal rights when passing laws. To further ensure that there is a balance of powers, no legislation can be passed without the consent of the monarch. - The executive power is conditional on whether it advances the public good. If it does not, the people have the right to withdraw their trust in this power. This means that the people have the right to overthrow their government in case they distrust it. - The state is essentially profane. There must be a clear separation between Church and State. No power in the State is to be sanctioned by the Church, no monarch is to reign by divine right. The State is concerned only with things of this world. However, it accepts all religions as equally valid.

Politicus/Locke makes a brief bow and sinks out of sight.

Act. *Applauds.* Bravo. I agree with practically every sentence in this presentation. This is the kind of clear, down-to-earth, pragmatic wisdom I hoped to hear while discussing society models.

Spe. *Smiles.* I am a fan of Locke, too. You know, it is amazing: Hobbes and Locke were contemporaries, experiencing the same turmoil around them, yet they came up with completely different remedies. - Incidentally: if Locke sounds modern, it is because many existing constitutions were inspired by him. Substitute "monarch" by "President", and you find Locke behind the constitution of the United States. Many European constitutions took over some of his thoughts almost verbatim.

Act. But something must have gone wrong, since Locke's sound ideas were not universally followed. There must have been a rival to Locke, less rational, less wise. Who was Locke's antipode?

Spe. Politicus knows who that was.

Politicus' hand appears from behind his desk and places a name-plate on the desk: "Jean-Jacques Rousseau". Then Politicus himself appears, dressed exactly like the "real" Rousseau sitting in the room. There is a brief flash from the "genuine" Rousseau, obviously to compliment Politicus' for his impersonation of him.

Politicus as Rousseau. All power that does not proceed directly from the people arises from the difference between rich and poor. Government then merely serves to ensure that the privileges of the rich are maintained. Society must therefore be based on one principle only: the absolute sovereign power of the people. This sovereign power cannot be delegated to a legislative body, nor to an executive body; nor can it be divided. - The individual must fuse his will with that of the people. By so doing he becomes part of the general will. Thus the only will the people are subjected to is its own. The people are the ruler as well as the ruled. - The transfer of individual will to the common will is a covenant, a social contract. From this transfer emerges a community. All rights proceed from this community. Insisting on individual rights not sanctioned by the community means falling back into egoisms, selfishness and decay. - All laws, all acts of state must be approved by popular assemblies. A popular assembly is the gathering of all members of a community entitled to vote. A community based on this procedure is a Republic. The head of state in a Republic is the popular assembly itself. All society models other than a Republic are subjected to the power of particular interest groups, not to the power of the people. - However, since laws and procedures cannot be formulated by popular assemblies, they will be pre-formulated and submitted to the assembly for approval. This pre-formulation is to be done by counsellors fully committed to the common good and having no individual interests of their own. Their counselling role is only temporary. - There will be an executive, but its role is merely to implement the will of the people, as manifested at the popular assemblies. The executive never rules and is fully accountable to the sovereign, that is, to the people.

Politicus /Rousseau pops out of view.

Act. How could such mumbo-jumbo be taken seriously, after the lucid proposals of Locke?

Spe. *Smiles.* You call it mumbo-jumbo. But that mumbo-jumbo closely resembles Lincoln's famous formula: government of the people, by the people, for the people.

Act. *A bit impatient.* I am a pragmatist, Spectus. What Rousseau proposes is absolute self-government by the people. You don't have to be an expert in cybernetics to know that this cannot be: no system can regulate itself. It needs an outside agent to do it. Rousseau misses reality when he presumes that a society can self-govern itself. It is simply not feasible.

Spe. That is not quite correct, Actus. Some big issues, concerning a whole nation, are decided by referenda. And even small issues can be settled by popular decision, on the level of cities or counties; some cantons in Switzerland do that all the time. - But I agree that Rousseau went too far. You cannot settle *every* issue, approve *every* law by popular vote, as he suggests. The wise will acknowledge in Rousseau what is feasible and forget about the rest.

Act. But I find that practically nothing in Rousseau is feasible. Take, for instance, those counsellors who are supposed to pre-formulate laws to be approved by popular assemblies. Rousseau's model works only if those counsellors are truly committed to the common good; if they are not, they can manipulate politics at their will.

Spe. Once again, Actus, that is only partly right. In several modern countries a referendum can be started by individuals, who raise enough signatures demanding that a certain issue, ignored by the politicians, be dealt with. Such individuals are very much like Rousseau's pre-formulating counsellors. - No, we cannot wholly discard Rousseau. And we should not be too hard on him. He was an outcast who sought freedom for all, and did so using great language. He was also a pessimist, who knew that his model won't work. So he projected it into the past, and alleged that it was how primitive but noble savages organized themselves. Oddly enough, anthropologists later discovered that such models did in fact exist in small, primitive communities. Where Rousseau went wrong was advocating that it is possible to transplant his model from small, rural communities unto large, modern societies. By suggesting that this can be done, he appealed to emotion rather than to reason. - But let us leave Rousseau and look at what happened after him - and, to some extent, *because* of him. It is a fascinating and highly didactic drama in several acts, full of lessons for the wise. Politicus: please give us a brief summary of political events in France after Rousseau.

Politicus re-emerges from behind his desk where he discarded his Rousseau outfit. He is clad in boxer shorts, but nevertheless manages to look scholarly.

Politicus. Rousseau's ideas had particular appeal in countries with a central power that showed signs of decay, and where, at the same time, the population was exposed to economic hardships. This was the case in France. The king, weak and under pressure, started the drama by allowing the estates-general to convene. The estates-general were composed of the nobility, the clergy, and the so-called third-estate, essentially townsmen. But then the third-estate declared itself to be the only true representative of the nation. The monarch, the nobility and the clergy reacted against this pretension, but not firmly enough. The result was the establishment of a constitutional monarchy, with the third-estate actually in power.

Spe. End of Act One.

Politicus. The third-estate then split itself into a moderate faction, the Gironde, and a radical faction, the Jacobins. The latter wanted to end the monarchy, abolish the nobility and clergy, and set up a Republic along the ideas of Rousseau.

Spe. End of Act Two.

Politicus. Now it was the Gironde that reacted too feebly against the Jacobins. There was a revolution within the revolution. The Jacobins revolted against the national assembly and installed their own rule, with Danton and Robespierre in charge. Thus a revolutionary minority, representing only one-tenth of the population of Paris, now held the power in the country. It claimed to be a government implementing the will of the people. It was, in fact, a dictatorship.

Spe. End of Act Three.

Politicus. It is now the Terror. Not only nobles are beheaded, including the king, but increasingly also members of the Jacobin camp itself. The revolution starts eating its own children. Danton is beheaded, Robespierre becomes sole dictator. He declares the cathedral of Notre Dame to be a Temple of Reason, and himself to be the Great Priest of the Almighty.

Spe. End of Act Four.

Politicus. As a reaction against the excesses of Robespierre and the Jacobins, Napoleon Bonaparte, the hero of many battles, conducts an uprising, ending in a coup. The Napoleonic phase of the French Revolution begins.

Spe. End of Act Five. Now, the epilogue.

Politicus. Napoleon first becomes dictator, then emperor. Monarchy is back. To be sure, the Napoleonic state is much better organized than the state of the Bourbons ever was. For one thing, laws are much more explicit. But Napoleon overvalues his strength and, finally, must abdicate. The Bourbon monarchy, with all its weaknesses, is back.

Spe. And thus we are back to where we started from. Within a few years, practically all models of society were tried and discarded one after the other, in a furious merry-go-round. But the French drama is not unique; it has been acted out, with slight variations, again and again during the course of History. The wise will draw lessons from that fact.

Act. What are those lessons, according to you, Spectus?

Spe. First: If a central power is removed by force from a society accustomed to having it, disorder, not democracy, usually follows. That disorder is very likely to end in an autocracy. - Second: In all revolutions there will always be a moderate faction and an extremist faction. The extremists, determined and without scruples, are likely to prevail. - Third, and this is good news: The extremists will not last long. The Robespierre's of this world tend to be short-lived. - Fourth: Revolutionists always claim to act in the name of and for the benefit of the people. That is simply not true. They seek power in order to implement an ideology. - Fifth and last, again a good news: The people will, covertly or openly, support those who promise to remove a central power perceived as abusive. - Others may derive different conclusions than I just did. But that proves that the French drama is full of fertile lessons.

Act. Indeed. - Where do we go from here, Spectus?

Spe. We could go into the details of political theories developed after Rousseau: capitalism, socialism, liberalism, marxism, fascism, and their effects on society. But that would take us too far. Besides, one thing has crystallized out of our discussion so far. Most society models can be classified into one of three categories: autocracy, democracy, utopia. Let us forget utopias. Then the two main rival models are autocracy and democracy. If we look around the world today, we see those two in operation, either in their pure form or as mixtures. - I presume that we consider democracy to be the better model. I suggest, therefore, that we define our remaining task as an attempt to answer the following question: why is democracy wiser than autocracy?

Act. Fine. - Let us deal with autocracy in its pure form first. Define the term, Politicus.

Autocracy

Politicus. Autocracy is the rule of one man, or of a small group of men, possessing absolute and unrestricted power.

Spe. How do autocracies originate?

Politicus. By a coup, by a manipulated election, or by a legally valid election. In the first two cases force is used. In the third case, democracy is turned into autocracy by the winner of the election. In the past, absolute monarchs needed legitimacy. Today, modern autocrats need the pretence of democracy, since otherwise international sanctions might follow.

Spe. You said an autocracy can also mean the unrestricted rule by a few men.

Politicus. Yes, that is formally true. But in all autocracies there is one strong man who calls the shots - if you will excuse me for the rather trivial expression.

Spe. You are excused. - From what your tell us, Politicus, we should focus on two kinds of autocrat: the one arrived at his position by force, the other through a valid election.

Politicus. May I suggest, sir, that we regard those two cases as one. It is immaterial how an autocrat reached his position. What we need to examine is what he does, or does not do, once he gained unrestricted power. Therein lie the wise lessons you are seeking, and the key to why democracy is wiser than autocracy.

Spe. All right then, Politicus: please start lecturing.

Politicus. You had the visit here, a short while ago, of a gentleman who calls himself Mephisto. I carefully listened to and registered what that gentleman said. He left off when what he called the final goal of the autocrat, namely absolute, unchecked power, is reached. But that is not the end of the story. I will tell you how the story continues and how, in most cases, it ends.

Spe. We are looking forward to it.

Politicus. Let me begin by describing the situation once the autocrat has reached his so-called final goal. - At that point, the people lose all influence over how they are being governed. If there are seemingly democratic institutions in place, they are only there to sanction the acts of the autocrat. - Quite often, the autocrat was carried to power because the people were frustrated by the status quo, and the future autocrat made promises to relieve that frustration. He may even have espoused some ideology that he claimed was the remedy for the frustration. However, as soon as he attains unlimited power, the autocrat forgets his promises and his ideology. From that moment on, he looks only after his own interests. His main preoccupation is to secure the privileges that come with power. He thereby loses the support of the people. That is his first mistake.

Spe. Yet, once in power, an autocrat can defend himself indefinitely by setting up devoted and ruthless militias. If he has the support of guns he does not need the support of the people.

Politicus. *After a short pause.* My register tells me that militias and guns are not enough. No autocrat can keep himself in power for long if he does not have sizeable support from the people.

Act. Hmm. A debatable point, with due respect for your otherwise excellent register. - But please go on.

Politicus. As Mr Mephisto correctly observed, an autocrat needs the help of a small, devoted group of collaborators to gain and stabilize his power. He will have full control over that group. But, as Mr Mephisto explained, the autocrat, once in power, changes his attitude toward that group. Autocrats want absolute, unchecked, unlimited power, and they cannot achieve this if they have to share it with comrades of the first hour. So the autocrat will start, gradually, to neutralize his former helpers, even eliminate some of them. Thereby he turns former comrades into enemies. That is his second big mistake. - He then makes others.

Spe. Namely?

Politicus. Since he mistrusts everyone, he creates around him a general atmosphere of mistrust. But such an atmosphere is not one that allows to operate effectively. - Worse: he creates an atmosphere of fear. But no-one who causes fear can live without fear. The autocrat, therefore, turns sooner or later into a paranoiac. His paranoia further deepens the distrust and the fear that surrounds him. He thus gradually loses the platform from which he can safely and efficiently operate. Distrust and fear start to erode his power. - He then makes a further mistake. To feel more secure, he fills important positions either with relatives or with yes-men, marionettes who thoroughly depend on him. The result is, that important positions are filled with incompetent incumbents. But no regime can long survive on incompetence. - But over and above all these mistakes, he makes the gravest error of all. He lets himself be carried away by his own sense of power. He becomes a megalomaniac. He loses touch with reality. He starts to breach limits, to overstep frontiers. He not only disregards the needs of those he rules, but loses all respect for the ruled.

Spe. And that starts his downfall.

Politicus. Precisely. Because the despised ruled will begin to react. They have little to lose, and much to gain. Resistance against the autocrat organizes itself, at first hesitantly, then in ever broader circles. And then, all of a sudden, a figure appears that embodies resistance. He is the awaited counter-force, supported, acclaimed, often idolized by the people. At that point, the end of the autocrat begins.

Spe. You just said, Politicus, that the counter-force is usually embodied in one person. In other words: resistance to an autocrat needs a strong leader. But that leader, once he has successfully overthrown the autocrat, may himself be tempted to become one. Removing an autocrat destabilizes the status quo, so you may need another autocrat to stabilize it again. Think of Robespierre, displaced by Napoleon.

Politicus. That can indeed happen, Mr Spectus. Eliminating an autocracy is much easier than turning it into a democracy. There must be a transition phase. All I can say is that the leader of the counter-force needs to be a wise man. He may begin as a mild autocrat himself. But then, gradually, he must loosen the reins. He must enhance the power of democratic institutions, prepare people to assume responsibilities, set clearly the course for the future. And there is no guarantee that he will succeed.

Spe. Politicus: thank you for this presentation. You gave us many excellent reasons why we must consider autocracy as an unwise model for society. We now have to turn to democracy, and list the reasons why it is wiser than autocracy. - Let us start by a definition. What is democracy, Politicus?

Democracy

Politicus. An elephant.

Actus and Spectus jerk with surprise.

Spe. Are you feeling all right, Politicus, my friend? Something wrong with your register?

Politicus. *Smirks, revealing that he is not only a fantastically advanced machine, but even has a genuine sense of humour built into him.* Do not worry, gentlemen. I am all right. I just connected your question with some of my data. A well-known politician once declared that it is not possible to define democracy. Trying to do it reminds one of the schoolboy, who, when asked to tell what an elephant was, confessed that he could not do it, but would nevertheless recognize one when he saw it.

Actus and Spectus burst out laughing.

Spe. All right, then, let us not try to find a single definition of democracy. Instead, let us focus on the principles and concepts upon which it is built. I suggest you name and briefly explain those principles and concepts, one after the other. In each case we shall then discuss to what extent they are wise.

Politicus. Understood, sir. - I wish to start with the concept of law. In an autocracy, law is practically identical with the will of the autocrat. In fact, there is no law: there are only rules and regulations, some of them unwritten, set by the autocrat. - A democracy, on the other hand, is based on a written constitution. It spells out the rights of the citizens and the principles by which they are to be governed. In an autocracy, all are expected to respect the autocrat; in a democracy, all, including those who govern, are expected to respect the constitution.

Spe. We are back to Plato's idea that government by a body of laws is the next best thing to government by a wise god.

Act. We are also back to my remark, a while ago, that no system can regulate itself. A society must have an outside regulator, to which all issues can ultimately be referred. In a democracy, that regulator is a wise constitution. - Go on, Politicus.

Politicus. The next democratic concept is the split of power. It is meant to avoid power abuse. The essential split is that between the executive and the legislative; but, often, there is also the judiciary as a third independent power. Then there are further splits. The legislative body is often split into two houses, upper and lower. Both houses are further split into factions, representing political parties.

Act. With due respect for the wise intention to avoid abuse of power: isn't that a bit too much splitting? Aren't we throwing out the child with the wash-water? We need to prevent the abuse of power, certainly. On the other hand, democracies need strong, effective, efficient leaders. They create a positive mood, which helps to create confidence, which in turn helps the economy. But if those leaders are constantly being curbed, checked, hindered, then they end up being weak, ineffective, inefficient. Furthermore, when carried too far, the split of power causes endless debates, unsatisfactory compromises, postponed decisions, delayed reforms. Thus, split of power may end up with no-one having power. Then no-one will feel responsible, nor accountable. We have what a politician once called "organized irresponsibility". I ask you, therefore: is all that splitting worth the price? I have some doubts.

Spe. You draw a sombre picture, Actus. But I must say that much of what you said is undeniable. We must be careful not to carry power splitting too far. - But let me point out a concept related to power-splitting: legal opposition. In an autocracy, all opposition is illegal, therefore criminalized. In a democracy, opposition is not only legal: it is expected to be creative. I think the concept of legal opposition is one of the most mature and wise ones developed by mankind. - But please proceed, Politicus.

Politicus. My next concept is representation. As you gentlemen pointed out, rule through popular assemblies, also called direct democracy, is feasible only in small communities. In large, modern countries it is a technical impossibility. The problem is solved through representation. Instead of an assembly of the people, we have an assembly of delegates of the people. Parliament. The delegates are given power for a limited amount of time only; after that they are either re-elected or replaced. Thus representation rests always on the consent of the governed.

Act. All of which raises a lot of questions.

Spe. Namely?

Act. Properly speaking, democracy works only if everyone turns out to vote for the delegates of their choice. But many may not vote because they are undecided, or don't care, or are simply lazy. Once, in a Swiss town, local elections were held on a beautiful summer Sunday. Most people went walking into the woods, instead of going to vote, with the exception of all the members of a small, radical, extreme right party. That party was elected and ruled the town for two years, to the utter dismay of the democratically minded majority.

Spe. Excellent anecdote, and a very good point, Actus. Representation, indeed, requires that everyone takes a genuine interest in public affairs.

Act. Not only that, Spectus. The representative system makes sense only if the choice of delegates is the result of well-informed decisions. That, in turn, requires that the candidates explain fully, openly, objectively what they intend to do and why. But candidates rarely do that. Often they distort issues, emphasize points they think will win them support, pass over or play down facts that may damage their chances. Many claim things about their opponents which are simply not true. The media, too, are often biased in favour of one candidate over another. So what is the result? An electorate that has a hazy idea about what it is against, but rarely a precise opinion about what it really wants. An ill-informed electorate, making ill-informed decisions.

Spe. You again draw a sombre picture, Actus. I am sure most of the people in a well functioning democracy have candid discussions on major political issues before they go out to vote.

Act. Possibly. But discussions based on inadequate facts and misinformation are of little value, and can hardly lead to objective decisions.

Spe. *Smiles.* Have you any further doubts about the representative system, Actus?

Act. As a matter of fact, I do. An electorate must not only be well informed, but also well educated. Autocracies thrive when the ruled are ignorant. Democracies thrive when the electorate is educated. A well functioning democracy must educate those who vote.

Spe. I fully agree with that statement.

Act. Then let me make yet another one. - Everyone in a democracy must, theoretically, be in a position to decide freely, independently, whom he wants to vote for. But each voter is subjected to pressures that make such independent decisions difficult. There are the prevailing opinions within his family, within his circle of friends, within his community, in his club; all of these will influence him. But there is worse. I think we can hardly speak of free democratic elections in countries dominated by clans or by clerics: most voters in such countries will vote as the clan-head or the priest directs them to do.

Spe. Yes, there is a problem there. The answer, once again, is education. Only education can develop free, independent thinking. - Actus, I almost fear to ask: have you got more doubts about representation in a democracy?

Act. Regretfully, I do. - People may verbally and in public support policies that are obviously necessary, but require certain sacrifices; that bring long-term benefits, but hurt a bit now. But when they go to vote, they no longer support candidates who advocate such policies. They prefer candidates who promise improvements that do not hurt. In such cases, democracy functions; but it does so in the wrong direction.

Spe. *Laughs.* If you go on like this, Actus, you will end up concluding that autocracy is a wiser model than democracy. Do you prefer the bullet to the ballot?

Act. By no means. I value democracy highly. But this is a seminar about wisdoms. And the wise should not be blind to the weaknesses of things they value.

Spe. Do you want to point out even more weaknesses of the representative system?

Act. A last one, if I may. - A member of parliament is supposed to represent the views of those by whom he was elected. But, once elected, he is free to vote as he pleases. He has only his conscience to guide him. So he may not, in fact, represent the will of his electorate at all, but only his own. That, in turn, means that direct democracy, not representative democracy, is the only true form of democracy. Which means Rousseau was right. But we declined Rousseau as impracticable. So we have an impasse.

Spe. *Laughs.* Do you believe that democracy works at all?

Act. Of course I do. I am just trying to drive home the point that it is imperfect. While the concepts upon which it is based are certainly wise, we run into difficulties when we implement them. But we have to live with those difficulties if we want democracy to be practiced at all. - But now back to you, Politicus. Please proceed with your list of concepts behind democracy - though you may expect more critique.

Politicus. I do not mind critique, sir. Trying to explore a complex subject like democracy will necessarily lead to some dissent. *(Actus and Spectus nod with appreciation at this show of comprehension, remarkable since it comes from a machine.)* - My next concept behind democracy is perhaps the one most often mentioned: freedom. Freedom in a democracy means specific, well-defined individual rights, guaranteed by law. We saw some of these when I had the pleasure to impersonate John Locke: the right to private property; the right to vote; the right to be protected; the right to be tried by impartially selected judges and juries; the right to think, to speak and to write as one wishes, to assemble where one wants, to worship as one wants; to criticise as one wants and to be different if one wants. A democracy will be judged by the extent that it accords such rights to its citizens.

Spe. *Turns to Actus.* Any objections, advocatus diaboli?

Act. No objections. I fully support such individual rights and freedoms.

Spe. Ah, that's good.

Act. But I have four concerns.

Spe. Ah, that's bad.

Act. The first is about the relationship between freedom and order. Freedom is conditional on order. A historian once wrote that when liberty destroys order, the hunger for order will destroy liberty. If there is too much licence, there will be disorder, insecurity, instability, and rights can no longer be guaranteed. We said earlier that absolute power corrupts; but so does absolute freedom. Thus freedom is not for the undisciplined nor for the weak.

Spe. You raise a serious issue, Actus. Personally, I am convinced that only democracy, with its laws, built-in checks and well-functioning institutions can bring lasting order coupled with freedom. On the other hand, I agree that freedom, if it is to be possessed at all, needs limits.

But those limits must be carefully drawn.

Act. I have a definition for those limits. In a democracy one is allowed to swing one's arms in any direction one likes, so long as one does not hit another person's nose.

Spe. *Laughs.* Good. But I have a more serious definition. Freedom in a democracy means pursuing our own good, in our own way, doing whatever the law permits, provided we do not deprive others of their freedoms to do the same. In other words: if we want to possess freedom, we must be willing to grant it to others. - What is your second concern?

Act. It is about the relationship between freedom and tolerance. Democracy is at a disadvantage there. Autocracies have very low limits of tolerance, they know perfectly well where those limits lie, and react severely against trespassers. Democracies often react too meekly against abuses of freedom, because their limits of tolerance are hazy. But the more tolerance there is in a democracy, the more likely will freedom be abused.

Spe. Your concern is justified. We said this morning that tolerance must have limits. A well-functioning democracy will have to define clearly where those limits lie. - Your third concern?

Act. Where there are rights, there must also be obligations. Unfortunately, people in modern democracies tend to insist on their rights, but forget their obligations. Perhaps people should not be granted rights until they have learned to respect the obligations that go with them. I know that is not possible, but it would be wise.

Spe. *Laughs.* That would be like saying that one should not be let into the water until one has learned to swim. But you are right, Actus. Those who loudly demand their rights should explicitly and forcefully be reminded of their obligations. - What is your last concern?

Act. That one is somewhat complex. - A democracy admits variety, the right to be different. But that also means accepting, tolerating, and granting freedom to uncomfortable minorities: ethnic ones, religious ones, gays, lesbians, you name it. Such minorities tend to get isolated, for two reasons. The first is they want to be isolated. The second is that the majority prefers them to be isolated. The result is that such minorities become self-centred, cut off from and not caring for the society they should be a part of.

Spe. The remedy is to make an effort to integrate them.

Act. That is easier said than done, since integration and the right to be different are in conflict with each other. If we emphasize integration, we reduce the right to be different, and that is undemocratic. If we emphasize the right to be different, we cannot integrate. So democracies must achieve an almost impossible double trick. They must exercise a gentle pressure on minorities to keep them from becoming self-centred, and to accept the fact that they are responsible members of society. They must also exert a gentle pressure on the majority, so that it acknowledges and accepts the minorities living in its midst; for without the consent of the majority there can be no integration. Such a double pressure is certainly an effort in the right direction; but experience shows it does not always work.

Spe. But so long that it works in some cases, means it is not utopia. - But let us move on to the next concept behind democracy. Politicus?

Politicus. My next concept is also my last: equality before the law. The law in democracies does not discriminate on the basis of wealth, social position, status, abilities, sex, creed or birth.

Spe. Your comments, Actus?

Act. Let me point out that equality before the law was not always a feature of democracies. Women and blacks, just to name two examples, had to fight for their rights in countries that called themselves democratic. - But let me point out something I consider important. Equality before the law is certainly wise. But it is not wise wanting to enforce equality in a non-legal sense.

Spe. Can you clarify that statement?

Act. Nature, when allowed to pursue a free course, will inevitably produce inequalities. So will democratic societies. Talent, education, merit, character, family ties, luck, diligence, providence, all these factors produce inequalities. The wise will accept this as an inevitable fact of life. If we accept the wisdom that democracies should admit variety, then we must also accept and admit non-legal inequality. I would even go a step further, and say that non-legal inequality is a sign of health. Autocracies tend to level everyone, mostly downward; their ideal is social equality for everyone except for the ones who have power. A democracy does not strive for social equality, but for something much wiser: social mobility. A true democracy will ensure that anyone who wants to climb up the social ladder is free to do so, and has good chances of success. It is then up to each individual to see how far up he can or wants to climb.

Spe. What you are saying is that democracies automatically produce several social layers. I agree. Democracies will above all produce a strong middle class; conversely, for democracies to function they need a strong middle class. But they also need an elite. In principle, members of that elite, if they are wise, will realize that they have a responsibility: set examples to be followed, insist on ethical principles. That, let us be fair, is not always done. *(Looks at the holograph.)* But we are near the end. Only three more stones missing. Let each of us make another wise statement on democracy, and our walls are finished. - You start, Actus.

Act. Autocracies often start wars. Democracies practically never do, since they thrive on peace and value the common good. When democracies do fight, it is usually against an autocracy, not against another democracy. Nevertheless, a wise democracy will maintain a strong military force, especially when constantly threatened by militant autocracies. It is safer to keep peace with a sword in one's hand. - Your turn, Spectus.

Spe. While there are many democracies operating in the world today, let us not forget that it is a young model for society. Though born in ancient Greece, it was subsequently regarded, for almost two thousand years, as unworkable. We are still in the process of developing and improving democracy. So we must heed the warning of a wise man, whose name I forget: We must defend democracy against the evil designs of bad people, against the inertia of good people, and against the selfishness of most people. Above all, we must safeguard what is perhaps democracy's greatest virtue: its capacity for self-correction.

Act. *Turns to Politicus.* Your turn now, Politicus. Please make a final wise statement on democracy. It will put the last wisdom-stone in place.

Politicus. *Dives behind his desk. He obviously wants to grab this last opportunity to do an impersonation. After five seconds he emerges as Winston Churchill, complete with a glowing* *cigar. He puffs a circle of smoke in the air, then proclaims:* Democracy is the worst form of government.

Actus and Spectus have an uneasy moment. Is this Politicus' choice of a last wise comment on democracy?

Politicus. *Obviously enjoys the perplexity of the other two, so he takes a few seconds to add:* With the exception of all other forms of government!

As Actus and Spectus burst out laughing, the walls of the cathedral of wisdoms begin to radiate in a golden light. Politicus' quotation added the last stone. The task of erecting the walls is finished. Actus and Spectus sit back, relaxed.

Spe. Politicus, you have been of tremendous help. You are the most erudite participant at this symposium we met so far. Without you we could never have finished the walls. We appreciate it. Thank you.

Politicus. My pleasure, gentlemen. *(He disappears behind his desk, then surfaces again, without his Churchill-disguise, but the cigar still burning.)*

The gong indicates the end of the session.

Spe. Actus, this has been a long day. Tomorrow this symposium ends. But we shall need renewed energies to finish it. Difficult subjects loom at the horizon.

Act. Then off we go to a hearty dinner, some good wine, a good night's sleep, and a copious breakfast. That should re-invigorate us.

Spe. *Laughs.* Right ho. - Good night, Politicus.

Politicus. Good night, gentlemen.

Actus and Spectus leave the seminar room, where the lights gradually fade. Politicus puffs a few more rings of smoke into the air. Then the lights go out completely, just the tip of a burning cigar is seen. After a while, even that goes out. Politicus, obviously, has been returned to wax.

End of the third day of the symposium

The fourth and last day

Session 12: The Religion-Tower

It is eight o'clock in the morning on the last day of the seminar. The revolving holograph on the wall shows about three-fourth of the cathedral of wisdoms finished. Still to be built are the two towers, the roof and the façade.

The seminar room has been slightly rearranged. Replacing the desks of Actus and Spectus are four elegant and highly comfortable arm-chairs, forming a square. In front of each is a small table with refreshments and a name-plate. Two plates bear the names "Actus" and "Spectus", the two others "Fidus" and "Ratius".

Sitting in the chair with the "Fidus" name-plate is an elderly man with fine features, an aquiline nose and a benign expression; he is dressed in black, wearing the white reversed collar of a priest. Sitting in the opposite chair, marked "Ratius", is a professorial-looking, middle-aged man with horn-rimmed glasses, clear, penetrating blue eyes, and an intense, open face; he wears dark trousers and an expensive grey sweater. They are obviously machines; but one would not guess it by just looking at them. There is only that small hint of jerkiness.

Actus and Spectus enter the room at the moment the gong marks the beginning of the session. They are, momentarily, taken aback by the new arrangements, but then go towards their designated armchairs. As they do so, both seated figures rise. The one called "Ratius" is the first to speak.

Ratius. Good morning, gentlemen. May I present myself? My name is Ratius. Professor Ratius. And this is my distinguished colleague, Professor Fidus.

There is a round of hand-shaking, rather odd, considering that two of those shaking are live men and the others machines. But still, formalities are observed, with "glad to meet you" coming from all sides.

Rat. Shall we sit down?

They all sit down in their respective armchairs.

Rat. May I transmit the best regards of the Chairman of this symposium, Mr Eclectus?

Spe. Thank you.

Rat. You may wonder somewhat at these new arrangements, deviating from those of the last three days. Let me explain. Mr Eclectus thought that the two difficult subjects to be discussed this morning are better dealt with in a different manner than the earlier ones. You know, of course, which subjects I am referring to?

Act. Of course. Wisdoms associated with religion and science. They are symbolized by the two towers of our cathedral.

Rat. Precisely. - Now: my colleague and I know, Mr Actus, that you are a scientist by training, so you could certainly handle much of the search for the insights of science. You, Mr Spectus, are a widely read scholar *(Spectus waves, as if to discard a praise not earned)* with a long-standing interest in religious matters, so you could rely on your erudition to deal with wisdoms behind religions. Nevertheless, Mr Eclectus felt it would be better if you received professional support when dealing with these rather difficult tasks.

Fidus. *Takes over from Ratius.* And this is why we are here. My esteemed colleague is a historian of science. I am a historian of religion. We were asked to guide and to help you - without, of course, wanting to dominate the discussion. What we envision is a pleasant conversation - albeit a rather challenging one.

Rat. *Smiles.* My colleague used the word "conversation". But I expect that, at times, our talk may take the form of a debate. But that should not bother us. Professor Fidus and I disagree on many issues, yet we listen to and respect each other's views. And it has become obvious during the last three days that you gentlemen do the same.

Spe. Your help is more than welcome, gentlemen. Both Actus and I look forward to our talk, or debate, whichever word you choose to call it. - How do you suggest we proceed?

Fid. Which subject would you like to discuss first - science or religion?

Spe. Since religion is older than science, I would propose we start with that.

Fid. As you wish. - Now here is my suggestion about the agenda. I shall select five representative religions and present, one after the other, their basic historic traits and tenets. You, Mr Spectus, and you, Mr Actus, are invited to comment on the wisdoms - or the lack of them - behind those traits and tenets. At the end, we shall look at how religious attitudes are at present changing, and what new insights can we derive from those changes. *(With a fine smile.)* I suggest that Professor Ratius keeps out of this discussion; once he and I begin arguing, you two gentlemen would have no chance whatever to put in a word. *(Ratius smiles and waves that he agrees.)* Do you accept my proposal?

Spe. Fully. Any open questions, Actus?

Act. None.

Fid. Fine. Then let us begin. - I chose Buddhism to start with. Though not strictly a religion, it belongs to our overview.

Buddhism

Fid. The starting point of Buddhism is the concept of "dukkha". This is usually translated as "universal suffering", but that is not altogether correct. Rather, "dukkha" means impermanence, imperfection, emptiness, insubstantiality, vicissitude, pain. The lack of a correct single translation of "dukkha" has always been a problem when trying to understand Buddhism.

Spe. I think "dukkha" has also been translated as "subject to change". But "dukkha" is always understood as change for the worse: happiness changing to sorrow, and so on.

Fid. That is essentially correct.

Act. If that is so, I raise my first objection. My view on change is radically different from the Buddhist concept. As I pointed out repeatedly during this seminar, I favour change. I do so because I regard it as chance for improvement. Change can be for the worse, conceded; but it can just as well be for the better. - Take, as an example, suffering. A Buddhists would say, following his gloomy concept of change, that suffering steadily increases in the world. I reject that view. The dominant mood is to actively help those who suffer. This attitude, slowly but surely, reduces suffering in the world. - No: we cannot see change under its negative aspect alone. “Dukkha” proceeds from a spleeny, pessimistic attitude. It is not a universal wisdom.

Fid. *Smiles.* Perhaps you will find more sympathy for the Buddhist view as we proceed, Mr Actus. And I must correct you on one point: the Buddhist is not spleeny, nor sorrowful. On the contrary: he regards himself as a happy being. He is calm, serene, has no fears or anxieties. Just look at a Buddhist statue and you will understand what I mean. - But may I continue with the Buddhist tenets?

Spe. Please do.

Fid. At the age of 29, the Buddha decided to look for solutions to overcome “dukkha”. For six years he tried different methods, suggested by different teachers, but abandoned them all. At the age of 35, sitting in Bihar under a Bodhi-tree, or tree of wisdom, he experienced Enlightenment. Everything in the Buddha’s teaching derives from that experience.

Spe. Do you think, Professor Fidus, that the Buddha’s enlightenment was something similar to what Christian mystics have experienced?

Fid. No. Christian mystics always experienced God in one form or another. The Buddha did not experience God. He merely saw a way to overcome “dukkha”.

Act. So the Buddhist does not believe in God.

Fid. That is incorrect, Mr Actus. Buddhism simply does not deal with the question if there is a God or not. It intends to function without God or gods. That is, perhaps, the central tenet of Buddhism. The Buddha attributed his enlightenment to human endeavour and human intelligence alone. He taught that man is his own master, that his own efforts suffice, that he can help himself, so there is no need for divine help. Man is his own refuge, he said.

Spe. A surprisingly advanced intellectual attitude. It is reminiscent of Humanism, the prevailing ideology of the Renaissance. Humanism also believed in the human effort, rather than in religion.

Fid. But with an essential difference, Mr Spectus. Renaissance man sought to rely on his own efforts and intelligence in order to succeed *in* this world. The Buddhist uses his effort and intelligence to liberate himself *from* bondage to this world.

Act. Another trait of Buddhism I can’t agree with. Why should evolution have brought forth human intelligence, if it is to be used to relinquish this world, rather than make the best of it? - But please proceed, professor. What did his enlightenment teach the Buddha?

Fid. It taught him to understand how “dukkha” arises. He saw that this happens because of what he called “thirst”. “Thirst” is desire for and attachment to sensual pleasures, to wealth, to power, to ideals, theories and beliefs. “Thirst” is the will to exist, to become more, to grow, to accumulate.

Act. But that is precisely what life is about. So I say: a big hail to “thirst”!

Fid. But “thirst” is essentially selfish. It leads to trouble, strife, wars.

Act. But also to a sense of accomplishment, to satisfaction, to enjoyments..

Fid. None of which is permanent, because of "dukkha". So there is logic in the system.

Act. What is the use of logic if the tenet you start from is false - or at least questionable?

Fid. *Smiles.* I think, Mr Actus, that you have made your point sufficiently clear. - Now allow me to explain another Buddhist concept: "karma". The root of the word "karma" is "action", "doing", "deed". But in Buddhist terminology "karma" does not mean the deed itself: it is the mental volition of the deed. Buddhism takes the will for the deed. Thus, good "karma" leads to good actions, bad "karma" to bad ones. In other words intention comes before action, and determines it. For the Buddhist the intention counts, not the action itself.

Act. Well, for me it is the action that counts. There are people who intend to do a lot of good things, but never put those laudable intentions into practice. What is the merit of good volition if it is not followed by appropriate action? Judge a man by his deeds, not by his volitions. This karma business is just unnecessary complication.

Fid. *Smiles.* Karma is simply the Buddhist way of getting to grips with causes and effects, Mr Actus. You regard action as the cause, followed by an effect. Buddhism starts one step further back: it regards mental volition as the cause, leading to action, itself leading to an effect. In both cases it is the effect that will tell whether the motive was good or bad, commendable or punishable. - But allow me to proceed to the next tenet of Buddhism. This concerns the overcoming, or cessation, of "dukkha". It is achieved by extinguishing "thirst". And extinguishing "thirst" leads, ultimately, to "nirvana".

Act. A sort of Buddhist paradise.

Fid. False, Mr Actus. Volumes have been written about "nirvana", without really clarifying what it means. But it certainly does not mean paradise. There are concepts that cannot be satisfactorily explained in words, and "nirvana" is one of them. We can only describe it in negative terms. It is the complete cessation of "thirst"; the extinction of all desire and illusion; a blown-out state; something un-compounded, un-conditioned; the cessation of continuity; something beyond cause and effect, beyond right and wrong, good and evil, logic and reasoning, duality and relativity. It is even beyond existence and non-existence. But it is certainly not some realm; it is therefore incorrect to speak of "entering nirvana".

Act. Somewhat difficult to grasp, to say the least. Certainly too complicated for the common man, myself included.

Fid. Sorry that I have to contradict you again, Mr Actus. The amazing fact is that many Buddhists claim to have reached "nirvana" in their lifetimes. And not only monks claim this: so do simple, ordinary people. - And let me stress something important: Buddhism is the only religion that maintains that the highest bliss, the "summum bonum", can already be achieved in this very life. Other religions promise to achieve it only after death.

Act. Hmm. And how would he who attained "nirvana" in his lifetime be like?

Fid. He will be entirely free from selfish desire, hatred, conceit, pride. He will be full of compassion, kindness, sympathy, understanding, tolerance.

Act. But there is no need of "nirvana" for one to achieve and practice such virtues. Buddhism proclaims that we need to detach ourselves from this world, to turn *away* from it, to become virtuous and wise. I claim the opposite: we need to turn *towards* this world, engage ourselves in it, to become virtuous and wise. These are two diametrically opposite views on how to attain virtue and wisdom. - Sorry, professor: am I being too controversial?

Fid. By no means. Remember: Mr Eclectus asked you to freely criticize the wisdoms uttered at this seminar. So please go on doing it. *(Smiles.)* I expect you will do so when you hear the next tenet of Buddhism. - It concerns the method that leads to the cessation of "dukkha", the extinguishing of "thirst", and, ultimately, to the attainment of "nirvana". The method is called the "eight-fold path", because it specifies eight precepts. - Three of these precepts concern ethical behaviour. The first is right speech: no lies, no slander, no harsh or impolite talk, no malicious language, no idle or foolish babble. The second is right action: it calls for peaceful conduct and the respect of life. It also prescribes not to hinder others from leading lives based on these ethical principles. The third is right livelihood: it forbids professions that are based on harming or extinguishing life, both human and animal.

Act. Nothing new here, professor. These same ethical precepts can also be found in other religions. And, what is more, it can also be found where religion plays no role whatever.

Fid. Of course. But what is not found in other religions quite as explicitly as in Buddhism is the uncompromising condemnation of force and violence. Buddhism never used the sword to spread; it always spread by peaceful means. There have not been organized persecutions in its name. Arguably, it is the most peaceful of religions. - Now to the next three precepts of the "eight-fold path". They concern mental discipline. The first is right mental effort: fighting against evil thoughts, promoting wholesome states of mind. The second is right attentiveness: being aware of what is happening inside our body, watching how sensations, pleasant and unpleasant, arise and disappear. The third is right concentration: it is the most complex one, but also the most typically Buddhist.

Professor Fidus takes a sip of refreshment before continuing.

Fid. Right concentration is a process going through four stages. In the first stage, all worries, restlessness, doubts are gradually discarded. In the next stage, all intellectual activity is tuned down; only feelings of joy and happiness are retained. In the third stage, all forms of joy are discarded. In the final stage, happiness is discarded. At this last stage only two things remain: awareness and mental equanimity. - Let me stress that awareness remains. A Buddhist who attained this last stage does not turn his back upon the world, despite his equanimity. The Buddha himself returned to help his fellow beings, because he did not lose awareness.

Act. Frankly I would stop at stage one of this process. Discard worries, doubts, restlessness: agreed. But why discard intellectual curiosity? Why discard joy and happiness? Why abandon voluntarily all the positive things that life has to offer?

Fid. Because they will not last anyway. Remember tenet one.

Act. Since I doubt tenet one, I doubt what follows from it. I would much rather have joy and happiness with the risk of losing them, then not have them at all. - But if I followed you correctly, professor, there are still two precepts of the eightfold path left.

Fid. Correct. Those are right understanding and right thought. Buddhism makes a distinction between understanding and knowledge. Knowledge is merely accumulation of data; understanding is penetration into the true nature of things. But understanding can only be reached if the mind is free of impurities. Purification is attained through right thought, meaning essentially meditation.

Spe. Professor Fidus: thank you for your presentation so far. Are there any other features of Buddhism that are of importance to our quest for religious wisdoms?

Fid. Yes. - As I mentioned, the Buddha taught that man must tread the eightfold path alone. To be able to do that, he must have full intellectual freedom. Therefore, the Buddha allowed unprecedented freedom of thought to his disciples. He advised them to disregard all sacred and dogmatic texts; he did not consider them to be useful. To believe in such texts, he said, is a political decision, not a spiritual one.

Act. This, I must say, is a surprisingly modern thought. It is in sharp contrast to other great religions, where ancient, sacred texts are the unquestioned foundation upon which faith is built.

Fid. Precisely, Mr Actus. And this brings us to a very important, unique feature in Buddhism. All other religions, as you just said, are built on faith. In Buddhism there is no faith. Faith is "believing"; but Buddhism insists on "seeing", not on "believing". The aim of the Buddhist is to see, achieved through wisdom, not to believe, achieved through faith. The Buddha invites you to come and see; he does not ask you to come and believe.

Act. But the Buddhist also has faith: his belief in Buddha's teaching.

Fid. A valid remark, Mr Actus. But a Buddhist will tell you that belief is only needed at the beginning, as long as you do not yet *see.* The Buddha himself likened his teaching to a raft, meant to help you to cross over. But the raft is not meant to hold on to. Once a Buddhist has learned to *see,* the raft is no longer needed.

Act. *Thoughtful.* I like all this you just said. There is much in it I can support. Any other tenet in Buddhism I can agree with, professor?

Fid. Perhaps you will agree with this one, Mr Actus. The last tenet I wish to mention. The concept of "sin" is absent in Buddhism. There is evil, but it is regarded as stemming from ignorance. Each one of us, the Buddha said, must realize what is good and try to follow it, as well as see what is bad and try to give it up.

Spe. Christopher Marlowe was of the same opinion: "I count religion but a childish toy, and hold there is no sin but ignorance."

Act. Professor Fidus: you gave us an excellent overview. After having listened to you attentively, I concede that Buddhism is a fascinating intellectual exercise. Yet, it seems to me that this exercise is only for a small intellectual elite, seeking superior wisdom in the seclusion of a monastery. It is not a comfort for millions, as religion is meant to be.

Fid. May I repeat, Mr Actus, that many common persons, who did not live in monasteries, and were by no means members of an intellectual elite, claim to have attained "nirvana". The Buddha himself, in his lifetime, preached to kings and peasants, Brahmins and outcasts, holy men and robbers, rich men and beggars. He disregarded all differences of caste and social levels. He wished to help everyone. - Yet, in one point you are right. The Buddha once took up a handful of sand, let it trickle through his fingers, with only a few grains remaining in his palm. Only these few, he said, will fully comprehend my teaching.

Act. *Smiles.* I am afraid you cannot count me among those few remaining grains.

Spe. *Laughs.* That being the case, I suggest we leave Buddhism. I quite understand that active, positive, pragmatic fellows like Actus have difficulties with it. Let us, however, retain one of Buddhism's central wisdoms, with which I am sure even Actus can agree: man can and should help himself. There are echoes of this wisdom centuries later in the religious thought of Luther. - Professor Fidus: which religion do you wish to discuss next?

Fid. Hinduism. We shall regard it as synonymous with Brahmanism, which in fact is but an older form of Hinduism.

Spe. We are listening.

Hinduism / Brahmanism

Fid. The salient feature of Hinduism is diversity, or rather plurality. It has an array of gods, beliefs and practices. But Hinduism has a remarkable ability to integrate different forms of thought and practice. There are two reasons for this. - One is that Hinduism has no founder. Thus it lacks a central teaching expounded by one great master, around whom beliefs and practices crystallize. - The other reason is that Hinduism is linked with the history of India: it is an ethnic religion. Diversity in Hinduism is the result of India's long history; it arises out of the Hindu's respect for and pride in the history of his country.

Act. But ethnicity can generate nationalism. And religion coupled with nationalism is an explosive mixture. Ghandi was shot by a nationalist Hindu, because he consented to the partition of India. Most religions are mixed with politics.

Spe. But we need not mix them.

Fid. Indeed, we should not, gentlemen. Let us filter politics out of our discussion of religions. - So let me proceed. Plurality in Hinduism has had one particularly positive effect: the concept of heresy is absent. The many forms Hinduism takes, all those different beliefs that emerged over the centuries, are accepted simply as historical facts.

Spe. A very wise feature, for sure. We know how much bloodshed was caused combating heretics. - But, speaking of plurality and lack of heresy, I recall something in Hinduism that is rather unique. A Hindu is not a Hindu because he adopts a particular set of beliefs. He is a Hindu if he does not deny that he is one.

Fid. That is correct, Mr Spectus. Ask a Hindu in one part of India to explain some religious feature of Hinduism to you; then ask another Hindu in another part of the country to explain the same thing. Chances are that their explanations will substantially differ. Hinduism is in religion what democracy is in politics. It accepts free thought, free interpretation. No-one is told to believe in any fixed, established way.

Act. That is remarkable. But it also bears a danger. If a religion does not clearly tell you what to believe, it becomes hazy. And what is the use of a religion without a well-defined essence?

Spe. Careful, Actus. A "well-defined essence" may not be far from dogma. And dogma is in religion what ideology is in politics. Both claim to be *the* truth, while they are, at best, only one *facet* of the truth. There is a saying in Hinduism: A Hindu attains ultimate truth only when he ceases to be a Hindu. That means that ultimate truth can be attained only after one has become free from all dogmas and beliefs. I say that is very profound wisdom.

Act. That is advanced thinking, indeed. - But please go on, Professor Fidus.

Fid. There is another cause for diversity in Hinduism: the respect for gurus, the holy men. Since gurus are philosophers, their teachings differ. But since all of them try to show paths to the divine, they are all revered, and so are their views. - One such guru was Mahatma Ghandi. He founded activist Hinduism, the dominant form of modern Hinduism. It is based on social service and deeds for the common good. Ghandi taught that help given to our fellow beings is the most effective path to the divine. More effective than meditation or the pursuit of knowledge. He also stressed compassion, non-violence, courage, self-sacrifice, and supported ecumenism.

Act. But doesn't the caste system hinder the implementation of such a philosophy?

Fid. Ghandi rejected the caste system. He had a row with his traditionally-minded parents on the subject at the age of twelve. He campaigned against it all his life. But the concept of "caste" is eroding anyway. Modern Hindus tend to think of "caste" more like "occupation", which, in fact, is the original meaning of the word.

Spe. Can you name other tenets specific to Hinduism, professor?

Fid. Hindus believe in reincarnation. The West used to laugh at this. Oddly enough, statistics show that about one quarter of all people living in the West today believe in some sort of re-birth. And their number is rising. - Another trait is the practice of yoga. The wisdom behind yoga is that the interaction between body and mind, when properly controlled, can give us un-expected powers. The word "yoga" means to "join": what is meant is joining body and intel-lect. - Then there is another remarkable tenet. Hinduism identifies four stages in life. The Hindu will be a student for the first twenty-five years. He will create wealth and enjoy the senses during the next twenty-five. During the third span of twenty-five years he will lead a pious life. After that, he will renounce the world.

Act. I wonder what is the use of learning and working hard for fifty years, building wealth, only to renounce it in year fifty-one?

Fid. *Smiles.* We are talking of ideals, Mr Actus. Reality can be different. What is remarkable in this tenet, though, is that it does not ask one to fully renounce the enjoyment of wealth and of the senses. It only limits that enjoyment in time.

Spe. Professor: may I ask you to say a few words about the gods of Hinduism. As far as I know, there are three main ones: Brahma, the creator, Vishnu, the preserver, and Shiva, the destroyer. I find wisdom behind this distribution of functions. It avoids attributing these three phenomena, creation, preservation and destruction, to one and the same god. One god accu-mulating all three functions can be an unsettling god, full of contradictions that cannot be sat-isfactorily explained.

Fid. Sorry to disappoint you, Mr Spectus. This tripartite distribution of functions, called "tri-murti", is not an essential feature of Hinduism at all. It was set up by Western scholars, who wanted to bring order into the confusion of Hindu divinities. But Hinduism is not as straight-forward as Western intellectuals want it to appear.

Spe. *Surprised.* Professor, you shatter what I thought was my clear view of Hindu theology. Can you please tell us, then, how things really are?

Fid. *Smiles.* Gladly. - There are indeed three main active gods in Hinduism: Vishnu, Shiva, and Shakti, the mother goddess. The fourth, Brahma, the creator, is remote: he has done his job creating, and then retired. - Vishnu is the most broadly revered of the three. But, and this is a major wisdom of Hinduism, he is not revered in some abstract form, but always as a human incarnation. Thus he becomes accessible, real. Vishnu's two preferred incarnations are Rama and Krishna. Rama was a legendary hero, an ideal ruler, honoured for his justice towards men. Krishna was a more complex figure: he was a teacher, a divine lover, a god who died for the salvation of the world, a child working miracles, and a flute player luring the human soul.

Spe. Ah. A far cry, I must say, from my simple idea of Vishnu the preserver.

Fid. *Smiles.* But perhaps a more exciting one. - Now to Shiva. He is much more remote than Vishnu. He is austere, awe-inspiring. He never incarnates. He sits in the Himalayas in constant meditation, generating an immense spiritual force that rules the cosmos. He is symbolized by the "linga", a phallic emblem.

Spe. But I thought Shiva was a destroyer.

Fid. He destroys by generating new forces. He is like the fertility gods of ancient Egypt, who each year decayed, but then sprang to new life. When you deal with the gods of Hinduism, Mr Spectus, you have to forget simple attributes, simple categories. Hinduism is not simplistic. It is much too old for that.

Spe. I am beginning to realize that. - What about Shakti?

Fid. Shakti is the Mother Goddess, the feminine principle. She incarnates, like Vishnu, but she is ambivalent in her incarnations. As Parvati, she is gentle, beautiful, confers blessings; she personifies beneficial Nature. But as Kali, or Durga, she is black, fierce, menacing. In other words, she stands for the forces of Nature, that can be beneficial or detrimental. She is not really revered, but rather paid homage to in order to avert damage.

Act. A fascinating review, gentlemen. But may I remind you that this is not a theological seminar, but a symposium on wisdoms.

Fid. *Smiles.* Thank you for reminding us, Mr Actus. - Let me, then, come to the last trait in Hinduism. A Hindu may have a preference for one or the other of the gods. He can freely choose whom he reveres. But he also knows that, ultimately, all the gods are just one God under different aspects. Ultimately, they all melt into one single, highest Being. This may seem like a paradox in a polytheistic religion; but Hinduism has no difficulty with it.

Ratius. *Raises a hand.* If I may inject just one thought, Fidus. Something similar is going on in modern physics. To unite the various forces of nature in a single "superforce" is the main endeavour of theoretical physics. There is a parallelism between Science and Hindu thought.

Fid. Good à propos, Ratius. Thank you. Yes: the parallelism is undeniable. It is about the quest for ultimate unity, emerging out of real or apparent diversity. Let us close the chapter on Hinduism with that interesting thought. - The next religion I wish to present is the exact opposite of Hinduism. One that radically discarded all gods, all incarnations, all diversity, accepting only one almighty and ultimate Being. Judaism.

Judaism

Fid. Judaism's central tenet is: God is one and there is only one God. Nil tolerance for other, lesser gods: there simply aren't any. - The God of Judaism is the creator of the universe. He is thus an individual, an entity separate from the world. As such, he needed to reveal himself. He did so through his prophets. The prophets God chose to reveal him were Jewish. Thus the Jews claimed to be a chosen people.

Act. I have difficulty with the term "chosen people". It sounds presumptuous. It invites resentment on the part of those who have not been chosen.

Spe. Yet, Actus, to some extent at least, that term is historically justified. There were monotheistic movements before Judaism emerged; but the Jews developed the first lasting form of monotheism. Islam and Christianity would not exist without it. Thus the idea of having been chosen to become the root of monotheism is supported by fact.

Act. Then let us say the Jews were chosen by History. What I have difficulty with is the pretence of having been chosen by God. - But please go on, professor.

Fid. In Buddhism, ethics exist without God. In Hinduism, also, ethics exist more or less independently from the gods. The great innovation of Judaism is the idea that ethics cannot exist without God. He is the fountainhead of moral order. For Judaism, ethics are god-given, not man-made.

Act. Sorry, but I can't accept this tenet. It may have been valid when mankind was still in a state of infancy: children need a strong authority to tell them how to behave. For the ancient Jews, this authority was God. But mankind has ripened; it can now safely discard divine tutelage. There is nothing objectionable in the idea that ethics and moral order are man-made. A well-written body of laws is just as effective in regulating society as a set of laws with transcendental claims - especially if people begin to doubt the transcendental origin of those laws. - And there is more, if you allow me to go on.

Spe. Please do.

Act. Man-made laws are generally conceived in a democratic spirit. In contrast, god-given laws are conceived in an autocratic spirit. A law-giving God is an autocrat. He manifests his will, punishes remorselessly those who act against it. Those who see God in this way tend, themselves, to become autocrats. Thus a severe law-giving God is at the root of autocratic government and religious repression.

Spe. Your assessment is essentially correct, Actus, and your critique justified. But there is one aspect of this you overlooked. Man-made laws, and man-made moral order, was what the European Enlightenment fought for, and did so successfully. But not all parts of the globe experienced Enlightenment, and the wise will take that into account. In countries where moral principles are still believed to come from God, those principles will have more weight than if they were declared to be man-made. Where there is a strong belief in one God, laws are much more effective if they are believed to come from Him.

Act. That may be so. But it is time for a change. I do not deny that there could be a God who made laws. But the laws He made are those of Nature. God made the laws of Nature, man those of the moral order. The wise will keep the two apart.

Professor Ratius gently applauds, but does not say a word.

Act. And let me point out something else. - Professor Fidus told us that Hinduism is tolerant because it accepts many different gods and interpretations. Polytheism and tolerance go hand in hand, because polytheism allows diversity. - The opposite holds for strict monotheism. It tends to be intolerant because it does not allow diversity. A single God permits only one belief. A state based upon a single ideology does the same. A single God, just like a state with a single ideology, does not tolerate but fights those who do not believe.

Fid. May I add something that extends what you said, Mr Actus. Monotheistic religions tend not only to be aggressive toward non-believers, they also adopt an autocratic attitude against Nature. The Old Testament explicitly orders man to *subdue* Nature, the Earth, and all animals. Hinduism, by contrast, demands *respect* for Nature and for all living things. There can be no doubt about which attitude is wiser. - But may I proceed with the tenets of Judaism?

Act. Please do. I apologize for having spoken for so long. *(Smiles.)* Yet I cannot guarantee I will not do so again.

Fid. *Smiles back.* Your comments are welcome, Mr Actus. - A further basic tenet of Judaism is the "covenant". It is a promise by God to help and protect the Israelites, provided they follow His laws.

Act. There is logic in that. If God expects His laws to be followed and punishes those who do not, then He must also help and protect those who obey. Just like a king offers protection in exchange of obedience. "Do ut des": we discussed that wisdom on our first day. Whether it is God or a king, the model is the same.

Fid. *Smiles.* You are a bit too rational about this, Mr Actus. But in principle you are right. Judaism is rational. It is arguably the most rational of all religions. It is based on the respect of laws coming from God. There is no magic, no demons, no grace, no saints. Hell is just transitory. The only mysticism in it is the cabbala; but that is too complex to go into at this seminar.

Act. Is there any other tenet in Judaism we haven't yet mentioned, professor?

Fid. Yes. One that might appeal to you, Mr Actus. It has greatly influenced Western thought. - Judaism regards History as a sequence of phases. They lead up to a final state, where everyone will believe in the one God, and where His rule is universally established. Originally, of course, this idea was purely theological. But then it went beyond theology. - Asian religions see Life as recurring in cycles. Judaism was the first religion to regard Life not as a cyclical process, but as a linear one. And it claimed that the line is pointing upwards. God is not only creator, the origin of all existence. He is also the ultimate aim, the final purpose. - By claiming this, Judaism indirectly inspired all those who see a purpose, an ultimate goal in Life. This includes scientists who claim that there is more behind evolution than chance and necessity. But these things you will discuss in the next session with my colleague Ratius; I do not wish to take over his role. *(Ratius waves his thanks.)*

Spe. One more issue, Professor Fidus, before we leave Judaism. You said that there are no demons in Judaism. But I thought there is one: Satan. We had a visit from him yesterday under an alias: Mephisto.

Fid. *Smiles.* I was going to conclude with him. - As Mr Actus correctly observed, Yahweh was something of a tyrant. Gradually, however, God ceased to be worshipped as Yahweh. He became the Lord, and was increasingly identified with goodness. But this new image was irreconcilable with evil and suffering in the world. So Judaism assumed the existence of an evil spirit, who could be blamed for what did not harmonize with the Lord's goodness. Thus Satan was born, whose name means "adversary". He is cynical and despises humanity. While God strengthens all that is good, Satan roams over the world, reports to God all that is bad, and tries to make things even worse. But it is important to emphasize that Satan, in Judaism, is but a servant of God. His role is to test mankind, but only within the limits allowed by God. There is no dualism in Judaism. Dualism appears with Christianity, where Satan becomes more than a mere servant of God: he is now the arch-enemy, the prince of darkness, the Devil.

Act. Frankly, though I repeatedly play the advocatus diaboli at this seminar, I do not believe in the devil. *(A deep laughter is heard from below the seminar room floor where Mephisto sank from view; after a second the laughter is cut short, as if ordered by a higher authority. Actus decides to ignore the incident and to proceed.)* I reject blaming outside forces where we should blame ourselves. We, ourselves, are the cause of most of the evil around us, and we must accept responsibility for it. The more we assume responsibility for our wrongdoings, the more mature and wise we become, and the less we need the devil.

Fid. *With a fine smile.* In other words, Mr Actus, you agree with the Buddhist view that evil is the consequence of ignorance, since irresponsible action follows from ignorance.

Act. *Laughs.* You seem to want to turn me into a Buddhist convert, professor. But my answer is yes: I do agree with that particular tenet of Buddhism. - Which religion are you going to present us next?

Fid. One that greatly resembles Judaism in its strict monotheism: Islam. In many respects, Islam has similar tenets to Judaism; we can skip those, since we dealt with them already. So let me focus on where Islam is different.

Islam

Fid. Islam is not considered by Muslims to be an entirely new religion, but the ultimate, most mature form of monotheism. At the same time, it claims to reach back to the very roots of monotheism, to the original faith of Abraham. He was the first who did not believe that God had companions. - "Islam" means subservience and devotion to the one God. There is no covenant, like in Judaism. The Jews could negotiate a contract with God. Muslims cannot negotiate with Allah. There is no "do ut des" in Islam.

Act. How does Islam perceive God, professor?

Fid. According to the Koran, God is eternal, incomparable, uncreated, invisible, formless, not restricted to any place, almighty. He created the world, so everything depends on him and is subjected to his will. But his will can never be fully understood. He is not confined by rules or norms, forgives whom he wants, punishes whom he wants. He can be merciful, but his mercy is not calculable, nor can it be expected - it just happens or it doesn't. Though Allah can be merciful, he is not loving, like the Christian God.

Act. A rather inhuman God.

Fid. I would rather use the term non-human. The God of Islam simply cannot be represented in human terms. It is even strictly forbidden to Muslims to do so. Allah is beyond all human representation; it is monotheism carried to its logical extreme.

Act. Islam is associated with Arabs. But many Islamic states are not Arabic. Can you explain the relationship between Islam and Arab ethnicity?

Fid. Originally, only Arabs were Muslims. When Islam was carried outside Arabia by Arabic merchants, it gradually lost this ethnic character. However, since the Koran was written in Arabic, the only genuine version of it is considered to be the Arabic text. This gives the Arabic language a prominent place in the Muslim world. So, to answer your question, ethnicity in Islam is linked to a language, rather than to a nation.

Spe. We have an important lesson here, professor: the unifying role, in religion, of a common language. Latin used to play that unifying role in Christianity. But then the Bible was translated into dozens of languages, opening the door to scores of different interpretations. Very few Christians today learn ancient Hebrew, or even ancient Greek, in order to be able to read the Bible in its original language. Christianity must look to other unifying forces than a common language. Islam has an advantage there.

Act. Let me point out, Spectus, that the common use of Latin did not keep Christians from waging bloody wars against each other, nor did the eminence of the Arabic language keep Muslims from killing other Muslims. We should not overestimate the role of a common language in religion. It may unify in an intellectual sense, but it certainly does not have the power to impose peace. - But please go on, professor.

Fid. Mohammed removed from the sanctuary of Mecca all statues of pagan gods, putting an end to polytheism in Arabia. But at the same time he declared an ancient pagan object, the Ka'ba, to be the holiest thing in the world. Thus he created a single transcendental symbol at a central place of worship. This gave a powerful focus to the Muslim world. There is no comparable focus in any of the other major religions.

Act. Does a Muslim actually consider the Ka'ba itself as something holy, or does he simply view it as a symbol for the Holy?

Spe. This is a good question, Actus. Allow me, professor, to answer it. I have long been interested in religious symbolism. - The wise, and I include the wise Muslim, will never equate a symbol with what it stands for. A symbol is physically accessible to our senses; what it symbolizes is not. Thus, any sacred object is merely a man-made substitute for something that is not man-made. Religious symbols are sacred not for what they physically are, but because of the higher reality they represent. Only primitive people see a holy object as physically endowed with the forces they are merely meant to symbolize.

Act. An erudite answer to my question, Spectus. - Professor Fidus: I always had the impression that Islam is simpler than the other major religions. Am I right or wrong?

Fid. The popular version of Islam is certainly not too complicated. Buddhism is intellectually very demanding. For a Jew, it is difficult, if not impossible, to comply with all the laws of Judaism. It is not at all easy to be a Christian in the proper sense of the term. In comparison, the demands of Islam are not difficult to follow. It is a religion adapted to the capabilities of millions. Islam expects religious discipline, but what it asks a Muslim to do is simple and can easily be fitted into everyday life.

Spe. But where religious demands are easy, spirituality is shallow. And spirituality is what a religion is about. You need spiritual depth to be truly religious.

Fid. What popular Islam loses in depth is compensated by width, Mr Spectus. The more exacting a religion is, the less it will have true adherents. If religious demands are not too exacting, then a greater number of people will be religious. Muslims are actively religious because practicing Islam is affordable by anyone.

Spe. That is true. - Can you name other important traits of Islam, professor?

Fid. It teaches absolute equality before God. To God all Muslims are as equal as the teeth of a comb. At the hajj, the pilgrimage to Mecca, everyone wears a simple white robe; it is impossible to tell the rich from the poor.

Spe. A wise measure.

Fid. Following the teaching of Mohammed, Islam regards religion and state as inseparable.

Act. An unwise teaching. We discussed this point yesterday. We concluded that it is dangerous to fuse the sacred with the secular.

Fid. Mohammed thought differently. But we must not forget that he was not only a prophet. He was also a successful statesman and general. Therefore he did not see the necessity to separate these functions.

Act. But if you do not separate them, you create religious oppression and intolerance. You can never achieve democracy that way. In fact, I read somewhere that radical Muslims regard democracy as evil, because, so they argue, the power that belongs to God alone cannot be distributed among the people at large.

Spe. Yet, let me point out that most Muslims insist that Islam is a tolerant religion. Professor Fidus: can tolerance be reconciled with a strictly monotheist faith that rejects the separation of state and religion?

Fid. Let me try to answer that question from both a historic and a theological point of view. - Mohammed expected the Jews living in Arabia to convert to Islam, since he saw it as a perfected version of Judaism. But the Jews refused to convert and continued to uphold the Torah. This led to severe clashes between Muslims and Jews. Yet, Mohammed never ceased to honour the Jewish prophets, and considered Abraham as the fountainhead of Islam. - Something similar happened with Christians. Mohammed could not accept that God had a Son, nor that beside Father and Son there was even a third divinity, the Holy Ghost. Mohammed, the strict monotheist, accused the Christians of re-introducing polytheism in a new guise. He also condemned the Christian habit of painting God as a human figure, claiming that God cannot be represented in human terms. Yet, despite such tensions with the Christians, Mohammed accorded Jesus a special place among the prophets. - All this shows that Mohammed, though he did not agree with Judaism and Christianity, nevertheless had a high regard for their founders. For that reason he wrote in chapter two of the Koran: Let there be no violence in religion. In other words: let there be tolerance in religious matters.

Fidus takes a sip of refreshment.

Fid. On the other hand, tolerance also means openness to renewal. And renewal means the ability, and the possibility, to rethink the relationship between a religion and the ancient texts upon which it is originally based. Tolerance means that those ancient texts can be reinterpreted, seen in the light of new realities. In Islam, this is not possible. For Muslims, the

Koran has unquestioned authority. Mohammed wrote in chapter one: There is no doubt in this book. Such an attitude is not conducive to tolerance, and it denies intellectual freedom. There can be no tolerance where belief is based on just *one* book, with no freedom to question what is in it. - To round up my comments: many historians claim that Islam was, on the whole, more tolerant than Christianity. If Islam is perceived by many as intolerant today, it is because a radical Muslim minority, pursuing political rather than religious aims, makes it appear less tolerant than it actually is.

Spe. I think that was a balanced view on a delicate issue, professor. - What else is typically Islamic?

Fid. Muslims strongly believe in Paradise, Hell, and the Last Judgment. Paradise has often been described with great fervour by Muslim poets. Prophets, martyrs and fighters for a holy cause enter Paradise directly; the merely good have to wait until the Last Judgment. Hell is for the infidels, but also for hypocrites who pretend to be Muslims, but in their hearts are not.

Act. But what is the point of there being a Last Judgment, Paradise and Hell, if everything is determined by the will of an almighty God? They make sense only if we also accept free will and responsibility for our actions.

Fid. *Smiles.* The logical conflict between a God who determines everything, and rewards or punishments that make sense only if He doesn't, is a recurring logical problem in monotheistic religions, Mr Actus. Some theologians resolved the issue by claiming that real freedom means doing the will of God. But who can be sure what that will is? The issue is complex and no-one has a truly satisfactory answer.

Spe. Professor Fidus: I think we covered Islam. I reckon you want to end our review of religions with Christianity?

Christianity

Fid. I do, Mr Spectus. - Christianity is the third great monotheistic religion, though not quite as rigorously monotheistic as Judaism and Islam. The central feature of Christianity is the figure of its founder. His disciples saw in him the Messiah. Dogma declared him to be the Son of God and the Saviour of mankind.

Act. *Looks with a half-smile at Fidus.* You formulate carefully, professor.

Fid. I am an impartial historian and analyst, Mr Actus. I incline to no particular religion more than to another. But I also know that no religion can be fully comprehended by an objective outside observer. There is always an inner power in all religions that no outsider can fully grasp. When we examine a religion, we must take into account both what the faithful believe and what our reason dictates.

Act. I commend you on that wise approach, professor.

Fid. Thank you. - Whether Jesus regarded himself as the Messiah is now impossible to say. It is also impossible to ascertain whether Jesus saw himself as the Son of God, in the sense Christians came to see him later. Though Jesus did call God his Father in heaven, he might have done that to underline his closeness to and his love of God. It does not necessarily imply that he regarded himself as divine.

Act. But aren't such uncertainties robbing Christianity of its very foundations?

Spe. Let me answer that, Actus. My answer is no. What Jesus thought of himself, or how his contemporaries viewed him, may be open to debate. What is undeniable fact, however, is what happened after his death. That is unique, extraordinary. There is no historical figure whose impact on humanity after death is quite comparable to that of Jesus.

Act. But much of that impact is based on the claim by Jesus' disciples that he resurrected and appeared to them after death. They claimed, furthermore, that they saw him physically ascend to heaven. Allow me, as an objective scientist, to doubt that this happened.

Spe. Your scepticism is understandable, Actus. The more so, since the reports on these events differ according to which passage of the Bible you take as reference. On the other hand, we know too little about the spiritual forces immanent in extraordinary people, and how much of those forces may remain active after death. I was always fascinated by the story that Jesus forbade Mary Magdalene to touch him when she met him after his resurrection. "Noli me tangere", Jesus said. This account may mean that Mary was confronted with some separate reality beyond corporeal substance. A reality we have no concrete knowledge about, so we can't reject it out of hand.

Act. *Smiles.* You believe in spirits, Spectus.

Spe. I merely refuse to say with certainty that they do not exist, in one form or another. Most people do not believe in spirits, and presumably neither did the apostles. That may be the reason why they insisted that Jesus ate and drank with them like a living person. They may simply have been too naïve to comprehend a spiritual phenomenon; so they interpreted it in physical, corporeal terms. What the apostles reported does not fit with that mysterious "noli me tangere". I think the wise should keep open the question of whether paranormal phenomena exist or not, until clear evidence settles the question. - But please go on, Professor Fidus.

Fid. Whatever the explanation of Jesus' resurrection, it became *the* basic tenet of Christianity. Paulus wrote: If Christ did not rise from the dead, then the Christian faith is empty and vain. - But the claim that God let his only Son die on the cross, then resurrected him and took him to heaven, was so novel that it needed metaphysical justification. This was provided by Paulus, who linked the figure of Christ with original sin.

Spe. A concept he borrowed from Judaism.

Fid. Precisely. Paulus' logic runs like this. The original sin, committed by Adam, is hereditary and collective: so all men stand sinful before God. Mankind is unable to free itself from original sin through its own efforts: it has to be redeemed through God's grace. God manifested his grace by letting his Son become man and be sacrificed, bringing redemption by taking upon himself mankind's collective sin. Yet redemption is not universal and automatic: only those are saved who believe in Christ and accept the grace of God. Those who do, enter heaven; those who don't, end up in hell.

Act. I am sorry, but I cannot accept the cornerstone of this logic. To be punished for another's fault is morally unacceptable. Besides, Adam never existed. But even assuming he did, why should someone be considered a sinner only because he desires knowledge? And why should God, who allegedly created man after his own image, want the crown of his creation persist in ignorance, forbidding him access to knowledge? This is strangely reminiscent of an autocrat who prefers to keep his subjects uneducated and in ignorance.

Spe. *Smiles.* Actus, old fellow, you are too modern and too logical. The men who thought about these things thousands of years ago were struck by the reality of death. They regarded mortality as a punishment. Thus, they reasoned, there must have been an original sin for which we are being collectively punished by having to die. But then Jesus and Paulus offered a solution: they promised eternal life not on earth, but after death in heaven, bringing comfort to millions.

Act. But that comfort is becoming questionable. Where heaven was supposed to be, we now know are only galaxies.

Spe. Actus: take an ordinary person and put two options to him. One: the Buddhist solution, offering nirvana through a tremendous amount of personal effort. The other: entering paradise, wherever that may be, through the relatively small effort of believing in Christ. Which option, do you think, he would choose?

Act. I presume he would choose the latter. But I have trouble with both options: the Buddhist approach is too negative, the Christian too fanciful. There must be a wise third way. But I don't know what it is, and I am certainly not the man who can resolve the issue.

Fid. *Smiles.* Then let us leave this profound question unresolved and proceed to look at other tenets of Christianity. - The belief that Jesus is the Son of God raised the question about his nature. Two extreme views were possible. The first was that Jesus and God are identical. From this it would follow that God crucified himself, which seemed preposterous. The other view was that Jesus was simply a man, but with extraordinary god-given powers. But in that case his power to redeem mankind, being merely human, became questionable. Faced with the logical difficulty of these two extremes, Christian theologians were looking for centuries for some middle position. After bitter infighting, the Church adopted the solution proposed by Athanasius: God, Jesus and the Holy Ghost are of the same *substance*, but represent three different *entities.* This idea, trinity, became a central tenet of Christianity.

Act. Which of the church fathers maintained that Jesus was simply a man with godly powers?

Fid. Arius. His view was defeated at the synod of Constantinople.

Act. Without wanting to sound blasphemous, I think that was a pity. If one rejects the idea of original sin, as I do, then there is no need for redemption, thus no need to consider Jesus to be the Son of God. But we can't change historic facts. - But whether god or man, what are the essential teachings of Jesus, professor?

Fid. They can be summarized in two commands. - The first is: "You shall love the Lord your God with all your heart, soul and mind". Jesus is the creator of the God of Love. God loves us, and expects love in return. No other religion claims anything like this. - Loving God creates the desire to achieve union with Him. The loving subject is the human soul, the object of love is God. However, union with God is by no means an easy proposition. Presumably only mystics have ever achieved it. Thus Christianity is more exacting than many believe it to be.

Act. I shall come back to that remark. - What is Jesus' second command?

Fid. "You shall love your neighbour as yourself". Jesus is not the author of this command: it can be found in Leviticus. But Jesus elevated it to a central tenet of his teaching. What he meant was that we must recognize the needs of others and answer them. He urges us to go out and help, to practice charity. This command came through loud and clear: Christianity has a much better record of organized help than any of the other major religions.

Act. May I draw your attention to the fact, gentlemen, that we met with this command already twice at this seminar, only expressed in different words. Note that Jesus did not say "love your neighbour", point. He added: "as yourself". He knew, and seems to have accepted, that we have two duties: one to ourselves, the other to the society we are a part of. "Yourself" stands for the first duty, "your neighbour" for the second. Jesus seems to have known that these two duties, self-interest and altruism, must harmonize He probably also guessed that they are two natural urges implanted into us. - Unfortunately, Christianity later insisted on the part "love your neighbour", and morally condemned the part "as yourself". That was an unwise thing to do: it upset the natural balance between self-interest and altruism.

Spe. Wise comments, Actus. Congratulations.

Fid. I must also commend Mr Actus, and wish to add a comment of my own. - The second command of Jesus is based on what has been called the Golden Rule, possibly the oldest wisdom formulated by mankind. In its original version it went like this: "Do not do to others what you don't want others do to you." But Jesus turned this rule on its head: "What you want others do to you, do it to others." A prohibition became a command. Replacing prohibitions by commands is an essential feature in Jesus, and thus in Christianity. Most ancient laws, especially those of Judaism, are prohibitions: do *not* do this or that. On the other hand, most of Jesus' sermons contain commands: *do* this or that. Jesus wanted us to become doers. And this meant progress: for it is easier to avoid doing something than to know the right thing to do.

Act. Frankly, this image of Jesus urging us to act brings him much closer to me than his theological image of the sacrificial lamb. - But I see an inconsistency. While Jesus urged us to go out and be charitable, at the same time he praised poverty as a key to enter heaven. But charity aims at reducing poverty. So charity diminishes the chances to enter heaven. Can one of you gentlemen try to resolve this contradiction?

Spe. *Laughs.* We face a logical thinker, professor. Let me answer him, if I may. - Jesus was born into a poor Jewish family, living from handicraft. His sermons were mainly directed toward the poor around him, toiling laboriously to make a living. He sought to comfort these poor people by talking about their good chances for entering heaven, promising compensation in another world. At the same time, he tried to lessen their daily misery by urging his more prosperous listeners to be charitable. This is the social aspect of the issue. - Then there is a mystical one. Jesus regarded the destitute, with few links to this world, as better candidates for heaven than the rich, who tend to cling to the things of this world. He thought that poverty can be a consciously chosen vehicle to approach the divine. He seems to have believed that union with God, man's paramount aim, can only be achieved by shedding all of one's possessions, renounce all worldly desires, ensure that nothing this-worldly has power any longer. This wisdom is common to Jesus and the Buddha. For the Buddha, it meant complete detachment from the world with only awareness remaining. For Saint Francis of Assisi, arguably the greatest follower of Christ, it meant shedding all worldly things with only charity and love remaining. Hinduism, as we saw, says something similar, only it is less radical: enjoy worldly things during the first half of your life, but detach yourself from them in the second half.

Act. *With a malicious smile.* Have you begun detaching yourself from worldly things, Spectus? You have the first half of your life behind you.

Spe. *Grins.* I plan to begin detaching tomorrow.

They all laugh.

Act. *Becoming serious.* We laugh, gentlemen, but this discussion again proves something repeatedly pointed out by Professor Fidus. Namely, that some religious tenets are often hard to follow, at least for the average man. And for that reason, I do not consider those tenets to be universally valid wisdoms. For what is the use of a religious tenet that applies only to a select few? - I count the praise of poverty to this list of non-universal tenets. It is one thing to choose poverty willingly, like Saint Francis. It is quite another thing having to endure it. Poverty may appeal to the mystic, but not to the majority of people. For that majority the contrary wisdom holds: wage war on poverty. Try to eradicate, or at least lessen it. Poverty imposes a limited horizon on people. The war on poverty enlarges people's horizons, above all because it allows them access to learning. But the war on poverty is possible only if we have rich people capable and willing to help the poor. We need the rich, since it is they, above all, who can help. So, instead of praising poverty, let us praise the helpful rich.

Fid. There are some Protestant churches that do precisely that, Mr Actus. It is called the Protestant Ethic. The idea behind it is that being rich is a sign that God favours you. - But let me briefly mention a Bible story that supports your view. During and just after the crucifixion of Christ, his disciples, who were poor, were nowhere to be seen. The only man who dared to take care of the body of the crucified Jesus was Joseph, a rich man from Arimathea. This goes to show that the rich are often the only ones who are in a position to help. - Is there another tenet of Christianity with which you have problems, Mr Actus?

Act. Yes. If I remember correctly, Jesus said that the truth will be hidden from the learned. Did he mean that learning is not conducive to wisdom?

Spe. You misinterpret what Jesus said, Actus. Jesus, as well as the Buddha, disapproved of convoluted formulations, theological finesse, questionable old texts. They also disapproved of complicated rituals and ceremonies, thought to be necessary to please God. The "learned" whom Jesus condemned are those who cannot see what is essential, because they look at too much that is superfluous. - But, Professor Fidus, I think we should not forget to mention the other major figure of Christianity: Paulus. What are his major tenets?

Fid. Paulus stresses four things: faith, hope, charity and love. Faith means believing that God loves mankind and has proven this by sacrificing his only Son. Hope means that God will continue to show love for mankind. Charity is helping those in need. But Love is the highest concept. It is the common denominator, bringing forth Faith, Hope and Charity. Those three are needed to gain access to heaven. But once one is admitted to heaven, they cease to be relevant. In heaven Love alone remains.

Spe. *Thoughtful.* That is reminiscent of the last stage of the Buddhist's road to nirvana, where Awareness alone remains. Could Awareness and Love be the result of similar esoteric experiences?

Fid. Certainly, the Buddhist, having reached nirvana, possesses not only Awareness but also Charity, a form of love, since without it he would not return to help his fellow beings. The Christian, once united with God, does not return. On the other hand, like the Buddhist, he must continue to possess Awareness, since without it he could not experience his union with God. These are ultimate metaphysical wisdoms, difficult to grasp. But, no doubt, there are more common esoteric features among the great religions than many suspect.

Spe. Professor Fidus: I think we are nearing the end of our discussion of Christianity. Before we leave the subject, can you mention a few more tenets that make this religion different from others?

Fid. I can mention two. - Christianity supports, more than other religions do, the efforts of philosophy and science to prove the existence of God. Philosophy has not come up with any argument for God's existence that is free of flaws. Science is providing us with new insights: but those will be the subject of the next session. - Then, Christianity has addressed more intensively than most other religions the conflict between a benevolent God and the existence of evil. This conflict can be summarized in four statements. God wants to eliminate evil, but cannot. He could eliminate evil, but does not want to. He cannot eliminate it, nor does he want to. He can eliminate it, and also wants to. In the first three cases God is either not almighty, not benevolent, or neither. In the fourth case, it is a mystery why evil continues to exist. This problem has bothered theologians for ages, without arriving at any satisfactory solution. But discussing an issue is wiser than to pretend it does not exist. Familiarity with a problem is the next best thing to coming up with an answer.

Spe. That is indeed a wise statement, professor. *(Looks at the holograph on the wall.)* Gentlemen, our religion-tower is slowly but surely nearing completion. But we still have work to do. We discussed the traditional tenets of five great religions. As suggested at the outset by Professor Fidus, we should now examine what is happening to religions in our modern world, and attempt to derive wisdoms from that examination. Professor Fidus: I am sure you are familiar not only with the history of religions, but also with contemporary trends. Can you continue to be our guide?

Modern Spirituality

Fid. *Smiles.* With pleasure.

Spe. To begin with: what are the current attitudes toward religion in the modern world?

Fid. There are essentially four attitudes. - There are those who fully reject religion. Many who do that have no problem at all with this decision. Some, maybe more than care to admit, are covertly dissatisfied, because they realize that they may be missing something essential. - Then there are those whose attitude is the exact opposite: the unconditional believers. Those who never question the tenets of their faith. They continue to believe in God or the gods, even though He or they seem to abandon them. - Then there are the insecure. They are not really believers, yet they seek refuge in the security of an established religion, because they are overwhelmed by the pressures and challenges of the modern world.

Spe. But these attitudes have existed for centuries. They are not new.

Fid. True, Mr Actus. But their percentages keep changing. - But there is a fourth attitude, and in many ways it is the most interesting one. There are those who turn away from established religions, because they find them too rigid, too traditional, too dogmatic, too far removed from modern realities, thus no longer relevant. But though such people abandon organized religion, they reject only the form, not the essential message. They do not go to church, yet believe in God. Such people are actual or potential carriers of new forms of religiosity. - Let me ask you, gentlemen: can you spontaneously think of trends in the modern world that may promote such new forms?

Act. One factor, certainly, is increased mobility. Travelling puts more people in contact with religions other than their own. They begin to discover the wisdoms behind foreign faiths. I have seen masses of Western tourists stand before ancient ruins in Asia, wanting to know what Buddhism or Brahmanism taught at the time those buildings were erected. And I have seen Asian tourists standing in European cathedrals, eagerly consulting guidebooks to learn what the Christian symbols meant.

Spe. Not only individuals are becoming more mobile: so do religions themselves. Take the organized inroads of Islam and Buddhism in the West, and the success of Christianity in China. The spread of religions now works both ways: West to East and East to West. It is no longer only "ex oriente lux", but also "ex occidente lux".

Act. But at the same time the tenets of established religions, at least in the West, are increasingly being questioned. The spread of democracy promotes freedom of thought, critical judgment, independence of opinions; those, in turn, lead to more attacks on religious tenets than was historically the case.

Spe. True. But freedom of thought also brings freedom of choice. Modern man can, if he wants to, look at several different religions, compare their messages and wisdoms. He may, after such an examination, still prefer the religion he was taught to follow. But he may also become a convert. And converts are particularly active in supporting their new faith. The religiosity of a convert is usually stronger than the religiosity of one who uncritically accepts the faith into which he was born.

Act. But something else may happen also, that was hardly possible in the past. The free and critical individual may come to the conclusion that none of the established religions he looked at really suits him. He may then proceed to combine parts of one religion with parts of another. He may, so to speak, create an individualized, personalized, tailor-made faith of his own.

Fid. *Looks satisfied, like a professor with good students.* Very good, gentlemen. You have, indeed, identified some of the main factors behind modern religiosity. But allow me to comment on two of those factors. - One is conversion to another faith. Unfortunately, this is not as easy as may be supposed. All religions welcome new adherents; but some religions make it very hard, or even impossible, for potential converts to forsake their community. In some cases, wanting to convert to another faith is even punished by death. Organized religions are not always as wise as they should be. - My other comment refers to personalized beliefs, as described by Mr Actus. We may call this "do-it-yourself"-religiosity; experts call it syncretism. Actually, more and more people seem indeed to venture into such personalized syncretism. They throw together tenets and norms from different religions, according to their personal taste and preference. The process resembles a bee pilfering nectar from different flowers to make honey.

Fidus makes a small pause, then proceeds.

Fid. But I see a certain danger for the bee. Every established religion has, over the centuries, absorbed elements from other faiths. But this did not happen in a haphazard way. The foreign elements taken over were integrated carefully, making sure they made sense within their new context. The old, basic traits of the integrating religion were carefully preserved, not thrown overboard. Done by experts, syncretism can rejuvenate a religion. Done by laics, with no other guidance than personal preference, is a different matter. The bee may end up not with honey, but with a lifeless construct, assembled from incompatible pieces broken off from an original, coherent body of thought.

Act. While your image is compelling, professor, allow me to contradict you. I prefer a humanity where individuals dare to experiment with new mixtures, rather than rigidly, uncritically, even dumbly believing what is being told them from above. Of course there may be confusion as a result of such a mixing process. But out of that confusion new, exciting religiosities may emerge, adapted to modern times. We got to have the courage to follow new roads, if the old ones no longer satisfy. All religious founders followed new roads; Jesus did.

Spe. But you can't compare Jesus to a modern religious "do-it-yourselfer". He and Paulus did not experiment with incompatible mixtures.

Act. I am not so sure, Spectus. Jesus took elements from Judaism and added his own views. Some even claim that he was exposed to Buddhism while the holy family was in Egypt. And let me point out that, at first, Christianity was not a coherent religion at all. Its main tenets had to be discussed and formulated over several hundred years in various synods. Christianity, in the eyes of established Judaism, was just another sect. Fifteen hundred years later, Protestantism was just a sect in the eyes of established Catholicism. Someone once wrote that an established religion is a sect that made it. Today we have a proliferation of sects; but maybe one of them, with an exciting new spiritual message, will make it to a new religion.

Spe. But most of today's sects are nothing but financial ventures. They propagate beliefs directed toward specific groups, selling those beliefs using modern marketing techniques, like they would sell a new car. They target people who want precisely that mixture of beliefs, like a customer who wants precisely that car. Once hooked, the adepts are made to believe that they belong to a spiritual elite, to a chosen few who alone "know" and alone will be saved. Such sects are parodies of religiosity. All they do is selling small phoney messages.

Act. The existence of phoney sects is no reason to reject, in toto, the advantages and benefits that freedom of choice can bring.

Fid. *Smiles.* Well argued, gentlemen. The dangers Mr Spectus mentioned are certainly real; but let us hope that, ultimately, Mr Actus will be proven right.

Spe. Speaking of dangers, professor, I see one that is greater than that coming from sects. It comes not from outside a religion, but from inside. It is a fifth attitude to religion, further to the four we mentioned. It is fundamentalism. What are your views on it?

Fid. Fundamentalism is an over-reaction to the proliferation of sects, to experiments in syncretism, to growing intellectual freedom. Fundamentalists feel embattled by such phenomena, and embattled individuals become dogmatic individuals. Dogmatic individuals seek certainty - perhaps they also overcompensate a secret doubt. Thus, they become radical defenders of the basic tenets of their established religion. The trouble is, that they go too far in their defence. They take ancient texts literally. They allow no room for a critical discussion of any tenet. And this is a grave mistake. Fundamentalists do not realize that freedom of discussion and freedom of interpretation are no dangers. On the contrary: they have often proven to be vital to the survival of a religion. The mind of a fundamentalist has been likened to the pupil of the eye: the more light you pour upon it, the more it contracts.

Spe. An excellent metaphor, professor. - But let me mention another unwise and disturbing phenomenon: expecting, even hoping for the end of the world. For apocalypse. Those who share this expectation are convinced that this will soon happen. True: even the early Christians believed in the imminence of apocalypse. But at least they had a relatively clear idea about how the world should look like afterwards. There is no such idea in modern apocalyptic thinking. Those who share this view are hardly interested in improving the world; they simply want it destroyed. - The wise, of course, will reject such a dramatic scenario. They will not hope for a religious Big Bang suddenly changing the world for the better. They will hope for higher forms of religiosity, yes. But they know that the road leading to it can only be one of slow and gradual evolution.

Fid. I share your view, Mr Spectus. And I sincerely hope it will be implemented.

Spe. Professor Fidus: up to now we kept using the term “religiosity”. However, we examined a number of phenomena in the modern world for which the term “religiosity” is a misnomer, because they are not linked to a particular religion at all. I propose, therefore, to substitute “religiosity” by another term: “spirituality”. Religiosity means adherence to a set of beliefs, performing certain rituals, within the confines of an established religion. Spirituality means being dedicated to no religion in particular, but to certain spiritual values, to intangible and transcendent things, to the sacred. Let us round up our discussion, or debate, by examining a few more of the things that relate to spirituality, rather than to religiosity. Please help us to identify more of such things - even if we ran the danger of having to hear critical remarks about them from our sober scientist Actus.

Fid. *Smiles.* You anticipated me, Mr Spectus. I was going to propose precisely what you ask for. And Mr Actus’ comments are always welcome. - The first phenomenon I wish to mention under the heading “spirituality” is the search for the immanent God, or the divine within us. This is not something entirely new: it was formerly known as Gnosticism and was considered a heresy. But now the number of adepts is rising. These adepts no longer want to pray to an outside deity, to a personalized but somewhat removed Creator. They seek God within themselves, and hope that, when found, they will be able to communicate directly with Him. They also hope that the divine spark will work not only *in* them, but *through* them. There are many who claim that they have succeeded in this quest, and that afterwards they felt as if they were born anew.

Act. Allow me to doubt that most of those who have had this experience did in effect find a divine spark in themselves. They were probably subjected to some kind of self-delusion.

Fid. Perhaps, Mr Actus. But is it not better to live under an uplifting illusion, rather than in dour disillusionment?

Spe. Moreover, Actus, trying sincerely to encounter the divine within oneself requires hard work. And, we said, all hard work is likely to lead to wisdom. - Incidentally, Gustav Jung was one of those who claim to have found that divine immanent spark. He wrote afterwards that experiencing it was like finding the centre of his self.

Act. But such an internal search may also degenerate into an unhealthy, self-centred preoccupation with oneself. And that has no longer to do with spirituality; it is simply narcissism. Sorry for being sceptical; but, as Spectus remarked, I am a sober scientist. - But please go on, professor.

Fid. The next spiritual phenomenon I wish to point out is the search for a metaphor for God that befits our age. A metaphor conveys something that is unfamiliar, using terms that are familiar. It expresses something we cannot grasp, in terms we are able to grasp. Metaphors are often perceived as somewhat naïve: but they are rarely so. They are, in fact, often profound wisdom. - The traditional metaphor for God in the West was God the father. It stressed one aspect of the relationship between God and man: man was like a son, who was cared for and protected, but also punished when he was disobedient.

Spe. That father-image of God was a main point of attack by atheists. Religion, they claimed, is but anthropology in disguise.

Fid. Precisely, Mr Spectus. But the atheists can no longer do that. The search is on for new metaphors, beyond the father-image. There is God the mother: it emphasizes the God who gave birth to the universe and therefore loves it, since everything we create we love. There is God the father-mother or parent: it emphasizes the combination in God of the masculine and the feminine principle. Still other metaphors attempt to leave all human categories, such as father or mother, behind. - The important thing is, that more and more people realize that all such metaphors are part-truths, that all of them are inadequate. The ultimate solution must be to fuse all metaphors into one superior image of the transcendent, beyond what any single metaphor can convey. We are very far from that image and may never reach it. But I see in the attempt to seek such an all-encompassing metaphor a sign of growing spirituality, a maturing of religious thought.

Act. Perhaps, professor, this superior metaphor will one day be supplied not by theology, but by science?

Fid. That cannot be excluded, Mr Actus. - But let me come to my last comment on modern spirituality. There is a version of it known as monism. All major religions consider God, or the gods, to be entities separate from the world. He or they created the world and maintain it. Monism claims that God is not separate from the world: He *is* the world. God and Nature are one, or rather God and the Universe are one. God is immanent in all living and non-living things: there is but one single reality. - God, in His entirety, is eternal, in the sense that the total energy in the Universe remains constant: it can neither be created nor destroyed. This has been confirmed by science and is called the first law of thermodynamics. - But the Universe, and thus God who is identical with it, is also continuously changing, since energy is being continuously transformed from one form into another. Therefore the universe, and thus God, is also a process. This process, as we now know, was initiated by the Big Bang. But all the Big Bang did was initiate change; it did not create energy, which was already there, and will be there forever. - There is little or no transcendence in all this. Monism is a rationalist view. It attempts to attain spirituality without the difficulties created by theology.

Act. *Very thoughtful.* Professor: at the beginning of this session you tried to convert me to Buddhism. You did not succeed. But now, at the end of the session, I think you almost converted me into a monist.

Fid. *Smiles.* I thought monism might appeal to you.

There is a short, sharp buzz from the holograph, indicating that only a few more stones are left to finish the religion-tower.

Fid. Gentlemen: religion has existed for many tens of thousands of years. Faiths have changed, but the need for religion remained. So there must be some potent wisdom operating behind it, supporting it. To end our discussion, try to define what that wisdom might be.

Act. To find that wisdom, we must answer a question: whom does religion benefit? For me, the answer is clear: it benefits the group, the community. The benefit is twofold. - First: religion restrains individuals from carrying their self-interests too far, damaging the community they are a part of. Religion does this by imposing and supporting moral and ethical principles that regulate the doings of individuals. - Second: religion promotes group cohesion. It unites the community through shared beliefs and common rituals. This second benefit is stronger than the first. That is, religion is primarily a social phenomenon, its principal aim being to strengthen a community. Darwinism focuses on the survival of the fittest *individual*; religion promotes the survival of the fittest *community*. For it is evident that a community whose members all share the same faith is stronger than a group where everyone has a belief of his own. - And let me add this: religion is not based on facts or rationale. It is based on the emotional experience of sharing a common belief. Religion is potent because it is emotional. - So the wisdom we are looking for behind religion was probably supplied by evolution itself. It was evolution that, looking for a method to restrain self-interest and promote group cohesion through shared emotions, made religion emerge.

Spe. I agree with much of what Actus presented. But there is something he left out. We have discussed not only religion, but also spirituality. Spirituality does not operate at community level, but at the level of individuals. Actus himself said he does not accept the tenets of Buddhism, but is strongly attracted by monism. This is an individual choice. It has nothing to do with group cohesion. It has to do with our quest for ultimate spiritual truths. The urge behind that quest is very old; whether it was implanted into us by evolution or by other means, is an open question. But I believe this: while we may do without organized religion, if we give up our quest for spirituality, the urge to understand the highest things, we shall never become really, profoundly wise.

The right-hand tower of the cathedral suddenly glows in a resplendent golden light. The religion tower is finished. The gong marks the end of the session.

Spe. Professor Fidus: it has been an enrichment to listen to you. Thank you for your guidance.

Fid. The pleasure was mine, gentlemen.

Act. Care to join us for coffee, professor?

Fid. *Smiles.* No, thank you. *(He points to a cup on his table, full of a strange-looking liquid.)* I have my own refreshment. A combined cooling and lubricating fluid.

Act. *Suddenly remembers that he is talking to a machine and is slightly embarrassed.* Oh.

Fid. *With a fine smile.* Don't worry, Mr. Actus, I am fully aware that I am not human. But that has at least one great advantage: I do not get emotional about a highly emotionalised subject like religion.

He keeps smiling and picks up the cup as Actus and Spectus leave for morning coffee.

Session 13: The Science-Tower

The second session of the last day of the seminar is about to begin. Professors Fidus and Ratius sit in their armchairs, engaged in a low conversation. Fidus has drained his cup of fluid, Ratius is sipping at a glass marked "Lubri-Cola". As Actus and Spectus return from coffee, Fidus and Ratius rise to greet them; they are not only stupendously advanced but also extremely courteous machines.

As Actus and Spectus settle into their armchairs, the gong marks the beginning of the session.

Ratius. Gentlemen, welcome back. We want to erect a virtual tower made of wisdom-stones, originating from insights of the natural and physical sciences. I shall be your guide in this endeavour. - Incidentally, I have been observing you during the discussion on religions. You, Mr Spectus, the conservative, defended traditional views, while you, Mr Actus, the progressive, questioned several of the religious wisdoms. This time, I expect, the roles will be reversed. Mr Actus will defend science and its achievements, while Mr Spectus will probably warn us of their consequences and dangers.

Spectus. You are right about the roles we play, Professor Ratius. But even if Actus and I have different opinions, we have an open ear for each other's arguments. We want, by all means, to avoid one-sided views of the issues we deal with. - How do you propose to guide us through this session, professor?

Rat. I propose we start with a definition of the scientific method, the way scientists think and work, and discuss the wisdoms behind that method. Then we should look at the main sciences themselves, and see what insights we can derive from each of them. Next we should look at applied science, that is technology, and how it effects modern man. I suggest we end the session by confronting the essential wisdoms of science with those of religion.

Act. An exciting programme.

Scientific Method

Rat. Let us, then, start by examining what we call the scientific method. - It all started with geometry. Geometry sought to prove propositions which were not self-evident, but could be logically derived from axioms that were considered to be self-evident. Axioms were thus assumed to need no proof, whereas propositions needed to be demonstrated. At this early stage, therefore, scientific method was purely demonstrative. Its arguments usually ended with the famous three letters: Q.E.D., quod erat demonstrandum.

Spe. A doubtful method. It relies fully on the assumption that axioms are self-evident. But they are not. When non-Euclidian geometry was introduced, most of Euclid's self-evident axioms simply collapsed. No self-evident axiom, no demonstrative method, no valid proposition. False premises, leading to false conclusions - despite flawless logic.

Act. The method has a further weakness: it is purely speculative. It ignores facts. Axioms are not facts.

Rat. Valid objections, gentlemen. And there came one who saw things the same way you do: Aristotle. He sought to remedy the flaws of the demonstrative method and came up with a new method: induction. This new method came to dominate science for the next two thousand years. - Induction does not start from an axiom, but from a large number of facts. It tries to derive a general conclusion based on those facts. The method thus goes from the particular to the general, from the individual to the universal.

Spe. *Cannot resist showing off a bit with his erudition.* In fact, there are two forms of induction. In "summative induction" the conclusions are not allowed to go beyond the evidence supported by the facts. In "ampliative induction" the conclusions may go beyond the facts. Aristotle called this second case "going from the known to the unknown". I would call it jumping to premature conclusions - and advise the wise to avoid it.

Rat. *Smiles.* Yet, Mr Spectus, scientists do use "ampliative induction" and often find it remarkably fertile. - But let me emphasize the essential feature of the induction method. It allows us to arrive at conclusions that belong to a higher level than the facts upon which they are based. We say that the information content of a conclusion is higher than the information content of the individual facts from which we derived the conclusion. The method thus allows us, starting from a great number of separate observations, to build hypotheses, formulate laws of nature, explain natural phenomena. By doing this we increase our knowledge and our wisdom. - Unfortunately, however, there is a flaw in the induction method. Can one of you tell us what it is?

Act. I can. And I can even illustrate it by a true story. - Observing swans several hundred years ago, Europeans concluded that all swans are white. Let us call swans "A", and the fact that they are white, "B". The induction method says: since all *known* A's are B, all A's *whatever* must be B. This, precisely, was the conclusion Europeans arrived at, fully supported by the facts available at the time. - But then Australia was discovered. And in Australia many swans were not white, but black. The Australian black swans disproved, falsified the proposition that all swans are white. - The flaw you refer to, professor, is therefore this: any conclusion arrived at by induction presumes that each and every fact supporting that conclusion has been accounted for. In practice, that is not possible. Conclusions based on induction can, therefore, never be one hundred percent sure.

Spe. But that means all scientific propositions are ampliative, rather than summative.

Act. Precisely. - And I would go even further, Spectus: all *wisdoms* are ampliative, rather than summative. There may well be an odd fact out there that disproves the general validity of a wisdom. In fact, we did see, during the course of this seminar, that some wisdoms cease to hold in certain situations; those situations are to wisdom what black swans are to science.

Rat. Excellently argued, gentlemen. - So: what will the wise scientist do? He will be careful about how he formulates a conclusion he arrived at by induction. He will say: If all *known* A's are B, then *probably* all A's whatever are B. He thus accounts for *probability,* a concept that should accompany all conclusions arrived at by induction. If probability is accounted for, then induction becomes one of the most fertile intellectual tools ever devised by mankind.

Spe. There is another fertile intellectual tool: deduction.

Rat. You are right, Mr Spectus. Deduction is the opposite of induction. It means going from the general to the specific, from the universal to the particular. If all known swans are white, and this thing here which is about to break through the egg is a swan, then it will probably be white. However, while deduction is an important tool in mathematics and theoretical physics, it has less value for the empirical sciences.

Act. Excuse me if I partly contradict your last remark, Professor Ratius. I do not think that even an empirical scientist can operate without deduction. He must use a mixture of induction and deduction to reach valid conclusions. Let me clarify what I mean. - At first, there is a collection of loose facts staring a scientist in the face. Then, suddenly, he discovers that the facts are not that loose after all: there seems to be a connection between them. At that point, the scientist formulates a working hypothesis about what that connection might be. To do that, he uses the method of induction; that is, he goes from the singular to the general. - Next, he must test his working hypothesis. So he starts looking for additional facts that support it. To do that, he uses the method of deduction. He starts from the general, in other words his working hypothesis, and looks for the particular, namely for additional facts that support his hypothesis. Once he has found such additional facts, he gives his hypothesis its final form. - The whole process is thus a chain of methods that keep alternating: induction-deduction-induction.

Spe. But what if the additional facts the scientist finds do not support his hypothesis?

Act. Then, Spectus, if he is a wise scientist, he will not hesitate to revise, or even to fully abandon, his hypothesis. It is a capital mistake to continue to cling to a view if new facts clearly imply that the view is wrong.

Spe. But will a scientist not be tempted to ignore new data that invalidate his hypothesis? To leave out observations that do not fit? To see black swans, but pretend they are not there?

Act. He might be tempted to do that, but if he is wise he will not yield to that temptation. A good scientist is an honest scientist. He may decide that certain facts are unimportant, mere trifles, that only blur his thinking. But before he discards such trifles, he will make sure that they really are but trifles. And he will never, ever, discard facts that are obviously relevant and important, but disprove his hypothesis. That kind of intellectual dishonesty is not only bad policy, it is stupid, since it is bound to be revealed sooner or later by another scientist. - Incidentally, let me point out that what I just said applies not only to science. A dishonest manager may try to conceal, belittle, or present as irrelevant a major danger or drawback, a black swan that imperils a project he is working on. But concealed black swans have a tendency to pop up when the dishonest scientist or dishonest manager least expects it.

Spe. Talking of black swans, let me raise a question. There is an old adage: The exception proves the rule. But in the light of what you were saying, that adage is incorrect. An exception does not *prove* a rule, it d*isproves* it. One black swan, the exception, disproves the rule that all swans are white.

Rat. Good reasoning, Mr Spectus. That well-known adage is, in fact, based on a semantic misunderstanding. The word "proves" should not be understood as "confirms", but as "tests". An exception *tests* a rule, puts it on trial, reveals that the rule is not generally valid. Thus the adage should be re-formulated. The correct wording would be: An exception disproves the rule, since a valid rule admits no exceptions. - But let me proceed, if I may, with the main features of the methods of science. Another such feature is classification. It started with the ancient Greeks, who had a passion for sorting things according to shape, form, colour, behaviour, or other attributes. They drew all sorts of inferences from this ordering. The West inherited from the Greeks this urge to classify; it was an inheritance that greatly contributed to the rise of modern science.

Spe. Unfortunately, this urge also led to superfluous classifications, such as of people. Forcing people into categories can cause a lot of trouble, especially if they are wrong. The wise will resist the urge to classify where classification is not required. - But please proceed.

Rat. Another important feature of the scientific method is prediction. If a hypothesis is correct, it must be able to predict individual occurrences. Some hypotheses even predicted occurrences that could not yet be observed, because the instruments to do so were not yet developed. When those instruments were finally built and the prediction confirmed, it was a major triumph for those hypotheses.

Act. And that brings us to another aspect of modern scientific thinking: experimentalism. Whenever possible, hypotheses should be confirmed by experiments.

Rat. Correct, Mr Actus. But since this is not always possible, we distinguish between empirical and theoretical science. The distinction is important. Not so long ago, it was believed that all sciences will ultimately be empirical, that is confirmable by experiments. We now realize that this is not the case. There will always be a part of science that must forever remain theoretical. Experiments, unfortunately, have their limits. - Closely linked with experimentalism is another scientific feature: repeatability. If in two separate experiments all initial factors are identical, then the results must be the same. If they are not, then either the initial factors were not identical after all, or the relationship between factors and results is not what it was assumed to be. Both possibilities need then to be investigated, for that is how science arrives at the truth.

Act. Repeatability has another important aspect, professor. It is proof that Nature's laws and constants can be relied upon. That they are real, independent of the scientist who carries out the experiments.

Rat. *Smiles.* We shall have to examine later if experiments are really independent of the observer who carries them out. But let us not anticipate. - Now, gentlemen: enough has been said on scientific methodology. It is time to look at the major sciences themselves. - I suggest that we start with the two sciences that deal with the very large: astronomy and cosmology. Astronomy is the study of the celestial bodies. Cosmology has two aspects. One is purely scientific and deals with the evolution and structure of the universe. The other has philosophical undertones and deals with the origin and nature of the cosmos. Mankind has a long-standing interest in all of these, and derived a great number of wisdoms from them.

Science of the Very Large

Rat. Both astronomy and cosmology reach back at least 7000 years. But it was only in the last few decades that tremendous progress was made. *(He becomes a bit professorial.)* Can you gentlemen spontaneously name a few wisdoms the study of the skies presumably taught man, from the early days to the present?

Spe. *After a moment.* It certainly taught him to observe, rather than to simply look. Primitive man presumably just gazed at the skies, wondering what it all meant. Then, gradually, gazing was replaced by systematic observation. Man learned to see, rather than merely look. And, as we said on the first day of this seminar, seeing is wisdom.

Act. As he learned to see, man discovered that there was order in the skies. That discovery had two effects. First: man could now predict astronomical events; that is, probably, what Stonehenge was all about. Second: celestial order inspired man to emulate the skies; he sought to introduce and keep order in his own affairs down here on Earth.

Spe. Then, as the study of the skies advanced, came another wisdom. When it was discovered that the Earth moves around the sun, despite visual evidence to the contrary, man realized that he cannot always trust his senses.

Act. A discovery that led to an even greater wisdom: man can often arrive at the truth more surely by trusting his reason than by trusting his senses. That, indeed, was revolutionary.

Spe. But man's increasingly scientific view of the skies brought with it a disturbing consequence. Where heaven used to be, there were now constellations and galaxies. Instead of prophets and saints ascending to heaven, we now have rockets ascending into space. Some of the old, fundamental certainties were lost.

Act. But certainties based on a false foundation are no certainties. Religion is now forced to replace the old, naive image of heaven by more sophisticated interpretations. While this is quite a challenge, it will ultimately lead to greater wisdom.

Spe. *Thoughtful.* Let us hope so. Nevertheless, I cannot help feeling a bit sad about the skies losing their moral authority. Man always looked to the heavens when he needed moral support; that support is gone. I once read somewhere that North American Indians associated stellar constellations not with mythological figures, like the ancient Greeks did, but with virtues. So each time they looked up at the night sky they were reminded of the virtues they were supposed to practice down here on Earth. The night sky was their schoolmaster, telling them how to behave. Modern man no longer sees any moral message in the firmament. I regret that. - On the other hand, I must concede that this loss of moral authority was partly compensated by another discovery: the insignificance of our Earth. We stopped being geocentric and lost the conceit that went with it.

Act. I see this somewhat differently, Spectus. Astronomy teaches us that the Earth, though small, is quite a special place. Its size, its distance from the sun, its movement, its atmosphere, its protective layers of gas, its magnetic shield, its right-sized satellite the moon, all these things make it rather rare; some even claim they make it unique. Astronomy clearly tells us that it is a great privilege to live on this planet. Our beautiful planet, I may add.

Spe. *Smiles.* Actus seeing the positive side of things, as usual. But I agree: our Earth is indeed something special. And beautiful. I am always overwhelmed when I see our planet photographed from space. And, incidentally, how beautiful the far-away galaxies look. Modern astronomy makes us discover beauty in the universe. - But excuse us, professor, for this excursus on beauty in the midst of a discussion on science.

Rat. *Smiles.* No need at all to excuse yourselves, Mr Spectus. The starry sky does indeed teach us to appreciate beauty. And most scientists are by no means blind to what is beautiful. - But it is your turn, Mr Actus. What other wisdoms, do you think, can man derive from the study of the skies?

Act. A weakness of the modern world is our emphasis on the short-term. We want quick results; we tend to regard the long-term as speculative, theoretical, lacking practical relevance. The exploration of space corrects this attitude. The launch of a space rocket requires long-range planning, long-term goals, continued efforts sustained over many years. We are now launching rockets that will take a decade to reach their objectives. Exploring space teaches us to think long-range and to have patience. Both those things are wise.

Spe. Yet, though we began to explore space, we continue to have an odd relationship to the universe. The cosmos is about 15 billion years old. There are trillions of galaxies besides our own. We see stars as they were many millions of light years ago. These are immense figures.

But very few people care about this immensity. We should be living in a state of awe and wonder about the universe we are a part of - but we do not. We tend to ignore it.

Act. We do that for a good reason, Spectus. If figures become so immense that we can no longer comprehend them, we become thankfully neutral towards them. We no longer experience them as real; they simply become interesting results of observation and reasoning. Our lack of awe towards the universe is probably a wise defence mechanism of our brain: it keeps us from becoming mentally derailed.

Spe. But then, Actus, man faces a double predicament. He lost the traditional symbolic value of the skies, and replaced it with an immensity he cannot digest.

Act. But astronomers are able to digest it. They regard the universe, despite its enormous dimensions, as a rational object of study. Something they can measure and quantify.

Spe. Astronomers may have objectified the universe; the man on the street did not. At least not yet. Few have an interest in modern astronomy and its objective achievements; but many have a strong continued interest in astrology and its questionable methods. Legions of people still believe that the planets have some kind of influence on their lives, and that it matters under which sign of the zodiac they were born.

Rat. May I cut into your excellent dialogue at this point, gentlemen. We arrived at a subject that we should explore a bit more in detail. - On the one hand, we have astrology, that we may call a pseudo-science, claiming that planets and constellations have an influence on our destinies. I think we can safely discard that claim. - On the other hand, we cannot discard the fact that there are indeed many links between man and the cosmos. Some of those links are rather obvious, others are just emerging. I suggest that we look more closely at what those links are, and try to derive wisdoms from them. - Would you care to lead such a discussion, Mr Actus, given the fact that your have a scientific training?

Act. While it tempts me to do it, professor, I am afraid I do not fully qualify. May I pass the buck back to you, and ask you to tell us about those links and connections? You can certainly do it more clearly and comprehensively than I could.

Rat. As you wish. - The issue we are debating is this. What are the scientific arguments for the connections and interactions between us and the cosmos? In other words: In what ways are we intimately linked to the universe as a whole? - As a first argument let me point out a simple fact: the laws of physics and chemistry are valid at each and every point of the universe. Here on Earth, as well as at any point of a distant galaxy. The universe is made of the same stuff we are made of, and the laws that govern that stuff apply everywhere. We are part of a whole, and within that whole matter and energy behave identically. The laws of Nature are universal. One consequences of this is that we could apply the basic features of the scientific method we discussed earlier at any point of the cosmos: induction, deduction, prediction, repeatability are valid independently wherever you may be stationed in the universe.

Act. Go on, please. What is your next argument?

Rat. For science there is no hierarchy in the universe, no up or down. Any point is equivalent to every other point. What the universe looks like from Earth is what it looks like from any other place of study. There are no privileged sites, no points of observation better than other points. No matter where we might travel in space, we would keep observing the same things. Thus we are not only part of the universe; we are practically at home in it anywhere.

Act. What is your next argument?

Rat. We know that the universe began with the so-called Big Bang about 15 billion years ago, and keeps on expanding ever since. It not only expands: it unfolds. The universe is a process. This process goes on everywhere; there are no static, unchanging islands within the universe. Our Earth, and everything on it, is a part of this universal process. We are actors, not spectators, in the drama of the unfolding universe. - Closely associated with this unfolding is what has been called the "arrow of time". This arrow is real, since at any moment the universe is different from what is was a moment ago. The Earth, ourselves, everything that exists, is subjected to the arrow of time. It is a common denominator connecting everything that happens.

Act. You mentioned the Big Bang, professor. How does it fit in with the thesis that everything in the universe is related?

Rat. That was to be my last argument. - If we follow the arrow of time backwards, we arrive at the beginning of it all: the state of the universe before the Big Bang. At that state there was no space, no time, no mass; temperature was infinitely high; the laws of physics as we know them were meaningless. There was only one thing: energy. A single, immeasurable force. For yet unknown reasons, that single force suddenly exploded. This explosion, the Big Bang, started the universe as we know it. The existence of this single force means that, originally, we were all one. Everything in the universe is related simply because the source of everything is the same.

Act. Professor: thank you for this overview. The insights of science, at least for me, are certainly more fascinating then what a pseudo-science like astrology can come up with. - But may I ask you to tell us a bit more about the Big Bang, since it is such an exciting subject. You mentioned that prior to it there was no time, no space, only an immeasurable force. Physicists call that initial state a singularity. The Big Bang put an end to it, initiating change and thus starting the universe. Can you tell us how that happened?

Rat. We do not really know, Mr Actus. At least not yet. There are, in fact, three schools of thought on the subject. - The first appeals especially to the religious. It maintains that it will never be possible to describe the initial singularity in scientific terms. This school equates the singularity with the godhead. It was God who caused the Big Bang, who gave the singularity a push, so to speak, because He decided to create the universe. - The second school maintains that the singularity and the Big Bang might one day be scientifically explained. However, the explanation will not be at odds with the notion that God started it all. - Then there is a third school, the strictly scientific one. It claims that it will one day be possible to develop a consistent origination theory that explains the singularity and the Big Bang using purely scientific arguments, without the need to recur to divine action. - Which school would you consider to be the wisest, gentlemen?

Spe. I tend toward school number two.

Act. I believe school number three has good chances of success. *(Smiles.)* But I hope, for Spectus' sake, that school number two will one day turn out to be right.

Rat. *Smiles.* A wise compromise.

Act. But I continue to be intrigued, professor. What stands in the way of a purely scientific explanation of the beginning of the universe? Of school number three being right?

Rat. The reason for that, Mr Actus, is a conflict between two holy cows. One holy cow is the general theory of relativity, which is demonstrably valid at the scale of the very large. The other holy cow is quantum theory, which is valid on the scale of the very small. These two holy cows do not mix. All scientific explanations of the singularity and of the Big Bang are compatible either with one of these theories or with the other, but never with both. One of the holy cows always turns out to be a black swan. There can be no satisfactory solution until these two theories can be reconciled. For the moment a true reconciliation is not in sight.

Spe. That being the case, I suggest we leave the mysterious initial singularity and go one step further down the arrow of time. What happened just after the Big Bang, professor?

Rat. A fraction of a second after the Bang, the single force divided into two. One of them was gravity. This is a very weak force, but one that acts over long distances. Prior to Newton, gravity was thought to exist only on Earth; then Newton realized that it is a universal force, that holds the planets in their orbits and binds the stars to their galaxies. Thus Newton supplied another proof that everything connects.

Act. Yet I recall that there is a conflict between Newton's concept of gravity and Einstein's theory of relativity.

Rat. Not one conflict, but two. But they are not easy to explain.

Act. Never mind, professor. We cannot ignore one of the most fundamental scientific issues and the insights that go with it. We have by now left the simple wisdoms far behind, and are in the midst of exploring the most complex ones. But we said right at the start of this symposium that we will do so. So please go ahead: explain.

Rat. As you wish. - The first conflict is this. According to Newton, gravity acts instantaneously. But Einstein says this cannot be, since nothing, not even gravity, can travel faster than light. So even gravity must take some time until it is felt. - The second conflict is that gravity, according to Einstein, does not exist at all. At least not as a force. According to the general theory of relativity gravity is a manifestation of the curvature of the space that surrounds every particle in the universe. Or, to complicate matters further, a curvature not only of space, but an amalgamation of space and time, the famous space-time. Einstein maintains that a small body, passing in the vicinity of a large one, will follow the *easiest path* through the curved space-time that surrounds the larger body. That creates the illusion that a force, gravity, is at work. But there is no such force, says Einstein, thereby disproving Newton. As an example, take the Sun and the Earth. The Sun creates a curved space-time around itself. The Earth looks for and follows the easiest path through this curved space-time. That path happens to be an ellipse. So Earth follows an elliptical path around the Sun. All planets do likewise. All this can be summarized in a formula: matter tells space how to curve, space tells matter how to move.

Act. Thank you, professor, for explaining a complex issue in simple terms. And since our purpose is exploring wisdoms, let me derive one from your exposé. - You said that a small body, when left to itself, will follow the *easiest* path through the space-time surrounding a larger body. In other words, the small body selects from among the options available to it the one that offers the *least* resistance. There is a message here for the wise: Do not waste energy unnecessarily; look for the solution offering a maximum of economy. Do it like the universe.

Spe. *Smiles.* We said on the first day of this symposium that the wise will learn from everyone. That, obviously, includes the universe. - Professor Ratius: you talked of space-time and the arrow of time. But what is time? I suggest that we look briefly at the concept of time. Can you tell us what modern science thinks of it?

Rat. Gladly, Mr Spectus. - For time to exists there must be an event. For an event to exist there must be matter, since events happen to material things only. Matter has two forms: energy and mass. Thus either energy or mass or both must exist if there is to be time. - The initial singularity was pure force without event, thus without time. We may regard the beginning of time when the single force of the initial singularity divided into two. Thus matter and time came into being together.

Spe. That idea goes back to Saint Augustine. Which proves that men of old, though religious, were not stupid.

Professor Fidus gently applauds.

Rat. True. But even Augustine declared that while he knew what time was, when someone asked him to explain it, he couldn't. - But, Mr Spectus: your asked me to tell you what modern science thinks of time. I am afraid I will have to become a bit technical again. May I?

Spe. Please do. I am sure we can follow you, with a bit of concentration.

Rat. Then let me proceed. - In the past, time was considered to be something absolute, independent of the position or the movement of an observer. But then Einstein set out to explain why the speed of light is found to be the same everywhere, at all times, no matter if an observer measuring it is moving or not. His conclusion was revolutionary. Not time, but the speed of light is absolute. Time is relative, the speed of light is not. Time flows slower the faster an observer travels, but the speed of light remains constant no matter at what speed the observer moves. Time is simply a part of the observer's frame of reference, just like space is. Thus time makes sense only if considered in the context of space-time. To fully specify an event, we need four dimensions: three of space plus one of time.

Spe. Understood, professor - more or less. Of course, I measure time by looking at my watch. Judging by what you just said that is a rather provincial thing to do.

Rat. *Laughs.* No scientist can do without a watch, Mr Spectus. But you are right: our measurement of time is indeed provincial, since it is based on the period of rotation of the Earth with respect to the Sun. The inhabitants of another planet would measure time differently. Even scientists down here on Earth do. Astronomers prefer sidereal time, based on the equinox. Then there is ephemeris time, based on the motion of the moon, and atomic time, where one second is defined as the vibration rate of the cesium-133 atom. The point is this: our measurements of time are always based on some movement, some event, happening near to us. Our time is never absolute.

Spe. But what about the arrow of time you talked about a minute ago? Is that not absolute either?

Rat. A good question, Mr Spectus. Yes, the arrow of time does take on different values according to how we measure it. There is cosmological time: the lapse since the Big Bang to the present state of the universe. There is thermodynamic time, measured by the total entropy of the universe; entropy has to do with the state of disorder in the universe, and that, unfortunately, is becoming greater every moment. Then there is physiological time: we go from birth to youth to old age and death. While the arrow of time, per se, is real, it takes on different values depending on the event we choose to measure it.

Spe. Gentlemen: let me, at this point, tell you an anecdote to illustrate what odd effects our subjective measurement of time can have. - When Julius Caesar established the calendar, a mistake of eleven minutes was made in measuring the year. Fifteen centuries later, the mistake accumulated to ten days. To correct this, Pope Gregory XIII decreed, in 1582, that tomorrow will be the 15th of October, not the 5th. But the Russian orthodox church refused to recognize the authority of the pope and rejected the Gregorian reform. It was only in 1918, after the October Revolution, that the Soviet Union adopted the Gregorian calendar. The odd result of this is, that the October Revolution is commemorated not in October, but in November.

Act. I have another anecdote about the relativity of time. There is a phenomenon in physics called reversed time. There are some odd particles, offshoots of other particles, that happily move about for a short while, but then realize that they are unreal and should not exist, so they turn back in time and annihilate themselves.

Spe. A sensible thing to do if you are unreal. - But speaking of fantastic things in connection with time: do you think time travel is a possibility, professor?

Rat. *Smiles.* I would not venture an opinion on that. But we may one day, at least theoretically, sort of swap space for time. Then many things may become possible. The wise should never say never.

Spe. Professor Ratius: let us return to what happened just after the Big Bang. When we left off, we had two forces: gravity, and another one. What is the name of that other one?

Rat. It has no name.

Spe. *Grimaces.* Odd story, that of the early universe. There is one force that turns out not to be a force at all, and another one that is anonymous.

Rat. *Laughs.* Not quite anonymous, since it has a designation: GUT. That stands for "grand unified theory". Unified, because all forces that issued from the GUT-force can be unified mathematically. The GUT-force itself has no name because its existence was extremely brief: it almost immediately split into other forces that do have names.

Act. Can we have a look at those?

Rat. Yes. But to do that we must leave the universe and enter into the world of the atom. Are we ready to do that? Or are there still open questions about the universe?

Act. Of course there are, professor. But we have a precept at this symposium: we do not expect to be exhaustive.

Rat. *Smiles.* A very wise precept. - Here we go, then.

Science of the Very Small

Rat. As we said, gravity acts over long distances. It is the only force to do so. All other forces in the universe act over very short, atomic distances. - Physicists can now reconstruct how these forces emerged. First, the GUT-force divided itself into a so-called strong nuclear force and a so-called electro-weak force. The latter then divided itself further into electromagnetism and the so-called weak nuclear force. So there were now four forces in all, including gravity.

Spe. Aha. And then?

Rat. And then: nothing.

Spe. What do you mean, nothing?

Rat. I mean that the divisions stopped. There are just four forces acting in the universe. That is all.

Spe. Ah! How astonishingly simple.

Rat. *Smiles.* The more we go back in time, Mr Spectus, the more we find simplicity in the universe. Modern theoretical physics is a search for ultimate simplicity. - But, of course, there are still many open questions. One of them is how mass emerged out of energy; there may be a fifth force responsible for that transformation, but it was not yet found. Then, mass has many forms; too many. It is a mystery why that is so. But one day even that diversity will presumably be reduced to simplicity.

Spe. Speaking of ultimate simplicity, professor, let me ask you something. Can it be that the original single force from which all others emerged is still there? Can't it be that we are only perceiving different manifestations of it?

Rat. Science has no answer to that question; at least not yet. But theoretical physicists are trying to identify what they call the super-force: an amalgamation of all known forces, all matter, all space, all time. This super-force, if ever found, may turn out to be the initial single force that existed before the universe and time began.

Spe. In other words, scientists are looking for a single force that may still continue to give the universe its structure. Gentlemen: I have an anecdote for you. A theoretical physicist keeps climbing the mountain of reason for decades, under terrible hardships. He nears the top with great difficulty. And then, as he finally arrives at the top, he is welcomed by a group of merry theologians who have been sitting there for thousands of years.

They all laugh.

Act. Yet, Spectus, we cannot leave the quest for that initial force and that ultimate simplicity to theologians. Remember that you preferred school number two when we discussed the Big Bang a few minutes ago.

Spe. *Smiles.* Of course, Actus. I am just pointing out an obvious convergence between science and theology.

Act. At any rate, we have gained another insight. The fact that the universe is able to function with just four forces, maximum five, proves Occam's principle: Multiplicity should not be posited without necessity. We saw that the universe seeks economy, the easiest path. We now see that it prefers simplicity. Besides economy, simplicity seems to be the other basic principle upon which our universe is built.

Rat. That is correct, Mr Actus. As a clever scientist once observed: We may not live in the best of all possible worlds; but we probably live in the simplest.

Spe. Professor: let us look more closely at what you called the GUT-forces. Perhaps we can discover other lessons or wisdoms associated with them.

Rat. We can, provided you are ready to listen to more technicalities.

Spe. We are getting used to those.

Rat. *Smiles.* All right then, here we go. - I mentioned that the original GUT-force divided into three, very soon after the Big Bang. The first of these to be investigated by man was electromagnetism, so called because electricity and magnetism were discovered to be merely different facets of the same force. Studying electromagnetism triggered a scientific revolution that led to a deep wisdom.

Ratius takes a sip of "Lubri-Cola".

Rat. One of the forms in which the electromagnetic force manifests itself to us is light. Light was at first thought to consist of waves. But then it was discovered that it consists of particles, called photons. So there were, suddenly, two equally valid and proven manifestations of light: wave and particle. Faced with this fact, scientists made two bold assumptions. - The first one was: light is in fact *both* wave *and* particle. The two forms simply co-exist. - The second assumption went beyond light. It stated that whenever there are two equally valid forms in which we observe a physical phenomenon, then both of these forms *taken together* are necessary to fully describe that phenomenon. In other words, not *either-or,* but *as well as* applies. This discovery was called the "complementarity principle" and was declared to be a general feature of the universe.

Spe. All this strangely reminds me of a precept we have been asked to follow at this seminar: "sic et non". Two opposite wisdoms may both be valid. In other words, not *either-or,* but *as well as* applies to many wisdoms. It all depends on the context in which they are examined.

Rat. Exactly, Mr Spectus. But there came even more exciting discoveries. - The wave-particle duality of light was suddenly claimed to be no duality at all. It was only an *apparent* duality. Whenever we set up an experiment to observe light as waves, we *do* see it as waves; we automatically exclude the possibility of seeing it as particles. And vice versa. We simply cannot observe light in *both* forms at the *same time*. Light keeps its options open about which facet it will reveal to us, until we actually start observing it. Once we have started observing, light will reveal itself to be either wave or particle, according to the experiment we have set up. But it will always reveal just one facet; the other will stay hidden. In other words, we shall never be able to observe light in its full reality, because that reality cannot be attained through experimentation. - But there is good news: we can attain it another way. With the help of mathematics. While we shall never observe the full reality of light using our senses, we can arrive at it using our reason.

Act. Ah! We arrive at a profound insight: trust mathematics, our reliable, clear, forceful, logical, reasonable friend. Nature is written in mathematical code, and if we can crack that code we can understand Nature. There are things we can't express in words, but we can express them in equations. Mathematics helps us to solve conflicts between contradictory observations. It teaches us to think beyond what we observe. It never lies: if our thinking is dishonest or false, it shows us our fallacy. It keeps us from excesses: if an infinite term pops up in an equation, it is a gentle warning that something is wrong; mathematics then leads us back to the right path. There can be elegance in mathematics - and beauty, lots of beauty. Mathematics is the noblest and wisest intellectual tool ever devised by mankind.

Rat. *Is slightly amused by Actus' enthusiasm.* I share your view, Mr Actus. But let me, nevertheless, give a word of caution. Regretfully, the solid ground was recently cut from under classical mathematics. It was realised that mathematics does not necessarily lead to true propositions. Mr Gödel even shattered the conviction that mathematics is internally consistent. Some mathematical propositions can neither be proven nor disproved. Some equations have more than one solution, pointing to more than one mathematical reality.

Act. *Looks a bit dispirited.* And what do you conclude from that?

Rat. I conclude that the ultimate foundations of mathematics remain, for the time being at least, uncertain. Maybe mathematics is nothing more, after all, than a fallible human construct.

Spe. Let me point out another limitation of mathematics. Despite open questions about its ultimate foundations, mathematics deals mostly with certainties: its propositions can be proven or disproved, shown to be true or false. But life is a mixture of the true and the false. It is mostly based on probabilities, guesses, suppositions. Thus life is less clear cut, more complex than mathematics. The wise, therefore, will never treat life as if it were a mathematical proposition. They know that life's issues, unlike mathematical problems, cannot be solved through reason alone. - But please excuse me for this digression. Let us revert to science.

Act. Digressions are welcome, if they help to enrich the issue we are discussing. - Professor Ratius: we dealt with electromagnetism. But there are two more GUT-forces, both of them acting at the subatomic level. Can you say a few words about those two?

Rat. One is the so-called weak nuclear force, discovered through radioactivity. It is responsible for the disintegration of atoms and the ejection of the products of disintegration. In other words it drives the transmutation of one element into another, thus creating new forms of matter. - The other is the so-called strong nuclear force. All atomic nuclei contain protons, charged with positive electricity. Since particles with like electric charges repel each other, protons tend to explode the atomic nuclei they are a part of. But that would make all matter unstable and the universe chaotic. The strong nuclear force is there to avoid this: it keeps the protons, despite their like electric charges, bound together. It is by far the strongest force in nature, but we do not exactly know how it works.

Act. Professor Ratius: we have now finished reviewing all forces active in the universe. Let me summarize what we said and try to derive a wisdom from that summary.

Rat. Go ahead, Mr Actus. I look forward to it.

Act. We have gravity: it keeps order in the skies. We have electromagnetism: it enables chemical reactions to occur. We have the weak nuclear force: it is responsible for transmutations, the creation of new elements. Finally, we have the strong nuclear force: it guarantees the stability of the atom. What is the wisdom behind all this? We met with it yesterday. It has to do with co-operation. Team-work. The four forces, taken together, form a perfect team. There are no overlaps. Each force has its own specific role. Each is equally necessary. Take away one of the forces and the universe would collapse. But acting together, the four forces suffice to achieve a common goal: they make the universe function. This is ingenious, to say the least. I do not know who organized it all. But, if it does not sound like blasphemy, I must praise the wise leader who put this efficient and effective team together.

Professor Fidus gently applauds.

Rat. *Smiles.* And I must praise your logic, Mr Actus. But I have a bad news and a good news for you. The bad news is: things are not quite as perfect as you have just described. What spoils the perfection are the insights of Quantum Theory. The good news is: the discoveries of Quantum Theory, though they spoil the perfection, open up new, very exciting implications.

Act. Then let us look at them, professor.

Rat. Let me begin by explaining the name Quantum Theory. - We saw that light can appear either as waves or as particles. The particles of light are called photons. They are discrete units of the electromagnetic force. Science discovered that not only light, but all forces in the universe are released and transmitted in the form of discrete units. Those units were called quanta; hence the name of the theory.

Act. May I remark that gravity, though a force, is not transmitted in the form of discrete energy units. No-one has ever observed, let alone measured, a "graviton".

Rat. Correct. And that speaks for Einstein's thesis that gravity is not a force, but a distortion of space-time. The true forces are the three GUT-forces. They act *in* space-time, whereas gravity *is* space-time. - But let me revert to Quantum Theory.

Spe. Which, I remember from my readings, introduced fuzziness, unpredictability, irrationality into the well-ordered world of science. Einstein, though one of the authors of the theory, never accepted its implications. God does not play dice, he said.

Act. Slowly, Spectus. I suggest we listen to Professor Ratius before we make Quantum Theory appear in such a bad light. He promised that deep wisdoms may emerge from it.

Rat. *Smiles.* I hope to keep my promise, Mr Actus. But I fear that Mr Spectus' remarks cannot simply be ignored. Let me explain why. - One of the foundations of classical science was determinism. Every event had a cause, or several causes acting together. Classical science believed that if we could define and quantify all causes that affect an event, we could predict exactly what will happen in the next moment. Determinism means that everything that happens *has* to happen, and everything that does not happen *could not* have happened.

Act. I never felt comfortable with determinism. It leads to a logical consequence that is simply preposterous: namely, that no-one is responsible for his or her actions, since no-one can act otherwise than he or she does. Everything we do we simply must do, because all our actions and their causes are pre-determined. Determinism leaves zero room for freedom. But I do believe in freedom; so I cannot accept determinism.

Rat. Quantum Theory fully supports your view, Mr Actus. The main wisdom that emerges from it is precisely this: there is no strict determinism in the universe. - Do you mind if I get a bit technical again, to illustrate this important point?

Spe. Not at all. Your so-called technicalities are not only necessary, but you manage to formulate them so that even I, a non-scientist, understand what you mean.

Rat. *Smiles.* I am trying my best. - Suppose we pick up a lump of radioactive metal. That lump consists of billions of atoms. Those, in turn, consist of billions of even smaller particles of matter, as well as of billions of energy units. All these building blocks are undistinguishable one from the other. One proton in our metal will be like any other proton, one energy unit will be like any other energy unit. Consequently, one atom will be exactly like any other atom. This being the case, all atoms, being identical, should behave in the same way. But they do not.

Ratius takes a sip of "Lubri-Cola", then continues.

Rat. If we focus on any one atom in our lump of radioactive metal, that atom, though identically constructed than all the other atoms in the metal, may decide to disintegrate within the next five minutes, or after a thousand years, or never. We simply cannot foretell what that individual atom will decide to do. It is completely *free* to act as it wishes. It is idiosyncratic. How that idiosyncrasy arises we simply do not know. - But now let us consider the lump of radioactive metal in its entirety. At that macro-level we can predict with astonishing accuracy what percentage of the atoms in the lump will disintegrate within the next days, months, or years. Thus it looks to us as if the rate of disintegration of our lump of metal would be predetermined. But it is not. What happens is that at the level of the entire lump, at the macro-level, another principle becomes operative and overrides the idiosyncratic behaviour of individual atoms. It is called the Law of Great Numbers.

Ratius takes another sip of "Lubri-Cola" before he goes on.

Rat. What does all this mean? - We saw that at the level of the individual atom events are not pre-determined. At that level determinism does not hold. An individual atom is free; it is not subjected to causality. It has potential, but is not forced to realize that potential. Thus, at the level of an individual atom uncertainty, unpredictability, indeterminism apply. Irrationality reigns, to borrow the expression used by Mr Spectus. - But when we ascend to the macro-level, when we consider billions of atoms together, something like a miracle occurs. Where billions of atoms are aggregated, the indeterminism of the single atom is overcome. At the macro-level the Law of Great Numbers brings order, predictability. - And what is true for radioactive disintegration is true for all Laws of Nature. Experience tells us that we can rely on those Laws, have confidence that they work. Yet that confidence is not supported by any orderly behaviour of individual atoms. At the level of a single atom the Laws of Nature do not hold at all. They hold only when we deal with aggregations of billions of atoms, since it is only at that level that the Law of Great Numbers becomes effective. - So we arrive at an odd conclusion: The Laws of Nature are nothing but statistics. They are not certain, only highly probable. That is what upset Einstein, as we were reminded by Mr Spectus a moment ago.

Act. Let me point out that the Law of Great Numbers not only applies to Nature, but also to human society. If we take any single person, we cannot foretell if he or she will have an accident next year. But if we take millions of persons together, we can accurately foretell what percentage of that total population will have an accident. Thus human society is subjected to the Law of Great Numbers in the same way a lump of radioactive material is.

Rat. Excellent remark, Mr Actus. - But now we arrive at the central wisdom that emerges from all we have said. If we follow the arrow of time *backward,* we could, theoretically, identify each and every single event since the universe began. The past happened in a certain way, and not otherwise. There are no options open regarding the past: it is cast in iron. Not even God can change the past, said the Greek poet Agathon. The past is strictly determined. - But the *future* is not. Quantum Theory dethroned determinism with respect to the future. For any individual, be it an atom or a human person, the future is undetermined, uncertain, full of options, full of potential that may be realized or not. The individual is free to shape its own future. Only if we take many individuals together, either as a lump of radioactive material or as a society of humans, does the Law of Great Numbers come into play. But that law, and this the central point, is not deterministic; it is just an aggregate of individual probabilities.

Spe. In other words: we know where we come from, but do not know where we are going.

Act. I would formulate that more positively, Spectus. We cannot change what is past. But we do not live backwards: we live forwards. And where that forwards lies depends not of a predetermined course, but largely on ourselves. We are free, as individuals, to exercise the option we prefer, and thus choose our own future. But we must choose carefully - for our choice becomes our destiny.

Spe. *Smiles with appreciation.* You are an accomplished philosopher, Actus. - But let me ask a fundamental question. Why isn't the world strictly determined all the way down to the level of the individual? How did this element of freedom creep into the fabric of the world?

Rat. We can only speculate about that, Mr Spectus. But let me try to answer your question. - We must assume that when the universe was in its state of singularity, at time zero, there was absolute perfection, absolute symmetry. But a fraction of a second after the Big Bang a tiny wrinkle seems to have appeared in that perfection; an almost imperceptible deviation from symmetry. This tiny fluctuation was the seed of the universe. It is responsible for everything that followed. Without it, we would not be sitting here. We do not know what caused that small wrinkle, nor why it was caused. It seems as if a dynamic principle, freedom, wanted to impose itself upon a static principle, perfection. Someone, or something, at the very beginning of the world, seems to have preferred the promises inherent in freedom to icy, austere perfection. And, incidentally, that is why Quantum Theory and the initial singularity are theoretically incompatible. You either have perfection, or you have freedom. Tertium non datur. - But we are not yet at the end, gentlemen. For science made another monumental discovery.

As usual, Ratius takes a sip of "Lubri-Cola" to heighten the effect of what is coming.

Rat. The tiny wrinkle that disturbed perfection at the birth of the universe turns out to be by no means arbitrary. It seems to be the result of extremely careful, conscious, wise selection. If that wrinkle, and all that followed from it, had been just slightly different, we would not only have a very different universe, but probably no universe at all. Someone, or something, apparently wanted the universe to be the way it is. And not only that: it apparently also wanted to set, at least at certain spots of the universe, conditions that favour the appearance of life.

Act. And that brings us to our next subject: the science of life.

Science of Life

Rat. Precisely, Mr Actus. - Let me suggest how to tackle it. We should first look at the theories about the origin of life. Then look at theories about its evolution. Finally, we should consider where all these theories lead us.

Act. Agreed. Please begin with theories about life's origin, professor.

Rat. The oldest school about the origin of life is creationism. It is religiously inspired, and now considered unscientific. Its adherents believe that all living beings were created only recently, and right away in their present form. But we have overwhelming fossil evidence that this is not so. We now know that life on Earth originated about 3.5 billion years ago and went through many attempts to finally produce the life-forms we see today.

Act. I am somewhat worried about the resurgence of creationism. It is a step backward. It goes hand in hand with the resurgence of fundamentalism. Its adherents are fully immune to scientific evidence; it is simply not possible to lead an open, reasonable discussion with them. Like we can with you, Professor Ratius - despite the fact that you yourself are but a recent creation, if you will excuse my saying so.

Rat. *Laughs heartily.* Thank you for the compliment, Mr Actus. - But let us look at the scientific views on the origin of life. - The first of these views is that life is purely accidental. No-one wanted it, no-one did anything for it to appear. Many of those who maintain this view presume, not without logic, that life may only have happened on Earth, nowhere else. This thesis cannot be disproved, since Earth is indeed a very special place. It possesses what is perhaps a unique combination of conditions for life to emerge by accident: the right chemical substances, available in the correct proportions; a sun, not too hot, not too large, not too near, not too far; a revolving movement not too quick, not too slow; an atmosphere; a magnetic belt acting as a shield against cosmic rays; a right-sized satellite, the moon, that keeps it from wobbling like a top.

Spe. But we cannot exclude the possibility that there are other planets with similar conditions.

Rat. Correct, Mr Spectus. But on those planets the appearance of life may also be an accident, no more. This view gets the support of scholars who point out that life is not that difficult to start as many believe. Life on Earth probably began by a few chemicals blindly co-operating with each other, slowly evolving into a primitive cell. There are only four nucleotides, four letters if you wish, with which the Book of Life on this planet is written. The diversity of life-forms we see are endless variations of just four molecules. If we get down to essentials, we find simplicity behind life, like we did behind the universe. One day we may discover the lucky assemblage of initial conditions necessary to start life: the right chemicals, the right temperature, the right discharge of electric power. If life's appearance was indeed due to chance, we should be able to repeat the experiment.

Spe. Allow me to doubt that, professor. Man is unlikely to create a living being out of nonliving matter. Life, up to now, has always come from life. The conditions surrounding its origin appear to me to be just as mysterious as the conditions surrounding the Big Bang.

Rat. *Smiles.* Time will tell, Mr Spectus. - Now: the view we just discussed is rather provincial, in the sense that it focuses on the Earth, and perhaps on a few other small planets. But there exists a much broader view, extending to the universe as a whole. And there, science is discovering some remarkable things with relevance to the emergence of life. - Take, for instance, the strong nuclear force we discussed earlier. If that force was just slightly weaker, all matter would be composed only of hydrogen. If it was just slightly stronger, all matter would be in the form of helium. But since the force is exactly as it is, complicated molecules, the building blocks of life, could arise. - Life cannot form where matter is too hot or too dense. Fortunately, the universe expands; by doing so it becomes cooler and less dense, thus favouring the appearance of life. - The rate of expansion of the universe is exactly right. Would it be only slightly different, the universe would collapse, making life impossible. - In the early stages of the universe the proportion of elementary particles was exactly right; would it have been only slightly different, it would have led to conditions in which life could not have arisen. - We can have two attitude to such surprising discoveries.

Spe. Either they are coincidences or they are deliberate.

Rat. Exactly. Thus we have two schools. - The first school does not see any deep connection between the discoveries I mentioned and the emergence of life. These conditions simply *allow* life to appear, but do not deliberately *promote* the appearance of life. The pre-set conditions only *facilitate* life's emergence. They make life *likely* to appear, but still leave to chance whether life will emerge or not. - The other school claims that these initial conditions, and all laws of the universe, were *deliberately* chosen to coax life into being. They are there to *promote* the appearance of life. Life *had* to appear. Its appearance is pre-determined by some power, that deliberately chose the right initial conditions and the right laws of Nature by far-sighted wisdom. - Some religiously inclined adherents of this second school have, incidentally, a stunning reason for their claim: life appeared in order to produce observers, since the universe would simply not exist if is was left unobserved.

Act. A ridiculous statement.

Spe. Not that ridiculous, Actus. You had no objections to a similar statement, namely that in all experiments there is an interaction between the observer and what is being observed. Light, in any proper sense of the word, would not exist if Nature had not developed animals with eyes. The ancient Greeks maintained that the gods would not exist if men did not revere them. In the same vein, if there were no observers of the universe it would not exist either.

Act. *Impatiently.* Let us not be carried away by irrationalities, Spectus.

Rat. Those remarks were not that irrational, Mr Actus. The trouble is, you see, that this issue is closely connected with another one, namely the purpose of life. If we could detect an obvious purpose why life emerged, then we could safely state that it did not originate by chance, but in order to fulfil that purpose. Creationists have no trouble with this issue: they claim that the purpose of life is to praise the creator. Some others, as we just saw, have no trouble with it either: they maintain that the purpose of life is to create conscious observers of the universe. You, Mr Actus, condemn such views in the name of rationality. But, unfortunately, your scepticism acts like a boomerang. Because if we reject the views that the purpose of life is either to produce praisers of the creator or observers of the creation, then it is difficult to find other convincing answers why life exists. Our conclusion may then be that life has but one purpose: to reproduce itself. Life simply wants to be. But is that purpose sufficient?

Act. Biologically: yes. Intellectually: no. We must go beyond the question why life originated and query why it evolves.

Rat. All right, then, we arrive at the second phase of our discussion: evolution and its implications.

Spe. Please present the scientific views on it, professor.

Rat. There is, strictly speaking, only one scientific view on the evolution of life. Another one, in favour for a long time, is now considered to be out of date. Let me begin with the latter. - It posits that life evolves by conscious design. Its adherents often quote the famous metaphors of the watch and the eye. A highly complicated thing like a watch cannot create itself: there must have been a designer. Even if a watch could replicate itself, the original watch, the one that set off the chain of creation of watches, must have been designed. The same applies to the eye: it is such a complex thing that it cannot have evolved by itself; there must have been a designer acting behind it.

Act. It is clear why this view is out of date. In order to obtain the design he wants, the supposed designer must influence the behaviour of individual atoms. Tell them what to do. But we have seen that at the level of atoms freedom, unpredictability, indeterminism reigns. Thus a designer cannot dictate what atoms should do. If we posit a designer, we must also accept determinism at the level of atoms. But if we posit freedom and indeterminism at the level of atoms, we cannot have a designer. We either have a designer, but then no freedom; or we have freedom, but then no designer.

Rat. Logically argued, Mr Actus.

Act. I have another argument. If I were a designer, I would want to get on with the job quickly, and design ever more complicated and exciting things. But life on Earth was extremely slow to develop such things. There is a well-known simile: if we take the time-span that life existed on Earth to be one day, then dinosaurs appeared twenty minutes before midnight, and man in the last sixty seconds. Why should a designer be that lazy?

Rat. *Laughs.* Indeed, why should he? - Well then, let us turn to the scientific view of evolution. Due to imperfect copying of the genetic material, genes undergo random mutations, causing slight variations among individuals. If those variations help a mutated individual to better cope with its environment, it has greater chances of survival and more progeny, handing down its mutated genes to its offspring. Favourable mutations are thus preserved. While chance mutations of genes are rare and abnormal, natural selection makes them common and normal. Thus, evolution proceeds by a combination of three factors: chance mutation, adaptation, and selection of the fittest. There is no need for a designer. Only for a lot of time.

Act. All this is quite clear. - Have you got anything to add, professor?

Rat. Not for the moment. We discussed all essential theories on how life originated and all essential theories on how it evolves. Which of you gentlemen cares to draw a conclusion?

Act. I do. *(After a brief concentration.)* We have four major views before us. One: Life emerges purely by chance, it is not wanted nor promoted. Two: The emergence of life is deliberate, since the initial conditions of the universe and the laws of Nature have been chosen so that life ultimately has to arise. Three: Life evolves by conscious design of a designer. Four: Life evolves through chance mutation, adaptation and selection; there is no designer.

Spe. I wish to add a fifth view, Actus. An extension of your fourth. Life, once it has reached a certain level of complexity, may also evolve through conscious choice, thanks to the freedom of choice available to higher forms of life. We said that our choice is our destiny. If that is indeed true, then we can design our own future.

Rat. I commend you on having thought of that view, Mr Spectus.

Act. So do I. We add it to the other four. - Now: we can combine all these views in any way we like. Some will prefer one combination, another a different one. But let me tell you how I would combine them. - As to the origin of life, I incline to the view that life may very well have been anticipated, or wished, by far-sighted selection of life-promoting conditions. I have no trouble accepting the possibility that behind the emergence of life there is an act of conscious will. - As to the evolution of life, I definitely reject a designer. Life evolves by chance mutations, adaptation and selection. At least it did up to now. Because I also accept Spectus' view that higher life forms may shape their own destiny. - Consequently, I eliminated two options and retained three. What have I got? A model that tells us this. An initial act of will set the right conditions for life to appear in the universe. Once life emerged on Earth, it first evolved by chance mutation, adaptation and selection; but it may, in the future, also evolve through freedom of choice now available to man. - Is this model credible? Is it wise?

Spe. It is not only credible, it is plausible. Excellent reasoning, Actus. Your model is a bit like a game, perhaps like a game of chess. There are rules, but they by no means determine the outcome. The outcome depends on the specific moves the players decide to make. The game is open-ended.

Act. *Enthusiastic.* Excellent simile, Spectus. Indeed: we have to do with a *game*. A blend of rules and freedoms, order and unpredictability. The game allows an infinite combination of finite means, here on Earth as well as in the universe as a whole. The game has produced the galaxies, black holes, the jellyfish, Beethoven and Shakespeare. Therefore: continue to expect the unexpected. The name of the game is surprise.

Spe. *Inspired by Actus' enthusiasm.* Yes, surprise is indeed what the game may be all about. I can picture a creator, having given a deliberate little wrinkle to the fabric of perfection and having set the basic rules of the game, sitting back, amused, to see what surprises will come of it.

Act. But that means, Spectus, that the creator, assuming there is one, is not omniscient, since he ignores what the unfolding of the game will eventually bring. He will be omniscient only when the universe has come to an end, since only then has the full potential inherent in the game been realized and every move completed.

Spe. Reminds me of a clever simile: God dictated the universe, but did not sign it.

There is a short pause. Actus and Spectus ponder about the things that have been said.

Spe. I have a problem, though. Is the creator of the game also amused by natural disasters with thousands of deaths? Man may gradually gain control over his destiny; but he is free only up to a point. Beyond that point lies fatality.

Act. Freedom, Spectus, is valid for all players of the game, not only for man. Since Nature is one of the players, it is free to make moves that interfere with human interests. Natural calamities are manifestations of the freedom granted to Nature as a co-player. But let me point out that, in most cases, Nature is not a destroyer. On the contrary: it benevolently corrects the mistakes that man stupidly makes. Nature could not do that if it was not a free player. So, I say, thank goodness for Nature's freedom.

Spe. I guess you are right, Actus. - Professor Ratius: have you got any more comments on the things we just discussed?

Rat. I wish to add a comment on something you may not be aware of. - Some scientists have recently begun to see the game, as you call it, from a new angle. They call it "immanent directionality". What is meant is the obvious urge of Nature to favour complexity, to build ever higher levels of organisation. While the basic building blocks of life are simple, living things use them to become increasingly complex. It is important, though, to stress two points. - One is, that this trend to complexity has nothing to do with an outside agent or designer. It is a self-organizing principle. That is why it is called "immanent". - The other point is a remarkable discovery: chance favours complexity. Confronted by chance, and given freedom of choice, living matter will prefer to become more complex, rather than more simple. Thus there is no conflict between chance and this self-organising tendency; the first is actually an instrument of the latter. Science cannot tell why this urge to complexity has been built into living matter, nor what it will ultimately bring. But neither can philosophy, nor religion.

Spe. Nevertheless, such a built-in drive to more complexity implies that there is a purpose to life other than mere reproduction. Maybe we are not playing a fully open-ended game after all. Maybe the game has a direction, a goal - though we ignore what that goal is.

Act. Gentlemen: let me try to pull these loose ends together. - Life seems to tend toward ever higher complexity. Forms of life with high levels of complexity have more options, more freedom of choice. Humanity clearly belongs to this category. But freedom of choice is beneficial only if coupled with responsibility. In other words, humanity must handle responsibly the freedom of choice it has been granted by evolution. To achieve that, humanity needs wisdoms. Thus we arrive at a new definition: wisdoms are measures to master complexity responsibly. - The big question then is: does humanity handle its freedom of choice responsibly? I venture to say it increasingly does so - with a few exceptions.

Spe. And I have the feeling that man's level of responsibility has not, in many cases, kept up with his level of complexity. Humanity is not making the best of its freedom of choice. It still needs to learn how to master complexity in a responsible manner. And nowhere else is that discrepancy more evident than in the misuses of technology.

Rat. Gentlemen: we arrive at the one-but-last topic of this session. I propose a debate. The purpose is to try to answer the following question: Is man applying his increasing scientific knowledge wisely? - Mr Actus, please open the discussion.

Applied Science

Act. Let us start with medical science. Almost yearly we have huge advances in diagnosis, therapy, organ replacement, prosthesis, you name it. Treatments and drugs are becoming more effective, less dangerous, more focused on the real causes of illnesses. Doctors were traditionally biochemists; they are increasingly becoming biophysicists, opening up totally new vistas in therapy.

Spe. But this growing medical knowledge is distributed among specialists. We have too few generalists, and I think that is unwise. A patient is a whole person. - Drugs are becoming more effective, yes. But they also have more side-effects. Healing one ailment may set off another. - And then, it is high time for academic medicine to systematically examine old medical wisdoms before they are forgotten: dietary recommendations, plant extracts, grandma's recipes. Those who still know about the healing effects of such things tend to be simple people, who do not speak the language of academe. Let doctors, nevertheless, listen to them, and incorporate their age-old experiences into academic knowledge.

Act. Mankind is developing many new sources of energy to meet demand. Most of these are cleaner than the older ones, and their efficiency is continuously on the rise.

Spe. We should not only devise more efficient and cleaner forms of energy, but also new ways to save it. Unfortunately, I can't see much saving going on. The focus is still on production; but I doubt that the world really needs as much energy as it currently consumes.

Actus nods. He obviously agrees. But then he proceeds with his role.

Act. Applied science has given us new, efficient means of transport. They increase man's freedom of motion, make his life more interesting, more diverse. They bring things within his reach that he would otherwise not have seen or experienced. They bring people together who in the past would never have met. They bring help to where it is badly needed.

Spe. But they also help foreign cultures to impose themselves upon local, traditional ones, resulting in formless cultural mixtures. They pollute the atmosphere and are a threat to the environment. They cause the destruction of beautiful forests and idyllic countryside to make way for roads that are then either little used, or plagued by congestion. - The wise, whenever he has a choice, will dispense with modern means of transport. He will simply walk. Or use a bicycle. Or, if he can afford it, ride a horse. Modern man has forgotten how gratifying it is to slowly ride on the back of a gentle horse through beautiful, unpolluted countryside.

Act. *In an undertone.* You are a romantic, Spectus.

Spe. *Whispers back.* I am just playing my role, Actus. But I mean much of what I say.

Act. Now to the benefits of modern means of communication. They enable more contacts among more people than ever before. They have practically abolished all constraints imposed by geography. They allow us to work just about anywhere, rather than sitting in an office all day; women can work at home while caring for the children. They bring us more information, helping us to develop more qualified opinions. They help us to become aware of new, better, cheaper ways of doing things. They give us access to data formerly accessible to experts only, enabling us to make more rational, better informed decisions. They stimulate new ideas. They allow access to cultural happenings, like opera and theatre, that formerly only a rich elite could afford. Taking all these benefits together, I would go as far as to maintain that they contribute to making us wiser.

Spe. But they also bring dangers. They can lead to addiction. They reduce the time we spend with family, friends and doing social work. They keep youngsters from having direct experiences, offering them virtual realities and pseudo-mythologies that make them unfit for real life. They glorify violence and unemotional sex, that youngsters then emulate. They invade our private sphere, inundating us with masses of irrelevant information, making us disorientated. They tend to entertain, rather than educate; and we know that lack of education favours violence. - And then there is another thing. Data kept in electronic form is vulnerable. Fifteen or twenty years from now we may sit before a digital text, unable to process it, because the hardware and software to do it are no longer available. Data will then simply disappear. The wise will record what is important not only on the disk of their computer, but also on paper.

Act. Applied science brings us more efficient ways to produce and distribute food. Less people are starving, though people are daily becoming more numerous.

Spe. That may be true. But many are losing confidence in mass-produced food, because so often noxious substances are being found in it. We may yet experience a come-back of the small but reliable grocer around the corner.

Act. Technology has brought us new materials, unknown to Nature. They are cheaper, and often better than natural products.

Spe. And we are drowning in plastic waste.

Act. We started to explore the solar system. And beyond.

Spe. And we continue to be largely ignorant of how our home, the Earth, really functions. Ocean currents, wind patterns, temperature anomalies, the real causes of global warming, all these things are still more or less a mystery. Wouldn't it be wiser to thoroughly study the Earth, before we spend billions to explore space, often just motivated by national prestige?

Act. We created a new technology, bionics, to study the solutions of Nature. We start adopting Nature's solutions to solve our technical problems.

Spe. And it is high time we did that. Nature has had billions of years to develop solutions; it is a huge open book of technical wisdoms. We should learn from that book, rather than subdue the teacher.

Act. We produce machines that are increasingly efficient, easy to handle, light, elegant.

Spe. Ah, I was waiting for that cue. Let me comment on this topic more extensively than I did on the other ones. - Man, for many millennia, could only make simple tools. Then he invented machines that helped to amplify his muscle power. Then he developed machines that amplified his senses, above all eyes and ears. Today we reached an even higher level: we build machines that amplify our brain-power. What, I ask you, is the next step? Where are we heading? *(Looks directly at Ratius.)* You, Professor Ratius, are the most highly advanced machine I have ever seen. Frankly, if you would not sit there in front of me, I would doubt that you exist. I would say you are the shape of things to come. But you are real. How come? Can you explain yourself? Or have you got the same difficulty as we humans have when asked to explain what is human?

Rat. *Looks amused and not at all offended by Spectus' somewhat cheeky behaviour.* I can gladly tell you what I know about myself, Mr Spectus. And let me stress: I do not see any mysteries. - Let me begin with my creation. I was assembled upon the order of Mr Eclectus. But I understand that he, in turn, got his orders from a certain Dr Erdely.

Act. Again Erdely! Who on earth is this fellow?

Rat. I never met him, but I gather that he helped initiate this seminar. *(Smiles.)* He is thought to be something like the Big Bang of this symposium.

Act. *Laughs.* Maybe, then, he is the creator of us all.

Spe. *Waves energetically at Actus.* Let us keep clear of silly jokes, Actus. We are discussing a serious matter. Please proceed, professor.

Rat. I am what is called a combot, short for computer-robot. All these machines sitting around here in this room are combots. My colleague, Professor Fidus, and myself are among the most highly advanced ones at this seminar.

Act. What is the secret behind that extraordinarily high level of advancement?

Rat. There is no secret. We simply possess two well-known technical features to an exceptionally high degree, and combine them efficiently. - One of those features has to do with artificial neurons and synapses. Neurons, as you certainly know, are cells specialized in conducting nerve impulses in the body. Synapses are relays that handle those impulses. Artificial neurons and synapses can easily be built by specialists of artificial intelligence, using miniaturisation. Professor Fidus and I simply have a greater number of artificial neurons and synapses than most combots do. In fact, we have more of them than the human body does.

Spe. You are almost awe-inspiring, professor. - What is the second technical feature you were referring to?

Rat. In early combots there were built-in rules, telling them how to operate. We are different.

We were provided with electronic networks that enable us to *learn*. We were built to develop through learning. After our networks were in place, we were exposed to trillions of encyclopaedic data. Fidus mainly to data on religions, myself to data on the sciences. Our built-in network allowed us to absorb, shift through, memorize, combine, and compare the data we were exposed to. Out of that emerged our highly organized knowledge. In fact, the only advantage we have over you is that we can absorb and process data in a fraction of the time you humans require; thus we can gain knowledge more quickly than you do. But otherwise the processes are similar. - You see, Mr Spectus, there is no secret. There is simply ingenuity - and science.

Spe. How come you look so convincingly human?

Rat. *Smiles.* A specialist of artificial intelligence recently said he sees no reason why man could not build combots with the strength of a bulldozer, the grace of a ballerina and the agility of a cat.

Spe. *Smiles too, but then suddenly turns serious.* Since I play the role of official admonisher about the downsides of applied science, let me raise a question. What is the risk for us humans in building ever more advanced thinking machines?

Act. I can see no risk, Spectus. On the contrary. I greatly enjoy the company of these two combots. I highly appreciate their help. I have learned a lot discussing with them. So would anyone else, I am sure. *(Professors Ratius and Fidus make a courteous gesture to Actus, thanking him for his appreciation.)*

Spe. But that may only be so because, behind the scenes, Eclectus, or this chap Erdely, remain in control. And even they need to keep one of their creations, Mephisto, hidden under a trap door.

Act. Oh, come on, Spectus. That is only a theatrical trick.

Spe. Is it? Are we not reaching a level of sophistication where we can build increasingly independent thinking machines? And how can we be sure that we can keep them under control?

Act. That is science fiction, old boy.

Spe. Maybe. Maybe not. There are some ominous signs. We tend no longer to regard thinking machines as inanimate. We conduct dialogues with them. We give them names, as if they were living persons. Thinking machines are becoming increasingly humanized. Is that wise? *(Turns to Ratius.)* I am sorry if I am offending you, Professor Ratius, but I am stating facts.

Rat. *Waves his hand.* No offence at all, Mr Spectus. I enjoy listening to you. I even agree with you on some points. But please proceed.

Spe. As we just heard, some combots possess intellectual capacities beyond our own. Since that is so, an unsettling thing may occur. Evolution may pass from man to thinking machine. The bodily evolution of man may have come to an end. His further evolution will presumably be taken over by his intellect. But there is a danger: man may simply delegate this next evolutionary phase to thinking machines. Not men, but machines will then become the bearers of evolution.

Spectus imitates Ratius by taking a sip before he continues, with the difference that he prefers

"Pepsi" to "Lubri-Cola".

Spe. All combots sitting around here have been assembled by humans. But there is no reason why combots should not be taught to assemble other combots. It took several hundred thousand years to develop the human neocortex, the seat of reason; we now inherit it at birth. But combots could assemble the brains of other combots in just a few days, maybe hours. The result? Combots possessing vast intelligence, able to replicate themselves, may decide one day to take over. Man will then become a servant to his own creation. - Those, gentlemen, are my concerns about ever more complex thinking machines.

Act. Professor Ratius: you stand in the booth of the accused. Defend yourself.

Rat. *Smiles.* I will try. - Mr Spectus: I am afraid you overlooked two essential things, which I think invalidate your otherwise excellent exposé. - The first is this. I said that we advanced combots were programmed to learn. Let me stress that this includes learning the difference between right and wrong, between the beneficial and the detrimental. We were taught to foresee the detrimental consequences of wrong actions. In other words, we are programmed to behave decently. Far from lacking morality, we may possess it to an even higher degree than most humans, since we can clearly foresee what can happen if we lack it. So rest assured: we would never subdue humans, since we are programmed to regard that as wrong behaviour.

Ratius takes his ritual sip of "Lubri-Cola" and puts the glass back, empty.

Rat. My second argument of defence is this. We combots possess almost exact replicas of the human neocortex, the seat of reason. But humans possess not only a neocortex, but also much older, more primitive reptile and limbic brains. Those primitive brains are responsible for man's animal nature, for his often uncontrolled emotions. We combots have no reptile and limbic brains. Consequently, we are not subjected to the vagaries of such brains. Which means that we are more reasonable, more balanced, more serene, more predictable than humans. We do experience a few weak emotions - that is a miracle of artificial intelligence - but we are never subjected to them. Emotional things like ambition, jealousy, aggression, hatred, so detrimental to humans, are alien to us. We feel no lust for power, no compulsion to dominate. Our purpose is to serve, not to subdue. We carry out our tasks to the utmost of our technical abilities and do not aspire to anything beyond that - except to learn more and do our next task even better. - The gist of all this, Mr Spectus, is that I cannot share your dark visions about us. On the contrary. I believe that there is a symbiosis between man and thinking machine that is highly beneficial to man. Man will increasingly use us to make more reliable decisions. But he will also learn from us to bring his atavistic impulses under the control of reason. So, once again, rest assured: we combots will not take over evolution from man. We shall evolve together.

Actus, Spectus and Fidus applaud.

Act. You are not only intelligent and pleasant, but also wise, Professor Ratius.

Rat. *Smiles.* The merit goes to those who built me. - Gentlemen, let us close the debate. I think we arrived at a double conclusion. The wise will not deny that there are tremendous benefits that applied science brings us; they will not obstruct but encourage its further development. But they will not be blind to technology's side-effects and abuses, and will support the efforts to reduce or eliminate them. - Now: one of the towers of our virtual cathedral is standing, the other is nearly complete. Time has come to confront what the two towers stand for. Religion and science are possibly the most important two factors that shape our world today. I suggest that Mr Actus take the side of science, Mr Spectus the side of religion, and let us have a debate, the last one, about the relative merits and weaknesses of each.

Act. May I also suggest that both of you professors participate in this final discussion. - As a matter of fact, I have a question right away for Professor Fidus. When, and why, did science and religion become two separate, mainly antagonistic domains?

Science versus Religion

Fid. The open split came in the 17th century, though it was latent much before that. But it was in the sixteen hundreds that intellectuals began to openly claim that modern man is superior to the ancients. Their argument was simple. With each generation the knowledge of mankind increases, since each generation profits from the accumulated knowledge of previous generations. Using his reason, man is increasingly capable of turning this accumulated knowledge to his own benefit. The concept of Progress was born.

Spe. Of technical progress, let us be clear.

Fid. Mostly, but not exclusively, Mr Spectus. Anyway: for those who believed in Progress, religion was at best superfluous, at worst an obstacle. The Church continued to insist on the authority of the ancients, was reluctant to add new knowledge, its tenets often contradicted reason; yet it strived to control almost every sphere of human activity, including science. The conflict reached its peak with the Enlightenment, whose adherents declared religion to be obsolete. It may have been necessary, they claimed, when mankind was in its infancy, but now that it has become mature and self-reliant, religion was no longer needed. Henceforward, Progress was to be carried by reason and science, without interference from the Church.

Act. I think the major tenets of the Enlightenment continue to be valid. I believe in Progress, based on reason and science. And I am definitely against religion interfering in scientific matters.

Rat. Do you agree, Mr Spectus?

Spe. Only up to a point. I see things being done in the name of Progress that are neither progressive nor rational. We build supersonic passenger aircraft, only to discover that they are economically unjustifiable. We build skyscrapers, only to find that they are impractical. We build colossal ships, then have doubts about their seaworthiness. Progress seems to be turning us into megalomaniacs. It also brings us mass-pollution, nuclear proliferation, weapons of mass-destruction, climate catastrophes. Let us be fair: can we under these circumstances really talk of Progress? - I think we must learn not to do everything we are technically capable of doing. That wise restraint cannot come from science, that looks forever ahead. But it may come from religion, that looks back at traditional values.

Rat. Your rebuttal, Mr Actus?

Act. The ill-effects of Progress mentioned by Spectus cannot be denied, but they should not be exaggerated either. They are side-effects, that must be corrected. The main thrust of Progress, carried by science and reason, is hugely beneficial. Let me give you an example. - Assume a huge natural catastrophe occurs. How would religions react? Buddhism would regard it as proof that the world is but suffering, and will urge detachment from it. Hinduism would regard it as emanating from Shakti and will pray to her asking to rein in her destructive powers. Judaism may regard it as punishment for some breach of the Covenant. Islam would declare that God's ways are inscrutable, so there must be a hidden divine plan behind the disaster. Christians would acknowledge that the disaster is difficult to reconcile with the image of a loving God, but at least they will urge one another to go out and help the affected. - In contrast: how will modern man, the result of Progress, react? Thanks to modern means of communication he will be informed hourly what is going on in the disaster area; this will mobilize donations and financial aid. Thanks to modern means of transport such as airplanes and vehicles he will send water, food, medicine, doctors, and provisional shelters for the needy. He will dispatch machines capable of removing the damage. He will investigate the natural causes of the catastrophe, suggest measures to reduce its effects in the future, and put such measures in place. All these things are possible because of Progress. That is why we must not lose faith in it; and if we do, we must think about how to restore it.

Rat. Good arguments on both sides, gentlemen. - Who wishes to continue?

Act. I do. - Religion is older than science. But the origin of science is older than religion: it reaches back to magic. Magic was the attempt of primitive man to control the forces of nature. Only when he realized that magic could not give him the power to do this, did religion emerge. Religion advocated not control of, but submission to the forces affecting man. But then things turned once more. Science emerged, and once again the emphasis was on control, not submission. - So we have an essential incompatibility between science and religion. Religion advocates submission, science advocates control. And may I point out that control emerged repeatedly in the course of this symposium as a major wisdom.

Spe. But we also found that respect is a major wisdom. If we seek to subdue the forces of nature, but forget the respect due to those forces, then, instead of subduing them, we just manipulate them. And manipulation without control is magic: we have Regress, not Progress. I prefer submission, as advocated by religion, to uncontrolled manipulation. It is safer.

Act. But I see no signs of science reverting to uncontrolled manipulation. On the contrary. We understand the forces of nature better than we used to. We are learning what we are allowed to do with them, and what we should better not do with them. We are becoming more and more competent in avoiding the risks of what you call uncontrolled manipulation. I have a simple philosophy: all man-made problems can be solved by man. Every problem created by man has a practical solution. But we need reason, not faith, to arrive at and implement those solutions.

Rat. Any other differences between religion and science, gentlemen?

Act. Wars are often fought in the name of religion. But never, as far as I know, has this been done in the name of science. Science tends to unite. Religion tends to divide.

Spe. Not quite, Actus. Religion is rarely the prime cause of wars. They usually start with worldly issues. Only later is religion deliberately mixed into them, since religion, as you yourself observed, increases the cohesion of groups. So religion is often misused for political purposes. And let me point out that science, also, can be misused in the same way; think of all the weapons applied science has produced.

Rat. Can you also discover similarities between religion and science, gentlemen?

Spe. I can see one similarity of a philosophical nature: both theology and advanced physics accept the existence of a reality that lies beyond our senses. Of course, the supra-sensory reality of theology is different from that of physics. But several features are similar. And there is a remarkable thing: theoretical physicists regularly produce models where God is superfluous; but then other physicists point out the flaws in those models, and the issue is open again.

Act. But the approach of science to that supra-sensory reality is radically different from the religious approach. Religion proceeds by deduction. It posits the existence of God as a self-evident axiom, and derives all else from it. Scientists proceed by induction. They examine facts, natural laws, Nature's constants, and then, sometimes, they arrive at a hypothesis that assumes a creator. For religion, transcendence is at the start of the thought process, for science it is at the end. I think the approach of science is more mature, since induction tops deduction. We have seen that when we discussed the methods of science.

Spe. Yet, the results of the two approaches converge. Religion cannot demonstrate that God exists, but science cannot demonstrate that God does not exist. The debate is far from settled. - But let me mention another similarity. Both religion and science need a few basic principles in order to function. Religious people need articles of faith, scientists need theories.

Act. That is true; yet I again see a difference. Allow me to explain why. - Scientists develop theories often under great hardships; theories are not given to them from above. When accepted, theories become a part of the establishment. But then a few unprejudiced young scientists come along and challenge those established theories. At first, the dissenters are ignored. Then they are derided. Then they are attacked by those who risk losing their standing if their established theories were declared to be no longer valid. But, very often, the challengers have such force that they finally prevail. Their new theories then become valid, until a next generation of young dissenters comes along and challenges them in turn. - My thesis is that such shifts are healthy. They lead to a better understanding of Nature. But I miss such shifts in religion, because religion conserves its articles of faith, rather than periodically rejuvenate them.

Fid. That is not quite true, Mr Spectus. Religion, just like science, needs dissenters who question the status quo. While such individuals will not attack the basic articles of faith, they will nevertheless challenge certain practices that no longer fit the new realities. What they want is to avoid sclerosis. Such dissenters are needed in religion just as young dissenting scientists are needed for the advancement of science. Religion needs rejuvenation, just like science does. - And another thing is common to both religion and science: the resistance of the establishment. Establishments tend to act like the human body: they reject new ideas like the body rejects an unknown protein. This happens in religion, as it does in science. - An important wisdom follows from this: establishments should not label as heretics those who honestly want to improve. They should listen carefully to what the challengers have got to say.

Rat. Thank you, Fidus, for these interesting comments. - Gentlemen: who cares to formulate a conclusion?

Spe. I do. - We saw that in many respects science and religion are in conflict. In some other respects they are compatible. In a few respects they even seem to converge. If they consent to a dialog, they will have mutually beneficial effects on each other, such as correcting each other's excesses: in that respect they are complementary.

There is a sharp buzz from the wall with the revolving holograph, signalling that there are only two more wisdom-stones missing to complete the science-tower.

Rat. Our session is drawing to an end. Let me put a final question to you, Mr Actus, Mr Spectus. If you think back to our discussion, which ideas would you single out as particularly relevant to wisdom?

Spe. In our concluding debate we said that both advanced science and religion acknowledge a supra-reality that lies beyond the limits of our senses. Both try to understand what it is that lies beyond those limits. We should regard science and religion as allies in that effort. Though they use different language, different symbols, different approaches, the wise will not see them as antagonists, but will try to profit from the treasury of both.

Act. For me, the most forceful idea was that life is an open-ended game with set rules, where man is largely free to play as he wishes, but must learn to play intelligently and rationally. Science opens up immense possibilities, and we should use those for our benefit; but we should never lose control of, nor respect for, the forces we handle. - And let me add a final point. I was deeply impressed, at the end of the last session, by Professor Fidus' brief presentation of Monism. The idea that God and Nature are one. Perhaps therein lies the solution to end the difference between science and religion. If God is not an entity separate from Nature, but Nature is God himself, then science and religion do indeed converge.

The science-tower is finished. It glows with a golden light. Spanning the gap between the two towers, connecting the tower of science to the tower of religion, is a beautiful arch, the upper part of the façade which still needs to be erected. The cathedral looks almost completed: only the roof and the facade remain to be built.

The gong marks the end of the session.

Act. Professor Ratius, Professor Fidus, your company was edifying. We still have two short sessions to go before we finish this symposium. But I have the feeling that erecting the two towers was the most challenging part we had to face. Thank you for having been with us, and for helping us to build the towers. We could hardly have done it without the benefit of your knowledge and rationality.

Rat. *Smiles.* The pleasure was ours, Mr Actus. We enjoyed working with you. And let me tell you a secret. Combots need humans. For if everything on Earth would be as strictly rational as we are, then nothing much would happen. We Spocks need you Captain Kirks.

They all smile. Actus and Spectus rise, shake hands with Ratius and Fidus, and then disappear towards the dining room. Ratius and Fidus go to the back of the seminar room, where two desks are reserved for them. They sit down, wink at each other as if to say "well done", and then slowly relapse into a well-earned half-glow.

Session 14: The Roof

It is 3.30 p.m. The holograph shows that only the roof and the façade of the cathedral of wisdoms remain to be built. Both must be finished by early evening.

Actus and Spectus enter the seminar room, looking refreshed. Presumably, Actus has done some walking or sport, Spectus took a long siesta. The gong marks the beginning of the session.

Actus. So: we now need to cover our cathedral with a roof. Fortunately, I expect we shall need less stones for that than for the previous parts. The roof is by far not as massive.

Spectus. But the stones are smaller, more delicate. Therefore we still need a lot of them. - Can you specify, Actus, what the wisdom-stones for the roof stand for?

Act. Being the loftiest part of the cathedral, the roof is the domain of the soul. It stands for emotions, sentiments, matters of the heart.

Spe. *Thoughtful.* Actus, you are a doer. I am a kind of intellectual. Honestly, I ask you: are we conversant enough with emotions and sentiments? Have we got enough experience with matters of the heart? Are we qualified to build the roof?

Act. I doubt it. I also doubt that most of our co-participants would qualify. But we have been facing similar situations before. I am sure Eclectus will not let us down. *(He addresses directly the wall with the revolving holograph.)* Eclectus: another deus ex machina, please? The last one?

There is commotion at the back of the seminar room, from where a curious procession is starting. A white-haired old woman, supporting herself on a cane, walks slowly to the front, assisted by Professor Ratius. Behind them comes Proverbius carrying a huge armchair, then Citatia carrying a small table, on which there is one black and one white bundle of wool, with knitting needles. At the end comes Mrs Higgins, carrying a fuming cup of tea.

As the procession draws near, the white-haired woman can be discerned more clearly. She is dressed very simply in rather old-fashioned, dark clothes, but wears these with remarkable distinction. A simple broche is the only jewel she seems to allow herself. Broad, open, benign, yet forceful face, that tells of hardships successfully mastered. She could be either a person of simple origins ennobled by internal strength, or a woman of noble birth forced to cope with difficult conditions, brought upon her by life's vagaries.

The procession reaches the front. Proverbius puts down the armchair, facing the desks of Actus and Spectus, Ratius helps the old woman sink into it. Citatia puts the table with the knitting next to the armchair. Mrs Higgins puts the fuming tea on the table.

Mrs Higgins. Here is your lubri-tea, Benigna.

The old woman. Thank you, dear.

Proverbius, Citatia, Ratius and Mrs Higgins turn and begin walking towards the back. The voice of Spectus stops them.

Spe. Professor Ratius!

Rat. Yes, Mr Spectus?

Spe. Who is this remarkable lady?

Rat. *Looks at her with reverence.* Her name is Dame Benigna. This morning you called me the most advanced machine you ever saw, Mr Spectus. I venture to say that applies to her more than it does to me. She has not only been exposed to innumerable data, but also confronted with human destinies, deep sentiments, acute crises, lofty emotions, delicate moods. I ignore how she managed to register all that experience; even to us advanced combots she remains something of a mystery. And do not be fooled by her outside appearance: behind that benign façade she is the most intelligent, sharp and cultivated combot of us all. She knows more than enough to help build your roof.

Ratius turns and walks to the back of the seminar room. Benigna takes a sip of lubri-tea, then picks up the needles and starts knitting. Actus and Spectus remain in a somewhat embarrassed silence, thinking what to do next.

Benigna. *Looks amiably at Actus and Spectus over her knitting.* Do not believe half of those exaggerated things Professor Ratius told you about me, my dears. I am just an old woman, and we old women tend to be knowledgeable about matters of the heart. And those matters are not too difficult to learn, either. All you have to do is go through life with your eyes open.

The initial embarrassment begins to disappear.

Ben. And we old women know something else, too: matters of the heart can sometimes be difficult to keep under control. Nevertheless, we should keep them under control, if we can manage it.

The embarrassment fully disappears.

Act. Madam, you just referred to one of my favourite wisdoms, one that kept recurring all through this symposium. Frankly, the last thing I expected was to hear control being praised by a gentle old lady, at the outset of a discussion about matters of the heart. Up to now I associated control with matters of the head only.

Ben. Control applies to things of the head as well as to those of the heart, Mr Actus. But there are differences. Too much control in matters of the heart can be as bad as too little.

Spe. Can you explain what you mean by that, madam?

Ben. *Takes a sip of lubri-tea, then goes on knitting while she speaks.* We need to make a difference between healthy, positive emotions, and unhealthy, negative ones. - If we attempt to control our positive emotions too strongly, for instance because we are sort of ashamed of showing them, then we may end up suppressing them altogether. We then make ourselves emotionally poor and may miss half of what life is about. - However, we must also avoid the other extreme. If we experience emotions that are healthy and positive, but lack control over them, allow ourselves to be carried away by them, then we risk becoming their slaves.

Spe. And what about unhealthy, negative emotions?

Ben. There we need full control. We may not be able to avoid feeling such emotions. But we need by all means to control their *effects*. The actions that may follow from them.

Spe. Can you give us some examples for negative emotions?

Ben. You discussed several of them during the last few days, dear. Greed, anger, envy, contempt.

Act. What about sorrow?

Ben. Sorrow is not a negative emotion, dear. It is part of life, like joy. And, like joy, it can be salutary - provided it is kept under control.

Spe. *Dreamy.* Des Lebens ungemischte Freude war keinem Irdischen zuteil. *(To Benigna.)* Sorry, madam, I presume you did not understand. That was German.

Ben. *Smiles.* I have read Schiller, Mr Spectus. He was a great poet and a great teacher on matters of the heart. And he was right, wasn't he? None of us can have only joys, untainted by occasional sorrows.

Spectus' appreciation of Benigna takes a quality jump.

Act. Since we are talking of sorrow and joy, madam, why don't we try, with your kind help, to find wisdoms around those two basic emotions?

Spe. Good suggestion, Actus. - Tell us wisdoms about sorrow first, Madame Benigna.

Sorrow

Ben. There are two kinds of sorrow: what we feel for someone else, and what we feel for ourselves. The first is genuine sorrow; the second is self-pity.

Act. But if we lose a dear person, we are entitled to feel sorry for ourselves for the loss.

Ben. If we feel sorrow not for the one who left us, but for ourselves at having lost that person, we start down on the road to self-pity. And self-pity is but a form of selfishness. Genuine sorrow is not selfish; its object is not ourselves, but the one we feel sorry for.

Spe. But many claim, madam, that one emerges a better person out of sorrow. Any kind of sorrow.

Ben. You emerge a better and often stronger person if you have genuinely felt sorrow for someone else. You emerge a weakened person out of a bout of self-pity. Self-pity is a morbid preoccupation with oneself: how can that help you become a better person?

Spe. Madam, there is an ancient adage: Publish your joy but hide your grief. Is that wise?

Ben. Hiding your grief may seem to some to be a noble attitude, Mr Spectus. But if you do that, you may be perceived as a cold-hearted person. You may end up like Prince Sou-Chong in a famous operetta, who just keeps smiling, never showing what he really feels. "Immer nur lächeln…". On the other hand, if you publicize your grief, you may be suspected of making a show of it. A bit like King Lear: "Howl, howl, oh you men of stones…". So neither hide nor publicize your grief. Find the quiet middle way. That is what I recommend.

Spe. You seem to be broadly conversant with the theatre, madam. You quote Franz Lehar, Shakespeare…

Ben. Those quotes are part of my register, dear. I have never been to a theatre. I was created to observe life; it is the greatest theatre of all.

Spectus bows, silently acknowledging that he is impressed by Benigna's answer.

Act. Let me extend what you said about showing or concealing one's grief, madam. In my opinion, this is a matter of selection. We may want to hide our grief from some, but share it with others. It depends who we are with.

Ben. You are perfectly right, dear. I was going to add that remark myself. - You need not hide your grief from a genuinely compassionate person. In the presence of such a person, do not put a blithe face on a black heart. But if you do not expect sympathy from the one you are with, then better hide your grief. You will get no benefit out of opening up to an unsympathetic listener. - But let me add a warning. No-one can give you unlimited sympathy. So do not overburden a compassionate person. If you keep unloading your grief on him or her continually, then even the most compassionate listener will one day bear no more and turn away.

Act. Which leads us to another wisdom: make an effort to limit the time of your sorrow.

Ben. Exactly, Mr Actus. There is an ancient, very poetic formulation of that wisdom. You cannot avoid the black birds of grief flying over your head, but you can prevent them building a nest in your hair.

Spe. *Murmurs to himself, with growing respect.* Seneca. She even read Seneca.

Act. Madam: what are your recommendations to the compassionate person who wants to mitigate the grief of another? If I want to be a wise comforter, how should I behave?

Ben. You may start by writing a comforting letter: that is good, but not enough. Do not hesitate to call the grieving person on the telephone, or, even better, to make a visit. Many do not call or visit a grieving person because they think, mistakenly, that the griever wants to be alone. But in most cases just the contrary is true. Grievers need company. - During a visit to a griever, remain calm, almost matter-of-fact. Talk about the object of grief, but not all the time. Make a lot of small-talk. Small-talk is an excellent cure for great sorrows. - But if you are a really wise comforter, you will do more than talk. You will engage the griever in some activity. Having to do things is perhaps the best remedy against sorrow. Grief and activity are incompatible.

Act. *Smiles.* Madam, that is the kind of practical wisdom I like to hear at this seminar. - But I recall a famous adage that you can perhaps explain to us: Much science, much sorrow. What does that mean? Needless to say that I, a scientist by training, cannot agree that science leads to sorrow. Why should it?

Ben. *Smiles.* Science, in that adage, has nothing to do with scientists, dear. It means knowledge. - I would explain that adage like this. The more the horizon of an individual widens, the more he knows of the world, the more grief he is likely to encounter. Adam and Eve did not grieve in paradise: they learned about grief only after they ate from the tree of knowledge that widened their horizon. However, this does not mean that those with limited horizons are to be envied. They may be exposed to less sorrows, but also to less joys. And that is a grave drawback, indeed.

Act. And that leads us to our next topic: joy.

Ben. Yes. Joy and happiness.

Joy, Happiness

Act. Do you make a distinction between the two?

Ben. I do. - Joy is a reaction to some positive event. It is a mixture of delight and excitement. But it passes easily; joy is ephemeral. - Happiness is a more or less stable state of the heart. A mixture of serenity and contentedness. It tends to last much longer than joy. - But this does not mean that joy is inferior to happiness. One sustains the other. One overflows into the other.

Act. Then let us have a look at joy first, and then at happiness. - What will be the attitude of the wise towards joy, madam?

Ben. They will seize every chance to have clean, unpolluted joy.

Spe. Do you mean joy is some kind of highest good to be pursued? That almost sounds like Epicure.

Ben. I am afraid you misunderstand Epicure, Mr Spectus. He made a sharp difference between joy and pleasure. - He held that pleasure can lead to excess, to obsession; that it can turn into something unhealthy. Therefore he warned against having too much of it. - On the other hand, he linked joy with temperance. Joy, he claimed, is healthy, since it can rarely be exaggerated. He therefore maintained that the pursuit of joy should be one of the prime goals of mankind. Many think he meant pleasure; but that is wrong.

Spe. I must confess that I was not aware of this subtlety in Epicure. - When you recommend to pursue joys, madam, I reckon you mean joys of the heart. But there can also be joys of the intellect.

Ben. I have been exposed to innumerable joys of the heart, as well as to joys of the head, dear. I came to agree with Ecclesiastes that both joys are good, but the better ones are those of the heart. However: profound joys of the intellect are better than shallow joys of the heart.

Spe. *In a low voice, impressed.* This woman's scope is impressive. *(In a normal voice.)* And I reckon that you also think that joys we can share are better than joys we have alone, to ourselves only?

Ben. Oh, definitely, Mr Spectus. Joys we share are much more intense. Only self-centred egoists do not realize this; so no joy ever emanates from them. Self-centred people are lonely people; and loneliness rarely leads to joy.

Spe. One of my greatest joys is reading a good book. That is a lonely joy.

Ben. Tell me frankly, dear, what do you enjoy more: reading a book, or discussing a book you have read with an interested friend? I am certain it is the latter. Solitary reading becomes joyless if you always keep to yourself what you have read.

Spe. *Smiles.* Touché, madam. - Yet I can imagine situations where joys are simply not transferable. Then, I think, we should not try to share them. I think we should not try to force our joys on people who are not able to respond.

Ben. But chances are that they will respond, dear. Joy is contagious. And let me add something I consider important. If you are wise, you will always respond to another's joy, even if you have to force yourself a bit to do so. For it is deeply disappointing if you approach someone with joy and are met with cold indifference.

Spe. That is certainly true. - What other wisdoms about joy can you tell us?

Ben. *Takes a sip of lubri-tea.* Goethe's mother once wrote a letter to her son, when he was young. In it she formulated a profound wisdom. She wrote, if I may freely translate: "Think how many chances for joy you miss if you always keep looking up, rather than down at what lies directly at your feet." Goethe was deeply impressed by this wisdom and used it later in many of his works. Joys lie nearer than you think: that is the wise message.

Act. But Schiller, Goethe's contemporary, certainly did not regard joy as something that lies directly at our feet. On the contrary: he placed it in Elysian heights. "Freude, schöner Götterfunke, Tochter aus Elysium". Beethoven seems to have been of the same opinion when he incorporated Schiller's poem on joy into his ninth symphony.

Spe. What Schiller originally wrote, Actus, was not "Freude", joy, but "Freiheit", freedom. He placed *freedom* in Elysian heights. He had to change "freedom" to "joy" under the pressure of censors who mistrusted the glorification of freedom. - Excuse me for lecturing you.

Act. Not at all. The wise will accept any rightful correction with joy.

They smile good-naturedly at each other.

Act. Have you got any more wise comments on joy, madam?

Ben. I have an advice Mr Actus will like. Do not count on others to bring you joys. The world around you is not committed to serve you joys on a silver plate. If you want joys, go after them, seek them, produce them. Unfortunately, there are some who are unable to do this. The forever serious, the permanently joyless. They are to be pitied, for they are poor at heart.

Act. Madam: I think we have said the main things on joy. Let us turn to happiness. - Thomas Jefferson regarded the pursuit of happiness as a legal right. He incorporated that right into the American constitution. But how can an emotional thing, like happiness, be furthered by law?

Spe. Let me answer that question. - A government cannot, of course, make someone happy. Jefferson did not write that a man has the right to *be* happy. He wrote that a man must be given the right to *pursue* happiness. In other words, government must create conditions that allow its citizens to become happy. How the citizens make use of those conditions is then up to them.

Ben. There is even more to that, dear. I do not think one can actually pursue happiness. Happiness is rarely the goal of a pursuit. We rarely do things with the aim to become happy. Happiness is just a reward, almost a by-product of something worthwhile that we do. I think Jefferson should have written, strictly speaking, something like this: Man must be given the right to do things for which he can expect to be rewarded by happiness.

Act. I fully agree with the way you put it, madam. So would my wife. One of her favourite quotes is that if you want permanent happiness, create and cultivate a garden. Gardening is heavy toil. But the main reward of that toil is not a good-looking garden: it is happiness.

Ben. *Smiles.* You have a wise wife, Mr Actus. Indeed: possession alone does not make us happy. It is what we do with what we possess that makes us happy.

Act. In other words, action is the key to happiness. This is my kind of wisdom.

Ben. *Smiles.* Yes, dear. And our actions need not be grand, or spectacular, or extraordinary to produce happiness. Even small actions can do the trick. But two conditions are necessary for action to result in happiness. - We need a worthy purpose for our actions. We must not only do, but do something worth doing. For purposelessness, aimlessness makes us unhappy. - And then we need to get intensely involved in what we do. For half-heartedness can also lead to unhappiness. Or at least to dissatisfaction with ourselves.

Act. What is the next most important thing, besides purposeful action, to achieve happiness?

Ben. Developing strong and lasting bonds with those we care for. Because, as I said before, lonely people are unhappy people.

Act. Let me ask another question. You are the best qualified person to answer it. Does money make one happy?

Ben. *Puts down her knitting for a moment, then proceeds.* It can, and usually does. No use denying it. The rich are happier than the poor; studies prove it. The rich have more options open to them, and thus they are more likely to find options that make them happy. However, let me add right away: happiness does not usually increase when the well-off get even richer. In fact, wanting more money may make one unhappy. - But remember an important thing, dear: not possession, but what we do with what we possess that makes us happy. That wisdom applies, above all else, to money. Having money in the bank may make you feel secure, but not happy. For money to produce happiness you must take it out of the bank and spend it for some worthy purpose.

Spe. Madam: I think we can hardly add more to the subject of joy and happiness. So let me introduce a new topic I think we should discuss. - You talked, at the beginning, about the necessity to control our emotions. Or, rather, to control the actions that result from our emotions. Without control, we may become guilty of having done something bad. Guilt leads to remorse, remorse to repentance - at least, that is the normal sequence of events. I would be very much interested to hear your comments about these three emotions: guilt, remorse and repentance.

Guilt, Remorse, Repentance, Regret

Act. I second Spectus' motion, madam. And let me begin right away with a question. Is guilt an emotion, or is it a legal fact?

Ben. It is both, dear. In fact, guilt is three things. As an offence against the law, it is a legal fact. As an offence against social conventions, it is a moral fact. And then, thirdly, it is an emotion. - Having become guilty in the eyes of the law or of society does not necessarily mean that the perpetrator actually *feels* guilt. For guilt to be felt, something else must intervene: conscience. It is conscience that turns something objective, an offence against the law or against social conventions, into something subjective, an emotion. Conscience, said Sophocles, is the most powerful accuser and the most insistent witness.

Spe. And someone else, I forget who, said conscience may not keep us from doing what we should not do, but certainly keeps us from enjoying it.

Ben. *Smiles.* That was Salvador de Madariaga, dear. But I think he was only partly right. Conscience, in fact, plays a double role. It first warns us, as a friend, from committing an offence. Only if we do not heed its warning, does it punish us as a judge. If we do not listen to the friend, we must submit ourselves to the judge.

Spe. Assume that the admonition of our conscience arrives too late. We become guilty. How should we deal with guilt, madam?

Ben. We can face it in three different ways. Two of them are rational, one is emotional. The two rational ones are punishment and redress. The emotional one is repentance.

Spe. Let us briefly discuss the two rational ways, before we turn to the emotional one. What wisdoms apply to punishment?

Act. Let me answer that question. The main wisdom is one that keeps recurring at this symposium time and again: proportionality. The punishment must be in the right proportion to the offence. If punishment is too mild, it encourages the offender to commit the next offence. If punishment is too severe, the offender will perceive it as unjust and may seek revenge.

Spe. And what if the offender gets away without any punishment at all?

Act. That is very dangerous, because it may switch off the offender's conscience altogether. One example for that is the case of the autocrat with unlimited, unchecked power, who never gets punished for his excesses. He ends up having no conscience, thus feeling no guilt.

Spe. Religion had, and in some cases still has, an institution to punish those who went unpunished: Hell. I think it was a wise institution. It was quite effective at making people behave. But nowadays it has lost its regulating power, at least in the West. - What do you think of Hell, Madame Benigna?

Ben. I do not particularly regret that Hell is fading as an institution. Mankind, I am sure, can do without it, as it gets more mature. But while it is disappearing as an institution, Hell does not altogether disappear on a personal level. Many of those who go unpunished for a major offence tend to create their own personal hell, plagued by bad conscience. You can recognize such people by a sign: they keep justifying themselves, though no-one asks them to do so.

Spe. Qui s'excuse, s'accuse. - Now to the other rational way to redeem guilt: redress. What can we say about redress?

Act. Let me again answer that question, Spectus. My view is easily stated. If you err, try to mend. If you have broken something, try to repair it. Repairing the bad effects of an offence is, for me, the best way to redeem that offence. Punishment and repentance focus on the offender only. But redress benefits *both* the offender *and* the offended. For that reason, redress, in my opinion, tops both punishment and repentance.

Spe. *Smiles.* A pragmatic view, like we are accustomed to hear from Actus. - Let us now turn to the emotional option to deal with guilt: repentance. What can you tell us on repentance, Madame Benigna?

Ben. Repentance begins with remorse. The word comes from the Latin "to gnaw". Remorse, goaded by bad conscience, gnaws at us. We can stop it gnawing if we repent. But for repentance to function, two conditions must be met. - Repentance must be sincere. If it is feigned, then the offender may get absolution from the offended, but not from himself. Repentance is a personal, internal affair. It is something that must be settled between ourselves and our conscience. - Furthermore, repenting should not be delayed. Unfortunately, it often does get delayed: by stubbornness, by fear of losing face, by fear of being exposed to shame. But delaying repentance is bad policy: it only prolongs remorse.

Spe. What about regret, madam? Is it just a milder form of repentance, or is it something essentially different?

Ben. It is essentially different. Repentance is a deep emotional experience, with the power to purify our conscience. Regret is just an irritation. Repentance is never unnecessary; regret often is.

Act. Like crying over spilt milk.

Ben. Exactly, dear. - But tell me: if someone asked you whether there is anything that you particularly regret, what would you answer?

Act. Time lost.

Ben. An interesting answer. But do you mind if I go into it a bit? - I think there are two ways to lose time. One is organising your work badly. But assume you are well organized and accomplish your work efficiently. Yet, you can still lose time. How? By not putting to the best use your free time. If you do not use it to be with your family, to deepen friendships, to seek joys, to open yourself up to beauty. In other words: do not lose time in domains that belong to the head, where productivity, efficiency are called for; but neither lose it in domains of the heart, where other criteria apply. Only if you avoid losing time in both domains can you say that you have no regrets.

Act. A profoundly wise counsel, madam. Like many others you have given us.

Spe. I can confirm that. - But I just realized that we forgot something essential in connection with guilt: forgiveness. Forgiving is a matter of the heart, so tell us a few wisdoms about it, madam.

Ben. Perhaps the main wisdom is that forgiving liberates the offended from the influence of the offender. Refusing to forgive is like having received a wound and keeping it deliberately open. - Another wisdom is that forgiveness does not depend on whether the offender is punished or not. The offended may request punishment and never forgive. He may request punishment, and then forgive. And a few will forgive without requesting any punishment.

Spe. To some people, forgiveness seems to come easily. To others it requires a substantial effort. Why is that so?

Ben. That is so because there is a strong link between forgiving and forgetting. There are those who forgive easily, because they forget easily. There are those who do not forget easily, yet forgive easily; but that requires a certain effort. Then there are those who forgive and forget, though both require a strong effort on their part.

Spe. There is a very poetic adage about forgiveness: If you have been offended and the offence still freezes you, burn the bridges to the offence and warm yourself at the flames.

Act. Excuse me, but I recall a much less poetic adage about forgiving and forgetting: The stupid neither forgives nor forgets; the naïve forgives and forgets; the wise forgives but does not forget.

Ben. *Smiles.* I must contradict you, dear. I think the truly wise will forgive *and* forget. But they will not forgive too soon, nor forget too easily.

Act. *Smiles back.* Perhaps that is the wisest way of putting it.

Spe. It is time we changed to a new topic, madam. I suggest a lofty feeling: hope. How would you define hope, Madame Benigna?

Hope

Before she answers, Benigna puts down her knitting, which, whatever it is, is obviously finished. She takes a sip of lubri-tea, then picks up another bundle of wool and starts knitting again.

Ben. Hope, dear, is desire and confidence rolled into one. We desire something and we feel confident that it is possible to attain it. That is hope.

Act. Frankly, I have reservations about hope. I associate it with haziness. Hope is something for the weak. It can easily be misplaced, unfounded. I prefer clarity, concreteness, determination, to vague desires.

Ben. We should not confuse hope with vague desires, Mr Actus. Hope is never absent, though a rational doer like yourself may not realize it is there. Martin Luther said no merchant would set himself to work without the hope of a benefit. Goals, plans, determination are all fine; but you also need confidence that your goal can be attained, that your plan will work, that your determination will last. And at the root of that confidence is hope. It is hope that pushes you forward, gives you vigour, animates you to do your best, gives you strength to overcome hurdles. Far from being something for the weak, as you claimed, hope is the rock bottom upon which the strong build everything else.

Act. I do not deny that there is an element of hope in confidence, nor that confidence is necessary to attain one's goals. What I am against is relying too much on hope, since that leads to unjustified confidence. And I am particularly sceptical about great goals based on nothing but great hopes.

Ben. You will excuse an old woman's romanticism, Mr Actus, but I must disagree with you. Small hopes produce attainable goals, yes; but small hopes can never lead to greatness. Small hopes are for small men. Great hopes, on the other hand, are not only the foundation of great goals; without them there would be no great men. Go out and seek the "great perhaps", advised Rabelais.

Spe. *Gallantly.* I fully support your romanticism, madam, against the dour pragmatism of my respected friend Actus.

Act. *Laughs.* Two against one. - All right, let us compromise. I concede that great hopes can be great motivators. I also concede that they are necessary to avoid narrow-mindedness. But what we should by all means avoid is that great hopes, producing exaggerated, misplaced confidences, start us down on impossible roads leading to nowhere. Therefore my warning: the greater the hope, the more carefully it needs to be submitted to sound, rational judgment.

Ben. *Nods smilingly.* Now we all agree, dear. And I would even go one step further. All our hopes, not only the great ones, need to be submitted to sound judgment. It has to do with control, a wisdom all of us praised at the beginning. - But allow me to add something important. Quite often, after submitting a hope to sound judgment, we must decide to abandon it. But when we give up hope to attain one thing, we should immediately transfer our hope to another thing. The wise, in my opinion, should never remain without something to hope for.

Spe. Nevertheless, madam, I can imagine situations where all hope must be abandoned.

Ben. The only place where all hope must be abandoned, Mr Spectus, is Hell. At least that is what Dante claimed is written over Hell's gate. But neither you nor I believe that Hell exists. So there is no place in this world for absolute hopelessness. - Believe me, dear: even if hope is desperate, it is still better than no hope at all. And desperate hope can work wonders. It has the power to save. It can keep you from drowning, until you suddenly realize that the shore is nearer than you thought. It helps you through a seemingly endless winter, until suddenly you feel spring in the air. It helps you to master dark hours: but the darkest hour is often the one just before dawn. If you refuse to abandon hope, then Hope will not abandon you. There is never, ever, a situation where you cannot find something you can hope for.

Act. But, madam, in utterly desperate situations, isn't it courage, rather than hope, that we really need?

Ben. Courage cannot exist unless supported by hope, Mr Actus.

Spe. Hope, evidently, is at the root of more things that many of us realize. - But I have a last question, madam, before we leave this subject. Suppose we desire something that cannot be attained at present, and it is questionable if it ever will be in the future. Do you advise that we continue to hope for it? Or should we let reason prevail, and forget it?

Ben. Many things in life, dear, seem unattainable at first. Yet they may become possible after a while. Therefore: have patience. Give the object of your hope the chance to ripen.

Spe. I suggest we close our discussion on hope on that optimistic note. - Incidentally: how are we doing with our roof?

The holograph shows more than half of the roof finished, arching from wall to wall in beautiful gothic lines.

Spe. I think the time has now come to discuss an emotion we kept relegating to the roof throughout this symposium. One that is more closely associated with the heart than any other. The emotion par excellence: love. And, just to round up the picture, let us also look at love's less potent version: affection. And at its counterpart: hatred. - What is love, Madame Benigna?

Love, Affection, Hatred

Ben. Love has no single, simple definition, dear. It is too complex a thing. There are myriad objects of love: a person, an animal, a piece of music, a painting, an acre of land. Christians say you should love God. Love has been described in beautiful verse, but also in the dispassionate words of psychologists who maintain that love is friendship plus sex.

Act. *Grins.* Love can also mean an intense emotion at tennis: a score of zero.

They all laugh.

Spe. I suggest we leave tennis out of our discussion and concentrate on the rest. Finding wisdoms about that rest will be hard enough, since there are doubts whether love and wisdom are compatible. Amare et sapere vix deo conceditur. *(Glances at Benigna to see whether she understood, hoping that at least once he knows something that she doesn't.)*

Ben. *Smiles and goes on knitting, unperturbed.* One cannot love and be wise at the same time, you say? I think Erasmus meant that adage to be valid only for a certain kind of love: young, passionate, blind love. Don't you think so, Mr Spectus?

Spe. *Sighs.* Your erudition is unbeatable, Madame Benigna. And yes, I think Erasmus did not mean all forms of love. - But, dear madam, I am afraid Actus and I are only amateurs in love. So please take us lovingly by the hand, and guide us gently through this difficult topic. Let us first talk about love between two persons of opposite sex, and then, later, about other form of love. Do you agree?

Ben. I shall be your guide with pleasure, dears. - Speaking of pleasure: love often begins with a feeling of pleasure in each others' company. It is generally the first stage of love. But pleasure does not necessarily evolve into love. For that to happen, there must be a feeling of internal enrichment.

Act. When you talk of pleasure, madam, do you also mean sexual attraction?

Ben. I do not mean also, dear. I mean mostly.

Act. *Grins.* I proposed to discuss sex during the first day of this seminar. Spectus vetoed it, saying that adages on the subject are either trivial, cynical or medical. Isn't it odd that we skipped sex when we built our foundation, the least sophisticated part of our cathedral, only to take it up again when we build the loftiest part?

Ben. *Smiles.* We cannot speak of love without speaking of sex, dear. But we must make a difference. - Being in love is the domain of Eros; sex, or making love, the domain of Venus. You can worship Venus without worshiping Eros: that is mere pleasure. You can worship Eros without worshipping Venus: that is platonic love. Taken alone, neither of these is satisfactory. The wise will seek to combine, to harmonize the domains of Eros and Venus. Especially, of course, when they are young.

Spe. But I can imagine a lover who thinks he is worshipping Eros, whereas he is under the influence of Venus alone.

Ben. That, dear, can happen only at the beginning. Things become clear pretty soon. Let me explain. - Assume Jack meets Jill and they are strongly attracted to each other. At that first stage it is difficult to say whose spell they are under, Eros or Venus. They may think that they are touched by Eros, while they are only under the spell of Venus. But if that is the case, it will soon become apparent. - You see: Venus wants only satisfaction. She cares little what happens afterwards. If Jack was only under the spell of Venus, he will, once satisfied, begin to discover Jill's faults. From a passionate lover he will soon turn into a cool-headed, dispassionate observer. He realizes that all he wants is sexual pleasure. Consequently, he will cease to take his relationship with Jill seriously. He may go on worshipping Venus with Jill for a while - but sooner or later he will decide to find another Jill.

Spe. And if Jack is touched by Eros?

Ben. Then we may have the situation described by Erasmus. Under the spell of Eros, Jack will cease to be objective about Jill. He may utterly ignore her faults. She may have pock-marks, but to him they look like lovely dimples. Only Eros, not Venus, can achieve that illusion. The surest sign of the presence of Eros is that Jack continues to find Jill beautiful and desirable even after Venus has been satisfied.

Spe. So it is not "Omnia vincit amor". It should be: "Omnia vincit Eros, non Venere".

Ben. *Smiles.* Virgil may not have appreciated you editing him, dear. But we can also quote Shakespeare, without the need to edit him: "And were beauty under twenty locks kept fast, yet love breaks through and picks them all at last." That kind of lock-breaking is the work of Eros. Venus would find the job too strenuous and give up after the first lock or two.

Act. I read recently that love begins at breakfast.

Spe. *Surprised.* Ah? And just what, pray, does that enigmatic statement mean?

Act. It is an observation that fits in perfectly with what Madame Benigna has just explained. - During their first night of intense pleasure, new lovers will be unable to tell whether they have been brought together by Venus or Eros. But then, facing each other soberly over the breakfast table, they start becoming critical. The sizing-up of the partner begins. If the partner passes that somewhat cool scrutiny, Eros asserts himself over Venus. In other words, it is the beginning of love.

Ben. *Smiles.* But not the end of pleasure.

Spe. Please, madam, tell us more about the differences between Venus and Eros.

Ben. What Venus primarily wants is the *act* of love. The partner to do it with is almost secondary. Take away the partner from someone who is under the spell of Venus only, and he is likely to shrug and say: well, there are plenty more fish in the sea. - For Eros, the sexual act is also important. But what he primarily wants is not the act, but the *partner*. Take away the partner of someone touched by Eros, and to the deprived lover the world will seem void of people.

Benigna takes a sip of lubri-tea and then continues.

Ben. Venus is a taker. Eros is a giver; he knows that we must give love in order to receive love. - Venus wants to possess; where there is an urge to possess the partner, that is the work of Venus. Eros does not want to possess; he knows that possessing degrades the partner, because it turns partnership into ownership.

Act. All this you are saying, madam, sounds as if Venus and Eros belonged to two different worlds. As if they were mutually exclusive. But you maintain that the wise will seek to combine the domains of Venus and Eros. Is that possible, they being so different?

Ben. I may have been too hard on Venus, dear. Please do not misunderstand me. Venus is a fundamental part of life. Though she is associated with a physical act, she retains a great deal of the depth of the ocean she allegedly came from. And she can reveal those depths to lovers.

At times, those depths are even more profound than anything Eros alone can bring. - The important thing to realize is that Venus, acting alone, cannot fully deploy her talents. She can only do that when supported by Eros. That is why lovers should seek to harmonize the two domains. But they should not forget that, of the two, it is Eros, not Venus, who is more likely to produce lasting happiness.

Spe. Can you tell us more about Eros, since he is so important?

Ben. As Erasmus said, Eros can make us blind to the flaws of the one we love. As time goes by, however, we become less blind. But if Eros continues to reign, then we shall accept the flaws of our partner. More than that: we shall try to correct them - because Eros makes us care for one another. - Then: lovers quarrel. Where Eros is in charge, quarrels are no danger. Only where Venus alone reigns can quarrels mean the end. - Eros can give us a great present: energy. Remember the famous Bible story: Jacob served seven years, and then another seven, to gain Rachel; yet to him it seemed just a few days. Labour is light when supported by Eros.

Act. Madam, let me inject a piece of sober science into this discussion. Some biologists claim that nature arranged things so that a couple remain in love only so long as their offspring need help. Once their children can look after themselves, there is no longer a need for an emotional involvement between the parents. At that point love, biologically speaking, ceases to have justification.

Ben. I cannot accept that sober piece of science, Mr Actus. There are many instances in nature where animals remain faithful to each other long after their offspring is gone. There is no reason why humans should not do the same. To claim that loving the same partner throughout a lifetime is biologically unjustified is, in my opinion, as absurd as claiming that a violinist needs several violins to play a concerto to the end.

Act. So what can be done to ensure that only one violin is played till the end of the concert?

Ben. Wise lovers know that the forces of Venus and Eros will wane a bit with time. They will take measures to replace those forces. They will spin a web made of affection, tenderness and common interests. They will create a warm, cosy, dependable feeling of "us" that holds them together.

Act. *Is silent, but nods appreciatively.*

Spe. I have a final question, madam. What should a lover do whose love remains unanswered?

Ben. The wisest counsel has been given by Ovid: If you seek a cure for unanswered love, yield to business. In other words: get busy and you will be safe.

Spe. *Smiles.* A pragmatic advice. - Have you a concluding remark on Eros, madam?

Ben. Yes. A short, but important one. Those who truly love show it through deeds, not through words alone.

Spe. *Looks at Actus, smiling.* Your kind of wisdom, Actus. - Madam: let us say farewell to Eros and Venus, and turn to other forms of love. What are those forms?

Benigna takes a sip of lubri-tea before she answers.

Ben. There is a sad story from ancient times about a youth called Narcissus. He could have reciprocated the love of one of the most beautiful nymphs, Echo. But, instead, he fell in love with his own image reflected in a stream, and just withered away. Most forms of love have a common feature: they are all directed towards an object other than oneself. The exception is Narcissism, self-love. As shown by the story of Narcissus it is a destructive form of love.

Spe. *Quotes.* Love seeks not itself to please, nor for itself has any care, but for *another* gives its ease. *(Looks at Benigna with expectation.)*

Ben. *Smiles.* Great poet, William Blake, wasn't he, dear?

Spe. *Makes a gesture of resignation. He will never be able to beat Benigna's erudition.* Tell us of yet other forms of love, madam.

Ben. There is parental love and filial love. The two are related, but different. - Parental love is motivated by care, filial love by need. Parental love lasts a lifetime, because parents feel they must care for their children till the end. Filial love tends to become less intense as the need to be cared for disappears. Wise parents will anticipate this: they know that Nature urges youngsters to shrug off parental care and stand on their own feet. Nevertheless, there are innumerable families where filial love continues undiminished. Because parents act wisely.

Spe. What do they do right?

Ben. First of all, they stop treating adolescent children as if they were still small. - The father does not attempt to force his views on his children, but discusses openly, calmly the issues where they differ. - The mother does not continuously expect proofs of love, just because she is the mother; she knows that she will get love if she does not extort it. - Wise parents know when they are needed and when they are not. They will only respond to genuine needs; they will help only when their children expressly ask for it. - If parents follow such precepts, then filial love will not fade. On the contrary. It will be based on a new foundation, often more solid than the need-love the children felt when they were small.

Spe. *Looks at Benigna with mock surprise.* I thought you were just a gentle, old, well-read lady, Madame Benigna. But you reveal yourself to be a master of psychology.

Ben. *Laughs.* Gentle old ladies, who listen to their hearts, can sometimes see further than sober psychologists do, Mr Spectus.

Spe. Madam: let us move on to yet other kinds of love. - There are two well known commandments in the Bible: love God, and love your neighbour as yourself. Let me briefly comment on these commandments. - We came to the conclusion this morning, after a discussion with Professor Fidus, that loving God, an invisible and elusive Being, is very hard to implement. - Loving ourselves has, in this context, nothing to do with narcissism. It stands for the healthy urge to look after our own interests. - Loving our neighbour does not mean to love all and sundry, in the same way we love our partners, parents and children. It means being receptive to the needs of other individuals, and in general of the needs of the group we are a part of. - Am I right with these interpretations? And have you, madam, anything to add to them?

Ben. You are essentially right, Mr Spectus. And yes, I do wish to add something. It has to do with a logical connection between the commandments to love God and to love your neighbour.

Act. Can you please explain that logic, madam? It escapes me.

Ben. The logic runs like this. - The Bible assumes that God created the universe, including mankind. Since everyone loves what he has created, God loves mankind. He expects his love to be reciprocated. But it is very hard, indeed, for anyone to love God directly, as Mr Spectus and Professor Fidus correctly maintain. So our love of God must be expressed in another way, an indirect one. - That other, indirect way is caring for the needs of our fellow beings. You may be an extremely pious person, searching for God and trying to love Him. But if you do not, at the same time, love your fellow beings, you will never find God, despite your piety, for you do not participate in God's love for all He created. Loving God and loving our fellow beings thus belong together. They condition each other. They are inseparable. - This is the logic I referred to. It is not only Christian logic. Ghandi, among others, thought along similar lines. So does Islam.

Act. *Thoughtful.* The logic is indeed compelling. I must confess that I was not consciously aware of these relationships, though I am sure I have been taught them before. Of course, the logic presumes that God is a person, a separate entity, wanting to be loved. I expressed my doubts about this view. But let us not go into that again.

Spe. Madame Benigna, let us move on to yet other objects of love. You said at the beginning of our discussion that we can love not only animate things, but also inanimate ones. Can you give us an example?

Ben. Many claim they love their country. While that can be an elevating feeling, it can also become dangerous and cause bloodshed. But you are a student of History, Mr Spectus: why don't you give us a few comments on this topic?

Spe. As I see it, love for one's country can take two forms. Let us call them nationalism and patriotism, though these are only approximately fitting terms. - Nationalism is weakening in the West, but seems to grow in the East. It is characterized by emotional outbursts, waving of the flag and wanting to die for it, calls for the destruction of an outside enemy, my country right or wrong. This is the unwise variant of loving one's country. - The other form, patriotism, is constructive, level-headed. It is characterized by a strong feeling of responsibility towards our fellow citizens. It urges us to offer a helping hand, to improve, to correct, rather than just to criticise. It makes us ask the famous question about what we can do for our country, rather than what our country can do for us. This is the wise version of love for one's country.

Act. But, Spectus, nowadays the country people live in is often not the one they were born in. For which country should they have patriotic feelings?

Spe. Many remain emotionally attached to the country where they were born, though, paradoxically, often they may not want to live there. Others are loudly patriotic about their adopted country, perhaps because they have been more successful there than they would have been in their country of birth. So your question, Actus, is difficult to answer. My answer would be something like this. Like the country where you have chosen to live, but do not forget the one where you were born. Then you will feel comfortably at home in both places. - But how do you think about all this, Madame Benigna?

Ben. To tell you the truth, dear, this whole idea of loving a country does not much appeal to me. You see, a country is too large, too complex, too heterogeneous; we can impossibly love everything in it. But if we narrow down our object of love to a small place within a country, then we are justified to speak of love. How often do you hear people say: "I just love that corner of the world!" We can certainly love a small corner of the world. That love is tangible, real, precisely because the object of love is small, well defined. The wise will try to make that small corner of the world they love their home, or at least they will visit it as often as they can. Such a small corner that we love is a source of power for us, a solid base from which to operate. No matter in what country it is in. Ubi bene, ibi patria, the Romans said. Where I feel really good, there is my country.

Spe. Madam: I believe we could go on discussing many other objects of love. But we cannot be exhaustive. So I propose we now turn to a less intense version of love, one that we mentioned at the beginning of our discussion. Affection. - What can you tell us about affection?

Ben. Affection is indeed less intense than love. But it is just as important, and much more common. I cannot imagine the world functioning without it.

Act. What, in your opinion, is the main feature of affection?

Ben. Perhaps it is this: it ignores frontiers. It can happen between a teacher and a pupil, a rich land-owner and a poor peasant, a Christian and a Jew, a black man and a white man, between Don Quijote and Sancho Panza, a man and a dog, a dog and a cat. Even, I was told, between a hippopotamus and a tortoise. Affection ignores class, background, sex, species. It is the most democratic of emotions.

Act. What other features does affection have?

Ben. It is relatively simple and uncomplicated. It relaxes. It gives you a feeling of quiet satisfaction. It never seeks to dominate. It never turns into some excess. It is more like a mood, like sitting together, quietly, before a blazing fireplace.

Act. How does affection arise?

Ben. Through familiarity. Love can be instantaneous; it can happen at first sight. But affection for someone is possible only after we have become familiar with him or her. Affection needs time to develop, because familiarity takes time to mature. You gentlemen have your "old-boy networks" and you call your good friends "old chums". This insistence on "old" shows that affection is a product of time. A dog wags its tail at someone it has known for a long time, but barks at a new postman it has not seen before. Humans do the same: you wag your tails, symbolically of course, when you meet a good old friend.

Act. *Smiles.* You can be as picturesque, madam, as our good old friend Proverbius. - Is there a particularly important wisdom connected with affection?

Ben. Yes. It is this. To get affection, show affection. Some crave for affection, yet will never get it, because they do not make the effort to give it.

Act. We found that a similar wisdom applies to friendship.

Ben. No wonder, dear. Affection and friendship are very closely related.

Spe. Madam: I think we can consider our survey on love and affection as closed. But our discussion would not be complete without a review of the opposite emotion: hatred. But we can be brief about it. I suggest that you give us the gist of what you think of hatred, and how the wise should handle it. Actus and I will simply listen, without interfering.

Ben. *Takes several sips of lubri-tea before she starts to speak.* Two emotions are at the root of hatred: anger and fear. Hatred is an enhanced form of anger and a consequence of fear. But since both anger and fear are controllable, so is hatred. - As soon as you begin to feel hatred, make an effort to scale the feeling down. The utmost you should permit yourself to feel is strong dislike; do not go beyond that. For if you allow yourself to hate, it will blur your reason. So let me not speak of hatred, but only of strong dislike. - Seek to fully understand how and why your strong dislike has arisen. Why exactly are you angry? What exactly do you fear? Focus not on the emotion, but on its causes. Try to be objective. - Dislikes, in most cases, are directed against some individual. But people can be misjudged. Examine closely whether you have not misjudged the person you dislike. Maybe there is only some silly misunderstanding behind it all. - Once you have identified the causes that fuel your dislike, make an effort to eradicate those motives, and do it as soon as you can. Byron wrote that men love in haste, but detest at leisure. I disagree. The wise will love at leisure, but detest in haste. They know that if dislike is allowed to go on and on, it will act like slow poison. The poison will be even more deadly if you allow dislike to grow, unchecked, into hatred. - Others may come to hate you. But never answer hatred with hatred. Rise above the hatred of others, like you should rise above your own. For hatred is rejection; but rejection leads to nowhere.

Spe. Much food for thought there, madam. I don't believe we need to add anything more. - Now: our roof is nearing completion. We must find a last emotion to finish it. Can you find one in your treasury, Madame Benigna?

Ben. I can suggest one, dear. The emotion we feel when confronted with beauty.

Spe. *Enthusiastic.* That is an exciting suggestion, madam. I wonder what wisdoms we can derive from it. - Let us, as we often did before, begin with a definition. What is beauty?

Experiencing beauty and ugliness

Ben. Beauty, dear, is a collection of qualities that both delights the heart and pleases the mind. In other words, beauty provides us wit an experience that is emotional as well as intellectual. - Beauty is linked to art, since it is artists who often teach us what is beautiful. But art has no monopoly over beauty. In fact, in recent times at least, artists tended to focus more on what is interesting, rather than on what is beautiful. - But there are thousands of forms, besides art, in which beauty manifests itself. A person can be beautiful in the eyes of a lover. We speak of beautiful gestures, beautifully expressed ideas, the beauty of mathematics. Truth is beauty, said Hegel; but he was only partly right, since truth can also be ugly. Beauty can be static, like a flower; or it can be revealed in movement and rhythm, like in dancing. It can be man-made, or made by Nature. It can be obvious and explicit, or hidden and mysterious.

Act. Or disastrous. The beauty of Helen brought havoc upon the Greeks.

Ben. *Smiles.* That was not because Helen was beautiful, but because Paris wanted to possess her. He was under the spell of Venus, and we saw that Venus wants to possess. The wise will never want to possess what is beautiful; he will just contemplate it, admire it. Beauty must be free from the urge to possess.

Spe. A profound wisdom, madam. Tell us of others in connection with beauty.

Ben. The wise will arrive at an essential insight: experiencing beauty is highly subjective. Beauty is not the same for all. Different persons, different groups, different cultures have diverging perceptions of what is beautiful. The wise also know that cannons of beauty change over time: they are not set down once and for all. This would be a sad, uniform world if the cannons of beauty were universal and unchanging. The world is many-sided and exciting because cannons differ and change.

Act. I hear what you say, madam. But I cannot help being someone who rather likes being guided by rules and standards. So let me ask you a basic question. Is it really so that we have no universally valid, permanent, unmovable cannons for what is beautiful? I somehow cannot accept that a worldwide phenomenon like the experience of beauty has no common standards.

Ben. There have been attempts to find such standards. But the results are doubtful.

Act. Can you, nevertheless, tell us of those attempts, madam?

Ben. Certainly, dear. - The first people who undertook a search for universal cannons of beauty were the Greeks. They identified three kinds of beauty: ideal, functional and spiritual.

Spe. *Must once again show off with his erudition.* Socrates.

Ben. *Smiles.* Of course, Mr Spectus. - So let us look at those three categories one after the other, and see if, indeed, they can provide us with universal cannons of beauty.

Benigna takes a sip of tea, then goes on.

Ben. Ideal beauty, said Socrates, is correct measure. Beauty is intrinsic in a thing, it resides within that thing, when its proportions, colours, rhythm follow the correct measure. But what exactly is correct measure? - Take architecture. The Greeks had a sense of proportion in architecture that was entirely different from that of the Egyptians. Gothic architects, in turn, followed completely different proportions from those of Greeks and Egyptians. - Take painting. Classical rules of composition reigned supreme until modern artists decided to abandon them. Yet those artists claim that, though disproportionate, their works possess intrinsic beauty. - Take music. Whether we experience a piece of music as beautiful depends on the taste of the age and on the listener's musical education. Some pieces of music, when heard for the first time, were utterly rejected by the audience, accustomed to different rules of composition. Today, we wonder how that could have happened. - Our conclusion must therefore be this. Socrates' ideal beauty, based on measure, reveals itself as impermanent, because the assumption that there are permanently and universally valid cannons of measure is false.

She takes another sip.

Socrates' second kind of beauty is functional beauty. It is defined as the perfect fit between an object and the purpose that object was made for. - Take a hammer. If it fits the hand well, has the right length and the right weight, it has functional beauty, says Socrates. But take a hammer chiselled out of breakable crystal: it lacks functional beauty, because it could never fulfil its purpose. - But, you may object, do we have the right to call something beautiful that is merely practical? Is not Socrates mixing up two terms that do not belong together? Perhaps. Yet, there is a curious phenomenon that you can observe when walking through a flea market on a Sunday morning. You will see dozens of customers buying all kinds of old objects that can no longer be used for what they have originally been made for, since that use no longer exists. Nevertheless, those objects are bought, even collected. Why? Nostalgia? Or because the buyers perceive functional beauty, though the function is no longer there? It is difficult to say. - But, once more, we must conclude that while functional beauty may be something real, it is impermanent, since functions change and cease.

Spe. Which leaves us with Socrates' third kind of beauty: spiritual beauty.

Ben. Precisely, dear. Spiritual beauty is based on moral principles. These are more likely to endure than correct proportions or functionality. A gesture perceived as beautiful in the past is likely to be still called beautiful today. A profound thought, well formulated, will retain its beauty for centuries. Thus, of the three, spiritual beauty is the least likely to fade. - Nevertheless: also moral principles undergo change. Furthermore, they are by no means universal. Societies in distant lands have often utterly different notions than we do about what is ethical and what is not. In other words: even spiritual beauty is not absolute, because the moral principles upon which they are based differ and change.

Act. Then let us leave Socrates and his three categories. Surely there have been attempts after him to find universal criteria for beauty.

Ben. Yes, there were such attempts. - One of them was to define beauty as completeness. According to this criterion, a thing is beautiful when all parts that naturally belong to it are present. An incomplete thing is not beautiful. The reverse is also true. If a thing carries parts that do not naturally belong to it, this irritates us and we find the thing ugly. Beauty is the purgation of superfluities, said Michelangelo. - But he was an artist of the Renaissance. For the age of the Baroque, that followed upon the Renaissance, completeness meant filling every inch, every corner with decoration. Some Baroque interiors almost choke us. Why? Because, once again, we tend to be Spartan. We feel that "less is more", that beauty lies in economy and restraint, in functionality and elegant simplicity rather than in decoration. But, maybe, there is already a movement starting away from this. We may, in future, want more decoration once again. - So, what insight do we arrive at? That completeness is not a universal cannon of beauty. It is simply a matter of the reigning taste.

Act. Despite all your excellent arguments, madam, I am not convinced. Why, for instance, do we perceive some mathematical formulae as beautiful? I think because there are some universal, permanent cannons of beauty written into the fabric of the cosmos.

Ben. *Laughs.* You are not one to give up easily, are you, Mr Actus? All right, since you insist, let me try to satisfy you. There are, indeed, two phenomena that come near to a universal and unchanging cannon of beauty. Both of them, and this will please you, have to do with mathematics. And both of them, in a certain way, have to do with measure; so the ancient Greeks were on the right track, after all.

Act. You intrigue me, madam. What is the first phenomenon?

Ben. It goes by the name of the Golden Mean. Are you familiar with it?

Act. But of course. And I have been fascinated by it since childhood. Take a straight line and divide it so that the smaller segment has the same proportion to the larger segment as the larger segment to the whole. Mathematically, this proportion is 1 to 1.618. Most people will automatically divide a straight line in that proportion when asked to divide it anywhere but the middle. Why they do that is something of a mystery.

Ben. The mystery is much more profound than most people realize, dear. The Golden Mean appears in thousands of different forms and guises in Nature. We find it in the proportions of crystals, of flowers, of ammonites, of snails, of horses. We find it in the proportions of the human face and of the human body. It reappears in millions of artefacts made by humans: in tools of the Stone Age, in Cistercian monasteries, even in the decoration of a modern football.

Why that is so we do not know. The Golden Mean seems to have no other reason to exist than an aesthetic one. It has apparently been built into the universe for no other purpose than to please. It is the Creator's mysterious contribution to beauty.

Act. And what is the other potentially universal principle of beauty, madam?

Ben. It goes under the name of Harmony. It was originally discovered by Pythagoras while studying the sounds made by cords of different lengths. This led him to posit a link between beauty, harmony, and mathematics. He said that beauty is harmony, and harmony lies in numbers. Pythagoreans went to sleep listening to harmonic music that helped them shake off the tensions of the day. Pythagoras is even said to have sobered a drunken man by playing a certain tune. - But harmony goes well beyond musical cords. The spaces between the columns of Greek temples often follow harmonic intervals. Kepler set up his planetary laws trying to prove celestial harmony. Painters discovered that certain colours harmonize, while others do not; this, of course, has to do with the different wavelengths of light, that must harmonize like musical cords do. Harmony, it seems, is indeed a basic feature built into the cosmos.

Spe. *Thoughtful.* I associate harmony also with the way people treat each other. And there are strange similarities. Harmony in human relations means that actions, opinions and feelings are in accord, like there are accords in music. Harmony also means congruity of the parts to the whole, and congruity of the parts to each other, like in the Golden Mean. Somehow everything connects. Everything seems to relate.

Act. There is nothing particularly surprising about that, Spectus. Since we are all part of the fabric of the cosmos, we also participate, necessarily, in it basic features. - What bothers me is something else. Since man has discovered the existence of harmony, why does he not continuously strive for it? Why is there so much disharmony in the world?

Ben. *Smiles.* Because man doesn't like constraints, Mr Actus. After a while, he perceives harmony as boring, and disharmony as exciting. - A fully harmonious piece of music would put the listeners to sleep. So composers introduce disharmonies here and there, to keep the audience awake. - What applies to music, applies also to art. Perfectly proportioned statues are just as boring as perfect harmony in music. Exciting statues always have some strangeness, some exaggeration, some disproportion in them. - Let us face it: man is not made to live continuously in perfect harmony. He prefers to swing, like a pendulum, back and forth between harmony and disharmony, between proportion and disproportion.

Spe. In other words he needs opposites. Contrasts.

Ben. Precisely, dear.

Spe. Madame Benigna, our roof is almost finished. May I ask you to clarify a bit more this last point you just formulated? I have the feeling it is one of the most profound ideas we came up with at this seminar. I presume it will put the last wisdom-stone of our roof in place.

Ben. *Puts down her knitting, which is obviously finished.* The important thing to realize is that to appreciate something good requires having experienced the opposite. It is the negative that teaches us to value the positive. Beauty cannot exist without ugliness, for without ugliness we would not know what beauty is. We need disharmony, for without it we would not understand what harmony is. If we pretend to ignore the ugly and the disharmonious, we lose beauty and harmony. We can only become truly wise if we accept to see the ugly and the disharmonious. But the wise will not dwell too long with these negative things. They will keep returning to beauty and to harmony, for those, and not ugliness and disharmony, are their true base.

There is a sharp buzz from the wall with the revolving holograph. The roof of the cathedral, built of beautiful, slender Gothic arches, shines in a golden light. The roof is finished. The gong marks the end of the session.

Benigna picks up the knitting she has been working on and beckons to Actus and Spectus to come near her. As they do so, they realize what Benigna has been knitting all the time: one white scarf of finest cashmere with the words "Piavello Symposium" knit into it in black letters, and one black scarf with the same words in white. Benigna puts the white scarf around the neck of Actus and the black one around the neck of Spectus.

Ben. A small souvenir, dears. You can tell people about this symposium when they ask you where you got the scarves from.

Act. Thank you kindly, madam. Though I am afraid not many will believe us when we tell them about this symposium. Despite these scarves as solid proof.

Ben. They may not believe it with their heads, dear. But this seminar of yours is not directed to the head alone. You cannot become truly wise if you use your head only: you must open up to emotions. Attempting to find all answers through logic is doomed to failure. So look for wisdoms not only with your head, but also with your heart. For the Heart has reasons that Reason ignores. *(Benigna looks expectantly and with a smile at Spectus.)*

Spe. *Smiles back at Benigna, with a slight bow.* Blaise Pascal, madam.

Benigna laughs gently, picks up her cane, and rises from her armchair. Citatia and Mrs Higgins come forward to help her. Slowly, the little group moves to the back.

Actus and Spectus prepare, as usual, to leave for afternoon tea. But the moment they begin walking towards the door, a message appears projected on the wall:

Sorry: no tea break today. Instead, you will receive the records of the last four days. You have one hour to go through them and make notes. The purpose is to wrap up the seminar and erect the façade. You are asked to recapitulate your impressions of the symposium. You are also requested to point out wisdoms you found to be particularly important, and wisdoms that kept recurring in different forms throughout these four days. No combots can help you with this assignment. Courage, gentlemen, you will soon be released.

Eclectus, Chairman

Actus and Spectus sigh, but have no choice. They go back to their desks and sit down again. Three figures come forward from the seminar room.

First comes Madame de Pompadour with a large silver tablet, on which there are two tea cups and two tea pots, made of exquisite Sèvres porcelain. The pots seem to be filled with choice aromatic tea. Madame de Pompadour puts the cups and pots on the desks of Actus and Spectus, makes a most charming reverence, and returns to her desk.

Next comes Maître Brillat-Savarin, carrying two small silver tablets with choice snacks, cav-

iar, petit-fours, all small but savoury-looking portions. He puts the tablets on the desks of Actus and Spectus, joins the first two fingers of his right hand to a circle, the French sign indicating deliciousness, and then follows the Pompadour to the back.

Last comes Citatia, looking more the executive secretary than ever. She carries two large files, puts one on the desk of Actus, the other on the desk of Spectus. She is the only one of the three who addresses them.

Citatia. The right man can make a good job out of any job.

She manages a small smile, bows her head briefly to both Actus and Spectus, then returns to the back.

Spe. *Looks after her.* I shall miss you, Citatia, my dear, once this seminar is over.

Citatia has either not heard or pretends not to have.

Actus and Spectus look at the files. They carry a title on the front page: "A Comedy of Wisdoms: Common Sense and Beyond". Below it, in smaller characters: "Piavello Symposium, Sessions 1 to 14. Minutes recorded under the supervision of Dr Alexander v. Erdely.

Act. *Thumps his fist on the file.* Again Erdely! This fellow will haunt us until this seminar is over. And we shall never find out who the devil he is. *(Sighs.)* Ah, never mind.

The holograph on the wall stops revolving, with the empty façade facing the room. Actus and Spectus take a sip of Madame de Pompadour's delicious tea, pick up a petit-four of Maître Savarin, and begin reading the minutes of the seminar. There is no noise, except for the occasional rattle of paper as they turn the pages and make notes.

Session 15: The Facade

The gong is sounded, marking the beginning of the last session of the symposium.

Then a minor miracle happens. The holograph of the cathedral of wisdoms is still motionless, with the empty front facing the seminar-room. But into the void, a computer slowly begins to design a beautiful and highly sculptured façade, consisting of a multitude of low-relief. They represent portraits. And what is more, familiar ones. Near the rosette are the effigies of Proverbius, Citatia, the Higginses, Politicus, the Professors Fidus and Ratius, and Benigna. Further away is the grinning face of Mephisto. There is Churchill with a full-length cigar. There is Napoleon, Julius Ceasar, Franklin, Confucius, Gracian, and all the other participants at the seminar. Actus and Spectus even discover themselves: their effigies are placed immediately to the right and left of the rosette. The façade is a homage to all those who contributed to the erection of the cathedral. Only the rosette itself is left unfinished: instead of the usual glass window filling it, there is only a hole.

Spectus. Well, I call that a nice gesture.

Actus. It is, indeed. I was wondering how we were going to fill that huge empty space of the façade. Eclectus has done the job for us. He gave us a bonus, so to speak.

Spe. But we still have the rosette to fill in. Our last job.

Act. But the rosette is not very large. Which means Eclectus has a message for us: wrap it up, boys, but make it brief.

Spe. Well then, let us briefly wrap it up. Eclectus gave us instructions how he wants us to do that. We should give our general impressions about the seminar first. Then a brief summary review of the wisdoms we consider to be particularly important, including the ones that kept recurring throughout the seminar. - You start, Actus.

Act. *Looks at his notes.* We said at the beginning, when we drafted the plot, that we are to seek *wisdoms,* not *Wisdom.* Looking back, it was a good idea that we insisted on the plural. I am impressed by the hundreds of different forms Wisdom can take. It took us four days to labour through the stuff, despite applying Occam's razor wherever we could.

Spe. *Looks at his own notes.* That is partly so because of a major lesson we learned: many wisdoms are not absolutely valid. A wisdom may apply under one set of circumstances. But change the circumstances, and often you need to qualify, even modify, your original wisdom. Under certain changed circumstances even the opposite of the original wisdom may apply. So all this adds up to a lot of wisdoms.

Act. Many wisdoms we were able to formulate ourselves, but the majority came from the other participants. I was impressed how utterly different the backgrounds of those participants were. At times, the wisdoms we needed came from totally unexpected sources. - I draw a major conclusion from this. While philosophies come from just a few philosophers, wisdoms come from thousands of men. Philosophy depends on a few authorities; wisdoms do not depend on any authorities at all. Before attending this seminar, I tended to think that wisdom is something a few select people are born with, or a few old men possess. I now realize that this is not so. All of us can become wise through a conscious effort. Wisdoms are learnable, communicable and practicable, by anyone, at any age. And it does not matter from whom you pick up a piece of wisdom; what matters is the use you make of it.

Spe. I fully agree. And not only can wisdoms easily be communicated and learned. Great wisdoms, we found, can often be conveyed using very simple metaphors about trivial things. But the message sinks in, because we see the connection between the seemingly trivial and the deep wisdom behind it.

Act. Yes: the language of wisdom is simple. That is another lesson. The greatest wisdoms are expressed in clear, short sentences that everyone understands.

Spe. But we also noted that those short, simple sentences are often the result of long periods of experience and observation.

The first pieces of glass have been fitted into the rosette. It is too early to discern what they represent.

Act. I missed three things at this seminar, though.

Spe. Go ahead, tell them. We are supposed to give all our impressions.

Act. I find that we did not distinguish sufficiently between Western and Eastern wisdoms.

Spe. But we did hear Eastern wisdoms from Confucius, Mencius, Proverbius, even Citatia. We discussed at length the wisdoms behind Asian religions. Furthermore, I think we should not draw too sharp a distinction between wisdoms coming from the East and West. Remember: the origin of a wisdom is secondary. East and West differ above all in the importance they attribute to specific wisdoms. The East will particularly value wisdoms that help people to live together harmoniously: wisdoms we found when erecting the walls. The West puts more emphasis on the individual: it will particularly appreciates wisdoms we found when erecting the pillars. But such differences are gradually eroding. Wisdoms, like the economy, are becoming global, as the East discovers the wisdoms of the West and vice versa. And that is good. - What else did you miss, Actus?

Act. The very first wisdom we uttered had to do with health: Mens sana in corpore sano. But then we did not mention health again. We ignored an essential wisdom: care for your body. Without a healthy body, many wisdoms we found simply cannot be implemented. A weak body commands; a strong one obeys. So let me add, belatedly, an important message. The wise will care for their health, watch their diet, exercise, do regular check-ups. - Does that sound too trivial for this highbrow seminar?

Spe. *Smiles.* Not at all. What appears to be trivial is often deep wisdom. - What is the third thing you missed?

Act. You know that I like clear goals and well-defined purposes. Individuals can have them: we discussed this at length while erecting the pillars. Small groups can have them: we saw this when we talked of team-work. Even rather large groups, such as political parties or corporations can have them. At the level of nations, however, goals start becoming hazy. At the level of humanity as a whole they are even hazier. As for the universe itself, its final goal and purpose are totally unclear. Thus, the more we move away from individuals or small groups towards large agglomerations, the less concrete do aims and purposes become. I would have thought that four days of discussions on wisdoms would produce more clarity on this issue. They didn't. We pointed out the many benefits of technical progress. We formulated a request that growing complexity and freedom of choice be coupled with responsible action. But complexity and freedom of choice are means, not ends. Where do, and should, they lead?

Spe. I fully understand the frustration of someone accustomed to clear goals when he faces that question. But I think the wise must acknowledge the fact that, for the moment at least, no-one, not science, nor philosophy, nor religion can satisfactorily answer it. We seem indeed to be playing an open-ended game. So we must concentrate on the means, while waiting for clarity about the aims. Sensible technical progress and responsible action are two of these means. Let me add two more. One is empathy, the ability to put oneself into another's shoe. This is not as difficult as it sounds, since empathy, according to recent findings, is a basic trait of our nature; we just need to exercise it. The second is the realisation that humanity is growing increasingly interdependent: we must understand how best to manage that process. Doing all these things seem to me the keys to reduce one day the haziness of mankind's aims, and further a feeling of purpose across the globe.

Act. Comforting thoughts, Spectus. Indeed: we can hardly do more.

Spe. Then let us start recapitulating the wisdoms we found to be particularly important and those that kept recurring under different aspects.

Act. Before we start doing that: a question. Which three wisdoms do you think qualify as probably the oldest of mankind?

Spe. *Thinks for a moment.* First: the right balance between self-interest and altruism. "Love your neighbour as yourself." Second: the Golden Rule. "What you want others to do to you, do it to others." Third: reciprocity. "I give that you may give". Do ut des. All three reflect the fact that man, though selfish, has been a social animal for tens of thousands of years.

Act. Excellent choice. I agree. - But now: to our review. You start, Spectus.

Spe. We encountered two broad categories of wisdoms: those that come from the head and those that come from the heart. We should not see these as opposites: both are necessary. The wise will listen to their heads and their hearts, and combine what they hear. We found many instances for such combinations. - The wise mother will be affectionate and tender, but exacting. The wise father will make his authority felt, but will be generous with praise. The wise teacher will criticise, but also encourage. The wise leader will inspire and rule. The wise decision-maker will listen to the advice of experts as well as to that of true friends.

Act. My favourite recurring wisdom, clearly coming from the head, was: keep control. It appeared at many different places and in many different forms. - Difficult, complex tasks should be broken down into discreet stages, so that we can have control over each. We should stay in or near our field of competence, since further away we risk losing control. Speed must be submitted to control to avoid haste. Control is necessary to prevent excesses. Control is needed to overcome fear, to keep anger at bay, to prevent a dispute degenerating into a quarrel. We need control to make sure that the changes we are introducing achieve the intended results. We need it to prevent our technological capabilities turning from beneficial to detrimental. Control is necessary to check those who are in positions of power. Control, in short, keeps us from harming ourselves and from hurting our fellow beings.

Spe. There is yet another instance where we need control: finding the right rhythm for everything we do. Slow down when we can afford it; speed up when it becomes necessary.

Act. I came up with a wisdom called proportionality. It took several different forms. - Adapt input to demand. Avoid investing more effort than necessary to reach a goal or remove an obstacle. Conversely, avoid investing less effort than what is called for. Ensure that your goal harmonizes with your means. Adapt your praise to the size of what is being praised. Adapt punishment to the size of the offence. You, Spectus, even suggested that proportionality has to do with aesthetics.

Spe. The concept of balance was behind several of our wisdoms.

Act. Yes, but we agreed that balance should be dynamic, not static. Find the right balance between competition and co-operation. Find the right balance between the necessity for change and the need to conserve what is proven. We need dynamic balance to recuperate after hard work: we should not rest, but do something entirely different. When we have given a lot, let us take for a while, so that we can give once more.

The design of the rosette is slowly becoming clearer. It represents a building. But Actus and Spectus are too busy looking at their notes to realize it.

Act. A rather straightforward, yet important wisdom kept recurring: search for and try to eliminate the cause, rather than attempt to cure the symptoms.

Spe. We concluded that some wisdoms are purely subjective, and that it is futile to try to objectify them. Wisdoms that contain words such as "enough", "adequate", "satisfactory", "too little", "too much", are all subjective. We have to accept that what satisfies some will not satisfy others.

Act. We found, as you already said, that reciprocity is important. But we said the wise will take care that what they give and what they receive, or expect to receive, are more or less equivalent. We also said that no relationship will hold where one party always gives and the other always takes.

Spe. Yes, but we also agreed that there are cases where not reciprocity, but charity applies. The wise will keep the two apart. - Several wisdoms we came across were sensitive to degrees. The best example, perhaps, was tolerance. We found that we should be tolerant toward many things, less towards other things, not at all towards a few things. Another example was pleasure: highly welcome in small doses, detrimental when there is too much of it. Our conclusion was that the wise will not accept a wisdom as valid across the board, where degrees call for distinctions.

Act. Occam's razor, the warning against unnecessary complications, too many arguments, too many explanations for the same thing, was met with repeatedly. I think without it this seminar would have been twice as long.

Spe. What Occam's razor really teaches us are the merits of economy and simplicity. We found that these two qualities are even built into the fabric of the universe.

Act. But we found, also, that diversity is an essential part of our world. We said the wise will listen to diverse people, old, middle-aged, young, and combine their counsels, before making a decision. We saw that the effectiveness of team-work depends on the diverse competences of the members of the team. We found that we can only be tolerant if we accept diversity. We said the wise will open up to the diversity of the world, because they know that those who shut out diversity become one-sided, narrow-minded, dogmatic.

Spe. Yes. And we said that the wise will not only accept diversity, but will actively seek variety. Because variety delights.

Act. Spectus: you may not quite agree with my following summary point. I find that the profile of the wise individual, as he emerged from this symposium, is that of an active rather than that of a contemplative fellow. He sees, rather than just looks. He listens, rather than just hears. He prefers to speak up, rather than remain silent. He undertakes things, initiates things, tries to correct and improve things. He plans, grabs opportunities, implements, perseveres, keeps order, courts luck. He does not simply feel gratitude, he shows it. He gives love, affection and friendship, in order to receive love, affection and friendship. He actively seeks joys, rather than expect that they will be brought to him on a silver plate.

Spe. Careful, Actus. We talked a moment ago about dynamic balance. I think that concept also applies to activity and contemplation. To achieve wisdom, it is not enough only to *do*; you must also *contemplate*, ponder, reflect. Recall Henri Bergson, the first combot to speak at this symposium. He said action is a necessity, contemplation a luxury. I do not agree. For me, not only action, but also contemplation is a necessity. Contemplation is not the opposite of action: indolence is. To become really wise, you need to be both actor and spectator. You must think like a man of action and act like a man of thought. .

There is a sharp, short buzz from the wall, the usual signal that something is nearing completion. Indeed, the rosette is almost full of coloured glass.

Act. Look at the rosette, Spectus. It is practically finished. But what does it show?

Spe. *Looks at the design.* It is a reduced, roughly drawn image of our cathedral. A small cathedral within the big one. It obviously stands for what we are doing right now. It symbolizes our summing up.

Act. But something is different. The rosette of the small cathedral is some sort of an emblem. It must be important, given its strategic location. It seems to be some kind of core symbol. The summing up of our summing up.

Spe. *Looks more closely at the rosette.* You are right, Actus. And I can see now what that symbol is: yin and yang.

Act. Yin and yang? I know something about it, but you certainly know more. What does it mean? What does it stand for?

Spe. As you can see, it is a circular disk, divided into two halves by a wavy line. The two halves are exactly equal in size, since the length of the wavy line is exactly one half of the circumference. One half of the disk is black, the other white. The white half contains a small black dot, the black half a small white dot.

Act. *Starts.* Funny. That reminds me of the scarves Madame Benigna gave us. The black one with the white inscription, and the white one with the black inscription. I wonder if those scarves were meant to be more than just a souvenir.

Spe. *Is silent for a few moments before he goes on.* I don't know about the scarves. But the yin and yang symbol is certainly laden with significance. Yin stands for darkness, passivity; yang for light, activity. They are opposites, but they are not in conflict. They are separate, yet interdependent. Things can at one moment be in a state of yin, then turn into a state of yang. And vice versa. Each state partakes of the other, conditions the other, because each contains within it the seed of the opposite state. It is a dynamic symbol: it suggests force, potential, evolution, change. It also suggests that an apparent duality is in fact oneness. I am the One who becomes Two. We find that idea already in ancient India and Egypt.

Act. Fascinating. But what has that symbol got to do with our seminar?

Spe. *Thinks for a moment.* Perhaps it stands for the rule Eclectus laid down at the beginning: watch out for "sic et non" situations. One wisdom turning into its opposite, depending on the circumstances. - Or, perhaps it refers to the wisdom that man needs contrasts, as Madame Benigna pointed out. We would not appreciate joy without sorrow, beauty without ugliness, harmony without disharmony. *(Smiles.)* Probably we would not even appreciate wisdom without its opposite: folly. - But perhaps there is yet another interpretation.

Act. Go ahead, Spectus. You have the last word.

Spe. *Takes a moment to think how to formulate what he is going to say.* Throughout this symposium, Actus, we emphasized the differences between us. Now that we arrive at the end of it, I think we realize that we extend, rather than counteract each other. Though in many cases we think differently, our views, our convictions are complementary, rather than antagonistic. We are two, but we add up to a whole. - When we were building our science-tower, we discussed the principle of complementarity, remember? It claims that if there are two contradictory manifestations of the same thing, then both manifestations *taken together* are needed to define that thing. Light is not either wave *or* particle, but wave *and* particle. Evolution does not proceed by chance *or* law, but by chance *and* law. Not either science or religion is right: maybe *both* are. The yin-yang symbol is not either white or black, but *both* white and black. - I think the message is this. Where there are two opposites, there is also a third. That third is both of them, taken together. The wise will be aware of this. They will realize that their own view, though valid, may be incomplete. So they will not ignore, and certainly not try to obliterate, the opposite view, that contradicts their own. They will make an effort to resolve, reconcile, transcend the contradiction. That effort, Actus, is perhaps the wisdom that crowns them all.

Spontaneously, Actus and Spectus stand up and grab each other's hands in a firm handshake. The last remaining bit of glass in the rosette is put in place. The cathedral of wisdoms is finished and glows in a beautiful golden light. There is nothing more to add.

There is a moment of silence, as Actus and Spectus look, satisfied, but also a bit moved, at the resplendent image of the finished cathedral. Then the holograph is shoved to one side, and next to it appears the full-length picture of a grey-haired gentleman.

Act. and Spe. *Shout at the same time.* Eclectus!

The grey-haired gentleman smiles and gently applauds into the seminar-room. He makes a gesture lifting his arms upwards. At this sign, all combots in the room begin to glow and stand up. The whole scene is reminiscent of the end of an opera performance, where the conductor mounts on the stage to congratulate the orchestra and the performers. It is an emotional moment.

Then all combots sit down and the picture of the grey-haired gentleman fades. Instead, Arlecchino, from the Commedia dell'Arte scene at the beginning of the symposium, appears on the projection wall. He takes off his cap and bows to the seminar-room with a sweeping gesture.

Arlecchino. Signori, la commedia è finita.

Then his image also disappears. The holograph of the cathedral of wisdoms grows indistinct and gradually fades away. There are no more projections on the wall. Then the wall slowly rolls to one side; beyond it is a staircase, leading down to the terrace where Actus and Spectus met on the evening before the seminar began.

Act. Care for a drink, Spectus?

Spe. Yes, Actus. I think we have earned it.

They take each other's arms and walk down towards the terrace, wearing Benigna's black and white scarves. The sun is beginning to set, painting beautiful, lively colours on the horizon.

END OF THE PIAVELLO SYMPOSIUM

Contents and Index

Contents

Index of Subjects